SCHIZOPHRENIA:
The First Ten
Dean Award Lectures

EDITED
BY
STANLEY R. DEAN, M.D.

MSS Information Corporation
655 Madison Avenue, New York, N.Y. 10021

Library of Congress Cataloging in Publication Data

Dean, Stanley R   comp.
   Schizophrenia.

   Bibliography: p.
   1. Schizophrenia--Addresses, essays, lectures.
I. Title. ✗[DNLM: 1. Schizophrenia-Essays. WM
203 S338 1973]
RC514.D34   616.8'982   73-6815
ISBN 0-8422-7115-5

TABLE OF CONTENTS

FOREWORD

Heart disease, stroke, and cancer cause the greatest number of deaths, but schizophrenia is the illness which involves the cruelest human suffering. The major thrust of the professional life of Dr. Stanley R. Dean, for whom these lectures are named, has been the understanding and cure of this disease. From the time of his training as a medical student studying psychiatry under Dr. Raymond W. Waggoner at the University of Michigan Medical School, through the years of his clinical practice, Dr. Dean cared for many difficult and perplexing cases which focused his attention on the illness. Compassionate about the suffering it caused and sensitive to the quandary of psychiatrists concerning its etiology, prevention, and cure, he became convinced that basic research and clinical investigations on it should be greatly expanded.

In 1957, therefore, he initiated the planning and establishment of RISE, Research In Schizophrenia Endowment. He was joined in this by some of his friends and former patients in his native Connecticut. RISE was dedicated to obtaining large funds through public subscription for all types of research which might solve the problems of schizophrenia.

I first met Dr. Dean in 1958 when I was privileged to serve on the Scientific Council of RISE along with a number of other psychiatrists. The program got underway rapidly and effectively due to the devoted commitment of many persons whom Dr. Dean had convinced of its importance. Beginning efforts were being made to outline a long-range scientific program of research on the illness when it became apparent that the purposes of RISE overlapped with some of the major research goals of the National Association of Mental Health. Discussions between the two organizations led to the decision by a majority of those involved in RISE that, even though schizophrenia constituted a special challenge, the best approach would be to mount a national campaign for support for all forms of mental health research rather than a single illness. With the expectation that schizophrenia would be given major emphasis, RISE dissolved and merged its activities with those of the National Association of Mental Health.

But Dr. Dean was not satisfied. He wished to make a further contribution specifically in the field of schizophrenia. He sought the advice of many people, including myself, during the time I was director of the Mental Health Research Institute at the University of Michigan Medical School, his alma mater. He finally decided to solicit funds to provide enough capital to finance in perpetuity an annual award for basic research accomplishments in the behavioral sciences contributing to our understanding of schizophrenia. Dr. Dean hoped that this would become the largest monetary award in the mental health field, as indeed it currently is. specifically for schizophrenia.

Dr. Dean asked the Fund for the Behavioral Sciences, a nonprofit foundation of which I am president, to administer this award and to receive gifts to capitalize the award. Our foundation agreed. At that time the other members of the Board of Directors of the Fund for the Behavioral Sciences were the Rev. Dr. C. Leslie

Glenn, Dr. Donald G. Marquis, Mr. Fowler McCormick, and Dr. Robert A. Winters. On the recommendation of Dr. Glenn — and to the frank astonishment of Dr. Dean — our Board of Directors decided without his knowledge to name the prize The Stanley R. Dean Research Award. Reluctantly, he acceded to this decision. He had wanted no such personal recognition for his efforts.

The Board of Directors of the Fund for Behavioral Science set up a procedure which would not in any way involve the directors in the determination of the recipients of the award. We wished simply to be the fiscal agent to ensure that the money was appropriately handled and that the award was properly administered. We felt it inappropriate for a foundation board to make scientific or professional decisions about award recipients. We accomplished this purpose in the following way:

We selected three outstanding specialists in the field of mental health as the first selection committee. It was chaired by Dr. Stanley Cobb, Chairman of the Department of Psychiatry of Harvard Medical School and Psychiatrist-in-Chief at the Massachusetts General Hospital. The other members were Dr. Henry Brosin, Chairman of the Department of Psychiatry at the University of Pittsburgh and Director of the Western State Psychiatric Institute, and Dr. Robert Livingston of the Department of Neurobiology at the National Institute of Mental Health.

The next year one of the members of this original committee rotated off and the recipient of the first award joined the selection committee. The next year the second member of the original committee dropped off and the second award recipient became a member of the committee. In the third year all three members of the committee were previous award recipients, and from that time forward they rotated on and off with three year terms.

This procedure continued for six annual awards. In 1968 arrangements were made for the award to be presented jointly under the auspices of the American College of Psychiatrists. The award recipients now are selected by a committee appointed annually by the Board of Regents of that College.

The award recipients during the first few years gave public lectures under appropriate mental health auspices in various cities. They now give lectures which are a highlight of the annual teaching seminars of the American College of Psychiatrists. In the past some of these lectures have been published in the journal *Behavioral Science*. Future publication will be arranged by the American College of Psychiatrists.

The list of the distinguished recipients of the award, which now has continued for ten years is as follows:

1962
Seymour S. Kety, M.D.

1963
David Shakow, Ph.D.

1964
Ralph W. Gerard, M.D., Sc.D., L.L.D., M.D. (Hon.)

1965
Leo Kanner, M.D.

1966
Franz J. Kallman, M.D.
(Posthumous)

1967
Eliot H. Rodnick, Ph.D.
Norman Garmezy, Ph.D.

1968
Gabriel Langfeldt, M.D.

1969
Manfred Bleuler, M.D.

1970
David Rosenthal, Ph.D.

1971
Sarnoff A. Mednick, Ph.D.
Fini Schulsinger, M.D.

The dedication and philanthropy of many persons have made this award possible. Not the least among these is Dr. Dean, himself, who has contributed generously in money as well as time. So too have Mr. and Mrs. Everett Callender of Greenwich, Connecticut. Mrs. Jane Callender has spent far more effort than anyone else in approaching donors and in carrying out the complex and ever-continuing work necessary to build up a sizeable capital fund like that which exists today. Without her the award would have never reached its present magnitude. Her husband, Everett Callender, has made the investment decisions for the foundation over the years with an expertness which has significantly enlarged the total capital beyond what would reasonably have been expected if usual investment policies had been followed.

Many have contributed to the Stanley R. Dean Fund for Psychiatric Research. The following is the list of sponsors.

SPONSORS

Mrs. Everett Callender, *Chairman*
Mr. and Mrs. Robert M. Blake
Mr. and Mrs. Edward Callender
Mr. and Mrs. Everett Callender
Mr. and Mrs. Hadley Case
Mr. and Mrs. Leslie Cheek, III
Mr. John H. Childs
Mrs. D. Dale Condit
Dr. and Mrs. F.H. Converse
Dr. and Mrs. Stanley R. Dean
Mrs. Oliver B. Elsworth
Mrs. E. Loren Fenn
Mrs. Everett Fisher
Mrs. J.B. Hawkins
Mr. Stuart L. Hawkins
Mr. and Mrs. Stanley Hoyt
Mr. and Mrs. Austin S. Igleneart
Mrs. Ernest Lee Jahncke, Jr.
Mr. and Mrs. Howard Steele Johnson
Mrs. Alexander Klemin
Miss Diana Klemin

The clinical and research activities of Dr. Dean have touched many fields, as his bibliography indicates. He has not only shown interest in schizophrenia, his main concern, but also in psychic research, marriage counseling, mental health of senior citizens, and international aspects of social psychiatry. He has also devoted time to RECOVERY, an organization for the rehabilitation of former psychiatric patients. He continues actively to pursue investigations into phenomena of the mind, normal and pathological, and to maintain his vigorous participation in many professional activities. Dr. Dean is a Clinical Professor of Psychiatry at the University of Florida and the University of Miami.

It is already clear that the Stanley R. Dean Research Award has had impact. It has drawn the attention of many to a career pattern — research on schizophrenia. A cumulative record is provided in this book of important scientific and clinical achievements contributing to our developing comprehension of schizophrenia which give promise that some day it can be cured or prevented. The articles in this book make it apparent that we are still far from that point, but they make it equally apparent that in the last decade a number of significant advances have made us a little more secure in our understanding of schizophrenic phenomena and a little more precise in our comprehension of what we must still learn. In this entire professional development the Stanley R. Dean Research Award has played its small but unique part.

James G. Miller, M.D.
Washington, D.C.
March, 1973

PREFACE

Since the time of the Bethlehem "Bedlam" Hospital in England and even long before, the so-called "normal" person has been curious about the behavior of the mentally ill — variously called the "mad," the "insane" and often times other derogatory names. In 1844 a group of 13 mental hospital superintendents assembled in Philadelphia to form what was to be the first American national medical association. Actually, it was established some three years before the American Medical Association. Since its inception, this organization has been particularly concerned about the etiology and treatment of various kinds of mental illness and has in many ways sponsored research and treatment programs, both through its individual members and through its association with the National Institute of Mental Health.

The type of mental illness which has caused most distress both to the individual and to his family is now known as schizophrenia, although for many years and even as recently as the early 20th century it was commonly called *dementia praecox*. Although this disease has been undoubtedly one of the greatest wasters of human life, both in terms of energy and of distress to individuals and to families, yet even today relatively little is known about its causation.

Many of us consider schizophrenia a generic term covering a number of diseases, while others think of it as a single disease with many variations. Undoubtedly there are many who have the disease who never come to the attention of the medical profession but are only considered bizarre or unusual in their behavior. In spite of its widespread nature and of its ambiguous symptoms, schizophrenia and those suffering from it occupy more time and energy of hospital personnel and their facilities than any other type of mental disease. So it becomes a truism that not nearly enough public money has been spent in research on the nature, cause and treatment of schizophrenia.

In an effort to stimulate more research in this troublesome area a well known New England psychiatrist, who had already done significant research in schizophrenia, Dr. Stanley R. Dean, convinced some of his friends and the parents of some of his patients to establish a fund which would offer a yearly award to the person or persons doing what a special committee considered to be that year's most valuable research in schizophrenia. That fund was incorporated into the Fund for Behavioral Science in 1962. The president of the Fund is Dr. James Grier Miller.

Each person chosen to receive the award was asked to give a lecture describing his scientific study. The first of these lectures were given separately, but in the last three years they have become a part of the annual teaching seminar of the American College of Psychiatrists. The award has been given on an annual basis, and this book contains the first 10 lectures in the series. It is a record of the progress which has been made since the first award in 1962.

Dr. Dean is to be congratulated on keeping the interest of renowned scientists involved in such important research which hopefully one day will establish a breakthrough in this serious scourge of mankind.

Raymond W. Waggoner, M.D.
Ann Arbor, Michigan
March, 1973

1962 DEAN RESEARCH AWARD

Professor of psychiatry at Harvard Medical School and director of the Psychiatric Research Laboratories of the Massachusetts General Hospital, **SEYMOUR S. KETY** *received his undergraduate and medical degrees from the University of Pennsylvania. After his tenure as a National Research Council Fellow at the Massachusetts General Hospital, Dr. Kety returned to the University of Pennsylvania where he spent eight years in the departments of pharmacology and physiology of the undergraduate and graduate medical schools. In 1951 he was appointed the first scientific director of the National Institute of Mental Health and Neurological Diseases in Bethesda, and established interdisciplinary research programs at these institutions. He directed the Laboratory of Clinical Science at the National Institute of Mental Health from 1956 to 1967 when he assumed his present position. Throughout his career, Dr. Kety has investigated the role of biological mechanisms in psychiatric illnesses and has contributed significantly to genetic-environmental interactions in the transmission of schizophrenia and the possible role of catecholamines in the affective psychoses. Acting on his belief that research is crucially important to the development of psychiatry, Dr. Kety was instrumental in organizing the Psychiatric Research Society and establishing the* **Journal of Psychiatric Research,** *of which he is the editor.*

BIOCHEMICAL STUDIES IN SCHIZOPHRENIA

Seymour S. Kety, M.D.

The concept of a chemical etiology in schizophrenia is not new. The Hippocratic school attributed certain mental aberrations to changes in the composition of the blood, but it was Thudichum, the founder of modern neurochemistry, who in 1884 expressed the concept most cogently: "Many forms of insanity are unquestionably the external manifestations of the effects upon the brain substance of poisons fermented within the body, just as mental aberrations accompanying chronic alcoholic intoxication are the accumulated effects of a relatively simple poison fermented out of the body. These poisons we shall, I have no doubt, be able to isolate after we know the normal chemistry to its uttermost detail. And then will come in their turn the crowning discoveries to which our efforts must ultimately be directed, namely, the discoveries of the antidotes to the poisons and to the fermenting causes and processes which produce them." In these few words were anticipated and encompassed most of the current chemical formulations regarding schizophrenia.

It may be of value to pause in the midst of the present era of psychochemical activity to ask how far we have advanced along the course plotted by Thudichum. Have we merely substituted "enzymes" for "ferments" and the names of specific agents for "poisons" without altering the completely theoretical nature of the concept? Or, on the other hand, are there some well-substantiated findings to support the prevalent belief that this old and stubborn disorder which has resisted all previous attempts to expose its etiology is about to yield its secrets to the biochemist?

An examination of the experience of another and older discipline may be of help in the design, interpretation and evaluation of biochemical studies. The pathological concepts of schizophrenia have been well reviewed recently. Prompted by the definite histological changes in the cerebral cortex, described by Alzheimer and confirmed by a number of others, an early enthusiasm developed which penetrated into the thinking of Kraepelin and Bleuler. This was followed by a period of questioning and the design and execution of more critically controlled studies leading to the present consensus that a pathological lesion characteristic of schizophrenia or of any of its subgroups remains to be demonstrated.

Because of the chronicity of the disease, the prolonged periods of institutionalization associated with its management, and the comparatively few objective crite-

ria available for its diagnosis and the evaluation of
its progress, schizophrenia presents to the biochemical investigator a large number of variables and
sources of error which he must recognize and attempt
to control before he may attribute to any of his
findings a primary or characteristic significance.

Despite the phenomenological similarities which permitted the concept of schizophrenia as a fairly well
defined symptom-complex to emerge, there is little
evidence that all of its forms have a common etiology
or pathogenesis. The likelihood that one is dealing
with a number of different disorders with a common
symptomatology must be recognized and included in one's
experimental design. Errors involved in sampling from
heterogeneous populations may help to explain the high
frequency with which findings of one group fail to be
confirmed by another. Recognition of the probability
that any sample of schizophrenia is a heterogeneous
one should seem to emphasize the importance of analyzing
data not only for mean values but also for significant
deviations of individual values from the group. The
biochemical characteristics of phenylketonuria would
hardly have been detected in an average value for phenyl-
alanine blood levels in a large group of mentally
retarded patients.

Most biochemical research in schizophrenia has been
carried out in patients with a long history of hospitalization in institutions where overcrowding is difficult
to avoid and hygienic standards cannot always be maintained. It is easy to imagine the spread of chronic
infections, especially of the digestive tract, among
such patients. The presence of amebiasis in a majority
of patients at one large institution has been reported,
and one wonders how often this condition or a former
infectious hepatitis has accounted for the various disturbances in hepatic function found in schizophrenia.
Even in the absence of previous or current infection,
the development of a characteristic pattern of intes-
tinal flora in a population of schizophrenic patients
living together for long periods and fed from the same
kitchen is a possibility which cannot be dismissed in
interpreting what appear to be deviant metabolic pathways.

The variety and quality of the diet of the institutionalized schizophrenic is rarely comparable to that of the
nonhospitalized normal control. Whatever homeostatic
function the process of free dietary selection may
serve is often lost between the rigors of the kitchen
or the budget and the overriding emotional or obsessive
features of the disease. In the case of the "acute"
schizophrenic, the weeks and months of emotional turmoil

16

which precede the recognition and diagnosis of the disease are hardly conducive to a normal dietary intake. Certain abnormalities in thyroid function previously reported in schizophrenia have been shown to result from a dietary deficiency of iodine, correctable by the introduction of iodized salt into the hospital diet. It is not surprising that a dietary vitamin deficiency has been found to explain at least two of the biochemical abnormalities recently attributed to schizophrenia. It is more surprising that the vitamins and other dietary constituents, whose role in metabolism has become so clearly established, should so often be relegated to a position of unimportance in the intermediary metabolism of schizophrenics. Horwitt has found signs of liver dysfunction during ingestion of a diet containing borderline levels of protein while non-specific vitamin therapy accompanied by a high protein and carbohydrate diet has been reported to reverse the impairment of hepatic function in schizophrenic patients.

Another incidental feature of the schizophrenic which sets him apart from the normal control is the long list of therapies to which he may have been exposed. Hypnotic and ataractic drugs and their metabolic products or effects produce changes which have sometimes been attributed to the disease. Less obvious is the possibility of residual electrophysiological or biochemical changes resulting from repeated electroshock or insulin comas.

Emotional stress is known to cause profound changes in man, in adrenocortical and thyroid function, in the excretion of epinephrine and norepinephrine, of water, electrolytes or creatinine, to mention only a few recently reported findings. Schizophrenic illness is often characterized by marked emotional disturbance even in what is called the basal state and frequently exaggerated anxiety in response to routine and research procedures. The disturbances in behavior and activity which mark the schizophrenic process would also be expected to cause deviations from the normal in many biochemical and metabolic measures: in urine volume and concentration, in energy and nitrogen metabolism, in the size and function of numerous organic systems. The physiological and biochemical changes which are secondary to the psychological and behavioral state of the patient are of interest in themselves as part of a total understanding of the schizophrenic process; it is important, however, not to attribute to them a primary or etiological role.

An additional source of error which must be recognized is one which is common to all of science and which it is the very purpose of scientific method, tradition and training to minimize — the subjective bias. There are reasons why this bias should operate to a greater extent in this field than in many others. Not only is the motivation heightened by the tragedy of this problem and the social implications of findings which may contribute to its solution, but the measurements themselves, especially of the changes in mental state or behavior, are so highly subjective, the symptoms so variable and responsive to nonspecific factors in the milieu that only the most scrupulous attention to controlled design will permit the conclusion that a drug, or a diet, or a protein fraction of the blood, or an extract of the brain is capable of causing or ameliorating some of the manifestations of the disease. This is not to suggest that the results of purely chemical determinations are immune to subjective bias, and the same vigilance is required to prevent the hypothesis from contaminating the data. In a field with as many variables as this one, it is difficult to avoid the subconscious tendency to reject for good reason data which weaken an hypothesis while uncritically accepting those data which strengthen it. Carefully controlled and "double blind" experimental designs which are becoming more widely utilized in this area can help to minimize this bias.

Obvious as many of these sources of error are, it is expensive and difficult, if not impossible, to prevent some of them from affecting results obtained in this field, especially in the preliminary testing of interesting hypotheses. It is in the interpretation of these results, however, and in the formulating of conclusions, that the investigator has the opportunity and indeed the responsibility to recognize and evaluate his uncontrolled variables rather than to ignore them, for no one knows better than the investigator himself the possible sources of error in his particular experiment. There are enough unknowns in our guessing game with nature to make it unnecessary to indulge in such a sport with one another.

The senior members of this laboratory: Julius Axelrod, Phillippe Carden, Edward Evarts, Marian Kies, Roger McDonald, Seymour Perlin and Louis Sokoloff, pursue fundamental research in the biological sciences and psychiatry. They have also participated in the development of the schizophrenia program of the Laboratory of Clinical Science, a program of biological research in schizophrenia in which they have been joined by Irwin Kopin, Elwood LaBrosse, Jay Mann and William Pollin. This program is designed to minimize many of the sources of error previously discussed while increasing the opportunity for true biological characteristics, if they exist, to be detected. One of the wards houses a

group of approximately fourteen clearly-diagnosed schizophrenic patients, representative of as many clinical subgroups as possible, chosen from a patient population of
14,000 with an attempt to minimize the non-disease
variables of age, sex, race, and physical illness, and
on the basis of careful family surveys to maximize the
likelihood of including within the group whatever
genetic subgroups of the disease may exist. They are
maintained for an indefinite period of time on a good
diet and under excellent hygienic, nursing, medical and
psychiatric care. Drugs or dietary changes are introduced only for research purposes or, when clinically
necessary, for short periods of time. The other ward
houses a comparable number of normal controls who
volunteer to remain for protracted periods of time exposed to the same diet and in a reasonably similar
milieu. We recognize, of course, that only a few of
the variables are thus controlled and any positive
difference which emerges in this preliminary experiment
between some or all of the schizophrenics and the normal
population will have to be subjected to much more rigorous examination before its significance can be evaluated.

A decrease in basal metabolism was found in schizophrenia by earlier workers although more recent work has not
confirmed this and theories attributing the disease to
disturbances in the fundamental mechanisms of energy
supply or conversion in the brain have enjoyed some
popularity, but on the basis of extremely inadequate
evidence, such as spectroscopic oximetry of the ear lobe
or nail bed. Our finding of a normal rate of cerebral
circulation and oxygen consumption in schizophrenic
patients was confirmed by Wilson, Schieve and Scheinberg,
and more recently in our laboratory by Sokoloff and
associates, who also found a normal rate of cerebral
glucose consumption in this condition. These studies do
not, of course, rule out a highly localized change in
energy metabolism somewhere in the brain, but cogent
evidence for such a hypothesis has yet to be presented.

Richter has pointed out the uncontrolled factors in
earlier work which implicated a defect in carbohydrate
metabolism as a characteristic of the schizophrenic
disease process. The finding in schizophrenia of an
abnormal glucose tolerance in conjunction with considerable other evidence of hepatic dysfunction, or evidence of a retarded metabolism of lactate by the
schizophrenic do not completely exclude incidental
hepatic disease or nutritional deficiences as possible
sources of error. Horwitt and associates were able to
demonstrate and correct similar abnormalities by
altering the dietary intake of the B group of vitamins.

Evidence for higher than normal anti-insulin or hyper-
glycemic activity in the blood or urine of a significant
segment of schizophrenic patients was reported in 1942
by Meduna, Gerty, and Urse, and as recently as 1958 by
Moya and associates. Some progress has been made in
concentrating or characterizing such factors in normal
urine as well as that from schizophrenics. Harris has
thrown some doubt on the importance of such anti-insulin
mechanisms in the pathogenesis of schizophrenia and it
is hoped that further investigation may clarify the
nature of the substance or substances involved and their
relevance to schizophrenia.

Defects in oxidative phosphorylation have been thought
to occur in this disease. Reports of alterations in the
phosphorus metabolism of the erythrocyte, await further
definition and independent confirmation.

The well controlled studies of the Gjessings on nitrogen
metabolism in periodic catatonia arouse considerable
interest in the possible relationship of intermediary
protein metabolism to schizophrenia, although earlier
workers had postulated defects in amino acid metabolism
in this disease. The hallucinogenic properties of some
compounds related directly or indirectly to biological
amines reawakened this interest and the techniques of
paper chromatography offered new and almost unlimited
opportunity for its pursuit.

The first group to report chromatographic studies of
the urine of schizophrenic and control groups found
certain differences in the amino acid pattern and in
addition the presence of certain unidentified imid-
azoles in the urine of schizophrenics. Although a normal
group of comparable age was used for comparison, there
is no indication of the extent to which dietary and
other variables were controlled, and the authors were
properly cautious in their conclusions. In a more
extensive series of studies, another group has reported
a significantly higher than normal concentration of
aromatic compounds in the urine of schizophrenic
patients, and suggested certain qualitative differences
in the excretion of such compounds. Others have
reported the abnormal presence of unidentified amines
or indoles, and one group, the absence of a normally
occurring indole in the urine of schizophrenic patients.
Not all of these studies appear to have controlled
possible drug therapy, urinary volume or concentration,
and few have controlled the diet. There are numerous
mechanisms whereby vitamin deficiencies may cause
substantial changes in the complex patterns of the
intermediary metabolism of amino acids. In addition,
the large number of aromatic compounds in the urine
which have recently been shown to be of dietary origin

20

suggest considerably more caution than has usually been employed with regard to this variable. Another point which has not been emphasized sufficiently is that chromatographic procedures which make possible the determination of scores of substances simultaneously, many of them unknown beforehand, also require somewhat different statistical analyses than those which were developed for the testing of single, well-defined hypotheses. It is merely a restatement of statistical theory that in an analysis for 100 different compounds simultaneously in two samples of the same population, five would be expected to show a difference significant at the 0.05 level! It is interesting to note that a more recent study was able to demonstrate considerably fewer differences between the urines of normal and schizophrenic populations and drew very limited and guarded conclusions. In our own laboratory, Mann and LaBrosse undertook a search for urinary phenolic acids in terms of quantity excreted rather than concentration, which disclosed four compounds significantly higher in the urine from the schizophrenic than that from the normals; two of these were found to be known metabolites of substances in coffee as were probably the other two as well; the presence of these four compounds in the urine was, in fact, better correlated with the ingestion of this beverage than with schizophrenia.

The hypothesis that a disordered amino acid metabolism is a fundamental component of some forms of schizophrenia remains an attractive though fairly general one, the chromatographic search for its evidence is interesting and valuable, and the preliminary indications of differences certainly provocative. Proof that any of these differences are characteristic of even a segment of the disease rather than artifactual or incidental has not yet been obtained.

The theory which relates the pathogenesis of schizophrenia to faulty metabolism of epinephrine is imaginative, ingenious and plausible. It postulates that the symptoms of this disease are caused by the action of abnormal, hallucinogenic derivatives of epinephrine, presumably adrenochrome or adrenolutin. By including the concept of an enzymatic, possibly genetic defect with another factor, epinephrine release, which may be activated by stressful life situations, it encompasses the evidence for sociological as well as constitutional factors in the etiology of the schizophrenias.

The possibility that some of the oxidation products of epinephrine are psychotomimetic received support from anecdotal reports of psychological disturbances associated with the therapeutic use of the compound, especially when it was discolored, and from some early experiments in which the administration of adrenochrome or adrenolutin in appreciable dosage was followed by certain unusual mental manifestations. A number of investigators failed to demonstrate any hallucinogenic properties in adrenochrome, and the original authors were not always able to confirm their earlier results.

Meanwhile, reports were emerging from the group at Tulane University, suggesting a gross disturbance in epinephrine metabolism in schizophrenic patients. Five years previously, Holmberg and Laurell had demonstrated a more rapid oxidation of epinephrine in vitro in the presence of pregnancy serum than with serum from the umbilical cord and had suggested that this was due to higher concentrations of ceruloplasmin in the former. There had also been a few reports of an increase in this protein in the blood of schizophrenics. Leach and Heath reported a striking acceleration in the in vitro oxidation of epinephrine in the presence of plasma from schizophrenic patients as compared with normals, and shortly thereafter implicated ceruloplasmin or some variant of ceruloplasmin as the oxidizing substance. Hoffer and Kenyon reported evidence that the substance formed from epinephrine by blood serum in vitro was adrenolutin.

All of the evidence does not, however, support the epinephrine theory. Despite the considerable new information regarding the metabolism of epinephrine in vivo which has been acquired in this laboratory and elsewhere in the past few years in animals and in normal and schizophrenic man, no evidence has been found for the oxidation of epinephrine via adrenochrome and adrenolutin in any of these populations. On the basis of Axelrod's delineation of the normal metabolic pathways of epinephrine and the availability of the triatiated catecholamine with high specific activity, an examination of its metabolism in 12 normals and an equal number of schizophrenics was completed. No significant qualitative or quantitative differences were revealed between these groups either in the rate of disappearance of labelled epinephrine from the blood or its metabolism. Although appreciable levels of adrenochrome have been reported to occur in the blood of normal subjects and to increase considerably following administration of lysergic acid diethylamide, Szara, Axelrod, and Perlin, using techniques of high sensitivity, have been unable to detect it in the blood of normals or of acute or chronic schizophrenic patients. A recent ingenious study of the rate of destruction of epinephrine in vivo found no difference between normals and schizophrenic patients in this regard. Finally, it has been shown in our laboratory by McDonald, and by the Tulane group themselves, that the low level of ascorbic acid in the blood was an important and uncontrolled variable in the rapid in vitro oxidation of epinephrine by plasma from schizophrenic patients. The fact that McDonald has been able to produce wide fluctuations in the epinephrine oxidation phenomenon from normal to highly abnormal rates in both normals and schizophrenics merely by dietary alterations in blood ascorbic acid level without any effect on the mental processes of either group is quite convincing evidence of the dietary and secondary nature of the phenomenon.

It should be pointed out that none of this negative evidence invalidates the theory that some abnormal product of epinephrine metabolism produces the major symptoms of schizophrenia; it does, however, considerably weaken the evidence which has been used to support it. In addition, there is the bothersome observation of numerous workers, and our own experience, that the administration of epinephrine to schizophrenics which, according to the theory, should aggravate the psychotic symptoms, is usually accompanied by considerably less mental disturbance than occurs in normal subjects.

The recent upsurge of interest in ceruloplasmin can be ascribed to the report which depended upon the oxidation of N,N-dimethyl-p-phenylenediamine by ceruloplasmin. Holmberg and Laurell had demonstrated previously that ceruloplasmin was capable of oxidizing a number of substances including phenylenediamine and epinephrine, but that this could be inhibited by ascorbic acid and Leach and Heath had reported a more rapid oxidation of epinephrine in the plasma of schizophrenics which they attributed to ceruloplasmin. All of these observations were compatible with earlier reports in the German literature of increased serum copper in schizophrenia, the demonstration that practically all of the serum copper was in the form of ceruloplasmin, and that this compound was elevated in blood during pregnancy and in a large number of diseases including schizophrenia. Following the announcement of the phenylenediamine test, however, interest in copper and ceruloplasmin rose and very soon a number of investigators reported this reaction or some modification of it to be positive in a high percentage of schizophrenics, although its value as a diagnostic test was discredited because of the large number of diseases, besides schizophrenia, in which it was positive.

McDonald reported his findings on three groups of schizophrenics, one from the wards of the National Institute of Mental Health, where they had been maintained on a more than adequate diet, and two groups from state hospitals. In none of the schizophrenic groups was there an increase in serum copper or other evidence of increased ceruloplasmin. The state hospital patients and one group of controls, however, showed low ascorbic acid levels and positive phenylenediamine tests which could be reversed by addition of ascorbic acid to the diet; the Institute schizophrenic patients had normal levels of ascorbic acid and negative phenylenediamine tests. It was clear that a high ceruloplasmin was not characteristic of schizophrenia and that the positive phenylenediamine test, where it occurred, could be completely explained by a dietary insufficiency of ascorbic acid.

In the Tulane group, the mean values for serum copper in schizophrenia decreased from a high of 216 ug/100 ml in 1956 to 145 ug/100 ml at the end of 1957, mean normal values remaining at 122 and 124 ug/100 ml during the same time. Other groups have found slight differences or no differences at all in ceruloplasmin or copper blood levels between schizophrenic and normal subjects, and no support for the ability of the phenylenediamine reaction to distinguish between schizophrenic and nonschizophrenic patients. It is not clear why some schizophrenics apparently show an elevated blood ceruloplasmin level; among the possibilities are dietary factors, hepatic damage, chronic infection, or the possible tendency of excitement to raise the blood ceruloplasmin as preliminary experiments appear to suggest.

Quite early in their studies, the Tulane group recognized that the potent oxidant effects of the serum of schizophrenics on epinephrine in vitro could not be satisfactorily explained by the ceruloplasmin levels alone. Leaving aside the importance of ascorbic acid deficiency on this reaction, they had postulated the presence in the blood of schizophrenics of a qualitatively different form of ceruloplasmin which they proceeded to isolate, to test in monkey and man and to which they gave the name taraxein. They have reported that when certain batches of this material were tested in monkeys, marked behavioral and electroencephalographic changes occurred. When samples of these active batches were injected intravenously at a rapid rate into carefully selected prisoner volunteers, all of the subjects developed symptoms which have been described for schizophrenia, including disorganization and fragmentation of thought, autism, feelings of depersonalization, paranoid ideas, auditory hallucinations and catatonic behavior.

A highly significant decrease in rope climbing speed in rats injected with sera from psychotic patients as opposed to that from nonpsychotic controls has been reported by Winter and Flataker. Their later finding that the phenomenon occurs with sera of patients with a wide variety of mental disorders, including mental retardation and alcoholism, and that there is a considerable variation in this index between similar groups at different hospitals, coupled with the inability of

at least one other investigator to demonstrate this
phenomenon in the small group of schizophrenic patients
under investigation in this laboratory, suggests that
the quite real and statistically significant phenomenon
originally observed may be related to variables other
than those specific for or fundamental to schizophrenia.

It has been reported that rabbits pretreated with serum
from schizophrenics do not exhibit a pressor response
following the local application of an epinephrine
solution to the cerebral cortex. This procedure failed
to differentiate between the sera of a small series of
normals and schizophrenics on our wards.

One attempt by Robins, Smith and Lowe to confirm the
Tulane findings using comparable numbers and types of
subjects, and at least as rigorous controls, was quite
unsuccessful. In twenty subjects, who at different
times received saline or extracts of blood from normal
or schizophrenic donors prepared according to the method
for preparing taraxein, there were only five instances
of mental or behavioral disturbance resembling those
in the original report on taraxein and these occurred
as often following the administration of saline, extracts
of normal plasma, or taraxein. It is easy to dismiss
these negative findings with taraxein on the basis of
the difficulty of reproducing exactly the 29 steps
described in its preparation; it is considerably more
difficult to dismiss the observation that a few subjects
who received only saline or normal blood extract developed psychotic manifestations similar to those reported
from taraxein.

During the preliminary investigations it was stated
that taraxein was qualitatively different from ceruloplasmin on the basis of unpublished studies. A physico-
chemical or other objective characterization of taraxein
would do much to dispel some of the confusion regarding
its nature. Is it possible, for example, that taraxein
is, in fact, ceruloplasmin, but derives its special
properties from the psychosocial characteristics of the
situation in which it has been tested?

Serotonin, the important derivative of tryptophan, was
first shown to exist in the brain in high concentration
by Amin, Crawford and Gaddum. Interest in its possible
function in the central nervous system, and even its
relationship to schizophrenia, was inspired by the
finding that certain hallucinogens, notably lysergic
acid diethylamide, could, in extremely low concentration
block the effects of serotonin on smooth muscle. Thus,
Woolley and Shaw in 1954 wrote: "The demonstrated ability
of such agents to antagonize the action of serotonin in
smooth muscle and the finding of serotonin in the brain

suggest that the mental changes caused by the drugs are the result of a serotonin deficiency which they induce in the brain. If this be true, then the naturally occurring mental disorders — for example, schizophrenia — which are mimicked by these drugs, may be pictured as being the result of a cerebral serotonin deficiency arising from a metabolic failure..."; while simultaneously in England, Gaddum was speculating, "... it is possible that the HT in our brains plays an essential part in keeping us sane and that the effect of LSD is due to its inhibitory action on the HT in the brain." Since that time additional evidence has appeared to strengthen these hypotheses.

Serotonin has been found to be considerably higher in the limbic system and other areas of the brain which appear to be associated with emotional states. Bufotenine, or dimethyl serotonin, extracted from an hallucinogenic snuff of West Indian tribes, was found to have some properties similar to those of lysergic acid diethylamide. A major discovery was the finding that the ataractic agent, reserpine, causes a profound and persistent fall in the level of brain serotonin, a process which more closely parallels the mental effects of reserpine than does its own concentration in the brain. By administration of its precursor, 5-hydrosytryptophan, the levels of serotonin can be markedly elevated in the brain with behavioral effects described as resembling those of lysergic acid diethylamide, a finding quite at odds with the original hypotheses. On the other hand, administration of this precursor to mental patients, along with a benzyl analog of serotonin to block the peripheral effects of the amine was reported in preliminary trials to suppress the disease, although the benzyl analog alone is apparently an effective tranquilizing drug in chronically psychotic patients.

Still another bit of evidence supporting the hypotheses of a central function for serotonin was the accidental discovery of toxic psychoses in a certain fraction of tuberculous patients with iproniazid, which led to the therapeutic use of this drug in psychic depression. Iproniazid is known to inhibit the action of monoamine oxidase, an enzyme which destroys serotonin, and has been shown to increase the levels of this amine in the brain.

There are certain inconsistencies in the information which has accumulated which argue against a simple or singular role for serotonin in schizophrenia.

Although the ability of the hallucinogen, lysergic acid diethylamide, to block effects of serotonin on smooth muscle prompted the development of the hypotheses relating serotonin to mental function or disease, a number of lysergic acid derivatives have since been studied, and the correlation between mental effects and antiserotonin activity in the series as a whole is quite poor. One of these compounds is 2-brom-LSD, which has 1.5 times the antiserotonin activity of LSD, and which can be demonstrated by this property in the brain after systemic administration, but which in doses more than 15 times as great produces none of the mental effects of LSD.

In addition to serotonin, norepinephrine is also markedly reduced in the brain following reserpine. In fact, the brain concentrations of these two amines follow each other so closely in their response to reserpine as to suggest some mechanism common to both and perhaps obtaining as well for other active amines in the brain. In one study, l-dopa, a precursor of norepinephrine, was capable of counteracting the behavioral effects of reserpine whereas the precursor of serotonin was ineffective. Nor are the effects of iproniazid limited to brain serotonin; a comparable effect on norepinephrine has been reported, and it is possible that other amines or substances still to be discovered in the brain may be affected by what may be nonspecific inhibitor of a relatively nonspecific enzyme. Chlorpromazine, which has the same therapeutic efficacy as reserpine in disturbed behavior, is apparently able to achieve this action without any known effect on serotonin. In addition, the provocative observation that iproniazid which elevates serotonin levels in the brain can cause a toxic psychosis loses some of its impact when one realizes that isoniazid, which does not inhibit monoamine oxidase and can hardly raise the brain serotonin concentration, produces a similar psychosis.

It seems reasonable that the serotonin as well as the norepinephrine in the brain have some important functions there and the evidence in general supports this thesis even though it also suggests that their roles still remain to be defined.

The urinary excretion of 5-hydroxyindoleacetic acid has been used as an indicator of the portion of ingested tryptophan which is metabolised through serotonin to that end product. Although the excretion of 5-hydroxyindoleacetic acid is normal in schizophrenic patients under ordinary circumstances, it may be altered by challenging the metabolic system with large doses of tryptophan. Under these circumstances, failure on the part of schizophrenics to increase their output of 5-hydroxyindoleacetic acid has been reported while nonpsychotic controls double it.

27

Kopin of our laboratory has had the opportunity to perform a similar study on schizophrenics and normal controls maintained on a good and reasonably controlled
diet and in the absence of drugs. In each group there
was a slightly greater than two-fold increase in output
of 5-hydroxyindoleacetic acid following a tryptophan
load and no significant deviation from this pattern by
any single case.

That the heuristic speculations of Woolley and Shaw and
of Gaddum have not yet been established does not mean
that they are invalid. The widespread experimental
activity which they stimulated has broadened and deep-
ened our knowledge of the metabolism and pharmacology
of serotonin and its effects on behavior and may lead
the way to their definitive evaluation in normal and
pathological states.

Genetics and schizophrenic disorders

Many of the current hypotheses concerning the schizophrenia complex are original and attractive even though to
this time evidence directly implicating any one of them
in the disease itself is hardly compelling. There is,
nevertheless, cogent evidence responsible to a large
extent for the present reawakening of the long dormant
biochemical thinking in this area and sufficiently convincing to promote its continued development. Genetic
studies have recently assumed such a role and it appears
worthwhile briefly to review them in the present context.

Earlier studies on large populations have reported a
remarkable correlation between the incidence of shizo-
phrenia and the degree of consanguinity in relatives of
known schizophrenics. These findings were not conclusive,
however, since the influence of socio-environmental
factors was not controlled. Better evidence is obtained
from the examination of the cotwins and siblings of
schizophrenics. The concordance rate for schizophrenia
is extremely high for monozygotic twins in such studies,
while that for dizygotic twins is low and not significantly different from that in siblings to which, of
course, they are quite comparable genetically. Even
these studies, however, are not completely free from
possible sources of error, which prevent a definitive
conclusion regarding the role of genetic factors in this
disease. One cannot assume that environmental similarities and mutual interactions in identical twins, who
are always of the same sex and whose striking physical
congruence is often accentuated by parental attitudes,
play an insignificant role in the high concordance rate
of schizophrenia in this group. This factor could be
controlled by a study of twins separated at birth of
which no statistically valid series has yet been
compiled, or by a comparison of the concordance rates in

monozygotic and dizygotic twins whose zygocity had been mistakenly evaluated by the twins, their parents and associates. Another possible means of better controlling the environmental variables would be a careful study of schizophrenia in adopted children with comparison of its incidence in blood and foster relatives.*⟩ Perhaps only a survey on a national scale would provide the requisite numbers of cases for any of these studies.

A less satisfactory resolution of this problem can be obtained by an appraisal of environmental similarities in normal fraternal and identical twins. A study of over 100 specific aspects of the environment of normal twins has been made from which it is possible to derive some general impressions. Although there is a difference in this crude measure of environmental congruence between identical and fraternal twins of like sex, it is not statistically significant and can account for only a small fraction of the large difference in the concordance of schizophrenia between these types of twins. On the other hand, there is a highly significant difference in environmental similarity between fraternal twins of like and unlike sex which is sufficient to account for the difference in concordance rate of schizophrenia between them, for which, of course, there is no tenable genetic explanation.

⟨Another possible source of error in the twin studies which have been reported is the personal bias of the investigators who made the judgment of zygocity and the diagnosis of schizophrenia in the cotwins.⟩ Until a more definitive study is done in which these judgments are made independently, a rough evaluation is possible at least for the diagnosis of schizophrenia, if not of zygocity, based on diagnoses arrived at in the various hospitals to which the cotwins may have been admitted before or irrespective of their involvement in the study — diagnoses which are not likely to have been contaminated by knowledge of zygocity. Kallmann was good enough to review the material collected in his 1946-49 survey from that point of view. Of 174 monozygotic cotwins of schizophrenic index cases, 103 or 59% had been diagnosed schizophrenic by Kallmann, while 87 or 50% had received a psychiatric hospital diagnosis of schizophrenia before any examination by him. On the other hand, he had made the diagnosis of schizophrenia

---

*⟨When such a study was carried out in collaboration with Rosenthal, Wender and Schulsinger, a significantly evaluated prevalence of schizophrenia-related disorders was found in the biological relatives of adopted individuals who became schizophrenic, but not in their adopted relatives.⟩

in 47 or 9.1% of 517 dizygotic cotwins as compared to a hospital diagnosis in 31 or 6%. Although the concordance rates based only on hospital diagnoses are decreased in both types of twins for obvious reasons, the striking difference between the two concordance rates remains. Slater has published individual protocols of his cases from which judgments of zygocity and schizophrenia can be made. Of 21 twin pairs who could be considered definitely uniovular, 15 or 75% were concordant with respect to the simple criterion of admission to a mental hospital, whereas in only 12 or 10.3% of 116 binovular or questionably binovular pairs was there a history of the cotwins having been admitted to a mental hospital for any psychosis. On the basis of this analysis of the two most recent series, it seems that only a small component of the great difference in concordance rates reported for schizophrenia between uniovular and binovular twins can be attributed to the operation of personal bias in the diagnosis of the disease in the cotwin.

Even the most uncritical acceptance of all of the genetic data, however, cannot lead to the conclusion that the schizophrenic illnesses are the result of genetic factors alone. In fourteen to thirty percent of cases where schizophrenia occurs in one of monozygotic twins, the genetically identical partner will be free of the disorder. Attention has already been called to the higher concordance with respect to schizophrenia and the greater environmental similarities in like sexed fraternal twins or siblings than in those of unlike sex, and from the same source a difference in concordance is reported between monozygotic twins separated some years before (77.6%) as opposed to those not separated (91.5%). Neither of these observations is compatible with a purely genetic etiology of the disease, and both suggest the operation of environmental factors. Rosenthal and Jackson have pointed out the striking preponderance of female over male pairs concordant for schizophrenia in all of the reported series whether they be monozygotic or dizygotic twin, sibling, or parent-child pairs. If sampling errors on the basis of a greater mobility of males can be excluded and the observations taken as a reflection of the true incidence of this phenomenon there are several explanations for it on the basis of social interaction but none on purely genetic grounds.

One cannot at this time review the extensive literature supporting the importance of environmental factors in etiology of schizophrenic disorders. To this reviewer, at least, it is quite as suggestive as the genetic evidence but by no means more conclusive, since few studies in either field have been completely objective or adequately controlled.

It is both interesting and important to note that even
if the conclusions of both the genetic and environmental
approaches to the etiology of schizophrenic psychoses
are accepted uncritically, they are not mutually exclusive. Both are compatible with hypothesis that this
group of diseases results from the operation of socio-
environmental factors on some hereditary predisposition
or by an interaction of the two so that each is necessary
but neither alone is sufficient. An excellent example
of such a relationship is seen in tuberculosis where
the environmental microbial factor is indusputed and
where Lurie has shown the importance of genetic susceptibility, so that a population sufficiently heterogeneous with respect to susceptibility and exposure to
tuberculosis yields results in contingency and twin
studies which, before the discovery of the tubercle
bacillus, could easily have been used to prove a primary
genetic cause and almost as convincingly as the results
of similar studies in schizophrenia. Interestingly
enough, studies of tuberculosis from the socio-environmental point of view would obviously secure data equally
convincing for the operation of exogenous, social and
economic factors. One hypothesis with respect to the
schizophrenic psychoses which remains compatible with
all the evidence from the genetic as well as the psychosocial disciplines is that these disorders, like
tuberculosis, require the operation of environmental
factors upon a genetically determined predisposition.

RESUMÉ

Although the evidence for genetic and therefore biological
factors as important and necessary components in the
etiology of many or all of the schizophrenias is quite
compelling, the signposts pointing the way to their discovery are at present quite blurred and, to me at least,
illegible.

Genetic factors may operate through some ubiquitous
enzyme system to effect general changes in one or another
metabolic pathway detectable by studies on blood or
urine, and it is to be hoped that the currently active
search in these areas will continue.

It is at least equally possible, however, that these
genetic factors may operate only through enzymes or
metabolic processes peculiar to or confined within the
brain or even within extremely localized areas of the
brain. We are in need of new hypotheses such as those
of Elkes, and many already discussed. In this connection,
gamma-amino-butyric acid appears to be just as interesting a substance about which to construct working
hypotheses as are the catechols or the indoles. Not only
has it been isolated only from nervous tissue, and its
metabolism there been investigated in some detail, but

its neurophysiological properties appear to be better
defined than are those of the other two groups, in
addition to which its inhibitory properties may have
special relevance to diseases where a failure in central
inhibition seems to be involved.

Amphetamine possesses remarkable psychotomimetic properties which should not be overlooked. Its ability to
produce a clinical syndrome often indistinguishable
from schizophrenia and a possible relation to the
naturally occurring catechol amines make it at least
as interesting as lysergic acid diethylamide.

In addition to techniques at present available in neurochemistry, neurophysiology, and behavioral pharmacology,
the development of others designed to yield information
on processes occurring within the psychotic brain will
be needed before our explorations in this field have
been exhausted.

But the biochemist must not lose sight of the possibility
which is certainly as great as any of the others that
the genetic factors in schizophrenia operate to determine
inappropriate interconnections or interaction between
chemically normal components of the brain, in which case
the physiological psychologist, the neurophysiologist,
or the anatomist is more likely to find meaningful information long before the biochemist. It would take many
biochemists a long time to find a noisy circuit in a
radio receiver if they restricted themselves to chemical
techniques.

These possibilities are mentioned only to indicate how
large is the haystack in which we are searching for the
needle; one cannot avoid a feeling of humility when one
regards the chance that any one of us has found or will
find it in a relatively short time.

That is no cause for discouragement, however. It is not
necessary that one be convinced of the truth of a particular hypothesis to justify devoting one's energies to
testing it. It is enough that one regard it as worth
testing and that the tools with which to do so be
adequate. Modern biochemistry with its wealth of new
knowledge of intermediary metabolism and its array of
new techniques for the separation and identification of
compounds and the tracing of their metabolic pathways has
provided the biologist interested in mental illness with
an armamentarium which his predecessor of only a generation ago could hardly have dreamed possible. If he
chooses among the approaches which may lead to a definition of the biological factors in schizophrenia, those
which will in any case lead to a better understanding of
the nervous system and of thought processes and behavior,
the present surge of enthusiasm will not have been mis-
directed.

1963 DEAN RESEARCH AWARD

An internationally acclaimed authority on schizophrenia, **DAVID SHAKOW**'s *work covers a span of three decades. He was among the first to discover and implement techniques for the application of quantitative measurement in psychological and physiological studies on schizophrenics. Though regarded as a pioneer in the entire field of schizophrenia, he received the Dean Award in special recognition for his contributions to experimental psychopathology and other theoretical aspects of that disease. The Dean Award is but one of many other honors accorded Dr. Shakow, including the Harvard Detur Prize; the HEW Superior Service Award; the Helen Sargent Memorial Award of the Menninger Foundation; the Vestermark Memorial Award; and the Distinguished Contribution Award of the American Psychological Association.*

PSYCHOLOGICAL DEFICIT IN SCHIZOPHRENIA

by David Shakow

INTRODUCTION

THE years since I first began to work with schizophrenia have gone by fast. I am naturally reluctant to count them! I shall try to give you at least a glimpse of some of the work I have been involved with during these years, mainly at Worcester State Hospital, but also at the University of Illinois, and most recently at the National Institute of Mental Health. In the face of a problem like schizophrenia, one can only humbly hope that he has contributed at least a few solid bricks to the final structure of understanding.

GENERAL BACKGROUND

Before going on to some of our data and their theoretical implications, I should like to remark briefly upon some of the special difficulties and complexities that we have found in the course of our research on schizophrenia —problems which I believe have plagued other serious investigators in this field. There are so many problems relevant to the conditions for carrying out dependable research in schizophrenia, that it would be quite possible to spend all my allotted time in discussing them. I cannot refrain, nevertheless, from at least touching upon a few of the problems I have discussed at some length in previous publications (Shakow, 1946, 1962). I believe that a large part of the many discrepant findings in this large and varied group of disorders stems from failure to take these factors into account. Not that even our own best thought-through and carefully executed designs haven't ended up in some way inadequate! I have not infrequently been appalled by some of the compromises with experimental design that circumstances have caused me to make.

Both interindividual and intraindividual *variability* are a major source of difficulty in research on schizophrenia. In our psychological studies, groups of schizophrenic patients have quite consistently given coefficients of variation three times that of normal subjects, and individual patients two times that of the normal ones. In studies of physiological functions, these have varied from one and one-half to more than twice that of normal subjects. Of the many sources of variation I shall only concern myself here with the two important ones of nosology and attitude.

Taken in its broadest sense, *nosology* has many facets. Initially there is the fundamental problem of the diagnosis of schizophrenia and its subtypes. Aware of this problem, we have made every effort, especially in our Worcester studies, to obtain reliable diagnoses of patients. In addition to certain definite exclusion criteria, we had specified standards for the general diagnosis of schizophrenia, as well as for subtype classification. Whenever there was a question about the schizophrenia diagnosis, the patient was not used in the research. If the patient did not clearly meet the criteria established for one of the four subtypes, the category of mixed, unclassified, or indeterminate was used.

We have a tendency these days to be condescending about subtype classification. In fact, there are even "nihilists" among us who would do away with all diagnostic categories, the less enthusiastic of these calling for at least the casting overboard of the subtypes. If diagnoses are to be made on the relatively careless bases so prevalent in many centers, then I would go along with this point of view. If, however, they are based upon carefully worked out and tested criteria, then they deserve considerable respect. I say this despite my original and continuing "dynamic" bias. For the clear-cut syndromes of behavior, for which such labels are referents, have definite value for research purposes, even carrying consistent dynamic and "style" implications for those interested. I am not claiming that there is not much room for improvement. Perhaps it will come through the factorial techniques, which, after some thought, we decided not to use at Worcester. What I do hold is that such perceptive clinicians as Kraepelin and Bleuler saw things that we might also see if we look carefully.

The growing trend for dichotomization in schizophrenia presents us with another aspect of the nosological problem. Although these dichotomies are helpful when used conservatively, analyses based on them too often show a tendency to oversimplify. Absolute constancy and consistency, whether within an individual or within a group of schizophrenics, is, of course, illusory. Schizophrenia, particularly in its less chronic phases, is a fairly continuous succession of action and reaction, of regression and restitution—processes which sometimes appear at an overt, easily discernible level, but most frequently at a more cryptic level. Should the patient come for study during a reaction phase, one may be led to place him in the opposite part of the dichotomy from that in which he characteristically belongs. For this reason several readings on a patient need to be taken.

These dichotomies and characterizations do have a distinct contribution to make. Although they have led to much discrepancy in the literature, careful examination reveals a surprising amount of overlap and synonymity among the various dichotomies. Still needed, however, are more rigorous criteria for class membership and more dependable methods for defining the criteria.

I should like to make a particular point about the chronic/acute dichotomy. These classes may be roughly separated by such a criterion as period of hospitalization. Even ideally, this measure tends to be approximate and arbitrary because the correlation of the classes of the dichotomy with the criterion is

at best mildly positive. To complicate the problem, we may be dealing with certain effects on functions which are more attributable to the long period of hospitalization than to the psychosis itself. Certainly many chronic patients show qualities which are not found in acute patients. Whether these are the direct and indirect effects of hospitalization, or whether they are developments of the psychosis that might very well have come about if the patients had not been hospitalized, remains an open question.

Another problem which troubles psychologists perennially is the part played by the *co-operation* or *attitude* of the subject. Almost all psychological tests and experiments require at least the passive participation of the subject. The data from such studies, except those directly investigating functioning at nonoptimal levels (a hazardous procedure, I must point out), carry the implication of having been collected under optimal conditions—external as well as internal. When there is suspicion that nonoptimal conditions are present, justifiable doubt about the validity of the findings arises. The argument may be offered that poverty in co-operativeness is intrinsic to schizophrenia; therefore, any attempt at the separation of its effects is at best academic. This thesis has validity to the extent that poor co-operation *is* intrinsic. The argument, however, runs into the difficulty of not making a distinction between the intrinsic effects of attitude and of other temporary or superficial interfering effects. In order to control for this factor in our studies, we consistently used an *A* to *E* rating scale which defined various levels of co-operation. The patients used in the studies reported fall mainly into the classes we labeled *A* and *B* co-operation, those showing either active interest in the task itself, or active effort because of secondary interest.

At this point a few words seem necessary about the kinds of studies we conducted and the kinds of patients we have generally used. The studies I shall be concerned with have been directed at answering questions of the *what* and *how* rather than the *why* and *about what* of the psychological functioning of schizophrenics. They are part of an effort to understand the nature of the schizophrenic organism, something about his psychological structure and function. Ego function has been emphasized, particularly single ego functions such as psychomotility and learning.

The patients we generally studied can be described as chronic. They had a mean age of approximately thirty, a mean schooling of nine to ten years, and a mean hospitalization age of approximately seven years. (Hospitalization age is defined as the time elapsed since first hospitalization for mental disorder.) The major advantage of working with chronic rather than acute patients is that because of the *relative* stability achieved, the intraindividual (and indirectly, the interindividual) variability is reduced.

EXPERIMENTAL FINDINGS

An examination of our actual studies, which ranged from the patellar-tendon-reflex latent time at one extreme to group behavior involving competitive and co-operative activity at the other, revealed four general categories of results. The first group includes areas in which from the very beginning no differences were found between the schizophrenic and the normal subjects. A second area of results was one in which differences found between the two groups initially or under ordinary conditions either disappeared with repetition, or were considerably decreased under certain special conditions. This group of findings I have characterized as showing "normalizing" trends. By "normalizing" I mean nothing more than that the originally different results obtained from the schizophrenics came to fall close to or actually within the range of normal performance. In the third group, differences were found between the schizophrenic and normal groups which *did* persist. Actually, a fourth category of "results" could be added here. This would include the situations in which the patient withdrew and would not co-operate, so that we were unable to get experimental data.

I shall now go on to present some of the data from each of the first three groups, based on both published and unpublished studies.

No differences

Contrary to what seems to be generally true in physiological and biochemical studies, we have tended to find very few variables in which no differences were found between groups of schizophrenic and normal subjects. Possibly this is to be expected, since the disorder has been defined in behavior terms.

But even if this is the case, certain cautions must be observed in defining "differences." We have already seen one in the discussion of "co-operation": the investigator must be careful in evaluating a response as to whether it is due to a lack of interest in responding adequately, or to an intrinsic inability to do so. Another relates to the need for conservatism in evaluating a "response" on the part of a schizophrenic. Even given satisfactory co-operation, this problem exists in relation to certain tasks. If one approaches a patient without having sufficient clinical sensitivity, it is quite possible to obtain considerably more pathological, and what may be termed experimentally "inadequate," responses than one would under "fairer" conditions. I should like to illustrate this by a relatively simple example from a study which we did on color-blindness in schizophrenia (Millard & Shakow, 1935), which I hope will also indicate a general principle of our way of approaching the study of schizophrenia.

In the course of our routine clinical studies of schizophrenics, in a relatively short time we ran into several patients who could be designated as "red-green" color-blind, by Miles' criteria in the Ishihara Test. Since we were intrigued with this finding and its possible genetic implications, we decided to carry out an extensive study with this test with schizophrenics, using other types of patients in the hospital as controls. Employing Miles' criteria (two or more incorrect responses, either color-blind or anomalous, excluding Plates X and XI) we obtained a 13 per cent incidence of color-blindness, as opposed to an 8 per cent normal incidence. This meant that we had a significantly greater number of color-blind schizophrenics. We felt uncomfortable, however, about the "anomalous-response" criterion. We recognized that anom-

TABLE 1
CONSTANTS OF THE DISTRIBUTION OF INDIVIDUAL THRESHOLDS IN VOLTS OF 22 SCHIZOPHRENIC PATIENTS AND
28 NORMAL SUBJECTS FOR TWO SESSIONS THREE MONTHS APART

	Patients		Normals	
	Session 1	Session 2	Session 1	Session 2
Min	61	55	65	60
Max	174	156	164	188
Mean	110 ± 5.7	102 ± 5.0	101 ± 4.6	103 ± 4.7
S.D.	26.8 ± 4.1	23.1 ± 3.5	24.1 ± 3.2	24.6 ± 3.3

alous and doubtful responses were much more likely to occur in a psychiatric population. We experimented with a number of other scoring systems but felt most secure about what we called the Worcester III criteria—two or more definite color-blind responses, excluding Plates X and XI. We felt rather strongly that we could not use the Miles criteria since the Gertrude Steinian law (a response is a response is a response is a response) held only in a limited sense for schizophrenics. In passing, may I mention my prejudice that this is one of the weaknesses in some of the operant conditioning work being carried out with schizophrenics. (And I say this as a *very* early, if only transient, operant conditioner with schizophrenics in the early '30's!)

To get back to color-blindness. When we used these stricter criteria we found no difference between the incidence in schizophrenic and normal subjects. I am arguing here for conservatism in making a judgment of pathology in those situations where we are offered a choice. Although most test and experimental situations do not offer us this kind of choice, caution is almost always possible. There are so many differences already; is there any need for increasing them unnecessarily?

Another area where we did not find any differences was in the patellar-tendon-reflex latent time. Huston (1935), when he carefully controlled for height of his subjects, found that there were no differences between schizophrenic and normal control subjects at this simple psychophysical level.

These and other experiments led us to decide that any differences existing between schizophrenic and normal subjects were more likely to be found at more complicated levels

than the simple sensory or psychophysical. We therefore turned our experimentation in these directions.

"Normalizing" trends[1]

We have characterized as showing "normalizing" trends those findings in which the differences originally found between schizophrenic and normal subjects have tended to disappear or become reduced under certain conditions. The normalizing factors that have struck us most forcefully appear to be of seven kinds. These factors are: (1) repetition, (2) passage of time, (3) co-operation, (4) time for preparation, (5) social influence, (6) stress, and (7) shock. I shall consider the seven factors separately and present one or two studies to exemplify each.

Repetition. In many of our studies—physiological as well as psychological—the first reading taken of a patient's performance in a task was found to be nonrepresentative of subsequent readings. Thus in a study of the threshold for direct current stimulation (Huston, 1934), the results of which are presented in Table 1, during the first experiment the patients had a mean threshold of 110 volts and the normal subjects a mean threshold of 101 volts. In the second session, three months later, the schizophrenic mean was 102 and the normal mean 103. It is thus seen that on repetition, without any essential clinical change in the patients, the patient mean fell essentially to the level of the normal subjects.

Let us take another type of study, this time a learning situation in which a kind of pur-

[1] A version of this section on normalizing trends was previously presented at the XVth International Congress of Psychology in 1957 (Shakow, 1958b).

38

TABLE 2
SCORES OF INDIVIDUAL SCHIZOPHRENIC PATIENTS AND NORMAL CONTROLS ON THIRTY-THREE-DAY
PRODMETER EXPERIMENT

		Co-operation	Mean Score First Day	Mean Score Lowest Day	Lowest Trial Score	Day Lowest Trial Score Reached
Patients	1	A	37	12	11	22
	2	B	38	13	11	24
	3	B	39	15	12	30
	4	B	34	16	13	17
	5	B	36	16	14	30
	6	C	39	17	13	27
	7	C	64	17	15	33
	8	C	43	18	16	18
	9	C	39	19	16	28
Normals	1	A	24	12	11	26
	2	A	30	13	11	24

suitmeter, the "Prodmeter," was used. In this experiment (Huston & Shakow, 1949) the subject is required to follow a revolving target with a pointer for ten trials of ten revolutions each. (The turntable stops when the pointer is not on the target.) The subjects were examined on 33 consecutive days, excluding Sundays. The results from Table 2, given in terms of the time taken for the task in seconds, are worthy of note. As indicated in the first column, the mean scores of the schizophrenic subjects for the first day are without exception higher (i.e., poorer), and generally much higher, than those of the two normal subjects. On the lowest day, however, the mean scores of the schizophrenic subjects are much closer to those of the normal subjects. An examination of the next two columns, which give the lowest trial score and the day on which the lowest trial score was reached, corroborates the general impression that the differences between the two groups tended to be reduced considerably with repetition. In fact, one of the patients actually did better than either of the two control subjects, both of whom were persons of unusually high intelligence and highly skilled in motor tasks. A number of the other patients came close to the scores of the normal subjects. Because of the small number of subjects the findings can, of course, be considered as only suggestive, and in need of replication. One does gain the impression, however, that given a sufficient amount of practice schizophrenic subjects can sometimes reach a "physiological limit" not very different from that of normal subjects.

Passage of time. Aside from repetition, with or without practice effects, we have also found what appears to be evidence that mere lapse of time can result in improvement in the performance of schizophrenic subjects. This phenomenon appeared in a pursuitmeter learning experiment (Huston & Shakow, 1948) which called for ten trials of ten revolutions each in following a target with a pointer. This task was repeated two times at intervals of three months. The data for the first two periods are given in Table 3, the scores being in terms of contacts made. (A high score in this case is a good score.) It will be noted that for the patients the mean for the tenth and last trial of Period 1 was 18.8, and the mean for the first trial of Period 2, following an interval of three months, was 24.1. They thus showed an actual gain of 5.3 points. For the comparable trials the normal subjects, on the contrary, showed a loss of 2 points—from 43 to 41. The trends of the curves for each of the other periods were in general at the same level. Whether this reminiscence effect was the result of the dropping out of interfering habits and irrelevant ruminations that prevented the patients from being able to show how well they had actually learned originally, or whether this effect was due to a kind of "consolidation" resulting from some continuing process, the

39

TABLE 3
PURSUIT SCORES, TRIAL-BY-TRIAL FOR 46 SCHIZOPHRENIC PATIENTS AND FOR 22 NORMAL SUBJECTS

Period	Trial	Patients		Normals	
		Mean ± S.E.	S.D. ± S.E.	Mean ± S.E.	S.D. ± S.E.
	1	12.9 ± 1.4	10.0 ± 1.0	30.0 ± 3.1	14.3 ± 2.2
	2	15.3 ± 1.8	12.2 ± 1.2	29.6 ± 2.8	13.3 ± 2.0
	3	15.5 ± 1.6	11.0 ± 1.1	34.0 ± 2.9	13.5 ± 2.0
	4	14.9 ± 1.5	10.5 ± 1.1	34.3 ± 2.8	13.3 ± 2.0
1	5	16.1 ± 1.7	12.1 ± 1.2	35.9 ± 2.5	11.7 ± 1.8
	6	17.2 ± 1.8	13.0 ± 1.2	34.1 ± 2.3	10.7 ± 1.6
	7	17.9 ± 2.1	14.5 ± 1.5	40.7 ± 2.7	12.6 ± 1.9
	8	18.7 ± 1.8	13.1 ± 1.3	42.5 ± 2.9	13.6 ± 2.1
	9	19.8 ± 1.9	13.6 ± 1.4	43.0 ± 3.2	15.2 ± 2.3
	10	18.8 ± 1.9	13.6 ± 1.4	43.0 ± 3.2	14.9 ± 2.2
	Mean	16.7 ± 1.6	10.8 ± 1.1	36.7 ± 2.4	11.2 ± 1.7
	1	24.1 ± 2.2	14.8 ± 1.5	41.0 ± 2.9	13.4 ± 2.0
	2	25.8 ± 2.2	14.8 ± 1.5	45.4 ± 3.4	15.7 ± 2.4
	3	26.3 ± 2.2	15.1 ± 1.6	45.2 ± 3.3	15.4 ± 2.3
	4	25.0 ± 2.1	14.1 ± 1.5	46.4 ± 2.8	13.1 ± 2.0
2	5	27.3 ± 2.3	15.5 ± 1.6	48.3 ± 2.7	12.6 ± 1.9
	6	29.6 ± 2.8	19.5 ± 2.0	49.3 ± 3.3	15.6 ± 2.3
	7	28.6 ± 2.7	18.6 ± 1.9	51.2 ± 3.4	15.8 ± 2.4
	8	29.3 ± 2.6	18.1 ± 1.9	52.7 ± 2.8	13.1 ± 2.0
	9	28.8 ± 2.7	18.6 ± 1.9	52.6 ± 2.9	13.7 ± 2.1
	10	31.4 ± 2.6	18.1 ± 1.9	60.0 ± 2.8	13.1 ± 2.0
	Mean	27.6 ± 2.2	15.1 ± 1.6	49.2 ± 2.6	12.1 ± 1.9

important point is that the phenomenon appeared in the schizophrenic but not in the normal subjects.

These first two of the seven normalizing factors—repetition and lapse of time—appear to be primarily outside the patient's control. The next series of categories that I wish to consider appear to require his involvement to some degree and are for this reason perhaps different in quality.

Co-operation. In all of our studies in which patients were involved, our general practice was to use a 5-point rating scale to characterize their participation in the task. For general purposes we labeled this characterization as "co-operation level." The term must be considered one which deals largely with the patients' involvement in the assigned task as determined by his effort and interest. A rating of A indicates active interest and maximum effort—generally the level of response obtained from normal subjects under similar circumstances. A rating of B indicates real effort by the subject but one deriving from sources other than a primary interest in the

task itself, probably from friendliness to the experimenter and a wish to be thought well of by him. A C rating indicates a docile, perfunctory, spasmodic effort, one where the patient requires some urging to complete the task. Ratings of D and E represent participation at even lower levels than that rated C. Performances with such ratings have rarely been included in reported data—actually E is never included and D only for very special purposes.

It has turned out in a number of our studies that when the co-operation level of the patient was at approximately that of the normal subject—that is, at the A level—the differences which were otherwise generally found between the total group of schizophrenic and normal subjects were reduced very considerably and sometimes actually eliminated. I shall present a few sample studies which bring out this fact.

The data for the first of these studies, one of steadiness (Huston & Shakow, 1946), is shown in Table 4. As you will see from the columns of the means, the performance was

TABLE 4

CONSTANTS OF THE DISTRIBUTION OF WEIGHTED
STEADINESS SCORES ACCORDING TO CO-OPERATION
LEVELS FOR 135 SCHIZOPHRENIC SUBJECTS AND
64 NORMAL SUBJECTS

	Co-op-eration	N	Mean	S.D.
Patients	A	26	118.7 ± 11.1	55.3
	B	48	73.2 ± 6.7	45.6
	C & D	61	29.7 ± 4.3	33.9
	Total	135	62.3 ± 4.7	54.3
Normals	A	64	120.0 ± 8.1	65.1

markedly different at the various co-operation levels—in fact, the differences were highly significant among the various patient groups. However, when a comparison was made between the performance of the patients rated *A* in co-operation (118.7) and the performance of the normal subjects (120.0), the difference was not significant—in fact, the scores were almost identical.

Time for preparation. Another experiment which showed a similar trend and involves still another factor is that on tapping (Shakow & Huston, 1936). The data are presented in Table 5. It will be noted from the column giving the mean scores that whereas the total schizophrenic group had a mean of 19.5 and the normal group a mean score of 28.9, the patients with an *A* co-operation rating had a score of 25.1. Although this difference was still significantly different from that of the normal subject group, it was now significantly reduced. Actually, if we take only the paranoid patients (the subtype giving the highest scores) who are rated *A* in co-operation, then the significant difference is wiped out.

The results obtained from the study of tapping puzzled us when we compared them with the results from a series of reaction time studies (which we shall have occasion to consider later) that we conducted at the same time. The reaction time differences remained significant even when co-operation level and subtype of schizophrenia were taken into consideration. Since tapping would, on the face of it, seem to be a form of continuous reaction-time activity actually requiring more persistent effort than isolated reaction time,

we were at a loss to account for the differences in the two sets of results.

For a time the only suggestion that occurred to us was that the distinction lay in a fundamental difference in the nature of the two experimental tasks. In the tapping experiment the subject was told that he should start tapping at a given signal and to continue tapping (for five seconds) until asked to stop. In several senses the schizophrenic was able here to set his own pace. He could actually start tapping when ready and was *not* penalized for any time he took for preparation. In addition, the apparatus was so constructed that the first 750 ms. of the tapping period was not counted. This provided the subject an additional period in which to prepare. In the reaction-time situation the subject was warned that a stimulus was coming. But here, of course, the stimulus called for immediate response, and the subject *was* penalized for delay. The pace of this task was in no way under the subject's control. It is quite possible that for the schizophrenic the opportunity to set his own pace, as opposed to having it determined from the outside, is very important. Obviously a systematic experiment should be designed to deal with this question. For the present, however, we are considering *self-preparation* one of the "normalizing" factors. We shall consider this hypothesis further at a later point in our discussion.

Social pressure. The usual way of obtaining involvement in a task by a patient is through the rapport and influence which the experimenter is able to establish. Another, more rarely used with schizophrenic subjects, is through providing a social situation in

TABLE 5

CONSTANTS OF THE DISTRIBUTION OF MEAN TAPPING
SCORES (TEN TRIALS) FOR SCHIZOPHRENIC PATIENTS
AND NORMAL SUBJECTS

	N	Mean	S.D.
Patients			
Total	125	19.5 ± .50	5.58
A co-operation	16	25.1	
Paranoid total	24	24.4 ± .94	4.60
Paranoid: *A* co-operation	8	27.5	
Normals	60	28.9 ± .55	4.24

41

TABLE 6

Speed in Seconds of Card Sorting by Schizophrenic Subjects Under Different Conditions of Learning

Condi-	Trials											
tions†	1	2	3	4	5	6	7	8	9	10	11	12
1	64.5*	60.0*	56.5	56.5	53.5	55.0	54.0	54.5				
2A	64.5	63.0	60.0	61.5*	43.5*	40.0*	44.0	48.0	43.5	44.0		
5	63.0	59.5	54.5	55.0	52.0	53.5	52.0	53.5*	42.5*	38.0	38.5	39.0

† 1. Learning Control Series ($N = 15$). 2A. Interindividual Competition Series (N = 6) Trials 5 and 6.
5. Group Competition Series ($N = 12$) Trials 9, 10, 11, 12.
* Significant differences between items.

which he is a member of a group of peers, where the social situation may press him into involvement. Radlo and I designed a study, as yet unpublished (partially described in Shakow, 1958b), which used card-sorting for the investigation of schizophrenic learning under conditions of both individual and group competition. The task consisted of speedily sorting sixty cards, each marked with a set of five digits, one of which set was either 1, 2, or 3. The cards were to be placed in compartments so labeled. The experiment was carried out with many groups and under a variety of conditions. For our present purposes it is only necessary to consider three groups, closely matched for initial scores. Table 6 shows the data from these groups.

Group 1, a group of schizophrenic patients in which no competition was introduced, served as the controls. Note the nature of the learning curve in this group. The asterisks indicate points at which there are significant differences between successive scores.

Group 2A was a patient group in a situation where *interindividual* competition was introduced. After going through trials 1-4 *individually* in separate rooms, three patients at a time were brought into an adjoining room for trials 5 and 6 and placed under conditions in which competition among them was emphasized. For trials 7 to 10 they again went back to their original rooms, where they worked individually under the previous conditions. It is to be noted that there was a drop in score (a low score, of course, being a good score) for trials 5 and 6 when compared with trial 4, and a rising, more or less flattened, curve thereafter. The patients appeared generally to retain most of what they had gained during

the period of competition. This may be interpreted either that once a patient, for whatever reasons, has achieved a level of performance he is able to maintain it, or that for the schizophrenic patient the competition situation "continues" despite the immediate physical absence of the competitors.

Group 5 represents patients in a *group competition* situation. In trials 1-8, six patients worked in individual rooms as previously and under similar instructions as in the control situation. (The similarity of the scores of Group 5 to the control group through these eight trials is quite striking.) In trials 9-12, two groups of three patients each competed as teams, each team using one set of sorting bins. A comparison of trial 9 of Group 5 with trial 8 of Group 1 (the control group) shows a spurt to a quite different level from the plateau achieved at trials 5 to 8 in both Groups 1 and 5. The differences were significant at this point. In general we believe these results tend to show the susceptibility of schizophrenics to both competitive and cooperative motivation; that is, they show a greater involvement in tasks and a higher level of performance under such conditions.

Stress. Although this is an area in which we have done a good deal of experimentation, we do not have any satisfactorily completed studies on chronic schizophrenics. We do, however, have a number of studies which are at least suggestive. But again, they call for replication.

Two studies using a targetball stress situation gave results similar to those we have just discussed. The targetball apparatus is designed to study achievement in relation to aspiration level. In addition, however, it is

42

so organized that the experimenter can manipulate the apparatus to make the subject either succeed or fail in relation to a "bogey" score, which represents the level of achievement of the "average" person. Subjects, whether schizophrenic or normal, generally become highly involved in the experiment. In our experiments in which this stress of failure was induced, it was found that such stress tended to improve the scores of the schizophrenic subject and to bring him closer to the normal. The stress appeared to improve the performance of the patients not only in a psychomotor task involving a special kind of pursuitmeter (see Sands & Rodnick, 1950, p. 675), but also on a *TAT* test involving thinking. In the latter the general quality of the stories, the clarity of the thinking, and the consistency with which the ideas were presented, all improved.

Shock. The last of the "normalizing" factors which I shall discuss is "shock." I shall present two experiments which offer evidence along this line.

The first of these is from a study by Rodnick (1942) on the effect of metrazol shock on habit systems. In this experiment two groups of 21 schizophrenic subjects each were initially trained, as Habit 1, to respond with a right-finger movement to a tone of 500 cycles and with a left-finger movement to a tone of 700 cycles. In this first session the subjects were given 100 trials, 50 for each tone. In a second session, 24 hours later, Habit 2 was established, both groups being instructed to reverse the direction of response to the tones. This training session consisted of 75 trials. One hour after the second session the subjects in one group were given metrazol injections. One and one-half hours later, both groups were retested to determine which habit was dominant. Ten trials were given, 5 to each of the tones.

As Table 7 shows, a statistically significant greater number of reversions to the first habit occurred in the group subjected to metrazol shock. Although the habit system here involved is of course a quite different order from that ordinarily associated with schizophrenic behavior, the value of the experiment lies in indicating that a metrazol shock (and perhaps other shock treatments) does have a differential effect upon older and more recently acquired habits.

TABLE 7
RESPONSES OF SCHIZOPHRENIC PATIENTS, SHOWING THE EFFECT OF METRAZOL SHOCK UPON A HABIT SYSTEM

Group	Less than 50 Per Cent Reversion to Habit 1	More than 50 Per Cent Reversion to Habit 1
Metrazol ($N = 21$)	7	14
Control ($N = 21$)	17	4

$\chi^2 = 7.88$ $p < .01$ (Yates correction for small n)

A study more closely associated with the complex habit systems of the schizophrenic is that carried out by Schnack, Shakow, and Lively (1945). We administered a battery of tests (the Stanford-Binet, the Kent-Rosanoff Word Association Test, and an aspiration-level test) to 50 male schizophrenic patients before and after treatment with insulin or metrazol. Our comparison of the two sets of scores revealed considerable changes in the direction of improvement of intellectual functions with treatment on most of the measures.

To test the significance of these changes, a further comparison was made with individually matched control patients who had had two successive examinations while under routine hospital care, but who had had neither form of therapy. These results showed that insulin and metrazol could only be held responsible for about one-third of the improvement in test scores—two-thirds being directly attributable to the ordinary hospital regime and familiarity with the test situation. The data further indicated that those with mental ages below 12-0 upon first testing seemed to benefit most from metrazol therapy. The patients with originally higher mental ages, however, were apparently disturbed by metrazol. Insulin, on the other hand, though helpful in both groups, seemed more effective with the higher intelligence group, when the changes occurring beyond those shown by control patients under routine care are taken as the criterion. Of the higher intelligence group, those more nearly normal had a better long-term reaction to insulin, but a poorer long-term reaction to metrazol.

Thus if we were to summarize what we have been saying about these normalizing factors we could say that they involve differing degrees of "heroics" which achieve at least "temporary effects"; they (1) allow a period for acquaintance and removal of strangeness; (2) permit personal motivation to enter, either self-induced, or from the outside by providing "stress"; (3) allow the subject to control the situation without his knowing it (if he knows, as we shall see later, he is likely to do his worst work); and (4) use extreme "shock" to bring the person out of his more recently acquired, nonadaptive habits.

Persistent differences

We have thus far considered two groups of psychological findings: those which showed no differences between normal and schizophrenic subjects, and those in which the differences either disappeared or tended towards the normal level under certain conditions. Let us now examine a third class of findings: those studies in which the differences were found to persist. By "persist" I mean that they endured under conditions generally similar to those which yielded the normalizing trend with the factors we have discussed.

Autonomic reactivity. Besides motor responses to a stimulus, for example reaction time, which we shall discuss shortly, there is a category of autonomic responses to stimuli in the context of experiments in which the subject is asked to relax and make no overt response. Over the years we have carried out a series of studies involving galvanic skin response, heart rate, and other such responses as affected through repeated stimulations by verbal ready signals, noise, tone, light, and pain. Let me give you examples from two studies, one carried out a number of years ago at Worcester State Hospital, and another more recently at the National Institutes of Health.

In the first study (Cohen & Patterson, 1937), the aim was to determine the rate of adaptation of schizophrenic and normal subjects to pain—in this case induced by pressing the skin with an algesimeter. There were ten subjects in each group of schizophrenics and normals.

As you will see from the graph in Figure 1, both groups of subjects started with a mean heart rate of 80. At the end of an hour of repeated stimulation the normals gradually came down to a level of 74, whereas the schizophrenic group fluctuated between 80 and 85, giving a reading of 80, the equivalent of their initial mean, in the last trial. Their actual mean level on the ward was 74.

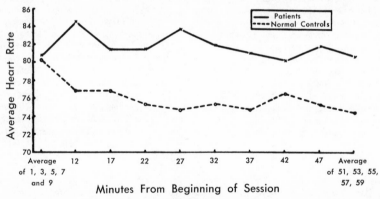

Fig. 1. Mean Heart Rate Changes of Schizophrenic ($N = 10$) and Normal ($N = 10$) Subjects Undergoing Repeated Pain Stimulation.

44

A recent study of *GSR* orienting reactions to visual and auditory stimuli (Zahn, Rosenthal, & Lawlor, 1962) employed a red light and a 300-cycle tone as stimuli. The subjects were 52 chronic schizophrenic and 20 normal subjects, both groups averaging a little over 40 years of age. The stimuli were presented 40 times each at separate sessions for a 1-second duration at $\frac{1}{2}$-minute intervals, with appropriate beginning and ending control readings. We might consider the results in two ways: in relation to the level of arousal or activation, and in relation to specific or orienting responses to stimuli.

Base conductance and frequency of nonspecific *GSR*s are two measures of skin resistance that have been found to be related to level of arousal. As is shown in Figure 2, using base log conductance as a criterion of arousal level shows that the schizophrenic subjects had a significantly higher arousal level in relation to the light stimulus. The normal subjects showed a progressive adaptation to both the light and tone stimuli that did not occur in the schizophrenics. The similarity of the curves for the tone stimulus to the one for the heart-rate-reaction to pain (see Figure 1) is striking. Let us take the

other measure of arousal—the number of nonspecific *GSR*s (drops in skin resistance of 400 ohms or more which did *not* occur within the first 3 seconds after the stimulus). Here again the patients showed a significantly higher arousal level.

How about the specific or orienting responses? These were defined as drops in resistance of 400 or more ohms beginning within the first three seconds after the onset of the stimulus. As Figure 3 indicates, here again the schizophrenics were more responsive over-all. The striking difference, however, is in the rate of habituation, which was significantly faster for the normal subjects.

An interesting comparison is the ratio of the specific to the nonspecific *GSR* response frequency per unit time. A clear difference existed in the direction of greater specific to nonspecific responsiveness for the normals. One likely interpretation of this finding is that the influences of internal or self-produced stimulation in relation to the influence of external stimulation is proportionately greater in the schizophrenics. This ratio seems more likely to be related to "preoccupation" rather than to "distractibility," although the latter cannot be ruled out altogether.

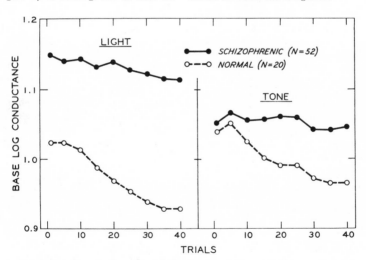

FIG. 2. Base Log Conductance of Schizophrenic and Normal Subjects to Repeated Stimulation by Light (Exp. 1) and Tone (Exp. 2).

45

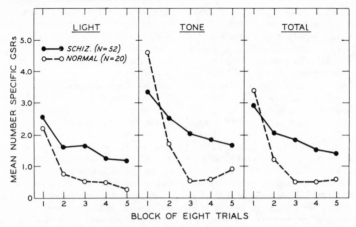

Fig. 3. Mean Number of Specific *GSR*s of Schizophrenic and Normal Subjects to Repeated Light and Tone and the Total of These.

Both these experiments seem to indicate that whereas the normal subject shows gradual autonomic adaptation or habituation to the stimuli, schizophrenic subjects do not seem to adapt in this way. The schizophrenic tends to continue to react at the end of the session—frequently for as long as an hour—at approximately the same autonomic level as he had at the outset. In this respect, the schizophrenic remains inordinately unaffected by the preceding succession of stimuli.

Reaction time. Another area in which we have found persistent differences is reaction time. An early exploratory study of simple visual, simple auditory, and discrimination visual reaction time (Huston, Shakow, & Riggs, 1937, pp. 40-57) found that the schizophrenic means in each of these three types of reaction were very much higher than those of the normal subjects, and that there was relatively little change over the three periods of testing, which were three months apart. A similar significant difference was obtained with the minimal reactions, the normal group having a significantly shorter mean minimal reaction time than even the best patients—those rated *A* in co-operation. Unfortunately we do not have long-term data involving daily

practice such as that on pursuitmeter learning. Such an experiment would be important in determining whether the schizophrenic can eventually achieve a normal level of performance.

In the first follow-up study on simple auditory reaction time (Huston *et al.*, 1937, pp. 57-79), there was, as is shown in Figure 4, significantly slower time for schizophrenic subjects at every one of six preparatory intervals (range 0.5-10 sec.) for both the regular and irregular procedures. In addition, an interesting phenomenon appeared which seemed to be related to what might be considered the maintenance of set. Our schizophrenic subjects seemed to have special difficulty in maintaining a major set, having instead a tendency to react to isolated stimuli, or at best to depend upon minor, less adaptive sets.

We noted in this experiment that whereas normal subjects were able to take advantage of the regular procedure by giving shorter reaction times at all intervals, the schizophrenic subjects had a breakdown point at the 2-second interval—that is, they gained no advantage from the regular, and of course much simpler, presentation. Beyond two seconds they seemed unable to take advantage

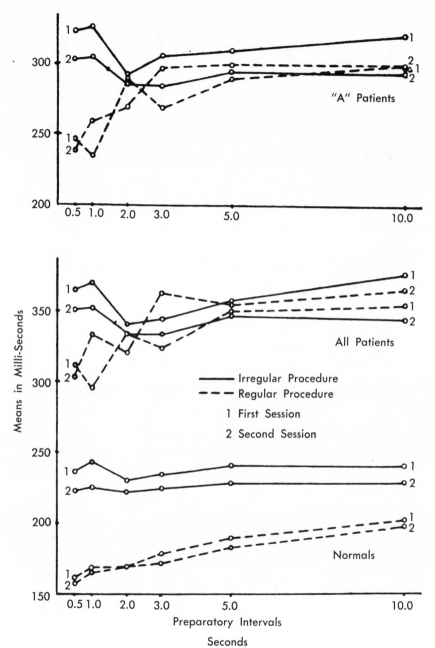

FIG. 4. Auditory Reaction Times for Total Schizophrenics ($N = 25$), A Schizophrenics ($N = 16$), and Normals ($N = 18$) for Six Preparatory Intervals, Regular and Irregular Procedure.

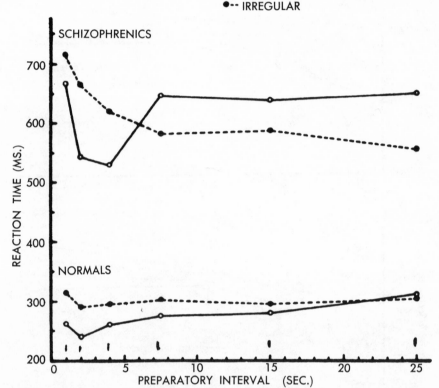

KEY

●— REGULAR
●-- IRREGULAR

SCHIZOPHRENICS

NORMALS

REACTION TIME (MS.)

PREPARATORY INTERVAL (SEC.)

FIG. 5. Mean Visual Reaction Times of 25 Schizophrenic and 10 Normal Subjects at the Various Preparatory Intervals of the Regular and Irregular Warning Procedures.

of the regularity of the presentation, giving reaction times as long as they did in the irregular series. These results held for all the patients, including those whose co-operation levels were judged to be equal to that of normal subjects.

A third study (Rodnick & Shakow, 1940) used simple visual rather than auditory reaction time, and extended the preparatory intervals to 25 seconds. As Figure 5 shows, this study in general corroborated the results of the first, except for a change in the point of juncture of the regular and irregular curves. The curves of the normals came together

somewhere between 20 and 25 seconds. We were now able to find a breakdown point in the normals. When the preparatory interval reached somewhat over 20 seconds, they were no longer able to take advantage of the regular procedure. In contrast, this point was reached by the patients at the 5-6 second level. Reaction times for both the regular and irregular procedures remained significantly longer at every interval for the schizophrenic patients. The major additional contribution of this study was the development of what we called a *set index,* based upon length of reaction time and the relationship between the

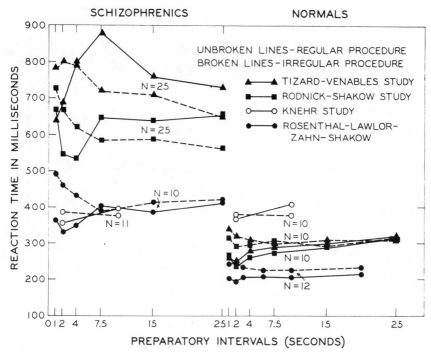

FIG. 6. Reaction Times of Schizophrenic Subjects During Regular and Irregular Procedures in Four Separate Studies.

regular and irregular periods. This index was able to differentiate the schizophrenic and normal subjects without overlap. This is the only instance that we know of in which such a finding on psychological phenomena has been reported in the literature.

Since this last study, which was done some time ago, numerous additional experiments have corroborated these findings. Huston and Singer (1945), Tizard and Venables (1956), and several additional studies (Zahn, Rosenthal, & Shakow, 1961, 1963; Zahn, Shakow, & Rosenthal, 1961; Rosenthal, Lawlor, Zahn, & Shakow, 1960) from our own laboratory at the National Institutes of Health have given the same pattern of results. Figure 6 shows most clearly the similarity in findings for regular and irregular procedures between several of these studies and the Rodnick-Shakow data. Of course, differences in reaction time

level because of differences in modality (and context) exist and must be partialled out. Only one study (Knehr, 1954) has obtained discrepant findings. The conditions and subject samples of this study seem so aberrant compared with those described in the other studies, however, that the results can probably be accounted for on the basis of these differences.

The set hypothesis we had formulated from our early studies posed two general questions: (1) How basic and pervasive was this disturbance in the ability to maintain a major set? and (2) With what other characteristics was the disturbance associated?

We know from our reaction time studies involving regular and irregular procedures that the schizophrenics, even at their own relatively slow speed, are unable to take advantage of the simplification that the regular

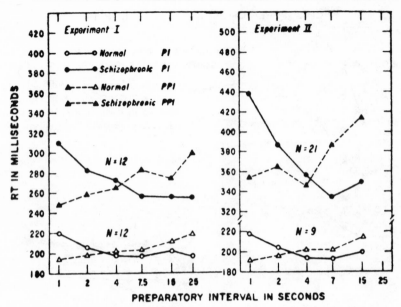

FIG. 7. Reaction Time as a Function of the Preparatory Interval (*PI*) Preceding Preparatory Interval (*PPI*) for Schizophrenic and Normal Subjects.

procedure provides. But how widespread is this disturbance? I shall first deal with this question as it is reflected in performance in relation to two other major aspects of the reaction time situation: the immediately preceding stimulus situation, and the preceding experimental context.

Let us consider the first question: Is the reaction time of the schizophrenic inordinately affected by the immediately preceding stimulus situation? In other words, is the generalized set he must maintain for optimal performance more readily disturbed by what has happened immediately before?

Woodrow (1914), in his early studies on preparatory interval, was able to obtain such an effect in normal subjects. In our own first study, on the other hand, we did not obtain this finding clearly in either normal or schizophrenic subjects. The fact that our experiment was not designed to test this hypothesis may account for this, however.

A recent auditory reaction time study in our laboratory at NIH (Zahn *et al.*, in press)

was directed primarily at answering this question. Twelve schizophrenic and twelve normal subjects were tested, using the irregular procedure with six preparatory intervals ranging from 1-25 seconds. Some of the results obtained from this experiment are seen in Figure 7. *PI* refers to the preparatory interval. The *PPI* refers to the preparatory interval of the immediately preceding trial. Thus at the 4-second point, the *PPI* curve represents the mean of all the reaction times for *all* intervals which were preceded by a preparatory interval of 4 seconds. This contrasts with the *PI* 4-second point, which represents the mean of the reaction times given specifically to the 4-second interval.

For both normal and schizophrenic subjects: (1) the *PI* and *PPI* slopes were significantly different from zero; (2) when the *PI* was short the reaction times were longer, whereas when the *PI* was long the reaction times were shorter; and (3) for the *PPI* the opposite effect was true—when *PPI* was short, reaction times were short; when *PPI* was long, the reaction times were long. When we contrasted the two subject groups, (1) we found a significant difference in absolute levels of reaction time; (2) the slopes of the *PI* curves were also significantly different, shown by the marked steepness of the schizophrenic curves as compared with those of the normals; and (3) the schizophrenics seemed to show a greater effect of *PPI*, though (because of group variability) the trend did not quite reach statistical significance. In a replication experiment, however, the difference was found to be significant.

The relationship between *PI* and *PPI* is best seen by looking at the two extremes of the curves—the 1-second and the 25-second intervals. At the 1-second interval on the *PI* curve, the schizophrenics gave the longest reaction times, but when the 1-second interval preceded other intervals (1-second point on the *PPI* curve), the shortest reaction times appeared. At the 25-second interval, the effect was just the opposite: the shortest reaction times were given to the 25-second interval on the *PI* curve; but when the 25-second interval preceded other intervals, the reaction times were the longest. Although the same general pattern was found in the normal subjects, there was a significant difference between the two in the degree of the effect.

The answer to the question we raised earlier, then, seems to be "yes": schizophrenics are inordinately affected by the immediately preceding stimulus situation in this type of task. I might say in passing that the replication study that I just mentioned gave essentially the same results.

Let us now turn from a consideration of the effect on set of a preceding single stimulus situation, to that of the effect of the preceding context—a repeated series of single, similar preceding stimulations. (This called, of course, for the use of the regular procedure.) To test out the relationship between set and this broader experimental context, we designed two auditory reaction time experiments (Zahn, Rosenthal, & Shakow, 1961) using regular preparatory intervals arranged in both ascending and descending series.

As the results from these studies were essentially similar, we need only discuss one of them here. This experiment, which used twelve schizophrenic and nine normal subjects, called for five preparatory intervals ranging from one to fifteen seconds. Three sessions were given: a descending series beginning with the longest preparatory interval and ending with the shortest; an ascending series beginning with the shortest interval and working up to the longest; and a repetition of the descending series. Some of the results of this experiment can be seen in Figure 8.

We will limit the discussion to the Ascending and the Descending 2 curves of both the schizophrenic and normal subjects. It will be seen that the schizophrenic reaction time for the smaller intervals was much shorter in the ascending series than in the descending series. In contrast, regardless of whether small intervals appeared first or last in the series, the normal subjects tended to give shorter reaction times on the shorter intervals than on the longer intervals. They did not seem to be influenced by the previous succession of longer preparatory intervals.

Figure 9 brings out this point in an even more striking fashion. Again let us limit ourselves to the Ascending and Descending 2 curves. For this analysis the six fastest-reacting schizophrenics were matched with a group of normal subjects (the normals turned out to be the seven slowest subjects) at the level of optimal performance in the ascending series—the 2-second interval. A mean reaction time of approximately 180 ms. was obtained in both groups. It later appeared that this matching held for the 1-second interval as well. This is the same trend shown in Figure 8, but it is even more marked for the schizophrenic curves. The major point to be made here, however, is that despite the matching of normal and schizophrenic subjects, the breakdown of schizophrenic performance on the ascending curve began at the next tested preparatory interval—the 4-second level. Reaction time increased significantly at that point. In a sense this is a corroboration of the findings of the earlier regular-irregular series studies, which also suggested that this is approximately the length of preparatory interval at which the ability of the schizophrenic to maintain a set breaks down.

We can say, then, that repeated exposure to a condition—the broader experimental context—appears to have a much greater effect on schizophrenic than on normal subjects.

In passing, I might point out that the disproportionately long reaction time with long preparatory intervals is not a function merely of the slow tempo of events in such a series. One might expect that a schizophrenic would more easily be seduced into slow responses by a setting that is somewhat "drawly." In order to check out this factor, we (Zahn,

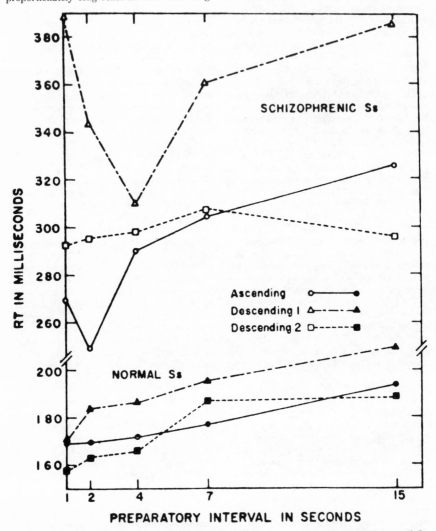

FIG. 8. Reaction Time as a Function of the Preparatory Interval for Two Descending Orders and One Ascending Order of Presentation.

Shakow, & Rosenthal, 1961) compared particularly the *RT*s of normal and schizophrenic subjects under the "usual" long *PI* condition with reaction times under a condition in which the tempo of events was the same, but where the *intertrial interval* was long and the *PI* short. The results showed that reaction time under the long *ITI*-short *PI* condition was virtually identical with that under an "optimal" short *ITI*-short *PI* condition for both

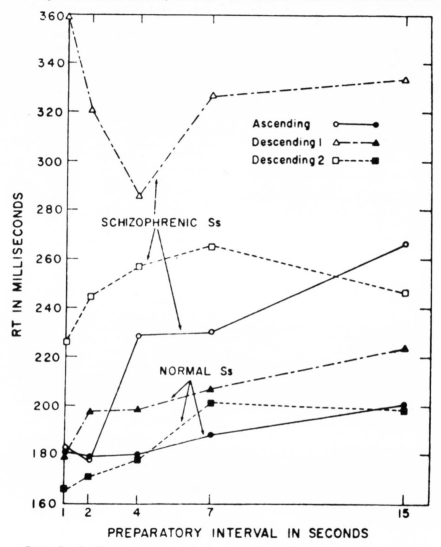

FIG. 9. Reaction Time as a Function of the Preparatory Interval (Subgroups of Six Schizophrenic and Seven Normal Subjects Matched on Reaction Time at 2-Second Preparatory Interval).

groups, and significantly faster than the short *ITI*-long *PI* conditions for the patient group. So we do seem to be dealing here with a problem connected with the length of the preparatory interval.

Having gained some notion of the pervasiveness of the phenomenon, we now can go on to consider some of the conditions which appear to be associated with this difficulty in maintaining set, as well as several conditions which do not seem to be so associated.

Despite Knehr's statement to the contrary, reaction time, and we may add set index, do not seem to be highly correlated with intelligence. In our Worcester studies we repeatedly obtained correlation coefficients of about .30 between reaction time and IQ. When co-operation was partialled out, these correlations fell to about zero. In one study at NIH (Rosenthal, Lawlor, Zahn, & Shakow, 1960), the correlation between set index and Progressive Matrices score was only .26, a nonsignificant correlation. Thus, intelligence seems to be a negligible factor.

Likewise, co-operation, which served as a "normalizing" factor with other functions such as speed of tapping and steadiness, cannot account for the difference between schizophrenic and normal reaction time performance. In the Worcester studies the correlation between co-operation and various kinds of reaction time consistently ran about .50. Despite this fairly high correlation, the patients we rated as *A*, those who presumably had a co-operation level not much different from that of normal controls, still showed a significantly longer reaction time—both simple and discrimination—than the normal subjects. The differential effect of preparatory interval on simple reaction time also held in spite of optimal co-operation. Thus co-operation, although related to level of reaction time *within* the schizophrenic group, does not seem to account for the difference between schizophrenic and normal performances.

In contrast to IQ and co-operation, there are two factors which seem more centrally related to reaction time performance and set.

The first of these may roughly—and broadly—be called "mental health." In the first study in which we had used the set index (Rodnick & Shakow, 1940) we had found that the two patients closest to the normal subjects in index were the two least deteriorated in the group. Because this was only a passing finding, we felt the need of a systematic study of set index in relation to mental condition. Therefore, as part of an NIH study of the reaction times and set index scores of a group of thirteen schizophrenic patients, we had eight judges—five attendants and nurses, one psychologist, and two psychiatrists—who had been in close contact with the patients rate their mental health. (With the psychiatrists we used the term "ego intactness" rather than "mental health.") We used a method of paired comparison so that every patient was matched with every other. There was high reliability, the median interrater correlation being .81. The correlation of "mental health" with set index was .89, and with reaction time .82.

In addition to what we called mental health or ego intactness, and probably related to it, is another factor which may be called "autonomy." Let me give you the background of our interest in this function.

As has been mentioned, our early Worcester studies included a tapping test that gave surprising results. Tapping had seemed to us to be only a more complicated and repetitive reaction time task. But we found that, in contrast to reaction time differences between normal and schizophrenic subjects which held at significant levels despite excellent co-operation, tapping did not hold up as a differentiating function. The differences tended to disappear with a high level of co-operation, especially with paranoid patients. The most likely hypothesis accounting for this seemed to relate to an intrinsic difference in the two experimental tasks. The reaction time situation was entirely experimenter-controlled, performance being measured from the point when the experimenter gave the signal to react. The tapping situation, on the other hand, allowed the subject a certain autonomy —of which, however, he was not aware. Although he was told to start when the ready signal was given, his performance was measured from the time he himself initiated the

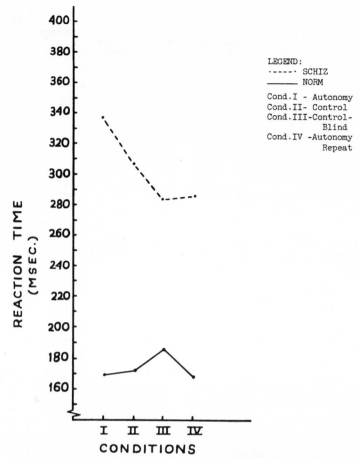

LEGEND:
· · · · · · SCHIZ
——— NORM

Cond. I - Autonomy
Cond. II- Control
Cond. III-Control-
            Blind
Cond. IV -Autonomy
            Repeat

FIG. 10.   Reaction Time as a Function of Experimental Conditions I (Autonomy), II (Control), III (Control-Blind), and IV (Autonomy) for Normals and Schizophrenics.

tapping. His own first tap activated the mechanism for counting taps.

A more recent auditory reaction time study (Cromwell, Rosenthal, Shakow, & Zahn, 1961) has relevance to this problem. The procedure called for three conditions: an *autonomy* condition in which the subject had freedom of choice of preparatory interval and freedom to start each trial on his own initiative; a *controlled* condition wherein the subject was told the length of the preparatory interval to come, but the interval was chosen by the experimenter, and each trial was initiated by the experimenter; and finally the *control-blind* condition which did not provide the subject with freedom to choose the preparatory interval, information about it, or freedom to initiate the trials. The last is, of course, the ordinary procedure in reaction time experiments.

Figure 10 gives, in order of presentation, the four conditions used (including a repeat

55

TABLE 8

DISTRIBUTION OF CATEGORIES OF RESPONSE ON THE ASSOCIATION TEST OF SIXTY SCHIZOPHRENIC PATIENTS FOR
FIVE SUCCESSIVE EXAMINATIONS (3-4 MONTHS AVERAGE INTERVALS) AND OF SIXTY NORMAL SUBJECTS FOR
TWO SUCCESSIVE EXAMINATIONS (2-WEEK INTERVAL)

	Examina-tion	Most Common		Individual		Unusual		Composite Index	
		R	Mean and S.E.	R	Mean and S.E.	R	Mean and S.E.	R	Mean and S.E.
Schizo-phrenics	1	0–38	19.5 ± 1.3	0–32	8.0 ± 0.8	0–82	15.8 ± 2.3	1–66	20.7 ± 2.0
	2	2–37	20.4 ± 1.2	1–32	7.7 ± 0.7	0–71	13.2 ± 1.9	0–62	18.6 ± 1.8
	3	0–45	20.8 ± 1.3	0–29	7.5 ± 0.7	0–97	14.7 ± 2.2	1–58	19.2 ± 2.1
	4	0–44	18.7 ± 1.4	0–24	8.1 ± 0.8	0–77	16.9 ± 2.4	2–69	21.1 ± 2.2
	5	0–41	20.0 ± 1.3	0–21	7.4 ± 0.8	0–82	14.6 ± 2.4	1–72	18.9 ± 2.1
Normals	1	3–61	27.8 ± 1.5	0–15	3.7 ± 0.4	0–58	9.7 ± 1.5	3–35	10.2 ± 1.1
	2	1–63	28.9 ± 1.6	0–13	3.0 ± 0.3	0–55	8.2 ± 1.4	3–37	8.0 ± 1.1

of the autonomy condition). The upper curve represents schizophrenic, and the lower, normal subjects. It will be seen that the normal subjects performed best under autonomy conditions and poorest under the control-blind; the schizophrenics, in contrast, did their best work under the control-blind condition. An index relating the autonomy and control conditions indicated that this difference between schizophrenic and normal subjects was significant at the 1 per cent level.

After each subject had completed the experiment, he was asked to state his preference for the autonomy or the control condition. The results indicated that preferences were in general consonant with performance in each group: the normal subjects stated a preference for the autonomy condition, whereas the schizophrenic subjects either preferred the control condition or had no preference. This difference in personal preferences of the normals and schizophrenics was significant at better than the 1 per cent level.

The conclusion that seems to come from these two autonomy experiments—the tapping and the reaction time studies—is that when the schizophrenic is made aware of his responsibility for a situation, he does most

poorly. However, when he is unaware that he is in a situation of autonomy, he does surprisingly well.

Kent-Rosanoff Association. Another of our studies (Huebner, 1938), parts of which were reported in Shakow (1958b), dealt with material from still another area of function, the association test. Table 8 presents data on sixty schizophrenic patients who were given the Kent-Rosanoff Association Test five times at 3- to 4-month intervals. The categories of response call for some clarification. "Most common" refers to responses which fall among the hundred most frequently given by the Kent-Rosanoff standardization group, those having the highest frequency in the tables. "Individual responses" are defined as those subsumed under the classificatory criteria given in the Appendix to the *Test Manual* but not actually given as a response by any one of the thousand standardization subjects. "Unusual responses" are those which are neither in the tables nor subsumed under the categories of the Appendix. The "composite index" is a weighted score which takes into account all three measures, the higher index scores being the more aberrant.

It will be noted that there was practically

no change in the mean scores of the schizophrenics over the period of 16 to 17 months which elapsed between the first and the last examinations. The intraclass correlation for the patients was .67. Unfortunately we do not have similar extended data on normal subjects. However, we did give two successive examinations two weeks apart to an equally large group of normal subjects. There was a significant drop in the composite index of these subjects, from 10.2 to 8.0. This occurred despite the fact that the intervening period was shorter, and the perhaps more important fact that in successive tests the normal subjects gave 42 per cent of their responses in identical form and the schizophrenics gave only 24 per cent of identical responses. The intraclass correlation for the normal subjects was .80.

Is there a common factor in these two situations—the reaction time and the Kent-Rosanoff Association Test—in which the schizophrenic appears to be particularly vulnerable? Although there may be many more aspects of difference than commonality, one common aspect does seem to exist: *the need for quick response to a demand from the environment.* Our data have suggested that there is an optimal preparatory interval for response, depending upon the complexity of the task. In normal subjects the optimal period seems to be of considerable range, going down to quite small periods. For the schizophrenic, however, this range is quite narrow, falling at the smaller end of the scale, but not the very small. If the stimulus follows too quickly upon the warning, the schizophrenic subject finds difficulty in choosing among the numerous (in the context of the task, irrelevant) associations which the stimulus arouses. If the stimulus does not come quickly enough after the warning, then there is the opportunity for irrelevant stimuli to obtrude and delay the reaction. Only if the time relationships are just right can one get an optimal solution from the schizophrenic subject. This situation may hold for the schizophrenic when compared with normal subjects, or may hold relatively for the schizophrenic within his own low level of performance.

Aspiration. I should like to close my presentation of detailed data with a report of a study of aspiration behavior carried out by Radlo and myself (reported in part in Shakow, 1958b). The findings of this experiment may provide some hint of the underlying dynamics behind the schizophrenic's reaction in the last two situations or, for that matter, in many of the variety of experimental situations that I have described. There were two parts to the experiment, both using the same subjects. In one a pinboard was employed; in the other a tapping apparatus. Since the results were almost identical for both situations, I shall report only some aspects of the pinboard study. The apparatus was a Johnson O'Connor pinboard. The subject was required to place single metal pins as rapidly as possible in a board with a metal face having holes of the proper size for a smooth fit of the pins. After a practice period, he was asked to indicate how many pins he thought he could place in the allotted time, this estimate being his aspiration level. He was then instructed to place as many pins as he could within the time limit. This was his achievement level. The analyses were based on the means of ten aspiration/achievement scores per subject.

TABLE 9

Success and Failure in Attainment of Aspiration Goals (Pinboard) of Schizophrenic and Normal Subjects

Group	N	Per cent of Successes	Per Cent of Failures
Normals	20	24	76
Patients, Type 1	17	35	65
Patients, Type 2	13	59	41
Patients, Type 3	7	79	21

Table 9 gives some of the results from this experiment. The patients were classified into three types: Type 1 consisted of those patients who set an average aspiration level above achievement level of one or more pin placements; Type 2 consisted of patients who set an average aspiration level equal to or up to one above their achievement level; Type 3 were patients who set an average aspiration level lower than their achievement level. You

TABLE 10
ASPIRATION RESPONSES AFTER SUCCESS AND FAILURE IN ATTAINMENT OF ASPIRATION GOALS (PINBOARD) OF
SCHIZOPHRENIC AND NORMAL SUBJECTS

Group	N	Per Cent After Success			Per Cent After Failure		
		Up	Same	Down	Up	Same	Down
Normals	20	83	17	—	8	76	16
Patients, Type 1	17	76	22	2	6	54	40
Patients, Type 2	13	66	30	4	—	45	55
Patients, Type 3	7	36	55	9	—	40	60

will note the differences between the normal subjects and the patient subjects, particularly between the normals and the Type 2 and Type 3 patients, in the ability to tolerate failure. There was a decidedly greater percentage of failures among the normal subjects. The details of the experiment are brought out more clearly in Table 10. Here the actual responses to success and failure are given. In all cases the differences between normal and patient subjects and between patient groups were statistically significant. Note particularly the reactions after failure of the patients.

What is the meaning of these data? It may be that the aspiration situation, because of its evaluative judgmental character and its relative clearness in indicating success or failure, approaches some of the dynamically important factors in schizophrenia in a more obvious and direct way. There is a possible relationship here between these studies and the studies of censure and implied censure by Rodnick and Garmezy and their students (Rodnick & Garmezy, 1957). We perhaps have evidence here of the attempt of the schizophrenic to play safe, to avoid failure and affect, because these have played such important roles in the development and maintenance of his condition. These are, of course, only speculations growing out of our findings. They are also, however, hypotheses which we must try to test experimentally if we are to discover the relationship between genetic developmental factors and the con-

temporary structure of the personality of schizophrenic subjects.

SUMMARY OF FINDINGS

General

In addition to the situation in which the patient withdraws and does not co-operate, we have considered a sample of experiments showing three types of findings about schizophrenic response in relation to normal response: (1) studies in which no differences from the normal were found from the very beginning—in which the schizophrenic patient responded adequately to the experimental situation; (2) those in which initial differences were found, but, under certain conditions, tended to disappear; and finally, (3) those in which initially-found differences continued to persist despite the provision of special conditions.

Let me summarize, through Table 11, some of the generalizations from the experiments I have reported and others I have not taken the time to report. From this sampling of response we can get a picture of the range of schizophrenic inadequacy.

I have already discussed the problem of set, the slowness of response as reflected in the reaction time situations, and the slowness of adaptation shown in the GSR and heart rate reactions, as presented in the first three items. While schizophrenics, when given enough time, appear in learning situations to be able to achieve a "physiological limit"

1. Longer to establish set; set difficult to maintain long—RT/interval; RT/discrimination
2. Slowness of response—RT
3. Slowness of adaptation—GSR/simple stimulus; heart rate/pain
4. Slowness of learning—prodmeter and pursuit-meter learning; Ferguson and Worcester $2C$ formboard; LI (Stanford-Binet)
5. Unrealistic perception—Rorschach:W-, F-, O-; Tachistoscope: No. error, uncommon error
6. Associative thinking—TAI (Stanford-Binet); TAS (Stanford-Binet)
7. Conceptual thinking—TC (Stanford-Binet); Alpha 3; Wegrocki
8. Weak goal behavior—interruption; substitution; play; $As \gg Ac$
9. "Weak ego"—tautophone: $1 < 3$
10. Loose affect—Rorschach: experience type
11. Individuality of response—Kent-Rosanoff; Rorschach: O, P
12. Variability—RT; prodmeter; tapping; etc.

close to that of normal subjects, there is still a slowness in the learning process. Item 4 lists tasks in which we have found evidence for this: prodmeter and pursuit learning experiments; an extended series of repeated administration of two complicated form boards (one of the Ferguson series and one developed at Worcester State Hospital—the Worcester $2C$); and the immediate learning items of the Stanford-Binet. Schizophrenics as a group also showed (item 5) a higher degree of unrealistic perception as was indicated by the larger percentage of minus responses in the "whole" (W), "form" (F), and "original" (O) categories of the Rorschach, as well as in the number of errors and the number of uncommon errors in a tachistoscopic experiment (Angyal, 1942). In associative thinking items on the Stanford-Binet (item 6), whether immediate (TAI) or sustained (TAS), they also fall down, as they do (item 7) on conceptual thinking (TC). Conceptual thinking difficulty was also revealed by results on Test 3 of the Army Alpha, and in a special study (Wegrocki, 1940) involving generalizing ability. Weaker goal behavior (item 8) was found in a Lewinian experiment on interruption (Rickers-Ovsiankina, 1937) and in an experiment (Shakow & Rosenzweig, 1937) on play.

Radlo and I (reported in part in Shakow, 1958b) obtained similar results in the study on aspiration level. We have interpreted as "weak ego" response (item 9) the significant trend in schizophrenics toward giving third-person rather than first-person responses on the tautophone, and we have considered the higher-experience-type index on the Rorschach (item 10) among the schizophrenics as evidence of "loose affect." "Individuality of response" (item 11) is quite characteristic of the schizophrenic, as we have already seen in the Kent-Rosanoff Association Test. It was also revealed by the greater number of "original" (O) and smaller number of "popular" (P) responses in the Rorschach. We have already commented on "variability" (item 12), a quality so highly characteristic of the schizophrenic group and so much more marked than in the normal.

Subtypes

I have already mentioned the considerable contribution of subtype to the striking inter-individual variation, as well as the intra-individual variation—at least in the psychological realm—found among schizophrenic patients. As I previously pointed out, it was our practice at Worcester, on the basis of careful diagnoses and rediagnoses according to carefully outlined criteria, to use the standard subtype classification, but with a liberal use of the additional categories: mixed, unclassified, and indeterminate. The latter, which is a category we developed, involved a history of clear membership in one of the subtypes but with the symptoms now abeyant.

To give some inkling of the range of such variation in chronic patients, it may be helpful to depict a few aspects of the different personality patterns of what we came to consider the two major subtypes of schizophrenia—the paranoid and the hebephrenic. In 58 measurements which we made on groups of normal, paranoid, and hebephrenic subjects, we found the paranoid to be nearer the normal in 31 instances and the hebephrenic nearer the normal in only seven instances. These findings related to measurements in which the normal appeared at one end of the distribution. In 20 instances in six quite

59

varied experiments, however, the paranoid and hebephrenic subject scores fell on *either* side of the normals. Thus, these two groups seem consistently to deal with situations in distinctive ways, giving quite different "styles" of response.

TABLE 12
PARANOID-HEBEPHRENIC COMPARISON

Paranoid	Hebephrenic
1. Intellectually preserved	1. Intellectually disturbed
2. Rigid	2. Loose
3. Persistent	3. Shifting
4. Limits environment	4. Broadens environment*
5. Responsive to personal meaning	5. Irresponsive to personal meaning
6. Accurate and cautious	6. Inaccurate and venturesome

* Either by being at the mercy of environment, or by establishing superficial contact with it.

Table 12 gives a highlighted qualitative profile of the two groups. The paranoid is quite rigid in his response, is relatively preserved intellectually, limits his environment with accuracy and caution, and has sufficient "pride" to protect his personality against the inroads of the environment. The latter is seen particularly in his mirror behavior, his play constructions, and his behavior in tachistoscopic experiments and in an aspiration study. His play constructions also show a sensitivity to personal reference. The hebephrenic subject, on the other hand, is quite disturbed intellectually (actually he is at an intellectual level somewhat below that of the general paretic), is inaccurate and venturesome, and, as seen in the same mirror and play situations, seems to be at the mercy of the environment, constantly being buffeted about by it. In play constructions he appears unresponsive to personal meanings. He consistently takes the "easy way" out, whether it be in preferring to do something that he has already done successfully, lowering his aspiration level after failure, or shifting from one situation to another without any plan. Even this much abbreviated account should lead to caution against any tendency to dis-

regard the subtype classifications as they have evolved over time.

THEORETICAL CONSIDERATIONS

I thought at first that I would limit myself to the presentation of data. However, I found that I could not leave it at that—that I could not neglect theory entirely. I have elsewhere considered schizophrenia in relation to some theoretical problems (Shakow, 1946), and more recently in the context of a theory of segmental set (Shakow, 1962). On this occasion, I would like to elaborate somewhat on these earlier discussions and present a few additional and complementary aspects.

Let us consider some of the implications for theory of the more specific findings we have described. It is in this connection that some aspects of the Coghillian theory of integrated-individuated action and Cannon's hypotheses concerning homeostasis are relevant.

You remember Coghill studied the salamander *Ambylstoma* with particular interest in the development of the nervous system as related to behavior. The relevant theoretical possibilities lie in what he reported of the antagonism between the processes of integration of the whole and individuation of the parts. Let us use Coghill's own words of some thirty years ago from his Presidential Address to the American Association of Anatomists (1933, p. 136): "The mechanism of total integration tends to maintain absolute unity and solidarity of the behavior pattern. The development of localized mechanisms tends to disrupt unity and solidarity and to produce independent partial patterns of behavior. In the interest of the welfare of the organism as a whole, partial patterns must not attain complete independence of action; they must be held under control by the mechanism of total integration. Parts become integrated with each other because they are integral factors of a primarily integrated whole, and they remain integrated, and behavior is normal, so long as this wholeness is maintained. But the wholeness may be lost through a decline of the mechanism of total integration or through the hypertrophy of mechanisms of

60

partial patterns." Coghill offers us here a suggestion which appears to fit much of what we have been describing for schizophrenia.

Likewise, Cannon's theory, which emphasizes the tendency of the organism to maintain stability at the vegetative level, even at the expense of economy of effort, also has importance for us in the present context. Cannon said (1939, pp. 302-303): ". . . I have called attention to the fact that insofar as our internal environment is kept constant we are freed from the limitations imposed by both internal and external agencies or conditions that could be disturbing. The pertinent question has been asked by Barcroft, freedom for what? It is chiefly freedom for the activity of the higher levels of the nervous system and the muscles which they govern. By means of the cerebral cortex we have all our intelligent relations to the world about us. . . . The alternative to this freedom would be either submission to the checks and hindrances which external cold or internal heat or disturbance of any other constants of the fluid matrix would impose upon us; or, on the other hand, such conscious attention to storage of materials and to altering the rate of bodily processes, in order to preserve constancy, that time for other affairs would be lacking. . . . The full development and ample expression of the living organism are impossible in those circumstances. They are made possible by such automatic regulation of the routine necessities that the functions of the brain which subserve intelligence and imagination, insight and manual skill, are set free for the use of these higher services."

In the light of the findings I have described, it seems reasonable to add to Cannon's description of the wisdom of the body a correlative description of the "wisdom of the mind." For Cannon has told only part of the story. The same trend towards freeing the higher centers appears to hold within the cerebrospinal system as well.[2] In the course of life cerebrospinal activity, at first focal, gradually becomes peripheral, and finally becomes automatized. At the time of automatization the central control necessary for the particular function becomes minimal and is thus released for higher activities. Only in times of emergency does it become focal again. In both the interofective and exterofective systems this process is a result of experience and practice. Automatization comes earlier to the interofective system, apparently being established during the early years of childhood; in the exterofective system the process continues in varying degrees throughout life. Somewhere Whitehead has said that civilization advances by extending the number of important operations which we can perform without thinking about them. He had reference presumably to this process of automatization.

On the psychological[3] side we can see certain overlappings and analogies with the physiological phenomena considered by Cannon. At our present stage of knowledge, however, satisfactory correlation of these aspects is, of course, difficult. But modern neurophysiology, with its extensive uncovering of neural areas apparently having crucial relationships to emotion and attention, its acceptance of a dynamic, constantly active complex of interconnecting systems, its emphasis on the high degree of interrelationship between the phylogenetically old and the neocortex, and the evidence it has uncovered for important internal (largely inhibitory) control mechanisms which exist throughout the system, is opening new vistas for correlation of the phenomena we have been discussing (Shakow, 1958a).

What, then, may one say about the general principles which seem to be behind the behavior of the schizophrenic as we have seen him? Without becoming specific about the actual physiological or psychological structures, I shall attempt to summarize these

---

[2] In Dempsey's (1951) discussion of homeostasis the implications of this principle for the exterofective system are also considered. The broader implications of homeostasis are discussed at some length in various sections of the volume edited by Grinker (1960).

[3] A detailed consideration of the physiological homeostatic difficulties of schizophrenic patients has been presented by Hoskins (1946). In the main, these data derive from essentially the same patients I have been considering.

61

principles in line with my own thinking and with what seems to me the spirit of both Coghill's and Cannon's theories.

The main point I wish to make is that in schizophrenia one sees a distinct weakening of the control center that serves the integrating and organizing function and provides for the establishment of what I have called "generalized" or "major sets." Accompanying this weakening is a tendency for the individuated patterns Coghill has described—I have referred to them as "segmented" patterns—to come to the fore and become inordinately important. This may occur in both the interofective and exterofective systems of both the psychological and physiological realms.

The process is of course not a simple, straight-line change. There is much "to-ing and fro-ing." In fact, this is one of the striking qualities of schizophrenia. But in general, the trend is expressed through the following stages which I shall describe briefly. The behavior shown is, of course, not exclusively limited to the behavior predominantly associated with each particular stage. Much overlap occurs and it is only these prominent features that characterize a stage. There is first a tendency to split off into individuated patterns, followed by a reactive strengthening effort on the part of the central control mechanism to control these split-off systems. This is in most cases unsuccessful. Then follows a diminution of the direction of energies to the outside environment, and finally the establishment of equilibrium through the dominance of the segmental patterns.

Associated with these stages are a variety of both experimental and clinical manifestations, some of which we have already discussed. The marked variability of response that we have found reflected in lower correlation coefficients across psychological functions; the inability to maintain set that subsumes the variety of phenomena we have considered particularly under reaction time; the slowing of response time as well as of adaptation and learning time; the difficulties with sustained and conceptual thinking; the weak goal behavior; the unrealistic nature of perception; and the individuality of response—all these appear to be evidences of this tendency towards segmentalization, or sometimes of the attempt to overcome it.

I have not hitherto discussed the more clearly defined experimental physiological findings. It might therefore be desirable to present just a few to round out the picture. Among the findings relating to physiological function there are some which have always impressed me. I refer to a set of significant differences in correlations relating to blood pressure and to body temperature. In carefully controlled studies by our group at Worcester under Hoskins we found the following correlations between individual systolic and diastolic blood pressures (Hoskins & Jellinek, 1933):

Normal

| Basal ($N = 323$) | .43 |
| Nonbasal ($N = 1398$) | .45 |

Schizophrenic

| Basal ($N = 180$) | .62 |
| Basal ($N = 100$) | .62 |

In body temperature (Linder & Carmichael, 1935) we found correlations between the oral and rectal readings of individuals to be:

	Normal	Schizophrenic
Mean of individual correlations	.56	.73
Correlations of mean ratings	.41	.91

Thus we see in these significantly higher correlation coefficients in schizophrenics what seems to be a kind of "robotization"—a "hydrostatic" type of relationship in blood pressure and a "thermostatic" type of relationship in temperature. Both would appear to be reflections of a process of segmentalization that takes these functions out from under the normal adaptive and modulating control. These processes become "independent" and less amenable to the central control needed for most effective adaptation. Our own experiments on *GSR* and heart rate, together with the "physiological withdrawal" documented by Angyal, Freeman, and Hoskins (1940), and the evidences for *high* central nervous system and autonomic nervous system *spontaneous* activity ("spontaneous" is here defined as the response called for by irrelevant stimuli) documented by Malmo, Shagass, and Smith (1951), are further examples of this segmentalized reactivity. There is, on the other hand, evidence for *low* central nervous system and autonomic *directed* activity—"directed" being defined as the adaptive activity called for by a relevant stimulus. This is seen, for instance, in diminished nystagmic response to caloric and rotatory stimulation, in lessened "sway" response to rotation (Angyal & Blackman, 1940; Angyal & Sherman, 1942; Freeman & Rodnick, 1942), and in other phenomena, many of which are described by Hoskins (1946).

On the clinical symptomatic side we see parallel segmental phenomena which can best be described in clinical terms. Segmental cravings, that are ordinarily not satisfied while total integrated control is effective, are now satisfied. There results a perverted use of the already automatically matured devices of the organism to satisfy these needs. Clinical symptoms take the form of preoccupation with ordinarily unconscious bodily processes—with the mechanics of processes rather than with their ends—sensory disturbances represented by hallucinations, peculiar thought patterns, and delusions. This immense variety of schizophrenic symptoms can in one sense be viewed as different expressions of only partial integration, or individuation, or breakdown of major sets—in other words, of segmentalization. The defensive goal-seeking of the schizophrenic ranges from almost total disintegration to highly organized but localized patterns of behavior. Only very rarely is total integration in the Coghillian sense present. There is an increased awareness of, and preoccupation with, the ordinarily disregarded details of existence— the details which normal people spontaneously forget—train themselves, or are trained, rigorously to disregard. These, rather than the biologically adaptive functional aspects of the situation, appear to take on a primary role. It is only when a patient develops a persisting aversion to food because the cafeteria menu lists a common item which we read as "soup" but which he can only see in its excretory significance as "so-u-*p*," that we begin to realize how very many of the thousands of details of daily existence get by us ordinary normals!

If we were to try to epitomize the schizophrenic person's system in the most simple language, we might say that he has two major difficulties: first, he reacts to old situations as if they were new ones (he fails to habituate), and to new situations as if they were recently past ones (he perseverates); and second, he overresponds when the stimulus is relatively small, and he does not respond enough when the stimulus is great. With regard to reactivity, the chronic schizophrenic is certainly not a "seething caldron." He resembles instead the "simmering pot" on the back of the stove which perpetually simmers at a low level. But it is a pot that does not ever provide one with a tasty *pot-au-feu*.

There is little doubt that the schizophrenic's is an inefficient, unmodulated system, full of "noise," and of indeterminate figure-ground relationships. What a confusing world must be the schizophrenic's when such basic modes of relating to the world are so seriously disturbed!

Nevertheless, we do at times see evidences for recoveries from some of these pathological characteristics of the psychosis. We have seen them, for instance, in the group of our own experimental studies that we have labeled "normalizing." Whether they appear spontaneously or as the result of "heroic" measures, we see them clinically in the not-too-rare occurrence of the "off-on" phenomenon —those instances in which the schizophrenic patient seems to have varying periods of relative clarity or normality. The central question for therapeutics is, then: What can we do to make these "on" periods persist? This, I am afraid, is a question that will remain unanswered for at least a few years more.

REFERENCES

Angyal, Alice F. Speed and pattern of perception in schizophrenic and normal persons. *Charac. & Pers.*, 1942, 11, 108-127.

Angyal, A., & Blackman, N. Vestibular reactivity in schizophrenia. *Arch. Neurol. Psychiat.*, 1940, 44, 611-620.

Angyal, A., Freeman, H., & Hoskins, R. G. Physiologic aspects of schizophrenic withdrawal. *Arch. Neurol. Psychiat.*, 1940, 44, 621-626.

Angyal, A., & Sherman, M. A. Postural reactions to vestibular stimulation in schizophrenic and normal subjects. *Amer. J. Psychiat.*, 1942, 98, 857-862.

Cannon, W. B. *The wisdom of the body* (Rev. ed). New York: Norton, 1939.

Coghill, G. E. The neuro-embryologic study of behavior: principles, perspective and aim. *Science*, 1933, 78, 131-138.

Cohen, L. H., & Patterson, M. Effect of pain on the heart rate of normal and schizophrenic individuals. *J. gen. Psychol.*, 1937, 17, 273-289.

Cromwell, R. L., Rosenthal, D., Shakow, D., & Zahn, T. P. Reaction time, locus of control, choice behavior, and descriptions of parental behavior in schizophrenic and normal subjects. *J. Pers.*, 1961, 29, 363-379.

Dempsey, E. W. Homeostasis. In S. S. Stevens (Ed.), *Handbook of experimental psychology.* New York: Wiley, 1951. Pp. 209-235.

Freeman, H., & Rodnick, E. H. Effect of rotation on postural steadiness in normal and in schizophrenic subjects. *Arch. Neurol. Psychiat.*, 1942, 48, 47-53.

Grinker, R. R. (Ed.). *Toward a unified theory of human behavior.* New York: Basic Books, 1960.

Hoskins, R. G. *The biology of schizophrenia.* New York: Norton, 1946.

Hoskins, R. G., & Jellinek, E. M. The schizophrenic personality with special regard to psychologic and organic concomitants. *Proc. Assoc. Research nerv. ment. Disease,* 1933, 14, 211-233.

Huebner, Dorothy M. Effects of repetition on the association test in schizophrenic and normal subjects. Unpublished master's thesis, Johns Hopkins Univ., 1938.

Huston, P. E. Sensory threshold to direct current stimulation in schizophrenic and in normal subjects. *Arch. Neurol. Psychiat.*, 1934, 31, 590-596.

Huston, P. E. The reflex time of the patellar tendon reflex in normal and schizophrenic subjects. *J. gen. Psychol.*, 1935, 13, 3-41.

Huston, P. E., & Shakow, D. Studies of motor function in schizophrenia. III. Steadiness. *J. gen. Psychol.*, 1946, 34, 119-126.

Huston, P. E., & Shakow, D. Learning in schizophrenia. I. Pursuit learning. *J. Pers.*, 1948, 17, 52-74.

Huston, P. E., & Shakow, D. Learning capacity in schizophrenia; with special reference to the concept of deterioration. *Amer. J. Psychiat.*, 1949, 105, 881-888.

Huston, P. E., Shakow, D., & Riggs, L. A. Studies of motor function in schizophrenia. II. Reaction time. *J. gen. Psychol.*, 1937, 16, 39-82.

Huston, P. E., & Singer, Mary M. Effect of sodium amytal and amphetamine sulfate on mental set in schizophrenia. *Arch. Neurol. Psychiat.*, 1945, 53, 365-369.

Knehr, C. A. Schizophrenic reaction time responses to variable preparatory intervals. *Amer. J. Psychiat.*, 1954, 110, 585-588.

Linder, F. E., & Carmichael, H. T. A biometric study of the relation between oral and rectal temperatures in normal and schizophrenic subjects. *Hum. Biol.*, 1935, 7, 24-46.

Malmo, R. B., Shagass, C., & Smith, A. A. Responsiveness in chronic schizophrenia. *J. Pers.*, 1951, 19, 359-375.

Millard, Mary S., & Shakow, D. A note on color-blindness in some psychotic groups. *J. soc. Psychol.*, 1935, 6, 252-256.

Rickers-Ovsiankina, Maria. Studies on the personality structure of schizophrenic individuals. II. Reaction to interrupted tasks. *J. gen. Psychol.*, 1937, 16, 179-196.

Rodnick, E. H. The effect of metrazol shock upon habit systems. *J. abnorm. soc. Psychol.*, 1942, 37, 560-565.

Rodnick, E. H., & Garmezy, N. An experimental approach to the study of motivation in schizophrenia. In M. R. Jones (Ed.), *Nebraska symposium on motivation.* Lincoln, Neb.: Univ. of Nebraska Press, 1957. Pp. 109-190.

Rodnick, E. H., & Shakow, D. Set in the schizophrenic as measured by a composite reaction time index. *Amer. J. Psychiat.*, 1940, 97, 214-225.

Rosenthal, D., Lawlor, W. G., Zahn, T. P., & Shakow, D. The relationship of some aspects of mental set to degree of schizophrenic disorganization. *J. Pers.*, 1960, 28, 26-38.

Sands, S. L., & Rodnick, E. H. Concept and experimental design in the study of stress and personality. *Amer. J. Psychiat.*, 1950, 106, 673-679.

Schnack, G. F., Shakow, D., & Lively, Mary L. Studies in insulin and metrazol therapy. II. Differential effects on some psychological functions. *J. Pers.*, 1945, 14, 125-149.

Shakow, D. The nature of deterioration in schizophrenic conditions. *Nerv. Ment. Dis. Monogr.*, 1946, No. 70.

Shakow, D. How phylogenetically older parts of the brain relate to behavior. Paper read at Amer. Assoc. for the Advancement of Science, Washington, D. C., December, 1958. (a)

Shakow, D. Normalisierungstendenzen bei chronisch Schizophrenen: Konsequenzen für die Theorie der Schizophrenie. *Schweiz. Z. Psychol. Anwend.*, 1958, 17, 285-299. (b)

Shakow, D. Segmental set: a theory of psychological deficit in schizophrenia. *Arch. gen. Psychiat.*, 1962, 6, 1-17.

64

Shakow, D., & Huston, P. E. Studies of motor function in schizophrenia. I. Speed of tapping. *J. gen. Psychol.*, 1936, 15, 63-106.

Shakow, D., & Rosenzweig, S. Play technique in schizophrenia and other psychoses. II. An experimental study of schizophrenic constructions with play materials. *Amer. J. Orthopsychiat.*, 1937, 7, 36-47.

Tizard, J., & Venables, P. H. Reaction time responses by schizophrenics, mental defectives, and normal adults. *Amer. J. Psychiat.*, 1956, 112, 803-807.

Wegrocki, H. J. Generalizing ability in schizophrenia: an inquiry into the disorders of problem thinking in schizophrenia. *Arch. Psychol.*, 1940, No. 254.

Woodrow, H. The measurement of attention. *Psychol. Monogr.*, 1914, 17, No. 5 (Whole No. 76).

Zahn, T. P., Rosenthal, D., & Lawlor, W. G. GSR orienting reactions to visual and auditory stimuli in chronic schizophrenic and normal subjects. Paper read at Society for Psychophysiological Research, Denver, October, 1962.

Zahn, T. P., Rosenthal, D., & Shakow, D. Reaction time in schizophrenic and normal subjects in relation to the sequence of series of regular preparatory intervals. *J. abnorm. soc. Psychol.*, 1961, 63, 161-168.

Zahn, T. P., Rosenthal, D., & Shakow, D. Effects of irregular preparatory intervals on reaction time in schizophrenia. *J. abnorm. soc. Psychol.*, 1963, 67, 44-52.

Zahn, T. P., Shakow, D., & Rosenthal, D. Reaction time in schizophrenic and normal subjects as a function of preparatory and intertrial intervals. *J. nerv. ment. Dis.*, 1961, 133, 283-287.

1964 DEAN RESEARCH AWARD

Dr. **RALPH W. GERARD**, *professor and dean emeritus of the University of California, Irvine, is one of the world's foremost physiologists. Internationally known for his pioneer work on the chemical and electrical activity of nerve and of brain, he has lectured widely and received a number of honorary degrees and foreign awards. Dr. Gerard has published several books and articles as well as serving as editor of many scientific journals. He is a member of the National Academy of Sciences and the American Psychiatric Association, and has served as president of the American Physiological Society and as consultant to various governmental institutions. Along with his investigative work, he has maintained a life-long interest in education, including in recent years the adaptation of audiovisual material and computer systems to learning and to processing information. Over the past decade he has written and lectured extensively in the behavioral and systems science areas and on their application to human affairs.*

THE NOSOLOGY OF SCHIZOPHRENIA: A CO-OPERATIVE STUDY

by Ralph W. Gerard

THE PROBLEM

THE disease schizophrenia is an ancient and universal one. There is evidence from Egyptian records that it was present among the people of the Nile. I have traveled widely in Asia, Australia, Europe, and the Americas, and have always made a point of inquiring about schizophrenia; certainly the same kind of illness exists in all these countries, and while it is not often possible to get meaningful figures, an incidence of about 1 per cent seems quite general.

The cause of schizophrenia is not known. The Egyptians thought it was gas in the ventricles of the brain; during much of the Medieval period it was believed to be a demon possessing the individual; later it was attributed to a bad colon or to bad teeth, or a bad nervous system, or a bad environment, or bad heredity—not all mutually exclusive. And the treatment depended pretty much on the mood of the day. For possession, the evil spirit was exorcized by whatever way seemed appropriate; teeth were extracted; colons were excised;

The research described here was done under the auspices of The University of Michigan (Mental Health Research Institute) and Ypsilanti State Hospital, and supported by U. S. Public Health Service grants MY-1971 and MY-1972. The author is indebted to Dr. Patricia M. Carrigan, Mrs. Lucy R. Watkins, and Mrs. Edna Kelly for their extensive editorial help and assistance in preparation of figures.

brains were exposed by trephining or lobotomy; shock was given; psycho- and sociotherapy were directed to environmental factors; drugs are being used; nobody has yet done a great deal about a hereditary cause.

The problem, of course, has been the absence of the kind of indicia which are familiar in the more physical aspects of medicine. No clear-cut pathology has been established in the autopsy room; indeed, the machinery of functioning could not be so irretrievably damaged, since even deteriorated schizophrenics can, under one treatment or another and for a shorter or a longer time, return to fairly effective functioning. The diagnosis has suffered from this lack of identifiable indicators, or pathognomonic findings, not only in pathology, but even in the clinical zone. There is nothing as nice and clean as the Koplik spot of measles, or the Kahn test for syphilis, or the presence of tubercle bacilli, or even such a characteristic as a tic of the left eye, or a proprioceptive hallucination. Hundreds, probably thousands, of measures have been developed and tested but none has been claimed to be 100 per cent diagnostic, even by a fond parent. Most, even the seemingly valid ones, were positive for only a limited fraction of schizophrenic subjects—50 per cent, 60 per cent, up to 85 per cent is the highest claim I know.

Perhaps, then, the reason one does not

69

find any test or measure that fits the total schizophrenic population is that one is dealing with a mixed bag of tricks. This was essentially the question when this study was initiated: Is it possible to go beyond Bleuler, when he introduced the term "schizophrenia" and spoke of the "group of schizophrenias," and somehow identify significant subgroups of schizophrenia? These might follow clinical divisions, but might not, since diagnosis is notoriously variable; in either event, a separation based on solid indicators would be invaluable.

I shall take a moment longer on this general point, because it is so tremendously important, and is not always simple to grasp. We think, in science, that our great forte is quantitation; that, in contradistinction to other walks of life, one measures and gets precise numbers with which to operate and predict. This is perfectly true, providing only that one is measuring the right thing! Entitation must precede quantitation. If one is measuring the wrong things, the finest measurements are nonsense—witness the fact that early last century outstanding scientists of Europe developed elaborate formulas to deal with the bumps on the head in the "science" of phrenology. Or recall the talk of the three umpires. Said the first, "Balls and strikes, I call 'em as I see 'em." The second, "Balls and strikes, I call 'em as they *are*." The third, older, one shook his head, "Balls and strikes, they ain't nothin' *until* I call 'em!"

Dividing a universe into meaningful subcategories is, in the broadest sense, classification, or taxonomy. In the narrower sense of classifying disease, it is nosology; and our research has been an effort in the nosological analysis of schizophrenia, hoping to find meaningful subgroups. Until one has a real class or group or entity to deal with, any research is likely to be as vacuous as the question, "What color is fruit?" Bananas and pears and oranges and apples must be considered separately. Similarly, the question, "What is the cause of a cough?" is sterile. Taxonomy is fairly old in modern scientific history. Linnaeus introduced his binomial classification system about two and a half centuries ago; only two centuries ago a book on nosology was published by Cullen; only

one century ago Morel made a comparable effort in the classification of mental illness, and introduced the term "dementia praecox"; and only at the turn of this century Kraepelin and Bleuler made their important contributions in the specific area of schizophrenia. I close this preamble by quoting Bleuler to you, from the 1911 edition of his book:

"At the present time, we cannot resolve the problem of dissecting schizophrenia into its natural subdivisions. . . . The various clinical pictures correspond at best to rather broad and crude subdivisions. . . . Even then, however, it is not a question of defining and delimiting different disease entities, but of grouping symptoms. This sort of classification corresponds in a way to the division of pulmonary tuberculosis into cases with and without fever, and with and without hemoptysis" (p. 227).

"Not many symptomalogical concepts of diseases have survived in other fields of medicine. Where no substitutes could be found for theory, they are being employed in full awareness of the fact that they are merely temporary formulations, not diagnoses. Yet, in psychiatry, such obvious conceptions must still be fought for" (p. 272).

"The subdivision of the group of schizophrenias is a task for the future. . . . Errors are the greatest obstacles to the progress of science; to correct such errors is of more practical value than to achieve new knowledge" (p. 280).

This is the challenge to which our group addressed itself. We were not studying the etiology, pathogenesis, treatment, prognosis, or symptomatology of schizophrenia—although the latter inevitably came into the picture. We hoped to identify a number of meaningful subgroups of schizophrenia—to separate oranges from grapefruit—to which it would be more profitable and reasonable to direct studies of etiology, pathogenesis, treatment, and prognosis. In a way, all we hoped to do was clear away underbrush. I think, at the end of this long road, often a painful and difficult one, that we have indeed made some real progress. This I shall now present to you, in extremely abbreviated form, and leaning heavily on illustrative data. (Preliminary reports on the main study, and some special ones, appeared in Gerard [1963] and elsewhere; all will be presented in a monograph to be published by the W. B. Saunders Co.).

THE STUDY

As to the magnitude of the problem, please recall that one fourth of first admissions to public mental hospitals are schizophrenics and, since they stay in hospitals longer than other patients, they constitute about half of the resident population. An appropriate attack became possible by virtue of generous support from the National Institute of Mental Health and the proximity of The University of Michigan and the Ypsilanti State Hospital and their willingness to pool scientific and clinical resources. The University, through the Mental Health Research Institute in particular, supplied much of the staff; the Ypsilanti State Hospital, some staff, the patients, and quarters. Table

TABLE 1

Staff of the Schizophrenia and Psychopharmacology Joint Research Project

Area Chief	Staff
Principal Investigator: R. W. Gerard	
Assistant Superintendent, Ypsilanti State Hospital: K. B. Moore, A. P. Dukay	
Director of Research and Training, Ypsilanti State Hospital: R. A. Moore	
Clinical Director, Ypsilanti State Hospital: V. W. Kershul	
Anthropometry: C. G. Ingram	
Biochemistry: A. Yuwiler	Monica D. Blumenthal, N. S. Ging, Mary Good, Idella Jenkins, Dorrit M. Jordan, N. S. Ling
Biological Assays: S. S. Fox	F. Altman, J. H. O'Brien, S. Fujita, J. Liebeskind, S. Schwartz, N. Williams
Pharmacology: S. Gershon	Ausma Rabe
Physiology: C. G. Ingram, G. K. Holmberg	E. Rodin
Psychiatry: N. Rosenzweig, K. B. Moore, A. P. Dukay	Elsa Broder, G. Brovins, J. Olariu, H. von Brauchitsch
Psychology: Eira I. Mattsson, S. G. Vandenberg	Patricia M. Carrigan, P. S. Houts, J. A. Marshall, S. May, Prem Radhakrishnan, W. J. Stansell, H. Styler
Ward and Diet Kitchen: Virginia Reuell, Carolyn Gervais	Joan Bontrager, R. Budson, J. McFadden, Dorothy Williams
Social History: Helen B. Fritz	Mary L. Anderson
Statistics: N. B. Mattsson	B. K. Radhakrishnan, N. A. Starr
Vision: L. H. Beck	
Administration: N. Rosenzweig, Lucy R. Watkins	G. R. Schieve (Ypsilanti State Hospital), Johnella D. Williams
Advisory Committee: A. P. Dukay, R. W. Gerard, E. L. Kelly, J. G. Miller, K. B. Moore, R. A. Moore, N. Rosenzweig, R. W. Waggoner, O. R. Yoder	

71

1 lists the main participants: I take this opportunity to salute and thank them for a loyal, hard, and continuous effort to get this job done. Thanks are also due the many technicians and students involved in the data collection and analysis, and to the nearly three hundred patients on occupational therapy status who served willingly and well in many capacities, especially in the statistics laboratory. Patients working there proved to be dependable and, conversely, such activities seemed to be highly valuable for therapy. Finally, much credit goes to the several groups who served as subjects—over six hundred prison and hospital inmates, as well as students, staff, and other normal controls.

Design

The design of the study, extremely simple in principle and equally difficult in execution, is indicated in Figure 1, a matrix of patients as columns and tests as rows, with idealized results. As mentioned earlier, none of the many tests for identifying schizophrenics had proved positive for all, or nearly all, patients tested. Also, most tests had been tried on different patient populations, so there was no evidence as to whether patients who failed to give results on test A were the same ones who failed to do so on test B and test C, while giving results on tests D, E, and F; or whether other patients, giving results on tests A, B, and C, failed to do so on D, E, and F. If such clusters occurred they would indicate different types of schizophrenia. The direct way to test this is to get an array of patients, from

as wide a population as possible, and give each as wide a battery of tests as possible. If results were as diagrammed, there would be little question that patients A, B, and F have one kind of schizophrenia and patients C, D, and M have another kind, with E a maverick. This was the design.

In principle, nonschizophrenic patients were not needed, since the goal was to structure a schizophrenic population, but there were good reasons for a control group. In the first place, we had to select, from an almost unlimited array of tests, those with some promise of discriminating subgroups. While tests which failed to discriminate schizophrenics from other patients might still have value in discriminating one schizophrenic subgroup from another (subgroups might vary in opposite directions from the norm and average out, as for hypnotizable subjects [Willey, 1951]), a test that discriminated for the whole population had a greater probability of serving to discriminate at the subgroup level. Second, if no cluster patterns emerged in the study, results on schizophrenics alone would be worthless, whereas comparative data on schizophrenics and nonschizophrenics obtained under controlled conditions would contribute to the over-all baseline differences between these groups. So a meaningful number of nonschizophrenics was included.

Procedures

We were first given a Research Ward of 25 beds at Ypsilanti State Hospital, but soon found it impossible to begin studies on patients moved there directly from anywhere in the hospital. So we asked for and were given an additional 70-bed ward, called the Annex Ward, to serve as an "anteroom" where patients could be kept for the time needed (usually about two months) to emerge from the effects of any drugs they had been receiving, to become accustomed to a constant diet, to each other, and to being in the research project (which was rather threatening to many of the patients, not to say a number of the physicians), and to permit the nurses, attendants, and experimental staff to get somewhat acquainted with them. The head nurse (first Virginia

| | PATIENT | | | | | | |
	A	B	C	D	E	F	M
TEST 1	-	-	+	+	-	-	+
2	-	-	+	+	-	-	+
3	+	+	-	-	-	+	-
4	+	+	-	-	-	+	-
5	-	-	+	+	-	-	+
6	+	+	-	-	-	+	-
N	-	-	-	-	+	-	-

Patients A, B, F and C, D, M fall into two groups

FIG. 1. Idealized Cluster Diagram.

Reuell, later Carolyn Gervais) and the ward psychiatrist (Alexander P. Dukay, then Elsa Broder and John Olariu) had much to do with the effectiveness of ward procedures. The patients were then rotated from the Annex Ward onto the Research Ward. Usually a group of five entered the Research Ward each Monday and normally stayed there five weeks. From the time of entering, patients were not merely on a constant diet, but on an identical diet every day. This was perhaps the only really distasteful part of the experience for the patients—they naturally didn't enjoy receiving the same breakfast, the same lunch, and the same dinner every day for five weeks. At first, cigarettes and coffee were prohibited; but when tests indicated that these did not influence the biochemical findings, or any others so far as we could tell, this very unpopular restriction was relaxed. The diet was rigorous, prepared in our own diet kitchen, and during the fourth week, when most of the tests were actually made, an attendant sat with each patient at each meal to make certain that he ate the entire weighed portions. Precautions (such as locked toilets to which attendants gave access) were also taken to obtain full 24-hour urine samples and to prevent sweets or other foods being smuggled in to the pa-tients, especially during this week. Violations did occur, but, by volume and other criteria, we were satisfied in practically all cases of adequate collection.

Patients not on a drug study were rotated back into the Annex Ward for some further tests at the end of the five weeks and finally returned to other wards of the hospital. Those on drug studies stayed in the Annex Ward for a couple of weeks and then returned to the Research Ward for a shorter time and a more limited repeat test battery. We would have liked much more of such "before and after" runs and, particularly, of longitudinal studies of variation, of which a small study was made by Carrigan (1964).

The actual operating procedures on the Research Ward are diagrammed in Figure 2. During the first week general ratings and baselines on the polygraph (blood pressure, respiration, skin resistance, and so on) were measured; during the next two weeks fairly routine measurements (some of the clinical tests, general physical fitness) were made; the fourth week was devoted to intensive measuring; and the fifth and sixth weeks to some continued polygraph measurements, nursing notes, etc. During the fourth week many measurements were made every two hours through the day, and some into the

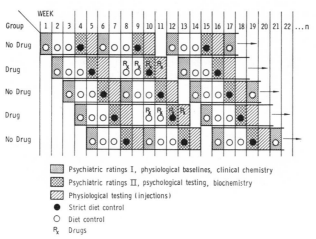

FIG. 2. Rotation Schedule for Data Collection.

TOTAL AVAILABLE POPULATION *	PATIENT SELECTION

United States, Michigan and Ypsilanti State Hospital: resident populations at beginning of study, plus new admissions during time of study (1.5 years).

Definitive Study: September 1959-March 1961

SEQUENCE OF ELIMINATION BY SELECTION CRITERIA:

	Total	Male
U. S. A. (266 Hospitals)	835, 000	425, 000
Michigan (8 Hospitals)	30, 500	16, 000
Ypsilanti State Hospital	5, 850	3, 000

Final Sample 208 Patients
(Number remaining after losses)

 Schizophrenics   Nonschizophrenics

1670   1330

SELECTION FACTORS RESPONSIBLE FOR ELIMINATIONS FROM YPSILANTI STATE HOSPITAL MALE POPULATION:

1. Maximum stay in hospital 10 years

750   850

2. Age range 18-50 years

560   465

3. Diagnostic criteria (Elimination of various sub-categories, especially among brain-damaged patients)

500   300

4. Other selection criteria (Physical and educational handicaps precluding participation, medication and treatment, etc.)

235   165

5. Losses from selected sample (Discharge. convalescent status, family care, refusal to cooperate, management problems, etc.)

108   100

*From U. S. and Michigan Public Mental Health Statistics, 1956-1959: Public Prolonged Care Hospitals for Mental Disease.

FIG. 3. Reduction of Ypsilanti State Hospital Population by Selection Criteria.

night: such close attention brought to light several interesting findings.

Between morning and evening, for example, the temperature fluctuations in non-schizophrenics and schizophrenics differ, with nonschizophrenic temperatures rising somewhat more in the afternoon than schizophrenics. There is also a shift in activity patterns (Budson[2]), particularly in schizophrenics: repetitive body movement and amount of speech decrease during the day, while eye movements (following people around) increase, suggesting a diurnal rise in rigidness. Finally, ratings on the Olariu scale, indicating degree of general pathology in a patient, showed that schizophrenics manifested increased pathology from the

[2] Richard D. Budson, A method for recording the ward behavior of mental patients: an objective and statistically analyzable approach. Unpublished manuscript, 1959.

first to the fourth weeks on the Research Ward while the nonschizophrenics moved in the other direction.

So much for the general measurement picture—these particular findings, although themselves interesting, are presented mainly as examples of the care with which these patients were followed.

Subjects

The primary problem was to identify our subjects. In the absence of the very kind of criteria we were seeking to establish, the only criterion for deciding whether or not a person is schizophrenic is the judgment of trained psychiatrists. The best we could do, then, in the initial selection of our experimental population was to demand concurrence in the independent judgments of three psychiatrists. If all said, "This is a schizophrenic," or "This is not a schizophrenic,"

74

the patient was accepted as a potential experimental or control subject; if the vote was two to one, the patient was out, although it was later decided to include some of these uncertain patients as a separate group of potential interest. Happily, as the patients went through a most intensive study, in few instances was there any basis for wishing to change the diagnosis.

During the period of the definitive study (a year and a half or so) about 2,000 patients were admitted to the hospital in addition to the 4,000 patients initially there, so a total of 6,000 patients was available (Fig. 3). To avoid problems associated with the menses, only males were used—a population of some 1,500 each of schizophrenics and nonschizophrenics. Progressive losses resulted from exclusion of those hospitalized over ten years (the only factor that distorted our final sample), those over 50 or under 18, patients with other diseases (diabetes, syphilis, tuberculosis, etc.), those who for one reason or another (violent, mute, feebleminded) could not be expected to take the test battery, and those who refused co-operation. Finally, we lost patients in the study because, although we gave no intentional therapy, the attention our subjects were getting seemed helpful and a number were discharged. So, from 3,000 patients, we ended up with 108 schizophrenics and 100 nonschizophrenics as the total possible sample. In spite of this great curtailment, there is excellent evidence that, in terms of age distribution, time of onset, clinical diagnoses, and subdiagnoses (everything except length of stay in hospital), we had a representative sample of the total population of the hospital—indeed, of the total U. S. mental hospital population. Unfortunately, we did not have a representative sample of the total schizophrenic population of this country; we necessarily stacked the cards against ourselves when we limited our subjects to a chronic hospital population. What subtypes of schizophrenia may have thus been lost, we cannot know; but only with the control of environmental situations made possible in a hospital could any valid findings be hoped for. So we chose the lesser of alternate evils.

TABLE 2
Social and Personal History Data
(72-Item Check List)

1. Evaluation of informant
2. Factual background data regarding patient, patient's family, and the childhood community setting
3. Family mental illness history
4. Patient's development
   Birth
   Physical development
   Intellectual development
   Physical health during childhood
   Personality pattern
5. Parental personalities and interaction in family setting
   Mother personality pattern—based on reported episodes
   Father personality pattern—and Kahn test of symbol arrangement
   Characterization of relationship
6. Parents' relationship to patient—patient to parents and sibling(s)
7. Patient's adjustment to school situation—socially and academically
8. Patient's adjustment to employment
   Job performance
9. Adolescent and adult social adjustment
   Pattern of sexual relationships
10. Onset of psychosis

Tests

Hundreds of tests of all varieties were explored before the final battery was selected; this is presented in outline in Tables 2 through 10. In the social history area (Table 2), ten major topics were examined in an

TABLE 3
Psychiatric Rating Forms

Mental Status Form
   Used by psychiatrists to describe in a few sentences patient's physical and mental status, and to establish diagnosis prior to admission to research program.
Lorr Multidimensional Psychiatric Rating Scale
   Completed by ward psychiatrist—original and revised versions.
Olariu Psychiatric Rating Scale
   Section A—based on standard psychiatric interview by ward psychiatrist.
   Section B—ward observation by attendant.
   Section C—personality assessment by psychiatrist and attendant together.
Other Scales
   Check-lists developed by staff for use during drug studies.

open-ended interview; this was carefully scored and reduced to numerical values on the rating scales developed for the project by Helen B. Fritz. Only quantitative data could be utilized for statistical analysis.

Psychiatric ratings (Table 3) were made by psychiatrists and ward personnel, using the Lorr scales and the Olariu scale developed by J. Olariu on the project, and well-liked by all our workers. Ward measurements (Table 4) also included, besides standard

observations, ratings on the Gorham scale and the Clyde Mood Scale.

The psychological battery (Table 5) included 28 tests, winnowed from five times that number explored in preliminary studies and including several developed by our staff (Eira I. Mattsson and S. G. Vandenberg) which proved to be valuable discriminators.

The physiological test battery (Table 6) included many vascular and respiratory measures taken, largely on the polygraph, under baseline conditions, under the influence of a variety of drugs influencing the autonomic nervous system, and under various kinds of psychological stress, such as mild shock.

The biochemical battery (Table 7) included many laboratory procedures on blood and on urine (a number developed by A. Yuwiler of our staff) which varied somewhat

TABLE 4

WARD MEASUREMENTS AND OBSERVATIONS

Measurements	Observations
Anthropometric	Once during week of rigid dietary control
Lorr Scales*	Schedules C and D—once during first week on diet, second rating during week of rigid dietary control
Olariu Scale*	(3 parts) By psychiatrists and attendants once during ward stay
Gorham Ward Behavior Rating Scales†	Every two hours, three days weekly, during week of rigid dietary control
Clyde Mood Scale‡	By patient, with attendant supervising, once during ward stay
Weight	Once weekly during ward stay, daily during week of rigid dietary control
Temperature, Pulse, and Blood Pressure	Once weekly during ward stay, twice daily during week of rigid dietary control. Temperature every two hours, with Gorham Scale, during week of rigid dietary control
24-Hour Urine Collection Sheets	Daily for five days during week of rigid dietary control
Blood Donor Sheets	Kept daily on all patients
Nurses' Notes	Once weekly by all shifts during stabilization weeks, daily by all shifts during three testing weeks
Doctors' Order Sheets	Whenever any medication given
Diet Data	Daily

* Multidimensional scales.
† Activity level, anxiety level, mental disorganization, predominant mood, interpersonal relationships, and anger scale, as modified by Project.
‡ Self-evaluatory scale of mood.

TABLE 5

PSYCHOLOGICAL TEST BATTERY

Intelligence and Thinking
  Ammons Picture Vocabulary
  Facial Expressions (Vandenberg, Mattsson)
  Graded Analogies
  Gray Oral Reading Test
  Kahn Test of Symbol Arrangement
  Kay Apparatus
  Picture Group Naming
  Roberts Cartoons
  Social Concepts
  Wechsler-Bellevue Intelligence Scale
  Word Classification
Memory
  Immediate Memory I (Schizophrenia Project Staff)
  Immediate Memory II (Schizophrenia Project Staff)
Perceptual Efficiency
  Changing Pictures (Mattsson, Vandenberg)
  Mooney Closure Faces
  Color-Form Movie
  Identical Forms
  Kinesthetic Aftereffect
  Rod and Frame
  Seguin Form Board
  Spiral Aftereffect
Psychomotor Performance
  Bourdon Dot Cancellation
  Dotting
  Mirror Drawing
  Reaction Time
  Stroop Color-Word Test
  Tapping
  Tweezer Dexterity

76

TABLE 6
Physiological Test Battery

Measures
  Blood pressure
  Electrocardiogram
  Ballistocardiogram
  Respiration rate and depth
  Skin potential
  Skin temperature
Conditions
  Resting Level—repeated to reduce anxiety
  Drug Tests
    Modified Funkenstein (epinephrine, norepinephrine, methacholine)
    Orthosympathetic blockage (piperoxan)
    Parasympathetic blockage (atropine)
    Central autonomic stimulation (yohimbine)
  Psychological Stress
  Repeated shock and tone

TABLE 8
Anthropometric Measurements

Length	Breadth	Girth
Height*	Shoulder width	Wrist
Sitting height	Chest width	Biceps*
Arm length	Pelvic width	Chest
Arm span	Humeral epicondylar width*	Waist
Leg length	Femoral epicondylar width*	Calf*
		Ankle

Skinfold fat	Weight*
Subscapular*	
Over triceps*	
Suprailiac*	

Rees-Eysenck Body Index
$$= \frac{\text{Stature in cms} \times 100}{\text{Transverse chest diameter} \times 6}$$
Androgyny Score (Tanner)
$$= 3 \times \text{Bi-acromial} - \text{Bi-iliac}$$
Somatotype (by Parnell's method using measures marked *)

at different phases of the study. Many anthropometric measurements (Table 8) were made by C. G. Ingram, and indices obtained from them. The androgyny score (essentially shoulder width compared to pelvic width—a measure of maleness or femaleness) and the Rees-Eysenck body index (a kind of sturdiness measure) proved especially interesting.

Numerous other tests were explored, many using patient serum or urine on various preparations. The ones marked † in Table 9

TABLE 7
Biochemical Test Battery

Blood
  Creatinine
  Bromsulfalein
  Serum oxidase
  Serum protein: albumin, globulin
  Glucose
  Cholesterol
  Uric acid
  Serum phosphorus
  Protein-bound iodine
Urine
  Volume
  Specific gravity
  Creatinine
  Sodium
  Potassium
  5-hydroxyindoleacetic acid
  Acid chromogens
  Epinephrine
  Norepinephrine
  Catecholamines
  Phenolsulfonphthalein

were explored in considerable detail, some constituting separate published papers. Several tests reported in the literature as highly discriminating for schizophrenics failed in our hands; some that we explored or developed did seem to discriminate but will need further confirmation. None of these tests was ready for use at the start of the definitive run, but those on visual threshold and on optic responses were included in later portions.

Besides tests made by our team, other investigators used biological materials from our patients which we sent them for their own measurements—on tissue cultures, blood antibodies, glucose permeability, etc.—or came to Ypsilanti to study our patients (Table 10). Such expanded testing was obviously of value to all; we had an excellent panel of tested schizophrenic patients on which others could explore new tests, and any added findings enhanced the information on our subjects. The only condition of our co-operation with competent investigators was that the added manipulations must not disturb the patients or interfere with our own testing.

TABLE 9
MISCELLANEOUS STUDIES BY MEMBERS OF THE STAFF OF THE SCHIZOPHRENIA AND PSYCHOPHARMACOLOGY RESEARCH PROJECT

Studies	Investigators
*Cat optic response and LSD	Fox
Cat intraventricular injection	Fujita
Cat intrareticular responses	Fox
†Rabbit cortex epinephrine response	Fujita
†Rat rope climbing	Jordan, Schwartz
†Rat resistance to stress	Liebeskind
Rat diaphragm O₂ with insulin	Ling
†Mouse intraventricular injection	Fujita, Ging
†Blood-brain-barrier glucose permeability	Holmberg et al.
†Scheinberg test	Yuwiler
Alkaline phosphatase	Yuwiler
Nonprotein nitrogen	Yuwiler
Nucleotides in general	Ling
Tetrahymenis pyroformes growth	Yuwiler
Loading tests	Yuwiler
*Dark adaptation	Beck
†Drug effects—Ditran, Tofranil, chlorpromazine, Tetrahydroaminacrin	Gershon, Broder, Yuwiler
*Chlorpromazine history	von Brauchitsch
Sensory conflict and related studies	Rosenzweig
†Intraindividual variability	Carrigan
34 additional psychological tests	

* Measurement included in definitive study.
† Investigated in some detail.

THE FINDINGS

Some particular findings

So much for the background and procedures of this study. In turning to results, I invite your attention first to some special findings before examining the full matrices. Table 11 presents some early results on anxiety, or emotional reactivity (Holmberg, 1961), which give encouragement to the possibility of precise measurement even without a pointer reading. Six independent observers with varied training (from a psychiatrist to technicians) rank-ordered 30 patients with excellent consistency. Moreover, their estimate of the anxiety level of a patient correlated significantly with some pharmacological indicators of anxiety.

Electrical responses in the optic system of

TABLE 10
STUDIES BY OUTSIDE INVESTIGATORS

Studies	Investigators
Patient Serum or Urine Studies	
Cerebrospinal fluid assays	W. Tourtellotte
Immunological assays	R. Haddad, Ausma Rabe
Toxic proteins	S. Cobb, G. Brooks, W. Fessel
Psychological Studies	
Sensory deprivation	W. Jackson
Thinking impairment	Essene Joseph
Bender-Gestalt	M. Hutt
Reminiscence	S. Mednick
Word association	S. Mednick
Stimulus generalization	S. Mednick
Word association	L. Gottesman
Zeigarnik effects	L. Gottesman
Wechsler factors	D. Saunders
Paranoid psychodynamics	H. Wolowitz
Depth perception	B. Weiner
Time estimation	I. Feinberg
Physiological Study	
Microtremor	H. Sugano

the cat's brain (the lateral geniculate body) to a light flash are enhanced by the hallucinogenic drug, LSD (Fig. 4). An injection of nonschizophrenic serum prior to drug injection did not alter this enhancement, but an injection of schizophrenic serum knocked it out (Fox, 1960). In the original series of 30 patients the dichotomization was almost complete. Later it held up only partially but did help discriminate some of the conventional clinical subgroups.

Another difference appeared in the concentration of toxic substances in schizophrenic and nonschizophrenic urine (Fig. 5). Injection of appropriate schizophrenic urine extracts intracranially into mice produced mainly excitation—a characteristic rapid jumping with a cry (the mice would seem to bounce once a second), often going

TABLE 11
SIGNIFICANCE OF CORRELATIONS WITH PRE-EXISTING ANXIETY LEVEL

Anxiety Rating Correlates with	p
Blood pressure increase with yohimbine	$< .01$
Heart rate increase with yohimbine	$< .01$
Heart rate increase with piperoxan	$< .005$
Heart rate change with methacholine	$< .01$
Heart rate change with atropine	$< .05$

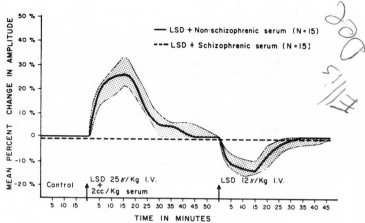

FIG. 4. Response in Cat Lateral Geniculate.

into convulsions and even death—or sometimes depression. Injections of extracts from nonschizophrenic urine generally produced depression or no change. This work was dis-

continued when S. Fujita, mainly responsible for it, returned to Japan, but he has since reconfirmed the findings there. The evidence favors two toxic substances, separated chro-

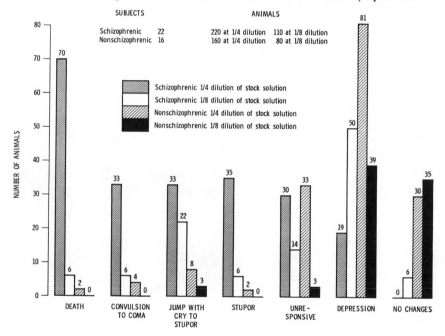

FIG. 5. Effects of Urinary Extracts on Mouse Behavior.

Chi Square Analysis
Blind diagnosis versus clinical diagnosis

*Right	Wrong	Right (questionable)	Open (no diagnosis obtained)
22	1	5	7

$N = 35$ (23 schizophrenics, 12 nonschizophrenics)

	Observed frequency	Expected frequency	$O - E$	$(O - E)^2$	$\chi^2 = \Sigma \dfrac{(O - E)^2}{E}$	$p < $ (1 df.)
1. Right	22	17.5	4.5	20.25	2.314	.20
Wrong ⎫ Right (questionable) ⎬ Open ⎭	13	17.5	−4.5	20.25		
2. Right ⎫ Right (questionable) ⎬	27	17.5	9.5	90.25	10.314	.005
Wrong ⎫ Open ⎬	8	17.5	−9.5	90.25		

* Right 11 schizophrenics, 11 nonschizophrenics   Wrong 1 schizophrenic
  Right (questionable) 5 schizophrenics   Open 6 schizophrenics, 1 nonschizophrenic

FIG. 6. Blind Diagnosis of Schizophrenic or Nonschizophrenic Based on Minor Tremor.

matographically (Fujita & Ging, 1961). A thorough chemical-pharmacological study is most desirable.

Still another biological measure was introduced by a second Japanese colleague, H. Sugano, too late to be in the main study. His teacher had noticed a fine, fast tremor which differed in schizophrenic and nonschizophrenic subjects, and Sugano measured this microtremor on our patients while ignorant of their diagnosis. As Figure 6 shows, his judgment of the clinical diagnosis (schizophrenic or nonschizophrenic) showed a high degree of accuracy.

A final biological discriminator was the dark adaptation threshold, studied by L. H. Beck. The lowest light intensity which a subject can detect when completely dark-adapted is not as low in schizophrenics as in

nonschizophrenics; but, still more important, if oxygen is inhaled for a few minutes, this threshold is lowered in the schizophrenic about to the normal level, but not altered in the nonschizophrenic (Table 12).

The matrices

The main results deal with the matrices of tests against subjects, or of correlations between tests and other statistical analyses. Figure 7 shows our statistician, Nils Mattsson, with about half of the computer printout. Computers are wonderful but can certainly drown one in information; it has taken

TABLE 12
EFFECT OF OXYGEN ON DARK THRESHOLD

	Increase or no change	Decrease
Schizophrenics	17	69
Nonschizophrenics	26	8

FIG. 7. Mr. Nils Mattson, Project Statistician, with Part of the Computer Printout.

TABLE 13
Cross-Correlations Between Psychiatric Ratings and Psychological Measures

Correlations	Expected by Chance	Obtained
.001	2	224
.01	16	411
.05	80	634

Psychiatric Rating	Psychological Measures							
	Full Wechsler	Dotting Speed	Facial Expressions	Social Concepts	Reaction Time	Memory II	Identical Forms	Mirror Drawing
Conceptual Disorganization (Lorr Scale)	− .52	− .52	− .60	− .55	− .52	− .49	− .47	− .51
Mental Disorganization (Gorham Scale)	− .46	− .54	− .58	− .51	− .60	− .49	− .32	− .44
Motor Disturbance (Lorr Scale)	− .44	− .40	− .49	− .44	− .42	− .31	− .33	− .39
Perceptual Distortion (Lorr Scale)	− .41	− .43	− .45	− .45	− .44	− .48	− .38	− .41
Withdrawal (Lorr Scale)	− .28	− .49	− .47	− .34	− .35	− .41	− .22	− .39
Withdrawal (Gorham Scale)	− .26	− .49	− .39	− .31	− .35	− .36	− .23	− .32
Resistiveness (Lorr Scale)	− .34	− .31	− .34	− .40	− .37	− .27	− .19	− .23
Melancholy Agitation (Lorr Scale)	+ .37	+ .28	+ .31	+ .32	+ .30	+ .20	+ .42	+ .11

Correlation matrix of some of the measures which produced most significant correlations between the above two areas
for p .05, r = .20; p .01, r = .25; p .001, r = .32.

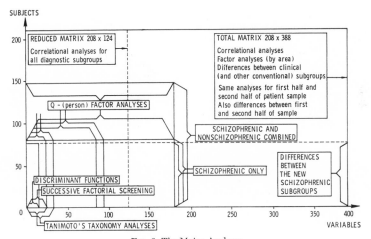

Fig. 8. The Major Analyses.

TABLE 14

RELATIONSHIPS BETWEEN SOCIAL CLASS AND
CHILDHOOD AND ADULT ATTRIBUTES, SCHIZO-
PHRENICS AND NONSCHIZOPHRENICS
COMBINED

Patients From Families of Higher Social Class

During child-hood	were more alert were better adjusted in school were more often chosen leaders by peers had better adjusted fathers
During hospitalization	score higher on intelligence tests have better memory (Olariu scale) show less mental disorganization show less motor disturbance have faster heart rate (baseline) have higher uric acid blood levels

us a couple of years to digest our results,[3] and we really have only covered the basic points.

As an example of the problem of obtaining meaningful ratings, I call your attention to one of our early efforts, and then a later one. Some fifty patients were interviewed by a psychiatrist in the presence of two others, each doing independent ratings on agreed-upon characteristics; three months later a like interview was held and rated. Rorschach tests on the same patients were rated separately by two psychologists, for the same characteristics. Roughly, the psychiatrists agreed with each other one-fourth to one-third of the time, the psychologists agreed over two-thirds of the time, but the psychiatrists and psychologists agreed with each other only about one-tenth of the time. Clearly the observers were dealing with an amorphous and not very well-defined set of criteria. A couple of years later, when the definitive test battery and rating scales had been developed and the psychological and psychiatric measures had been sharply defined, the agreements shown in Table 13 were obtained. Psychological variables are across the top of the correlation matrix, psychiatric ones down the side, and an r as

[3] IBM card decks remain at the Mental Health Research Institute and can be made available for further studies.

low as .20 has a probability of occurrence less than .05 if the variables are not related; an r of .32 has a probability less than .001. Clearly, most correlations are well above this level, so psychological and psychiatric criteria can agree when made precise enough to measure something.

An abbreviated picture of the total study is presented in Figure 8. On the vertical axis are subjects, over 200 in the total definitive run, and on the horizontal axis are tests, almost 400 separate measures. The full matrix, 208 times 388, represents the number of actual values we obtained and used in the full analysis. These had to be averaged, correlated, and examined across each variable, and by various groupings and major classes; so we found ourselves dealing with half a million correlation coefficients. Even though the computer calculated these, their interpretation remained a job for human brains. Besides the total matrix—the relation of all tests to each other and to all subjects—a number of smaller matrices were used for analysis of particular populations (such as all schizophrenics, or those with complete tests), using smaller arrays of

TABLE 15

RELATIONSHIPS BETWEEN CULTURE GROUP AND
CHILDHOOD AND ADULT ATTRIBUTES

Schizophrenics from a Less Integrated Culture Group	Nonschizophrenics from a Less Integrated Culture Group
had parents with poorer social relationships got along less well with peers in childhood have less education	
	are less active, more regressed, and generally more overtly psychotic (7 Olariu scales) perform better on psychomotor tests perform poorly on dark adaptation test have higher parasympathetic index have smaller blood pressure change with norepinephrine
have lower blood uric acid levels	

TABLE 16
Psychological Test Performance and Childhood and Adult Attributes, Schizophrenics and Nonschizophrenics Combined

Patients Who Function Better on Psychological Tests

During childhood and early adolescence	were more alert received more education and performed better in school were brought up in families of higher social class with more cultural interests
During hospitalization	show less psychopathology (mental disorganization, withdrawal, perceptual and motor disturbances, etc.) as rated by attendants and psychiatrists have lower blood pressure baselines before physiological stress experiments excrete more sodium and potassium, and creatinine (especially during day) have higher blood uric acid levels have shorter arm span, broader shoulders, smaller wrist girth are slightly younger and hospitalized for a slightly shorter time (but correlations considerably smaller than expected)

TABLE 17
Correlational Patterns for Faster Reaction Time

Schizophrenics with Faster Reaction Time	Nonschizophrenics with Faster Reaction Time
	come from families with more cultural interests were more alert as children
show strikingly less psychopathology (especially mental disorganization, withdrawal, and motor disturbance) as rated by attendants and psychiatrists perform better on other psychological tests (trend relatively inconsistent, and little or no correlation with perceptual performance)	show less psychopathology as rated by attendants and psychiatrists, although relationship not as striking perform better on other psychological tests (trend strong and consistent and correlated with perceptual performance) have broader shoulders and higher androgyny scores have lower blood pressure baseline and lower parasympathetic index
have higher urine volume and excrete strikingly more creatinine, sodium, and potassium	have strikingly higher blood uric acid levels

TABLE 18
Creatinine Excretion and Childhood and Adult Attributes, Schizophrenics and Nonschizophrenics Combined

Patients Who Excrete More Creatinine

As children	had better peer relations had better adjusted fathers
During hospitalization	*show less psychopathology (withdrawal, mental disorganization, etc.) as rated by attendants and psychiatrists *perform better on tests of intellectual functioning and memory *have faster reaction time †are physically larger individuals

* Day excretion only.
† Night excretion only.

especially discriminating tests for even sharper scrutiny. The matrices used in the progressive search for meaningful subgroups—Q-analysis, taxonomic analysis, discriminant function analysis, and finally successive factorial screening, which gave us our final subgroups—are all identified in the figure. I shall consider, first, results on the total population, then on smaller but still mixed populations, then on the schizophrenic population *in toto*, and finally, as divided in various ways.

TABLE 19
Blood Uric Acid Level and Childhood and Adult Attributes

Schizophrenics with Higher Blood Uric Acid Levels	Nonschizophrenics with Higher Blood Uric Acid Levels
attained better job status were identified with more integrated culture groups have mothers who performed in maternal role more adequately have higher activity level show greater mental disorganization (Gorham scale) show more animated response to cartoons have better immediate memory have longer legs have bigger calves have larger proportion of lean body weight excrete more potassium	achieved higher education levels come from families of higher social class had better health in childhood show greater emotional reactivity (Holmberg scale) have faster reaction time have better vocabulary

83

TABLE 20
ANTHROPOMETRIC DATA AND CHILDHOOD AND ADULT ATTRIBUTES

Patients Who are Larger, and Have Higher Androgyny Scores

As children	met their environment more successfully were more often leaders among peers were more alert were less anxious
As adults	had better jobs prior to hospitalization have been hospitalized for less time have a lower parasympathetic index

The total matrix

The number of significant cross-correlations between main areas was well beyond chance expectancy. For example, correlating all measures in social history with all in psychiatry would give over 5,000 cross-correlations. Since a value significant at $p = .001$ would be expected once in 1,000 times by chance, five such values might be anticipated among 5,000. The number actually obtained was 67, and similarly strong patterns characterized the matrix generally.

This is perhaps the first time such widespread data have been available on a modest population, and a number of surprising correlations came out. These findings are for hospitalized male psychiatric patients in general. Although they were not further explored here, since they are not specifically related to schizophrenia, they cry for extensive followup.

Social class of the family, for example, shows a strong relationship to childhood and adult attributes (Table 14). Higher social class is associated with a "better" childhood, with better performance in the hospital, etc. Even without drawing conclusions as to cause and effect, the relationships found are extremely interesting. Table 15 shows comparable material for loosely integrated culture groups, by schizophrenic and non-schizophrenic subjects.

Other interesting relations are seen in Tables 16 through 20. Patients who functioned better on psychological tests had a better childhood experience and, as adults in the hospital, showed less psychopathology, lower blood pressure, excreted more sodium and potassium and, particularly, creatinine, had higher blood uric acid, and differed in physical measurements (Table 16). Table 17 presents correlational patterns for reaction time specifically, shown separately for schizo-

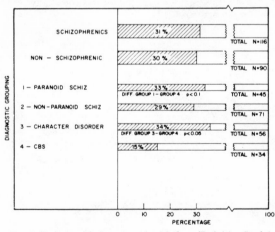

FIG. 9. Patients with Overpossessive Mothers (Definitive Study).

84

TABLE 21
Psychology Factors and Their Highest-Loading Variables

Factor and Tentative Label	Variables
Verbal intelligence	Wechsler-Bellevue Vocabulary
	Gray Oral Reading Test
	Ammons Picture Vocabulary
Nonverbal intelligence	Wechsler-Bellevue Block Design
	Identical Forms
Memory	Immediate Memory II
	Immediate Memory I
Color reactivity	Color-Form Movie, color vertical
	Color-Form Movie, color horizontal
Form reactivity	Color-Form Movie, form horizontal
	Color-Form Movie, form vertical
Perceptual closure	Mooney Closure Faces, female
	Mooney Closure Faces, male
Speed of psychomotor performance	Dotting, preferred speed
	Dotting, fastest speed
Speed of psychomotor response	Reaction Time, standard delay
	Reaction Time, variable delay

TABLE 23
Some Important Attributes of Each Q Factor*

Q-Factor	Attributes
1	Positive pole: mostly nonCSB and P
	Negative pole: mostly non$P$ and CBS
	General psychological functioning, especially intellectual
	General psychopathology
	Family social class
2	Positive pole: mixed diagnoses
	Negative pole: mostly non$P$
	Emotional reactivity (Holmberg scale)
	Social adjustment in childhood
	Body size and general body build
	Orthosympathetic activity
3	Positive pole: mostly NS (many CBS)
	Negative pole: mixed diagnoses
	Alcoholism
	Contrast between intelligence and memory functions
	Withdrawal and anxiety
	Socioeconomic environment in childhood
	Parasympathetic activity
	General autonomic response to physiological stress
4	Positive pole: S and CBS
	Negative pole: mixed diagnoses
	General psychological functioning
	Conceptual disorganization
	Autonomic lability
	Glucose
5	Positive pole: mixed diagnoses
	Negative pole: S ("classical")
	Contrast between general intelligence and other psychological functions
	Motor disturbances
	Orthosympathetic activity
	Glucose
	Education level achieved and motivation toward learning in childhood
6	Positive pole: mixed diagnoses
	Negative pole: S
	General psychopathology, especially withdrawal
	Memory and motor functions
	Autonomic response, especially to psychological stress
7	Positive pole: mostly S
	Negative pole: mostly S
	Nonverbal intelligence
	Motor functions
	Autonomic response to stress
	Urine volume
	Childhood reaction to frustration
8	Positive pole: mostly NS
	Negative pole: mostly S
	Alcoholism
	Motor functions
	Age
	Circulatory response to drugs
	Age-linked biological deterioration

phrenic and nonschizophrenic groups. A strong relation between high creatinine excretion and better intelligence, adult functioning, and childhood experience is shown in Table 18; and a somewhat comparable one for blood uric acid, in Table 19. We believe these correlations are real and important and invite extensive further exploration—some based on our own data.

A final group of findings, relating adult status to the childhood situation, is summarized in Figure 9 and Table 20. One is a negative finding about the schizophrenogenic

TABLE 22
Anthropometry Factors and Their Highest-Loading Variables

Factor and Tentative Label	Variables
General size	Weight
	Chest girth
	Waist girth
Linear development	Height
	Arm length
Trunk width	Shoulder width
	Leg length
	Chest width
Limb robustness	Bicondylar diameter, femur
	Calf girth
	Ankle girth
Skinfold fat	Skinfold fat, suprailiac
	Skinfold fat, triceps
	Skinfold fat, subscapular
Age	Age

TABLE 23—*Continued*

Q-Factor	Attributes
9	Positive pole: mostly S ("classical") Negative pole: mixed diagnoses Contrast between general intelligence and other psychological functions Withdrawal, no active disturbance Occupational achievement Body build Disturbance in respiration Biological inactivation, deterioration
10	Positive pole: mostly S Negative pole: mostly NS Some psychiatric disturbance Mother's involvement in patient and home Family conflict Autonomic response to stress
11	Positive pole: mixed diagnoses Negative pole: mixed diagnoses General psychopathology Body build Temperature and respiration response to psychological stress

S—schizophrenics
NS—nonschizophrenics
P—paranoid schizophrenics
nonP—nonparanoid schizophrenics
CBS—nonschizophrenics with chronic brain syndrome
nonCBS—nonschizophrenics without chronic brain syndrome
* Correlates listed are those which tend to distinguish a given Q-factor from all others, contributing to its uniqueness as a cluster.

role of a demanding, oversolicitous mother: we found no difference in the incidence between the schizophrenic and nonschizophrenic subjects (Fig. 9). Actually, a great amount of social pathology was seen in our patients; but a control study (by Helen B. Fritz and Eira I. Mattsson, of our staff) matching patients with unhospitalized men in comparable work and social groups showed about as much social pathology in the normal group, though rather differently distributed.

One lucky enough to be born a sturdy youngster (rather than gangling or fat)—the stocky, freckled, good-American-boy type—may have a smoother road ahead in life. As a child he is more readily accepted in the peer group and is often a leader, and as an adult has more success (Table 20). Perhaps such a physique rolls through the traffic of life more as a truck than a compact.

Factors

I turn next to various ways of analyzing the matrices. First, a full factor analysis was carried out on the test results in each area. In several instances, factors emerged clearly and were easily interpretable; the eight factors in psychology are shown in Table 21, and the six in anthropometry in Table 22. In other areas, notably biochemistry, the factors were fuzzy and contained such mix-

TABLE 24
SOME STATISTICALLY SIGNIFICANT DIFFERENCES BETWEEN SCHIZOPHRENIC AND
NONSCHIZOPHRENIC PATIENTS

Schizophrenics Have Significantly	
More or Higher	Less, Smaller, or Slower
Childhood behavior difficulty in peer relations brooding conformity and nonaggressiveness maladjusted mothers *Psychiatric characteristics* withdrawal conceptual & mental disorganization motor disturbance anxiety (Gorham scale) *Physiological functions* body core temperature (but lower skin temperature) disturbed respiration at rest improvement in night vision after breathing oxygen	*Psychological test performance* reaction time manual speed concept formation and reasoning ability social understanding *Anthropometric characteristics* chest girth *Biochemical measurements* urine volume, day sodium, day potassium, day and 24-hour serum phosphorus

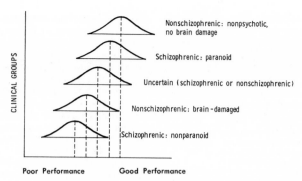

CLINICAL GROUPS

Nonschizophrenic: nonpsychotic, no brain damage

Schizophrenic: paranoid

Uncertain (schizophrenic or nonschizophrenic)

Nonschizophrenic: brain-damaged

Schizophrenic: nonparanoid

Poor Performance   Good Performance

FIG. 10. Relative Performance Levels of the Five Clinical Groups on Psychological Tests: The Most Typical Sequence of Group Means.

tures of test items that no meaning could be given them.

Next, the patients were factored against tests (a Q-analysis) as a first effort to find subgroups. This was still done on the total population, schizophrenics and nonschizophrenics combined, and each of the Q-groups (Table 23) was bipolar. Some poles did seem to represent one or another type of schizophrenia, but the picture was not sharp and some subjects appeared in no group, others in more than one, so further analysis was pursued on just the schizophrenic subpopulation.

TABLE 25

BEST DISCRIMINATORS, BY AREA, BETWEEN PAIRS OF FIVE CLINICAL GROUPS

Social History	Psychiatry	Psychology
Family social class	*Gorham Scales:*	Reaction Time
Peer social adjustment (childhood and adolescence)	Interpersonal relationships	Wechsler-Bellevue Full Scale I.Q. and most subtests
Aggression pattern with peers	Mental disorganization	Facial Expressions
	Anxiety level	Social Concepts
Predominant heterosexual relationships	*Lorr Factors:*	Dotting Speed
	Conceptual disorganization	Kahn Test of Symbol Arrangement
Predominant mood in childhood	Withdrawal	
	Olariu Clusters:	
Parental social adjustment	Regressed deteriorated	
	Overt psychosis	
	Chronic organic	

Anthropometry	Physiology	Biochemistry
Skinfold fat	*Resting level:*	Sodium, day
Leg length	Skin temperature	Urine volume, day
Calf girth	Per cent disturbed respiration	Urine volume, 24-hour
Androgyny score	*Drug response:*	Creatinine urine, day
	Parasympathetic index	Creatinine blood/urine ratio
	Blood pressure change with norepinephrine	Urinary acid chromogens
	Respiration rate change with yohimbine	
	Blood pressure baseline before yohimbine	

87

TABLE 26

SOME CHARACTERISTICS OF PARANOID SCHIZO-
PHRENICS SIGNIFICANTLY DIFFERENTIATING
THEM FROM NONPARANOID SCHIZOPHRENICS

Paranoid Schizophrenics

As children	Were more alert
	Were better adjusted with peers
	Had higher family social class
	Were exposed to less parental conflict
As adults	Are more physically active
	Are less withdrawn
	Have better social understanding
	Show less mental disorganization
	Earn higher scores on intelligence tests
	Have faster psychomotor performance
	Have a lower parasympathetic index
	Have greater urine vòlume (day)
	Excrete more sodium
	Have higher serum phosphorus level
	Excrete more 5-HIAA

Schizophrenics vs. nonschizophrenics

Of the measures we finally settled on in each area, something like 30 per cent discriminated between schizophrenic and nonschizophrenic subjects at a p of .05 or better (Table 24), evidence of successful test selection. Some of the effective discriminators reappear as subgroup discriminators. In fact, as an early guide to subgrouping and to test selection, we divided our total population into clinical subgroups. Besides schizophrenics and nonschizophrenics, there was the group of uncertains, mentioned earlier; the nonschizophrenic group divided rather naturally into those with chronic brain syndrome, and others; and the schizophrenic group we divided simply into paranoid and nonparanoid (all other schizophrenics).

The psychological test performance of these five groups shows a clear order (Fig. 10), schizophrenics being consistently poorest and nonschizophrenics without brain damage, best. These five groups were discriminated by a considerable number of our

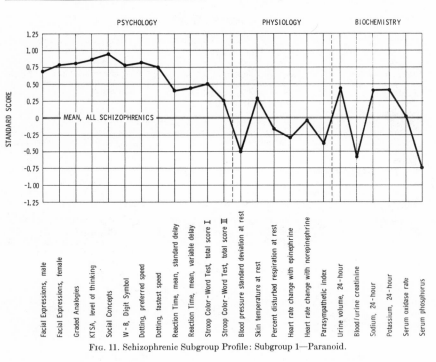

FIG. 11. Schizophrenic Subgroup Profile: Subgroup 1—Paranoid.

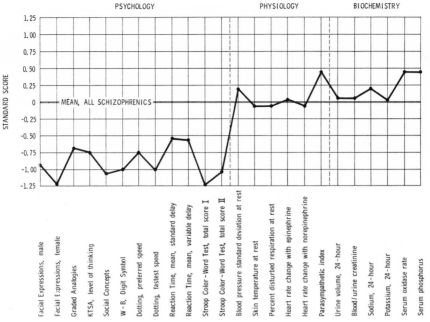

PSYCHOLOGY   PHYSIOLOGY   BIOCHEMISTRY

FIG. 12. Schizophrenic Subgroup Profile: Subgroup 2—Nonparanoid.

tests; the best discriminators are given in Table 25.

Schizophrenic groups

At last we can zero in on just the schizophrenic population, comparing first the paranoid and the nonparanoid clinical groups. Table 26 shows the main discriminators of these. This was encouraging, for at least two kinds of schizophrenia that had been separated on the basis of clinical criteria were also separated by our tests. After all, one would not have expected that wise clinicians over the centuries had utterly "missed the boat," but that some of their subdivisions would, indeed, have meaning. It was very satisfying to find that in many respects, our results do fit with the clinical subgroups, while differing in useful ways.

Finally, for a group of schizophrenics on which we had complete results, and for a small group of discriminating tests limited to the areas of psychology, physiology, and biochemistry, successive factorial screening

was applied and seven subgroups emerged. The first, clearly a paranoid type, is shown in Figure 11. The mean performance of all the schizophrenics in the matrix on each test is the double horizontal line; that of the subgroup, the jagged curve. On psychological measures, on the whole, this group performed much better than the average for all schizophrenics. On physiological measures, and even more on biochemical ones, values oscillated strikingly above or below the group mean.

By contrast, the second subgroup (Fig. 12)—a nonparanoid one—shows very poor psychological performance; mostly normal physiological responses, but with a high parasympathetic index; and high values for serum oxidase (Humoller) rate and serum phosphorous on the biochemical side. The remaining groups likewise had different test profiles. Differences were especially marked between the four nonparanoid groups.

Appropriate statistical measures show that practically 90 per cent of the patients were

TABLE 27
DISTRIBUTION OF 76 SCHIZOPHRENIC SUBJECTS ACCORDING TO THEIR HIGHEST
DISCRIMINANT SCORE, BY SUBTYPE AND FUNCTION

Schizophrenic Subtype	Discriminant Function							N	Proportion Right
	1	2	3	4	5	6	7		
1. Paranoid	12	—	—	2	2	—	—	16	.75
2. Nonparanoid	—	15	—	—	—	1	1	17	.88
3. Nonparanoid	—	—	10	1	—	—	—	11	.91
4. Paranoid	2	—	—	8	—	—	—	10	.80
5. Paranoid	1	—	—	—	8	—	—	9	.89
6. Nonparanoid	—	—	—	—	—	7	—	7	1.00
7. Nonparanoid	—	—	—	—	—	—	6	6	1.00
							Total:	76	.87

Ten subjects were misclassified according to their discriminant score (only one was misclassified as to paranoid or nonparanoid subtype in general). The chi-square of this distribution is 352.0 with 36 degrees of freedom (highly significant).

correctly placed in the appropriate subgroup (Table 27), and only one patient was in the wrong group, as between paranoid and nonparanoid. If perfectly assigned, all would be on the diagonal from upper left to lower right. Table 28 summarizes some of the important characteristics of each of the seven groups, and the measures that significantly discriminated them. There are clear and meaningful orderings in the social history and psychiatric variables, as well as in the biological and psychological ones.

Many more details will appear in the monograph reporting this study, and some relations still are being revealed; but I must comment on a memorandum submitted on June 18, 1963, by H. von Brauchitsch, the first psychiatrist to examine the outcome of this analysis. He had not previously seen the assignments to the seven subgroups; and I remind you that the assignments were made in terms of psychological, biochemical, and physiological measurements—no psychiatric data contributed to the grouping. His preliminary impression of the clinical characteristics of the subgroups was as follows:

"Although it can be regarded as neither statistically nor methodologically satisfactory, the *prima vista* results were impressive beyond expectation. Contrary to the psychiatric evaluation of the Q-analysis, the seven groups evolving from the recent analysis appeared to present well-defined and easily recognizable clinical entities."

He gave the seven groups tentative names,

TABLE 28
SOME IMPORTANT CHARACTERISTICS OF
EACH SCHIZOPHRENIC SUBGROUP*

Subgroup	Characteristics
Group 1: Paranoid	Uniformly good psychological functioning Low serum phosphorus Variable blood pressure
Group 2: Nonparanoid	Uniformly poor psychological functioning
Group 3: Nonparanoid	High creatinine blood/urine Low urine volume Low potassium Low sodium
Group 4: Paranoid	Good intellectual functioning, but only average psychomotor functioning Low urine volume
Group 5: Paranoid	Fast dotting speed High urine volume High sodium High potassium Low serum phosphorus High reactivity to stress
Group 6: Nonparanoid	Low reactivity to stress High parasympathetic index
Group 7: Nonparanoid	Low skin temperature Impaired symbolic thinking and reasoning High serum phosphorus

* Characteristics listed are those which tend to differentiate a given subgroup from all others in this analysis.

and although only three of these seemed adequately descriptive to the research team, I present them as some indication of the psychiatric attributes. The italicized names are the group-approved ones: Group 1 (paranoid), Compliant; Group 2 (nonparanoid), *Overt Psychotic*; Group 3 (nonparanoid), *Depressed*; Group 4 (paranoid), Extrovert; Group 5 (paranoid), *Manic*; Group 6 (nonparanoid), Introvert; and Group 7 (nonparanoid), Insecure.

Here, then, is a distillate of some seven years work by a team that at peak included over forty participating scientists.

In a recent volume that reviews past efforts at classification and emphasizes the futility of formally dividing the realm of mental illness, Karl Menninger (1963) quotes his teacher, Earnest Southard: "Perhaps I believe that the world can get forward most by clearer and clearer definition of fundamentals. Accordingly, I propose to stick to tasks of nomenclature and terminology, unpopular and ridicule-provoking though they may be" (p. 3). Menninger goes on to say, "Southard was indeed ridiculed for his efforts."

I think we have cleared away much speculative underbrush and laid a factual foundation on which future investigators in this field can build. We have not attempted to draw theoretical interpretations; we say only, "Here is a picture of schizophrenia. We have amassed extensive measurements under controlled conditions and think we see seven clear subgroups. Anyone who does research or theorizing in the future (including ourselves) can advance from this base— we hope it will prove helpful."

REFERENCES

Carrigan, Patricia M. Intraindividual variability in schizophrenia. *Diss. Abstracts*, 1964, 25, 2, 1330. (Order no. 64-8142)

Fox, S. S. LSD alteration of optic potentials (cat lateral geniculate); block by schizophrenic serum. *Fed. Proc.*, 1960, 19, 262.

Fujita, S., & Ging, N. S. Presence of toxic factors in urine from schizophrenic subjects. *Science*, 1961, 134, 1687–1688.

Gerard, R. W., *et al.* The nosology of schizophrenia. *Am. J. Psychiat.*, 1963, 120, 16–29.

Holmberg, G. K., & Gershon, S. Autonomic and psychic effects of yohimbine hydrochloride. *Psychopharmacologia*, 1961, 2, 93–106.

Menninger, K., Mayman, M., & Pruyser, P. *The vital balance: the life process in mental health and illness.* New York: Viking, 1963.

Willey, R. R. An experimental investigation of the attributes of hypnotizability. Unpublished doctoral dissertation, University of Chicago, 1951.

1965 DEAN RESEARCH AWARD

LEO KANNER, *M.D., professor emeritus and Honorary Consultant at The Johns Hopkins University School of Medicine, was born in 1894, in Klekotow, Austria and received his medical degree at the University of Berlin. Following early work in electrocardiography and gastroenterology in Berlin, he came to the U.S.A. in 1924, as senior assistant physician at the Yankton, South Dakota, State Hospital. Invited by Dr. Adolf Meyer to join the staff of the Henry Phipps Psychiatric Clinic in Baltimore, he founded in 1930 the Children's Psychiatric Service in the Department of Pediatrics. In 1935 he published the first textbook of child psychiatry in the English language, now in its fourth edition. In 1943, he described early infantile autism, which since then has become a widely discussed and extensively investigated syndrome. Dr. Kanner has received many honors and awards from learned societies and universities in this country and abroad, and is still teaching at the Johns Hopkins University. He also founded the* **Journal of Autism and Childhood Schizophrenia** *in 1971 and serves as its editor.*

INFANTILE AUTISM AND THE SCHIZOPHRENIAS

by Leo Kanner

In a paper published in 1943, entitled "Autistic Disturbances of Affective Contact," I reported from the Children's Psychiatric Service of the Johns Hopkins Hospital observations of 11 children (8 boys and 3 girls) who had in common a pattern of behavior not previously considered in its striking uniqueness. The symptoms were viewed as a combination of extreme aloneness from the beginning of life and an anxiously obsessive desire for the preservation of sameness. I concluded the discussion by saying: "We must assume that these children have come into the world with an innate inability to form the usual, biologically provided affective contact with people, just as other children come into the world with innate physical and intellectual handicaps. If this assumption is correct, a further study of our children may help to furnish concrete criteria regarding the still diffuse notions about the constitutional components of emotional reactivity. For here we seem to have pure-culture examples of inborn autistic disturbances of affective contact."

In my search for an appropriate designation, I decided in 1944, after much groping, on the term *early infantile autism*, thus accentuating the time of the first manifestations and the children's limited accessibility.

The term autism was introduced by Eugen Bleuler, who wrote: "Naturally some withdrawal from reality is implicit in the wishful thinking of normal people who 'build castles in Spain.' Here, however, it is mainly an act of will by which they surrender themselves to a fantasy. They know that it is just fantasy, and they banish it as

soon as reality so demands. I would not call the effects of these mechanisms 'autism' unless they are coupled with a definite withdrawal from the external world."

This definition does not quite account for the status of our patients. For one thing, withdrawal implies a removal of oneself from previous participation. These children have never participated. They have begun their existence without the universal signs of infantile response. This is evidenced in the first months of life by the absence of the usual anticipatory reaction when approached to be picked up and by the lack of postural adaptation to the person who picks them up. Nor are they shutting themselves off from the external world as such. While they are remote from affective and communicative contact with people, they develop a remarkable and not unskillful relationship to the inanimate environment. They can cling to things tenaciously, manipulate them adroitly, go into ecstasies when toys are moved or spun around by them, and become angry when objects do not yield readily to expected performance. Indeed, they are so concerned with the external world that they watch with tense alertness to make sure that their surroundings remain static, that the totality of an experience is reiterated with its constituent details, often in full photographic and phonic identity.

All this does not seem to fit in with Bleuler's criteria for autism. There is no withdrawal in the accepted sense of this word, and a specific kind of contact with the external world is a cardinal feature of the illness. It may therefore appear at first glance that I followed the example of the pseudo-etymologists who claimed that the Latin word for dog derives from the animal's inability to sing (*Canis a non canendo*) and the word for grove from the absence of light (*Lucus a non lucendo*). Nevertheless, in full recognition of all this, I was unable to find a concise expression that would be equally or suitably applicable to the condition. After all, these children do start out in a state which, in a way, resembles the end results of later-life withdrawal, and there is a remoteness at least from the human portion of the external world. An identifying designation appeared to me to be definitely desirable because, as later events proved, there was danger of having this distinct syndrome lumped together with a variety of generalized categories.

It can be said in retrospect that the brief history of infantile autism can be separated into three consecutive phases.

1. While the case reports, their phenomenology, and their etiologic implications almost immediately received the attention of the profession, it naturally took some time before similar observations could be made and communicated. For this reason, the earliest reactions dealing with the issue did not appear in print for several years. Meanwhile, studies were continued and intensified at the Johns Hopkins Hospital. For a period of approximately one year a special ward was set aside at the Henry Phipps Psychiatric Clinic for close investigation and therapeutic experimentation. In a 1946 paper, I discussed the peculiarities of metaphorical and seemingly irrelevant language of autistic children, and in a 1949 article, having by that time become acquainted with 55 patients who could be so diagnosed with reasonable certainty, I tried to set forth my ideas about the problems of nosology and psychodynamics of early infantile autism.

2. This state of affairs changed abruptly in 1951. No fewer than 52 articles and one book were concerned specifically with the subject between then and 1959. The first European confirmations of the existence of the syndrome came in 1952 from van Krevelen in Holland and from Stern in France.

In the same year, Clemens Benda included in his book, *Developmental Disorders of Mentation and Cerebral Palsies*, a brief chapter with four illustrations, entitled "The Autistic Child". In it, he wrote: "The great question is whether autism is a part of the schizophrenic syndrome complex or should be considered a separate entity. A decision of this question cannot be made without a more thorough discussion of what constitutes childhood schizophrenia."

This sage advice was not heeded by many authors. While the majority of the Europeans were satisfied with a sharp delineation of infantile autism as an illness *sui generis*, there was a tendency in this country to view it as a developmental anomaly ascribed exclusively to maternal emotional determinants. Moreover, it became a habit to dilute the original concept of infantile autism by diagnosing it in many disparate conditions which show one or another isolated symptom found as a part feature of the overall syndrome. Almost overnight, the country seemed to be populated by a multitude of autistic children, and somehow this trend became noticeable overseas as well. Mentally defective children who displayed bizarre behavior were promptly labeled autistic and, in accordance with preconceived notions, both parents were urged to undergo protracted psychotherapy in addition to treatment directed toward the defective child's own supposedly underlying emotional problem.

By 1953, van Krevelen rightly became impatient with the confused and confusing use of the term infantile autism as a slogan indiscriminately applied with cavalier abandonment of the criteria outlined rather succinctly and unmistakably from the beginning. He warned against the prevailing "abuse of the diagnosis of autism," declaring that it "threatens to become a fashion." A little slower to anger, I waited until 1957 before I made a similar plea for the acknowledgment of the specificity of the illness and for adherence to the established criteria.

To complicate things further, Grewel, in the hope of avoiding confusion between true autism and other conditions with autistic-like features, suggested the term pseudo-autism for the latter. Even this term came to be employed haphazardly, and conditions variously described as hospitalism, anaclitic depression, and separation anxiety were put under the heading of pseudo-autism.

All this resulted in the need for a careful evaluation of the reports of cases presented as samples of autism. A sifting of the literature of the 1950's compels one to eliminate many alleged illustrations as descriptive of something other than that which they were intended to portray.

3. The 1960's have witnessed a considerable sobering up. The fashion deplored by van Krevelen has gradually subsided. This is perhaps caused in part by the fact that those who go in for the summary adoption of diagnostic clichés have now found another handy label for a variety of abnormalities. Instead of the many would-be autistic children who are not autistic, we have the ever-ready rubber stamp of "the brain-injured child." While this certainly is regrettable, it has at least driven the acrobatic jumpers onto another bandwagon and has left the serious study of autism to those pledged to diagnostic accuracy. Hence, it is easier to single out properly designated cases, not lost in the shuffle of a peculiarly miscellaneous deck, for an investigation of their pathognomonic characteristics. And indeed, in the past few years, the diagnoses made have been more uniformly reliable and the discussion has been considerably less obfuscated by the smuggling in of irrelevant materials.

However, the question of nosological allocation of infantile autism has continued to be a matter of puzzlement. This is especially true of the formulations regarding its relation to schizophrenia.

Anyone attempting such a formulation ought to bear in mind Clemens Benda's quoted suggestion that a decision will have to depend on a discussion of what constitutes schizophrenia. One cannot get away from the need for semantic clarification and for a historical and ideological review of the meaning attached to all that is involved when this term is used. Has the meaning been stationary since the word was coined or have there been fluctuations and modifi-

cations? Is schizophrenia to be conceived as a unitary disease or as a generic noun encompassing a variety of kindred entities? Would all psychiatrists respond to these questions with unanimity?

In the 1890's, Kraepelin undertook the magnificent architectural job of erecting a solid structure of psychiatry from the many building stones lying around in disarray. Guided by the search for basic similarities and dissimilarities, he found a common denominator in a number of psychotic conditions which impressed him as sharing a "deteriorating process." Among them he included the catatonia of Kahlbaum (1863), the hebephrenia of Hecker (1871), the simple deterioration of Pick (1891) and Sommer (1894), and paranoid states associated with disorganization. He subsumed the whole deteriorating group under the term dementia praecox. As soon as this was accomplished, Kraepelin found it necessary to retain the above syndromes, not as the separate units as which they had been previously presented but as subdivisions of the *specific* disease, dementia praecox.

Before we proceed, it is important to pause for an examination of the meaning of the word "specific." Some of the dictionaries offer among their definitions two which, if used interchangeably, are apt to produce—and are indeed producing—semantic quandaries. One says: "Designating a definitely distinguishable disease." The other says: "Of or pertaining to a species, or group, of which the members have common characteristics and are called by a common name."

Kraepelin viewed dementia praecox with its subdivisions essentially as specific in the sense of the first-quoted definition. When Bleuler suggested the term schizophrenia in 1911, he announced that he looked upon it as a common name for a species and emphasized his point by speaking not of schizophrenia in the singular but of the "group of the schizophrenias." He declared significantly: "This concept may be only of temporary value inasmuch as it may later have to be reduced," adding parenthetically, "(in the same sense as the discoveries in bacteriology necessitated the subdivision of the pneumonias in terms of various etiologic agents)."

This prediction indicates a profound grasp of medical history and may prove to be prophetic in the long run. For much of the progress of medicine has been characterized by the singling out of circumscribed diseases from a welter of ill-defined generalities, by the gradual transition from the assumption of the homogeneity to the recognition of the heterogeneity of conditions which have certain broad aspects in common. We are far removed from the time when learned treatises were published, entitled *De febribus* or *De pestibus*, dealing with febrile illnesses and contagious diseases as if they were all of them identical in nature and origin. The falling sickness, once regarded as a single entity, is now divided into a variety of dysrhythmic conditions of different provenances. Before Langdon Down's description of mongolism in 1866, mental defectives were thought of as if, to paraphrase Gertrude Stein, the feebleminded were the feebleminded were the feebleminded; since then, neuropathologic, metabolic, genetic, and psychological studies have managed to do away with the illusion of the sameness of all mental deficiency.

There is at present cause to believe that similar developments are in store for the concept of schizophrenia, resulting in the "reduction" envisioned by Bleuler. Moreover, concrete demonstrations of this trend are beginning to be supplied in the area of child psychiatry.

When Kraepelin created the concept of dementia praecox, he did so entirely on the basis of his work with adults. At no time was there any reference to its occurrence in children. He mentioned once, as a hunch rather than on grounds of careful statistics, that of 1,054 patients $3\frac{1}{2}$ percent had shown signs of "psychic weakness" before ten years of age. All that Bleuler had to say about this in his sizable monograph is contained in a footnote, which reads: "The disease rarely becomes manifest in childhood. Yet there are cases in which a primary schizophrenia can be traced back to the earliest years of life." On the page above this footnote Bleuler reported an estimate according to which the onset of schizophrenia could be found in 4 percent of the case histories to go back to the age of "before 15 years." Obviously, when any thought was given to children at all in connection with dementia praecox or schizophrenia, it was done so largely in terms of retrospect and not as a result of direct examination at the time of the anamnestically recorded incipiency. Childhood schizophrenia was not something seen and clinically investigated as such but rather merely hinted at as an occasional prelude remembered by the relatives of adolescent and adult patients.

Between 1905 and 1908, Sante de Sanctis tried to accomplish for children what Kraepelin had done for adults. He gathered a number of cases which had in common symptoms of lack of affect, negativism, stereotypy, talkativeness, delirium, hallucinations, and catatonic features. As etiologic factors he enumerated hereditary predisposition, acute or chronic toxic diseases, and "factors inherent in child development." He combined all cases under the name dementia praecocissima, a sort of miniature version of dementia praecox. His reports were followed by additional illustrations of his own and other Italian investigators, and a few cases were published under this caption by German, French, and Swiss authors. De Sanctis felt that the clinical picture was indistinguishable from dementia praecox but he was not sure that the adult and the infantile forms had the same causative background.

A review of the contemporary and subsequent literature shows that the notion of dementia praecocissima proved to be of limited viability and has now been discarded altogether as a valid collective designation. Most of the patients turned out to be specimens of an assortment of neuropathologically identifiable, more or less progressive, congenital or acquired anomalies of the central nervous system. Some of them (e.g., Schilder's disease) could not have been known to De Sanctis because they were not isolated until after the time when he incorporated them in his classification. Clinical neurological tests, biopsies, or autopsies removed them from the category; the concept of dementia praecocissima continued to be "reduced" to a point where it lost its justification altogether. In view of later attitudes, it is significant to note that the finding of a clearly definable organic disorder automatically excluded an ailment from the diagnosis of childhood schizophrenia.

This became evident again when the Viennese educator (*Heilpädagoge*) Heller described in 1908 a group of children presenting "an almost photographic identity of course" with the following features: After normal development during the first two or three years of life, there was a rapid change of behavior with anxiety, motor restlessness, loss of speech and of sphincter control, and general regression, leading in a short time to complete dementia, while the children showed no clinical signs of physical disturbance and retained an intelligent facial expression. Heller's disease or dementia infantilis (a term coined by Weygandt), though extremely rare, was observed by others as well and was entered in the textbooks as the earliest form of childhood schizophrenia. It remained there until Corberi in 1931 discovered in four brain biopsies "acute diffuse degeneration of the ganglion cells.' Schilder averred categorically in 1935: "I assume as a matter of course that dementia infantilis has nothing to do with schizophrenia but is an organic process."

This is a pivotal statement around which hinges the whole philosophy of the distinction between organic and functional psychoses. Schizophrenia was classed as a functional psychosis by definition. Ergo, if you find in a patient signs of an organic process his condition logically has nothing to do with schizophrenia.

Two departures are possible from here. One goes in the direction of viewing the term functional as a temporary, perhaps even a bit embarrassing admission of the inability to find an organic substratum; this spurs a search for one so that, if it is discovered, the adjective functional can be dropped. This is, after all, the gist of Kraepelin's postulate of a metabolic disorder, of Bleuler's prophecy, and of much that is happening today in the realm of schizophrenia research. The other departure goes in the direction of regarding "functional" as synonymous with nonor-

ganic; this has encouraged a search for environmental, psychogenic noxa as the explanation of schizophrenic phenomena. The one focuses on the quest for internal, centrifugal springs of psychotic behavior; the other on the shaping influence of external, centripetal forces. Until recently, the twain did not meet and were bogged down in an irreconcilable antithesis.

This antithesis did not become conspicuous until the early 1940's. Until that time, when there was talk of childhood schizophrenia, curiosity was extended mainly to patterns resembling adult syndromes. Strohmayer's treatise on the psychopathology of childhood, which appeared in 1910, and the 1926 (second) edition of Ziehen's textbook of the mental diseases of children discussed juvenile (hardly ever infantile) schizophrenia in Kraepelinian terms. Strohmayer did not hesitate to say that, except for senile, arteriosclerotic, and true paranoid psychoses, all mental illnesses known in adults can be encountered in children with the same symptomatology. Ziehen viewed schizophrenia as an "acquired defect psychosis," together with paralytic, epileptic, traumatic, meningitic, and toxic dementia, in contrast to diseases not resulting in intellectual defect. He spoke of the latter (e.g., mania, melancholia, delirious states, paranoia, and obsessive psychosis) as "functional." This runs counter to the usual inclusion of schizophrenia among the functional psychoses.

However, in the late 1920's and in the 1930's more and more voices were raised in favor of a distinction between adult and childhood schizophrenia, attributable to maturational and experiential factors. There was growing agreement that the Kraepelinian subdivision was not suited for the preadolescent years, and efforts were made to find a grouping more in harmony with direct observations. In Germany, Homburger, one of the pioneers of child psychiatry, decided to use the type of onset and course of illness as a starting point, rather than the symptoms noted at any given time. He thus suggested two different groups, one with acute onset and another with insidious onset. Partly in consequence of Homburger's lead and in part independently, Ssucharewa in Russia, Lutz and Tramer in Switzerland, and Despert in this country underlined this grouping in their discussions of childhood schizophrenia. Patients of the first group, mostly older children, have seemed to make a good adjustment prior to the appearance of recognizable psychotic symptoms. In the second group, there is a gradual withdrawal from contact with reality, a progressive loss of interest in play, an increasing tendency to brood, a preoccupation with abstractions, and obsessively repetitious ruminations. It was deemed essential for the diagnosis in both groups that a period of relative normalcy had preceded the beginning of the illness.

This was the situation around the start of the 1940's, at the time when I published the first cases and introduced the concept of infantile autism. One year earlier Bender had summed up the general professional attitude in a few sentences which deserve to be quoted because of their clarity and succinctness. She wrote: "There are those who do not believe in childhood schizophrenia, not having seen a case. At the best, none of us has seen very many cases in which we could make a definite diagnosis, not knowing the acceptable criteria. There are others who, having seen certain types of mental disorders in children, prefer to call them schizophrenia-like psychoses of childhood."

While Bender and others began to look for acceptable criteria, a sizable group of workers, temporarily influential especially in this country, joined in a chorus chanting the refrain, *Cherchez la mère* (which I tried in vain to silence in 1941 in my book, *In Defense of Mothers*). Poohpoohing description as an obsolete pastime of atavistic nosographers, they started out with interpretations in which the mother-child relationship was put on the pedestal as the only valid etiologic consideration. The underlying idea was: Why bother about questions of genetics, organicity, metabolism, or anything else if we can proceed promptly with the psychogenic denominator common to all disturbances of the ego? Thus arose a tendency to set up a pseudodiagnostic waste basket into which an assortment of heterogeneous conditions were thrown indiscriminately. Infan-

tile autism was stuffed into this basket along with everything else. On the East Coast, Beata Rank, creator of the notion of "the atypical child," comprised in this hodgepodge "all more severe disturbances in early development which have been variously described as Heller's disease, childhood psychoses, childhood schizophrenia, autism, or mental defect." On the West Coast, Szurek announced: "We are beginning to consider it clinically fruitless, or even unnecessary, to draw any sharp dividing lines between a condition that one could call psychoneurotic and another that one could call psychosis, autism, atypical development, or schizophrenia." Such looseness threw all curiosity about diagnostic criteria to the winds as irrelevant impediments on the road to therapy which was applied to all comers as if their problems were identical. The therapeutic cart was put before the diagnostic horse and, more often than not, the horse was left out altogether. With a perfunctory bow in the direction of "heredity and biology," we were urged to give up the concern for the differentiation of any kind of behavioral deviation. By decree, mother-infant involvement was to be accepted as the sole key to everything that goes on within and around the neonate; it alone was supposed to determine his destiny. Modify it therapeutically by using the right technique, and the child has a chance to become adapted to the requirements of suburban propriety.

In contrast to this summary disavowal of biological factors, Bender, assuming the possibility of an underlying diffuse encephalopathy, defined childhood schizophrenia as follows: "A disorder in the regulation of maturation of all the basic behavior processes, represented in children by a maturation lag at the embryonic level, characterized by a primitive plasticity in all patterned behavior, determined before birth and activated by a physiological crisis, such as birth." With anxiety as the organismic response to such crises, secondary symptoms were called forth as defense mechanisms which served Bender as a basis for the grouping of childhood schizophrenia into three types: (1) the pseudodefective or autistic type; (2) the pseudoneurotic or phobic, obsessive, compulsive, hypochondriacal type; (3) the pseudopsychopathic or paranoid, acting-out, aggressive, antisocial type.

This formulation accomplished a number of things. It managed to dispose of the idea that childhood schizophrenia must be viewed as *either* functional *or* organic. It implied that at the present state of our knowledge one can—and must—take into consideration the likelihood of a fusion of innate physiological and postnatal emotional factors. It suggested a grouping based on observed phenomena differing in character and in course.

Questions have arisen, however, with regard to the ease with which the diagnosis was suddenly bestowed upon a relatively vast contingent of patients. Bender, who in 1942 had, as she said, "not seen very many cases in which we could make a definite diagnosis," announced later that by 1951 "over 600" schizophrenic children had been studied in one single psychiatric unit, that of the Bellevue Hospital in New York. By 1954, she had as many as 850 cases on her list, which means an addition of about 250 in the short span of three years. It is highly improbable that all of them would be acknowledged as being schizophrenic by many other experienced child psychiatrists, and yet it cannot be denied that Bender has made careful investigations and has conscientiously adhered to her established criteria.

Out of this emerges a rather disturbing dilemma. We seem to have reached a point where a clinician, after the full study of a given child, can say honestly: He is schizophrenic because in my scheme I must call him so. Another clinician, equally honest, can say: He is not schizophrenic because according to my scheme I cannot call him so. This is not a reflection on anyone in particular. The whole concept has obviously become a matter of semantics.

It is not unreasonable to hope that the bracketing out of the syndrome of infantile autism portends a way out of the dilemma. Returning to the two definitions of the word "specific," we can state unreservedly that, whether or not autism is viewed as a member of the species schizophrenia, it does represent a "definitely distinguishable disease."

This disease, specific—that is, unique, unduplicated—in its manifestations, can be explored per se. Unimpeded by the perplexities of nosological assignment, investigators can agree on its own phenomenology, search for its own etiology, and follow its own course in ordinary and experimental settings.

This is in keeping with the trend to which Eugen Bleuler's son, Manfred, referred when in a comprehensive review of theory and research between 1941 and 1950, he wrote: "The formulation of schizophrenia has rid itself during the past ten years of the hypothetical idea that a disease termed schizophrenia is available for investigation; instead, it has turned its focus on the study of separate diseases within the group of the schizophrenias."

Once it is acknowledged that infantile autism is a separate disease (and then only), the controversy about its rightful position in any hierarchic nomenclature becomes a matter of personal preference and will remain so until we have acquired more substantial knowledge of fundamentals and depend less on speculation and dialectics.

There are those who insist that infantile autism is one of the schizophrenias, even though this means giving up the original idea that childhood schizophrenia develops after a period of relative normalcy. There are some who, because of the poor response by many patients to psychometric assessment, want it placed among the mental deficiencies. And there are those who refuse it a domicile in either group.

Rimland (1964, p. 68) believes "that there is sufficient information at hand to demonstrate clearly that early infantile autism is *not* the same disease or cluster of diseases which has come to be called childhood schizophrenia, and that autism can and should be distinguished from it at all levels of discourse." Further on (p. 76), he states that "it is clearly accurate and desirable to treat infantile autism and childhood schizophrenias as separate and quite unrelated disease entities." But is childhood schizophrenia a separate disease entity?

The singling out of autism has been followed by a number of other attempts to describe specific conditions lifted out of the schizophrenic package. Mahler reported in 1949 a syndrome which she named "symbiotic infantile psychosis," distinguished by a symptomatology which she thought to be centered around a desperate effort to avert the catastrophic anxiety of separation. In the same year, Bergman and Escalona discussed "children with unusual sensitivity to sensory stimulation." In 1954, Robinson and Vitale introduced a number of "children with circumscribed interest patterns." It may well turn out that this is just a beginning and that other syndromes will be detected and studied on their own merit.

There is, indeed, no "disease entity" called childhood schizophrenia, just as there is no disease entity called mental deficiency. It would not occur now to anybody to look for a uniform background for such anomalies as phenylketonuria, galactosemia, and familial oligoencephaly. By the same token, it is hardly feasible to house together an assortment of dissimilar phenomenologic conditions grouped loosely as childhood schizophrenia, be that on the basis of genetics, neuropathology, biochemistry, psychoanalysis, existentialism, or what have you.

Infantile autism serves as a paradigm. Unfortunately, cause and effect are not as easily ascertainable as Fölling has been able to make them for phenylketonuria. But we have at least a well-defined clinical picture of beginnings, symptoms, and course which in their totality are unmatched and therefore specific in the same sense as phenylketonuria is specific—that is, "a definitely distinguishable disease." Efforts have been made recently by Polan and Spencer and particularly by Rimland (1964) to refine the diagnostic criteria and to compile a check list of symptoms as a guide for differential diagnosis. Since my own publication in 1946, valuable studies have been made of the language peculiarities of autistic children, especially in the German monograph by Bosch, *Der frühkindliche Autismus*, which appeared in 1962. In 1951, I reported observations on the conception of wholes and parts in early infantile autism. In 1954, I attempted to review autism from the point of view of genetics or at least genealogy. Others have investigated the effects of drugs on autistic children. There have been a number of follow-up studies through, and some beyond, adolescence. A valuable contribution was made in 1953 by Ritvo and Provence about form perception and imitation. The occurrence of autism in twins has been reported.

I was greatly impressed from the start by an observation which stood out prominently and that I made a point of in my first report. Among the first 11 cases, the parents of my patients were for the most part strongly preoccupied with abstractions of a scientific, literary, or artistic nature, and limited in genuine interest in people. Even some of the happiest marriages were rather cold and formal affairs. I remarked: "The question arises whether and to what extent this fact has contributed to the condition of the children. The children's aloneness from the beginning of life makes it difficult to attribute the whole picture exclusively to the type of the early parental relations with our patients." As time went on and more autistic children were seen, the coincidence of infantile autism and the parents' mechanized form of living was startling. This was confirmed by most observers. These were realities which were impossible to ignore. Yet there were some exceptions. Approximately 10 percent of the parents did not fit the stereotype. Besides, those who did reared other normal or, at any rate, nonpsychotic offspring. Moreover, similarly frigid parents are often seen whose children are not autistic.

Aspects of interplay between patients and their parents have been studied by various investigators, and on the basis of these studies four viewpoints have emerged. One theory regards parental behavior as a reaction to the children's peculiarities and of no etiologic significance; this would be justified if it were not for the established fact that the parents' personalities had displayed the characteristic traits long before the arrival of their autistic children. At the other extreme parents, particularly mothers, are considered the basic cause of pathogenicity; the assumption is that a healthier maternal attitude would have precluded the disorder. A third group feels that the patient, endowed with an innate disability to relate to people, is further influenced adversely by the parents' emotional detachment and the resulting manner of handling him; this in no way discounts the possibility of a reciprocal awkwardness of living together. A fourth theory looks upon the children's psychoses and the antecedents' emotional aloofness as stemming from a common, biologic, genetically determined source; some of the parents indeed give one the impression of autism that has escaped psychotic propensities.

Without going into further details, all of which are fascinating and instructive, the following points can be made with regard to the present state of affairs.

1. It is now generally agreed that a unitary disease entity, schizophrenia, does not exist. Analogously, there is no such unit as childhood schizophrenia.

2. For the time being, however, this caption cannot be discarded. It is "specific" only in the sense that it "pertains to a species, or group, of which the members have common characteristics and are called by a common name." After all, we still speak of mental deficiency, knowing well that the term, a semantic convenience, includes etiologically and clinically heterogeneous conditions.

3. Bender's pioneering work has helped do away with the either-or antithesis of functional and organic by recognizing the fusion of innate as well as experiential components.

4. Attempts have been made to subdivide clinical varieties comprised under the term childhood schizophrenia: cases with acute and insidious onset; "organic and non-organic" (Goldfarb & Dorsen, 1956); pseudodefective, pseudoneurotic, and pseudodelinquent types. These, I believe, have important though only temporary value in that we may anticipate a splitting off of specific syndromes—"specific" in the sense of a "definitely distinguishable disease."

5. Infantile autism has been split off from the cluster and offers itself for investigation of its unique features. It has an identity of its own.

6. Some of the remaining controversies are based more on semantics than on intrinsic essentials.

In closing, I would like to quote from a paper, entitled "Schizophrenia as a Concept," which I presented at a symposium in 1959. I said there: "Child psychiatry is showing the way to the practical application of Bleuler's vision of the plurality of the schizophrenias. It is encouraging to note that similar attempts are beginning to be made with regard to the adult schizophrenias. The smug certainty about a disease schizophrenia has been definitely sloughed off. For the time being, there is still much groping and more or less emotionally tinted clinging to cherished opinions. But so long as facts are scarce, it is inevitable that there be differences of opinion about the delineation of the concept itself, about etiology, and about therapeutic procedures. It is my opinion that in the foreseeable future the same thing will happen to the schizophrenias as has happened to the hyperpyrexias, the insanities, and the amentias and that, when we stop searching for an identical cause and treatment of different ailments tied together in the schizophrenia bundle, we may expect the opening up of new and clearer vistas. But this, also, is only an opinion."

REFERENCES

Rather than list the voluminous literature on infantile autism and childhood schizophrenia, I would like to call the reader's attention to three good bibliographic sources on the topic.

Bradley, C. Schizophrenia in childhood. New York: Macmillan, 1941. Pp. 137–145.
Goldfarb, William, & Dorsen, Marilyn M. Annotated bibliography of childhood schizophrenia. New York: Basic Books, 1956.
Rimland, Bernard. Infantile autism. New York: Appleton-Century-Crofts, 1964. Pp. 237–265.

1966 DEAN RESEARCH AWARD

FRANZ J. KALLMANN *was born in Neumarkt, Germany in 1897, received his medical degree at the University of Breslau, and began psychiatric training and practice in that city. He later joined the clinic of Professor Karl Bonhoeffer in Berlin, studied with Ernst Rüdin in Munich, and started his investigations into the inheritance of schizophrenia. By the time of the publication of his major Berlin family study in 1938, he had migrated to the United States and for the remainder of his career was associated with the New York State Psychiatric Institute and Columbia University. He became noted for studies of twins, and in addition to his continued work in schizophrenia, he provided evidence for the role of genetic factors in manic-depressive psychosis, involutional psychosis, homosexuality, and the aging process. He was one of the first to be concerned with problems of genetic counseling, and was a pioneer in the establishment of psychiatric services for the deaf. Dr. Kallmann died in 1965 at the age of 67.*

JOHN D. RAINER *first met Franz J. Kallmann in 1952 and was immediately impressed by the broad framework which his thinking provided for psychiatric research and understanding. Their close collaboration began in 1955, and Dr. Rainer succeeded to the post of chief of psychiatric research (medical genetics) at the New York State Psychiatric Institute after Dr. Kallmann's death. In addition to a concern for responsible genetic counseling in a psychotherapeutic milieu, his special interests are in the application of the principles of human genetics to the problems of etiology, diagnosis, and course of development in psychiatry and psychoanalysis. Dr. Rainer was born in Brooklyn and received his medical degree from Columbia University.*

THE CONTRIBUTIONS OF FRANZ JOSEF KALLMANN TO THE GENETICS OF SCHIZOPHRENIA[1]

by John D. Rainer

MY first thought tonight I am sure is in all of your minds—how great a loss we suffer not to have had Franz Kallmann continue his productive life and be here to speak himself of his work and his ideas. His death on May 12, 1965 closed a long and productive career. I can only speak for Mrs. Kallmann and for all of those who have worked with Dr. Kallmann in acknowledging deep appreciation for the honor being paid tonight to his life and his work. He learned of course of his nomination for this award a few months before he died, and I feel that his knowing about this important recognition contributed much to the remarkable sense of fulfillment and accomplishment with which he was able to face his final illness.

The work of Franz Kallmann was so closely fused with his own life experiences, his scientific and medical ideals, his delights and his enthusiasms, that it would be impossible to do for him what he would have done tonight—to place in his own perspective almost 40 years of investigation on two continents. I shall try to describe that portion of his research dealing with schizophrenia, recalling perhaps some data or emphases that have been relatively neglected. Before that, however, a few words about Kallmann as a person might supply some hints about why he worked and how he

[1] Because of the length of Dr. Kallmann's bibliography, all citations in the text of this paper will be referred to by number rather than date. (Editor).

worked, what he was driving at, and by what interests and energies he was moved.

Franz Kallmann was a many-sided person. He was a scientist in the broadest sense with a fertile imagination, a thorough knowledge of subject matter and method, a scanning interest in all of human activity, and the constant ability to frame richly suggestive hypotheses and to formulate careful research plans for their investigation. At the same time, he was always a good physician, a knower of men, a student of human fortitude and weakness, a family counselor, and a clinical psychiatrist in the noblest tradition.

Some years ago, Kallmann prepared an autobiographical chapter, for a volume which was never published, entitled "That Rare Specimen—a Psychiatrist Concerned With Genetics." This chapter obviously just antedated the general rapprochement between clinical psychiatry and genetics sparked by the refinement of laboratory techniques as well as the detailed study of individual differences among infants and children. Kallmann's most general contribution throughout the years was to catalize that rapprochement between psychiatry and genetics, a task made uniquely possible for him by his intimate professional affiliation with national and world leaders in both of these disciplines.

In that autobiographical chapter, Kallmann said: "It will be found that a close relationship exists between the two disciplines, psychiatry and genetics.] What is a good psychiatrist? In my opinion he has to be a good physician and, above all, a medical man who takes a humanitarian interest in the psychological and emotional problems of his patients. What is a good human geneticist? While his essential prerequisite is a scientific attitude or scientific detachment, in the final analysis scientific data are drawn from people and are intended to be applied to people. Here, to my mind, is the link between the work of the psychiatrist and that of the human geneticist."

Kallmann went on to describe his early life in Silesia with many revealing personal details. Suffice it to say here that he was the son of a hard-working and socially-minded physician and surgeon, beloved in his town. He received a classical education. Memorizing the Iliad in Greek, defending his dissertation in Latin were part of his preparation and foreshadowed the keen linguistic ability so evident in his own writings, all the more remarkable for being couched in an adopted tongue. Kallmann received his medical degree at the University of Breslau in 1919 and embarked upon psychiatric training there, showing an early interest in the forensic field. After his marriage and some busy years in private practice, he decided in 1925 that he wanted to join the clinic of the eminent Professor Karl Bonhoeffer in Berlin where the highest standards of clinical psychiatry were fostered. Bonhoeffer, apparently a demanding but broad-minded teacher, saw to it that Kallmann enrolled in a special training course at the newly founded Berlin Psychoanalytic Institute where he studied under Rado and Alexander. Kallmann also studied neuropathology under Creuzfeldt and began a lifelong interest in the study of schizophrenia. His first approach was anatomical. Creuzfeldt had held the theory that the disorder was caused by a disproportional growth of two phylogenetically different parts of the brain and had developed an intricate technique of dissection. At the time, therefore, Kallmann was dividing his days between clinical service and work in histopathology. At visiting hours, he recalled, "the head nurse knew she could reach me in the laboratory when relatives of patients wanted to talk to a physician. Swayed by some pragmatic notions of her own, she often announced a group of waiting visitors with the statement, 'Doctor, the familial taint is here.' It was just because that nurse was so domineering that I undertook my first family study to 'disprove' the inheritance of schizophrenia" (76, p. 18). Although, according to Kallmann's reminiscences, Bonhoeffer thought the desire to blend psychiatry with genetics was somewhat unusual, he did not turn down his request to apply for a fellowship at the Research Institute in Munich, later known as the Max-Planck Institute, which was then headed by Ernst Rüdin. It was at that time that Kallmann organized the first family study based on the incidence of schizophrenia among the children and grandchildren as well as the brothers and sisters of a sample of patients suffering from that disorder. At first assisted only by his wife, he gradually enlisted the aid of a group of loyal nurses in the Berlin hospitals. Commuting between Berlin and Munich, he developed the methods of statistical procedure and field investigation, the careful diagnostic appraisal, and the psychiatric insight which marked his first and subsequent studies. By 1934, he was becoming increasingly anxious to leave Germany, where he found the political abuse of genetics for racial purposes, including sterilization laws for the mentally ill, not at all consistent either with the Hippocratic responsibility of the physician or with the genetic data on schizophrenia which he was beginning to collect. In 1936 Kallmann came to the United States and with the generous support and assistance of many leaders in American psychiatry, neurology, and medicine—including Dr. Nolan D. C. Lewis, Dr. David Levy, and Dr. Franz Boaz—he joined the staff of the New York State Psychiatric Institute and the faculty of Columbia University. He brought with him to this country the manuscript of his first master volume, *The Genetics of schizophrenia* (12). With some assistance, he translated the book into English and it was published in New York in 1938. I would like now to look into that study in some detail.

Having failed to disprove his head nurse,

Kallmann introduced this volume with a discussion of the need for scientific exploration and a disclaimer that the discovery of genetic predisposition to schizophrenia signifies therapeutic nihilism. "We need hardly mention," he said, "that even a successful clinical program of psychosomatic therapy in the field of schizophrenia would (not) minimize the practical value of modern hospital care based on efficient methods of symptomatic treatment, complete psychological understanding of psychopathological mechanisms, and a well-planned system of improved, mentally hygienic living conditions" (p. 3). Since schizophrenia had the tendency to manifest itself relatively late in life and since its clinical forms and severity varied so much, Kallmann felt even at that time that a eugenic program would be difficult and undependable. On the other hand he insisted that a sine qua non for any intelligent thinking on the subject was to determine not only the nature and genetic pattern of the mental abnormalities transmitted to the descendants, direct and collateral, of schizophrenic patients but also to determine something about the relative fertility of such patients and their families. Since it was not and is still not possible to identify the genotypical structure in each family member, Kallmann relied on the only genetic method available, the empirical determination of the hereditary prognosis of families of affected individuals, the contingency method devised by Rüdin.

The material for the 1938 study consisted of 1,087 index cases or probands, making up the total number of schizophrenic case histories available in the archives of the Herzberge hospital in Berlin for the years 1893 to 1902. Since they represented a random group untouched by any selective process, these patients could indeed be designated as "probands" according to the criteria of the contingency method. It remained only to follow the indicated relatives of each of these cases regardless of the difficulties involved. Kallmann describes, with so large a series of probands, how hard it was to trace family members; nevertheless this was done. Kallmann explicitly states that unlike some previous studies, the cases which he followed did not represent only those who were most accessible or those who had surviving chil-

dren or other relatives; such a group would be overweighted with paranoid schizophrenics who are usually the oldest and have had the most children before their first hospitalization.

The diagnosis of schizophrenia was made according to consistent standards and excluded all schizophrenics developing after the age of 40, thus avoiding "climacteric and presenile psychoses frequently having a schizoform character" (p. 11). All records were personally reviewed and a diagnosis was made without reference to the earlier diagnosis or to any notes on hereditary conditions in the family of the patient. Cases with specific neurological symptoms, particularly those associated with alcohol or syphilis, were excluded. After four years of work the total number of persons in the entire material amounted to 13,851, made up of the 1,087 probands, their husbands, wives, and parents, their direct descendants, their siblings, and their nephews and nieces. A little more than half of the probands had no children and hence no direct descendants.

The cases were divided along medical and symptomatological lines into hebephrenic, catatonic, and paranoid groups, in which there was a degree of disintegration of personality during the course of the disease; and the simple group which ran a mild course without any considerable deterioration, recovering without gross defect. In describing the hebephrenic and catatonic groups, Kallmann laid stress on "a relatively early and definite check in the development of personality; on emotional inadequacy with affective disharmony and change of the primary psychic activity; on disorders of association, and on a progressive deterioration of personality clearly associated with the process of schizophrenia" (p. 21). For hebephrenia he regarded affective dementia as a particular characteristic, and he did not consider the presence of chronic or occasional hallucinations and unorganized delusions as a ground for excluding hebephrenia. In catatonia the decisive point was psychomotor dementia—"cases in which motor disturbances were prominent, namely the agitated, stuporous, and cataleptic forms" (p. 21). Paranoid cases, as well as simple cases, were marked by the absence of definite dementia, the former determined by the predominance of paranoid delusions, but without domination by hallucinations and with onset before the age of 40. The simple group, finally, was restricted to patients who, since their discharge and for at least 30 years, had remained "permanently free from gross psychotic disturbances. They must have continued tolerably useful in their social and occupational relations and nevertheless, have shown the definite stamp of the earlier schizophrenic process" (p. 23). The decisive diagnostic criteria remained "a more or less marked bent in their life-curve, in the presence of some slight symptoms of schizophrenic deterioration" (p. 23). The total group (see Table 1) consisted of 493 hebephrenic cases, 253 catatonic, 150 paranoid, and 151 simple, plus 40 doubtful cases which were omitted from further statistical analysis. Females predominated, ranging from 57 percent of the total in the catatonic group to 62 percent in the paranoid, and the females tended to be from one to five years older than the males. Kallmann attributed this sex distribution to his decision to omit automatically all persons with a history of alcoholism or syphilis, most of whom were males. Discussing at length the social background, occupation, and medical history of the ancestors of his probands, he concludes: "for the present we can prove schizophrenia only in a bare 10 per cent of the immediate ancestry of schizophrenic patients, but the total number of ancestors obviously tainted with the hereditary predisposition to schizophrenia and belonging to the heredity circle of schizophrenia comes, in the direct line, to at least one-third of the parents, uncles and aunts" (pp. 42–43). Ruling out earlier vague attempts to consider every form of psychopathic abnormality or organic nervous disease in the ancestors of schizophrenics as manifestations of a hereditary taint, he considered these as the minimum figures for diagnosed schizophrenia. He found them at this point to be consistent with a recessive mode of heredity in which there would be no reason to expect to find schizophrenia in the parents of an index case, and in which most affected individuals would be born to carrier or heterozygotic parents. Further evidence for the recessivity of schizophrenia was supplied later in the book.

TABLE 1
DISTRIBUTION OF THE PROBANDS ACCORDING TO SEX AND FORM OF SCHIZOPHRENIA

By Groups	♀		♂		Total
	Absolute	Per Cent	Absolute	Per Cent	
H	300	60.9	193	39.1	493
C	143	56.5	110	43.5	253
P	93	62.0	57	38.0	150
S	92	60.9	59	39.1	151
D	19	47.5	21	52.5	40
Total Number	647	59.5	440	40.5	1087

From Kallmann, *The Genetics of Schizophrenia*, New York: J. J. Augustin, 1938, p. 23.

Before turning to the important data on the frequency of schizophrenia in descendants of his schizophrenic index cases, Kallmann discussed at length the fertility and mortality of the probands and their descendants. His chief findings in that section (see Table 2) were that the mortality of the children of all index cases exceeded the corresponding mortality for the general population by about 10 percent. As far as fertility was concerned, while the paranoid and the simple schizophrenic patients married about as often and had about as many children as the general population, in the hebephrenic and catatonic groups only half as many of the patients married, and the birth rate was about three quarters that of the normal; one third of the children born to the latter groups of schizophrenic patients were born after the onset of the disease, while the paranoid cases had most of their children before onset.

Foreshadowing his future concern with responsible genetic counseling, Kallmann said at this point "we need hardly mention that a general and legal compulsory sterilization simply cannot be considered as the eugenic method which would be applicable to the heterozygotic taint carriers predisposed to schizophrenia. We must reject it if only because this procedure seems unsuitable on human, medical, and methodological grounds even for the hereditarily diseased patients themselves. We are rather inclined to believe that in countries with high ethical standards and moral disciplines, the liberty

110

TABLE 2

DIFFERENTIAL FERTILITY OF PROBANDS IN
COMPARISON WITH THE GENERAL
POPULATION

	Celibacy Rate	Birth Rate per Marriage	Child Mortality 0–4 Years
Schizophrenic Probands [1892–1902]			
HC Group	60.1%	3.0	45.6%
PS Group	23.9%	4.6	42.5%
General Population of Berlin*			
1880	—	4.04	
1890–1900	29%	—	34.0%
General Population of Prussia [1896–1901] [Woytinski]			
Rural Inhabitants	—	5.3	—
Urban Factory Workers	—	4.4	—
General Population of Germany [1884–1900]	—	4.4–4.8	—

* Annual Statistical Report of the City of Berlin, Vol. 88, Pages 21 and 89.
From Kallmann, *The Genetics of Schizophrenia*, New York: J. J. Augustin, 1938, p. 66.

of the individual to determine his own fate within the limits of his natural sovereign rights and the voluntary submission of every citizen to public measures adopted for the perpetuation of common happiness and security belong to the finest and most indestructible ideals of mankind. Accordingly, the methods of education in biology, official bureaus of eugenic guidance and marriage counsel, mandatory health certificates before marriage and, if necessary, the legal prohibition of marriage seem preferable to us both on personal and scientific grounds" (pp. 68–69). At the same time, although there seemed at that time to be selective factors lowering the marriage and birth rate —not only among the patients themselves but as Kallmann found, among their brothers and sisters—this limitation of reproduction was in no sense adequate to eliminate spontaneously the predisposition to schizophrenia. We shall see that one of Kallmann's last studies was a reevaluation of the marriage and fertility patterns of schizophrenics in New York State.

Among the challenging implications of the case material at this point was Kallmann's first observation that there was a steep rise in mortality from tuberculosis in comparison with the average population, not only for the schizophrenic patients, but for their

children as well (see Table 3). The mortality in the children occurred mostly in the second decade of life and was almost five times that of the general population. The increase was also considerable in brothers and sisters of the index cases. The only other cause of death in which the index cases as well as their siblings showed an increase was suicide. Kallmann was interested in these figures both as indicating possible lethal factors tending to limit the number of schizophrenic persons in the population, and also as representing possible biological correlations, especially in the case of tuberculosis.

The key chapter in *The Genetics of Schizophrenia*, Chapter 4, describes the frequency of schizophrenia in the direct and indirect descendants of the probands. The chapter is introduced by some methodological and diagnostic statements. The rationale for such elaborate studies is given by the statement, ["since genetics cannot estimate the frequency of disease in the descendants simply by theoretical figures of hereditary prognosis, nor disclose it by cross-breeding of pure strains, we are confined at present to obtaining the probability of disease for the various descent groups of schizophrenics by the accurate interpretation of experience" (p. 99).] Kallmann describes the Weinberg Abridged Method to correct for variations in the age distribution; namely for the

TABLE 3

TOTAL MORTALITY FROM SUICIDE AND
TUBERCULOSIS IN THE VARIOUS
DESCENT GROUPS

	Suicides		Mortality From Tuberculosis, Based on Deaths between 10–59 Years
	Based on All Births	Based on Deaths between 10–59 Years	
Children of Probands...	1.3	11.6	58.5
Grandchildren.........	0.3	8.3	60.0
Siblings................	1.8	8.0	33.0
Nephews and Nieces....	0.8	6.6	38.7
Panse's General Population of Berlin.........	0.4	2.4	14.3

From Kallmann, *The Genetics of Schizophrenia*, New York: J. J. Augustin, 1938, p. 91.

fact that among the relatives of the index cases, there are some who will be too young to have developed the disease clinically, so that a pure prevalence figure would represent too low an estimate of those who would develop schizophrenia if they lived through the age of 45. Briefly described, the interval from the 15th to the 44th year was considered as the danger period for the manifestation of schizophrenia. In determining the total number of relatives in a given category, one counted therefore only half of the persons who were between the ages of 15 and 44. All persons who were 45 or older were reckoned in full, while those who were below the age of 15 at the time of ascertainment or at the time they dropped out of sight, were omitted entirely. A detailed discussion of the abridged method of Weinberg and a comparison with other methods designed to accomplish the same correction are given in this chapter. Regarding diagnosis, Kallmann pointed out that in the chapter to follow all children and grandchildren of index cases classified as schizophrenic could be found described clinically, one by one, in a series of accurate vignettes, so that his diagnostic tenets could be checked at any time and could be employed similarly by other investigators for further genetic studies. Kallmann stated at this point, "the accuracy of psychiatric diagnosis depends much more on whether psychopathologic attributes are correctly interpreted and evaluated in proper technical terms than on whether the right final diagnosis is deduced from the sum of the identified symptoms. The best diagnostic system is worthless if it is incorrectly applied and, in the last analysis, the accurate recognition and appraisal of schizophrenic manifestations must depend on the subjective delicacy of touch and personal ability of the individual investigator" (pp. 101–102). He went on to discuss the diagnosis of schizoid personality, a category included in all of his statistics, although he was unable to decide whether "an eccentric borderline case is a homozygotic carrier of the predisposition to schizophrenia with inhibited manifestation, or the most definite type of a germinally affected taint-carrier (heterozygote), or perhaps only a symptomatic schizoid type without direct connec-

tion to the heredity-circle of schizophrenia." In respect to the proof of diagnosis, "psychiatry and genetics are in about the same position as internal medicine was in the pre-bacteriological era when there was the difficulty of deciding whether a suppurative coating on the tonsils was diphtheritic or nonspecific, or whether an infectious fever was caused by influenza bacilli or other types of bacteria. For want of other criteria, it is necessary for the psychiatrist to utilize experiences of extensive clinical observation, studying the various psychopathological manifestations most carefully, and limiting the sources of error as far as possible" (p. 104).

The statistical findings in this chapter are fairly well known in general, but their detailed breakdown is worth repeating. For the *children* of the index cases, the following expectancy figures for the four clinical subgroups were derived (see Table 4): hebephrenic 20.7 percent, catatonic 21.6 percent, paranoid 10.4 percent, simple 11.6 percent. The close approximation between the hebephrenic and catatonic expectancy and between the paranoid and simple expectancy led Kallmann, at this point, to bracket the

TABLE 4

COMPARATIVE TAINT SURVEY IN THE VARIOUS
DESCENT GROUPS OF THE PROBAND
FAMILIES

		The Present Study (Estimated According to the Abridged Method)			
	Total Number of Adults under Observation		Expectation of Schizophrenia		
		Total Material		Clinical Sub-Groups	
			Total Material	Nu-clear Group	Periph-eral Group
Children	1000	16.4%	20.9%	10.4%	
Grandchildren	543	4.3%	5.1%	2.9%	
Great Grandchildren	29	—	—	—	
Siblings	2581	11.5%	12.9%	8.9%	
Half Sisters and Half Brothers	101	7.6%	7.6%	—	
Nephews and Nieces	1654	3.9%	4.7%	3.4%	
Normal Average Population		0.85%			

Adapted from Kallmann, *The Genetics of Schizophrenia*, New York: J. J. Augustin, 1938, p. 145.

two former groups together as the nuclear group and the latter groups together as the peripheral group. The expectancy of schizophrenia in the offspring of a patient depends, of course, upon the diagnosis of the other parent. In those cases in which the other parent had some psychiatric manifestation, the expectancy was 21 percent overall, while for those in whom the other parent was normal, it was 11.9 percent. For illegitimate children it was highest of all, 26.3 percent. A significant finding noted at this point was that there were no significant risk differences between children of male and female probands, nor between children born before and after the disease onset of the proband. The overall expectancy for children of schizophrenics was 16.4 percent, about 19 times as high as the schizophrenic expectancy in the general population, taken on the basis of a number of studies quoted in the text as 0.85 percent.

In the case of grandchildren the expectancy figures were 4.3 percent for schizophrenia, still about five times greater than the general population, although if one omitted those grandchildren who had a schizophrenic parent as well as the proband grandparent, the rate dropped to 1.3 percent.

In his discussion of siblings, Kallmann preceded the figures with his statement that theoretically the frequency ought to be greater in the siblings than in the children if one is dealing with a recessive hereditary trait; with about a one percent normal average frequency in the population, he calculated that the frequency of heterozygotes would be about 18 percent if there were complete manifestation and the marriage rate of heterozygotes were normal. Actually these last two conditions were not met, since marriage rate, fertility, and disease manifestation varied according to the individual disease form and in the different generations. The overall figures established by the survey were 11.5 percent for the sibs; 7.6 percent for the half-sibs; 19 percent for the sibs of those cases with one schizophrenic parent. Turning to the four clinical subdivisions, the schizophrenia rate in the sibs was 12.6 percent for hebephrenic; 13.4 per cent for catatonic; 8.9 percent for paranoid; and 9.5 percent for simple. It is of interest that the figures for schizoid personality in the sibs and for that matter in the children of index cases did not vary significantly among the four diagnostic groups.

The rate for nephews and nieces of schizophrenic patients was 3.9 percent. However, these figures actually ranged from 1.8 percent for those nephews and nieces who had phenotypically normal parents to 21.4 percent for those with one schizophrenic parent and 50.0 percent for those with two schizophrenic parents. These figures, Kallmann said, "form the final link in the chain of our differential taint study on the various crossbreeding proportions among the descendants of schizophrenics, terminating with a rather conclusive proof of the recessive hereditary transmission in schizophrenia" (p.133).

Chapter 4 concludes with a noteworthy theoretical discussion of the nature of the [hereditary predisposition factor in schizophrenia.] Kallmann gave further substantiation for the fact that the schizophrenia rate in sibs is indeed higher in the nuclear group than in the peripheral group and ascribed this to a biological cause rather than to a social pattern having to do with selection of marriage partners, age of manifestation, and the like. Nevertheless, he found that the four different disease forms do not form different hereditary predispositions; the children of hebephrenic or paranoid patients are not always in turn hebephrenic or paranoid, and two or more schizophrenics in the same series of children do not manifest the same form of psychosis. As a matter of fact, he pointed out that only about half of the schizophrenias in the children and grandchildren correspond to the disease form of the probands, while, even in the same sibship, the number of similar psychoses is only 73 percent. He concluded, therefore, that the individual form of schizophrenia is determined not solely by the special nature of the hereditary predisposition, but by a series of other factors. These are not racial, he said in this 1938 book, quoting with tongue in cheek a German writer who said only Nordic people develop pure types of schizophrenia; rather he went on to indicate his belief that the phenotypic manifestation depended on varying hereditary constitutional characteristics of the individual, in-

conclusion

113

cluding the "inner environment," with the "phenotypical and somatogenous components of the individual constitution" (p. 152). A discussion followed of the recessive nature of the basic inherited factor versus the theory of dominance with incomplete penetrance and some of the dihybrid theories that were offered. Kallmann supported the former theory and mentioned here for the first time some twin figures, those of Luxenburger and Rosanoff, in which the concordance for schizophrenia in identical twins was about 70 percent. "The inhibition of manifestation," Kallmann said, "in more than a quarter of identical twins with a homologous predisposition to schizophrenia, is to be explained only by the assumption that these cases lack exciting dispositional factors" (p. 153). There were only 41 twin pairs among the descendants in the present investigation; 19 sets died in childhood, and in 12 others only one twin survived the 20th year. Of the remaining ten pairs, seven were of the same sex, but of these only one pair showed any psychiatric abnormalities, the rather famous identical twin sisters, Kaete and Lisa, raised since infancy by two different uncles and concordant for catatonic schizophrenia, there were two opposite sex discordant pairs.

Since another source of presumed homozygotes was the offspring of two schizophrenic parents, Kallmann investigated the schizophrenia rate among this group and in his total material found it to be 68.1 percent, again short of the expected 100 percent. Kallmann's detailed formulation explaining the variations in manifestation by assuming constitutional factors as determining elements in the development of the individual disease form is worth further description. "The constitution of an individual is viewed," he said, "as the phenotypical resultant of the impact of all environmental influences on the sum of all genetic strains." "Hebephrenic and catatonic psychoses," he speculated, "tend to occur when there is in certain organs a particular inferiority that is based on a specific hereditary predisposition and is constantly exposed to the influence of dispositional physical processes running their course in every body and frequently excited by unfavorable components of the environment." In those severe forms, however, this occurrence might be confined, he said, "to individuals whose physical constitution does not provide, especially during the critical stages of generative endocrine change, for repressive factors adequately resistant to the urge toward manifestation of the schizophrenic predisposition. Correspondingly, the paranoid and simple schizophrenias might occur only after the original restraining mechanism has ceased to operate, either through gradual exhaustion of the physiological forces before and during the climacteric and presenility or in simple schizophrenic cases, under the impact of sudden somatic processes markedly reducing the resistance of the total organism for a period of time. . . . To express these concepts of the phenotypical development of schizophrenia most simply, we may say that the mode of manifestation tends to be variable and depends in each instance on the result of the individual interplay among genetic, constitutional, and environmental factors" (pp. 161–163).

The following chapter described in detail all descendant cases as well as some of the other interesting families and pedigrees, including twins; and the one after that discussed the absence of an increase in other psychopathological abnormalities in schizophrenic families—namely, epilepsy, syphilis, feeble-mindedness, and psychopathy. Kallmann then turned to the study of the genetic relation between schizophrenia and tuberculosis and concluded with his thoughts about the constitutional resistance factors in both conditions. Indeed he found the mortality from tuberculosis considerably increased in all the categories of relatives of schizophrenics, greater in the nuclear group than in the peripheral group, and greatest in those categories of relatives with the highest expectancy of schizophrenia. He suggested that the anatomical substratum for the low resistance in both of these conditions was an "inherited tissue insufficiency rather than a similarity of physical structure or some toxic endocrine organic change per se" (p. 256) and that the most plausible explanation at the time was that an impaired reactive ability or weakness of the reticuloendothelial system was the common constitutional basis. Kallmann quoted in this chapter the experimental findings of Meyer who found by the use of the Congo red method that the capacity for storage in schizophrenics was diminished and by use of the cantharidin blister technique of Kauffmann, that there was an inadequate reactive capacity of the cells of the reticuloendothelial system—possibly correlated with a deficiency in the production of antibodies. At that time, the methods employed for testing the efficiency of the reticuloendothelial apparatus were crude and Kallmann regarded the theory as only a working hypothesis, one to which he returned many years later.

The book we are describing concludes with a discussion of clinical and eugenic implications. Kallmann reiterates that sterilization of schizophrenic patients would eliminate only from two to three percent of the total number of schizophrenics and that the results would in no way justify the means. Clinically, he describes the interaction between heredity and environment as follows: "It is too often forgotten that only predispositions are inherited and never attributes as such, and that the phenotypical manifestation of the trait in the individual depends on the sum of all the given environmental conditions" (p. 264). The inhibition of schizophrenia in over 30 percent of the offspring of two schizophrenic parents corresponding with the twin figures that others had obtained indicated to him the importance of other somatic or dispositional factors. Eugenic measures by systematic enlightenment of individual families did not interfere, he said, "with the clinical problem of psychiatry to prevent and combat the manifestation of the schizophrenic trait in the tainted individual born in spite of prophylactic measures. To achieve the therapeutic optimum, all psychiatric efforts must be concentrated on identifying the somatic processes responsible for the phenotypical development of the hereditary predisposition . . . (intervening) to improve gradually the remedial success already achieved in a minority of schizophrenics by nonspecific mutation treatment (insulin, sulfosin) or other methods . . . in order to reach the goal of modern medicine: simultaneous prevention and healing" (pp. 268, 272).

I have gone into a great deal of detail in describing *The Genetics of schizophrenia* since, in the first place, the book has long been out of print and is not easily available, and, in the second place, it contains many leads to future investigations and many formulations, as well as detailed data, which are worth reviewing in discussing Franz Kallmann's investigations and career. Moving on, in one of his first papers written in the United States, (13) Kallmann said he was convinced that systematic instruction of marriage partners would be enough to effect an adequate reduction of postpsychosis fertility rate and that early marriage should not be recommended to young schizophrenic females as a therapeutic procedure. He recommended in 1938 (11) the availability and use of contraception for those couples who could understand the nature of the problem.

By 1941 Kallmann had already begun to study manic-depressive disease (20) and for our purpose we may indicate some of the differential diagnostic criteria he set down at that time. Manic-depressive disease was marked for him by alternating episodes of depression and elation which do not show real hallucinations, dissociation, delusions, or a definite tendency to mental deterioration. He referred to his ongoing twin study for indeed, upon coming to New York State, he decided to obtain a larger group of individuals presumably predisposed to schizophrenia by searching for the identical twins of schizophrenic patients. He wrote at that time that the main purpose of twin studies was not to show concordance but to study those pairs that differ in onset or production, in order to prevent or to heal the condition, and that curability and inheritability were not incompatible.

An interesting paper in 1941 (21) written together with Drs. Barrera, Hoch, and Kelley on the role of mental deficiency in the incidence of schizophrenia reported no correlation between these two, except by coincidence. In 1942 (22) Kallmann described further his concepts of the heredo-constitutional mechanisms of predisposition and resistance (see Figure 1). He considered a scheme in which the schizoid personality was either a heterozygote with little resistance or a homozygote with strong re-

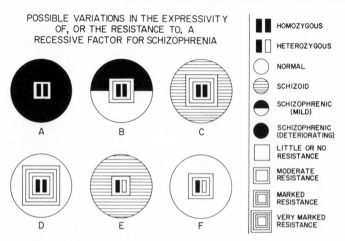

POSSIBLE VARIATIONS IN THE EXPRESSIVITY
OF, OR THE RESISTANCE TO, A
RECESSIVE FACTOR FOR SCHIZOPHRENIA

■■ HOMOZYGOUS

■☐ HETEROZYGOUS

◯ NORMAL

⊖ SCHIZOID

◐ SCHIZOPHRENIC (MILD)

● SCHIZOPHRENIC (DETERIORATING)

☐ LITTLE OR NO RESISTANCE

▢ MODERATE RESISTANCE

▣ MARKED RESISTANCE

▣ VERY MARKED RESISTANCE

Fig. 1. From Kallmann, and Barrera, *Amer. J. Psychiat.*, 1942, 98, 546.

sistance; the schizophrenic, a homozygote with little resistance; and the mild schizophrenic, a homozygote with intermediate resistance; and he discussed the possibility of a normal clinical appearance in a homozygote with strong resistance or a heterozygote with intermediate resistance. The resistance, in any case, he considered as a multifactorial constitutional mechanism. He pointed out that in the twins which he was currently studying, the nonschizophrenic twin was always the physically stronger, taller, and heavier, and far more resistant to infections and other ailments than the twin who did develop schizophrenia. A number of case studies with pictures were presented at that time, and, in connection with Sheldon, the patients were somatotyped and schizophrenic found to be correlated with the asthenic type, resistance with the athletic. During those years, Kallmann was engaged concurrently in a large-scale twin study of tuberculosis per se and in a prototypic family study reported in 1943 with Reisner (25), he found 87 percent concordance for tuberculosis in monozygotic twins; 26 percent in dizygotic twins ranging from 20 percent in opposite-sex pairs to 30 percent in same-sex pairs, 26 percent in full siblings, 12.9 percent in half-siblings, 7.1 percent in marriage partners—all compared with

1.37 percent in the general population. In this paper he described his perfected twin family method, soon to be reported in connection with the schizophrenia study.

In 1946 there appeared what is perhaps Kallmann's best-known publication (30), a paper on the genetic theory of schizophrenia, read the previous year at the annual meeting of the American Psychiatric Association. The report summarized the result of 10 years' intensive survey of twin index cases. By describing them as "collected from the resident populations and new admissions of all mental hospitals under the supervision of the New York State Department of Mental Hygiene" (p. 311). Kallmann did not do justice to the many hours and months of personal journeying through the hinterlands accompanied always by his wife and variously by distinguished psychiatrists like Slater, Strömgren, Hurst, and Svendsen. In the 794 twin index cases there was an excess of females over males of almost 20 percent. About 70 percent were unmarried, and 68 percent of the total number belonged to the nuclear groups.

The actual prevalency rates for schizophrenia uncorrected for age in the various twin index cases were as follows: parents, 9.1 percent; husbands and wives, 2.0 percent; step siblings, 1.4 percent; half-siblings,

TABLE 5

SCHIZOPHRENIA RATES FOR RELATIVES OF
SCHIZOPHRENIC TWIN INDEX CASES

	Number	Rates*	
		Uncorrected	Corrected
Parents	1191	9.1	9.2
Spouse	254	2.0	2.1
Step Siblings	85	1.4	1.8
Half Siblings	134	4.5	7.0
Full Siblings	2741	10.2	14.3
Two-Egg Cotwins	517	10.3	14.7
One-Egg Cotwins	174	69.0	85.8

* Uncorrected = all schizophrenia and all persons over age 15.
Corrected = definite schizophrenia and $\frac{1}{2}$ persons age 15 to 44 + all over 44.
Adapted from Kallmann, The genetic theory of schizophrenia. *Amer. J. Psychiat.*, 1946, 103, p. 313.

4.5 percent; full siblings, 10.2 percent; dizygotic cotwins, 10.3 percent; monozygotic cotwins, 69.0 percent (see Table 5). The figures which are more generally known are those which have been corrected by the abridged Weinberg method: parents, 9.2 percent; husbands and wives, 2.1 percent; stepsibs, 1.8 percent; half-sibs, 7.0 percent; full sibs, 14.3 percent; dizygotic cotwins, 14.7 percent; monozygotic cotwins, 85.8 percent. It is of interest to note that a reexamination of the records of the cotwins done in later years showed that out of 103 monozygotic cotwins diagnosed as schizophrenic, all but two had themselves been in a mental hospital; likewise all but 4 of 47 affected dizygotic cotwins.

Kallmann explained the difference between the 68 percent risk previously obtained for the offspring of two schizophrenic parents and the 85.8 percent risk for monozygotic cotwins by the fact that the parents had already been distinguished by having had the chance to marry and produce offspring, and were probably marked by better genetic resistance factors than the nonselected series of twins. Emphasized again was the importance of the fact that the morbidity rate in monozygotic cotwins, as in the offspring of two schizophrenic parents, was less than 100 percent. From a biological standpoint, Kallmann said, the finding classifies schizophrenia as both preventable

and potentially curable. The implication was that the main schizophrenic genotype is not fully expressed either in the absence of any particular factor of a precipitating nature or in the presence of strong constitutional defense mechanisms which, in turn, are partially determined by heredity. Kallmann took pains to point out that the risk figures "do not mean however that heredity is effective in only 70 to 85 percent of schizophrenic cases or that it is essential merely to the extent of 70 to 85 percent in any one case" (p. 315).

As one might put it today, the measures represent the interaction between genetic and nongenetic factors in determining variability within a given population, and not a division into two mutually exclusive categories. Most striking of all was the observation that "over 85 percent of the siblings and dizygotic cotwins did not develop schizophrenia, although about 10 percent of them had a schizophrenic parent, all of them had a schizophrenic brother or sister, and a large proportion shared the same environment with these schizophrenics before and after birth." There was no correlation between schizophrenia in the cotwin and instrumental delivery or premature birth. The concordance in dizygotic twins seemed to be independent of their sex (see Table 6). The total concordance was 14.3 percent for male pairs, 14.9 percent for female pairs; for opposite sex pairs, it was 10.5 percent where the male was the index case, 10.2 percent where the female was the index case; for same sex pairs it was 17.4 percent for male pairs, and 17.7 percent for female pairs. In the monozygotic pairs, there was some difference between separated and nonseparated twins, bearing in mind that in this series separated twins were those who were not living together for five years prior to disease onset in the index twin. The rates were 77.6 percent for separated pairs, 91.5 percent for nonseparated pairs, the overall figure having been given as 85.8 percent. Only in 17.6 percent of the monozygotic twin pairs was the age of onset simultaneous. In 52.9 percent it ranged from one month to four years, and in 29.4 percent the difference in age of onset was over four years. Regarding the clinical course of the disease,

TABLE 6
VARIATIONS IN THE SCHIZOPHRENIA RATES OF SIBLINGS AND TWIN PARTNERS ACCORDING TO SEX AND
THE SIMILARITY OR DISSIMILARITY IN ENVIRONMENT

	Siblings of Twin Index Cases			Dizygotic Cotwins			Monozygotic Cotwins		
	Male	Female	Total Number	Male	Female	Total Number	Sepa-rated	Nonsepa-rated	Total Number
Same sex	15.9	16.3	16.1	17.4	17.7	17.6	77.6	91.5	85.8
Opposite Sex	12.5	12.0	12.3	10.5	10.2	10.3	—	—	—
Total Number	14.0	14.5	14.3	14.3	14.9	14.7	77.6	91.5	85.8

Adapted from Kallmann, The genetic theory of schizophrenia. *Amer. J. Psychiat.*, 1946. 103, p. 316.

there were important similarities in the monozygotic pairs and great dissimilarities in the dizygotic pairs, pointing again to the multifactorial constitutional resistance factors. For the first time an excess of consanguineous matings was found among the parents of the index cases, with about 5.7 percent of the twin index pairs originating from consanguineous matings of nonschizophrenic parents. Kallmann's general conclusion to this paper was as follows: "Psychiatrically it should be evident that the genetic theory of schizophrenia, as it may be formulated on the basis of experiment-like observations with the twin family method, does not confute any psychological concepts of a descriptive or analytical nature, if these concepts are adequately defined and applied. There is no genetic reason why the manifestations of a schizophrenic psychosis should not be described in terms of narcissistic regression or of varying biological changes such as defective homeostasis or general immaturity in the metabolic responses to stimuli. Genetically, it is also perfectly legitimate to interpret schizophrenic reactions as the expression of either faulty habit formations or progressive maladaptation to disrupted family relations. The genetic theory explains only why these various phenomena occur in a particular member of a particular family at a particular time" (p. 320).

These principles were developed further in a paper written in 1948 (40), in which Kallmann discussed such concepts as the ability to be normal, behavioral plasticity, genes and fate, and the genetic approach to therapy. In this paper and a paper published in the American Psychopathological series on failures in psychiatric treatment (45), he pointed out the close correlation between sudden weight loss and onset of schizophrenic symptoms in some of the twins whom he followed. In the latter paper he also discussed some of the unconscious objections to heredity that he found among his fellow psychiatrists and reiterated that there was no fixed relation between a gene itself and the character caused by it, that "therapeutic action against an inherited disorder is possible either by rendering the underlying main gene less penetrant or by changing its expression through carefully directed management of vital environmental factors or through methodical stimulation of secondary modifiers" (p. 136), and that the need for studies of dissimilar twins was very great.

Those were the years in which the postwar ascendancy of interest in psychodynamics coincided with the low point of attention to genetic factors in psychiatry, and indeed they were difficult years for Kallmann as a pioneer in this area. Nevertheless while continuing to collect schizophrenic twins, he was engaged in a number of other fruitful activities including the study of over 2000 senescent twin pairs, the founding of the American Society of Human Genetics, and participation in an increasing number of national and international meetings.

At one of those conferences, the First International Congress of Psychiatry in Paris in 1950, Kallmann summarized not only the twin material in schizophrenia, but the smaller series of manic-depressive twins that he had meanwhile collected. In his report to that congress (56) he addressed himself to the problem of nosology, deriving from the twin data on the one hand a biological disparateness between schizophrenia and manic-depressive psychosis and on the other, a partial association between schizophrenia and involutional psychosis. While he came to consider that manic-depressive psychosis was genetically homogeneous and conditioned by a dominant gene with incomplete penetrance, he felt that "the diagnostic category of involutional psychosis is either less homogeneous clinically or more complex pathogenetically than are those of schizophrenia and manic-depressive psychosis. . . . There is some reason to believe that a few involutional cases might actually be late-developing and attenuated processes of schizophrenia precipitated only by the impact of the involutional period of life, which threatens loss of security" (p. 13). He had found no twin pairs with both schizophrenia and manic-depressive psychoses, no increase in manic-depressive psychosis in the families of schizophrenic twins or vice versa, but some increase in involutional psychosis in the families of schizophrenics. Recapitulating some of his diagnostic criteria, he wrote at that time, "Except for paranoid syndromes occurring in previously nonpsychotic persons during the involutional and senile periods of life, all the 'mixed' psychoses causing a disintegrative bend in personality development were regarded as basically schizophrenic processes and were generally classified as such unless clearly symptomatic or associated with gross organic pathology. In accordance with this latitude in diagnosing a schizophrenic psychosis, the classification of schizophrenia was not reserved solely for the episodic and deteriorating forms of hebephrenic, catatonic and paranoid coloring but it was extended to include the simple, atypical, and 'schizo-affective' varieties showing only a very slow tendency to deterioration, the acute confusional states precipitated by extreme stress, and the 'panneurotic' borderline cases without delusions or hallucinations described by Hoch and Polatin as the pseudoneurotic type of schizophrenia. . . . Our diagnosis of schizo-

phrenia rested on the constellative evaluation of basic personality changes observed in association with a whole group of possible psychopathological mechanisms, rather than on the presence of any particular type of symptomatology. As a general principle greater diagnostic importance was attached to the demonstrable effect of a 'bending' curve of personality development than to any surface similarities to pathognomonic textbook descriptions, especially when this bend was found in conjunction with such malignant features as xenophobic pananxiety, loss of the capacity for free associations, inability to maintain contact with reality, (autistic and dereistic attitudes toward life), or a compulsive tendency to omnipotential thought generalization" (pp. 8–9). In that Paris address, Kallmann said that "in future twin studies . . . emphasis should be placed on clarifying the intricate interplay of gene-specific biochemical dysfunctions, general constitutional (adaptational) modifiers and precipitating outside factors arising from the effect of certain basic imperfections in the structure of modern human societies" (pp. 22–23). With now 953 schizophrenic index cases the corrected expectancy rate for parents was 9.3 percent, for half sibs 7.1 percent, for full sibs 14.2 percent, for dizygotic cotwins 14.5 percent, and for monozygotic cotwins 86.2 percent.

This major summarizing paper was followed within two years by the Thomas W. Salmon Lectures at the New York Academy of Medicine which were published in 1954 as a monograph (76). In this book, Kallmann reviewed his own data and those of other investigators in schizophrenia in the framework of a volume discussing at length general concepts of heredity in mental disorder and genetics in mental health planning. Kallmann dealt for the first time there with the problems of childhood or preadolescent schizophrenia. He noted that the excess of males in this younger group as opposed to the excess of females in the older schizophrenic patients was as yet unexplained, and he mentioned that he was conducting an investigation of preadolescent twin index cases in which the majority of the concordant twin pairs were of the male sex and the concordance rates of both zygosity groups apparently lower than for the adult forms of schizophrenia.

The complete report on preadolescent schizophrenia was published in 1956 by Kallmann and Roth (96) and described 52 sets of twins, 17 monozygotic and 35 dizygotic. By that time Kallmann was inclined to explain the excess of males in terms of an increased biological vulnerability. He stated that "the diagnostic criteria were generally on the conservative side . . . very young children who presented a picture of psychosis with mental deficiency, perhaps simulating a severe intellectual defect as a result of a very early schizophrenic process, were not included in the sample. . . . All diagnoses were made by one investigator and strictly on the basis of the clinical history of the child, without prior knowledge of the family background. A distinct change in the behavior of a child who previously seemed to develop normally was regarded as a crucial diagnostic feature. The most frequently observed symptoms were diminished interest in the environment, blunted or distorted affect, peculiar conduct especially in motor activity, diffuse anxiety with phobias and vague somatic complaints, bizarre thinking with a tendency toward exaggerated fantasies, and hallucinations." There appeared to be no etiological significance in the birth order of the index cases, and the ages of their parents at the time of their birth were within the normal range. The expectancy rates for schizophrenia in the cotwins of the preadolescent cases were: dizygotic twins 22.9 percent, monozygotic twins 88.2 percent. These were uncorrected figures; since this study dealt with schizophrenics under the age of 15, it was not thought advisable to correct age differences by the abridged Weinberg method. If one considered only preadolescent schizophrenia in the cotwins, the rates were 17.1 percent for dizygotic twins, 70.6 percent for monozygotic twins. In parents the schizophrenia rate was 8.8 percent, in sibs 9.0 percent. (For the study of sibs, the 52 twins were supplemented by 50 single-born preadolescent schizophrenics). In the course of this study two observations were made which pointed the way to some of

Kallmann's later investigations. First a small rise in the schizophrenia rate of the parents of the preadolescent cases was found over that noted in previous studies. It was suggested that this increase might indicate that the present population of schizophrenics had a slightly better chance of becoming parents then was true in previous samples. Four years later Kallmann was to begin a study of changing mating and fertility trends in schizophrenia. In the second place, the quality of the parental homes of the preadolescent schizophrenic cases was investigated and a close relationship found between inadequate homes and severe maladjustment, between unstable parents and schizophrenia in the children. While these findings were compatible with both genetic and environmental theories, it was noted that two thirds of the normal twins and other brothers and sisters came from the same inadequate homes.

Returning to the adult form of schizophrenia, Kallmann wrote (79) that the vulnerability to schizophrenia might be described psychodynamically as an integrative pleasure deficiency leading to adaptive incompetence, a formulation for which he gives credit to Sandor Rado. Indeed Rado, Kallmann's former teacher and then the Director of the Columbia University Psychoanalytic Clinic, had formulated his theory of the "schizotype" based on his pupil's work and marked by the particular psychodynamic constellations of the pleasure deficiency and a proprioceptive defect.

In the 1950's, keeping pace with certain current trends in genetics, Kallmann was discounting the importance of the difference between dominant and recessive inheritance, preferring the dynamic approach of the Goldschmidt school which tried to understand phenomena in terms of "gene-specific molecular processes and developmental systems with all their interaction, embryonic regulation, and integration. In this frame of reference, the concept of Mendelian heredity (with or without simple segregation ratios) becomes more or less synonymous with 'chromosomal heredity.' Pertinent environmental factors which mold, and formative elements which secure behavior-

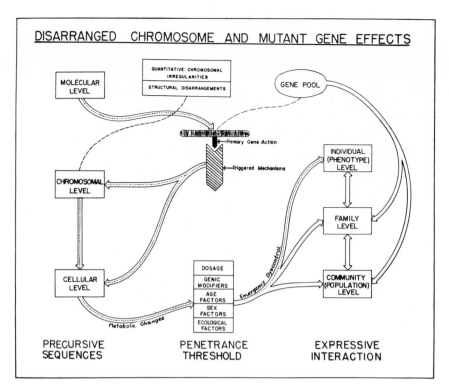

DISARRANGED CHROMOSOME AND MUTANT GENE EFFECTS

MOLECULAR LEVEL

QUANTITATIVE CHROMOSOMAL IRREGULARITIES
STRUCTURAL DISARRANGEMENTS

GENE POOL

←Primary Gene Action

←Triggered Mechanisms

INDIVIDUAL (PHENOTYPE) LEVEL

CHROMOSOMAL LEVEL

FAMILY LEVEL

CELLULAR LEVEL

DOSAGE
GENIC MODIFIERS
AGE FACTORS
SEX FACTORS
ECOLOGICAL FACTORS

COMMUNITY (POPULATION) LEVEL

Metabolic Changes

Emergency Dyscontrol

PRECURSIVE SEQUENCES

PENETRANCE THRESHOLD

EXPRESSIVE INTERACTION

FIG. 2. Adapted from Kallmann, in *Comparative Epidemiology of the Mental Disorders*, Grune & Stratton, New York, 1961, p. 236.

able malleability on the human level are viewed as 'end products of the same evolutionary process' " (122, p. 341).

In the American Handbook of Psychiatry (121) he wrote: "For several reasons it still seems appropriate to interpret the main adaptive defect in a potentially schizophrenic person as the result of a basically recessive unit factor, although it is quite irrelevant with respect to the overall genetic theory whether the given main gene is classified as primarily dominant or recessive, or fails altogether to show simple segregation ratios. The modern concept of human heredity does not hinge 'upon the counting of simple Mendelian ratios' and it seems that most pathological conditions

in man are neither fully dominant or completely recessive but only relatively so, depending 'upon the facility with which the trait is detectable in the heterozygote;' " and "the question of how to designate a mode of transmission that seems distinguished by a specific unit factor for the entire syndrome, plus a number of modifying genes responsible for the variable clinical expressions of the main genotype, is more or less a matter of semantics" (p. 191).

The late years of the 1950's and the early 1960's brought with them the well known advances in genetics including the study of human chromosomes, the increased understanding of the molecular biology of heredity, and the current search for knowledge about control and feedback mechanisms. In his writings between 1960 and 1965, Kallmann incorporated these modern concepts of genetics into his theoretical framework and taught them to psychiatrists. He conceived of the interaction of biochemical, molecular, subcellular, and cellular mechanisms with threshold factors to produce the individual behavioral phenotype and the family and social expressions thereof, as indicated in a diagram adapted from one of his more recent publications (138) (see Figure 2). It was appropriate that for the 25th anniversary of the department of medical genetics a symposium on expanding goals in genetics in psychiatry (145) included discussion not only of the genetics of disordered behavior, but of the most recent progress in basic cytological and biochemical genetics from various parts of the world.

In the last five years Kallmann devoted most of his attention to two consuming projects, a marriage and fertility study of schizophrenic patients and a psychiatric and genetic study of the deaf. The former study was formulated in accord with growing concern for the problems of genetic counseling, a field in which Kallmann had much to say. He regarded genetic counseling as a form of psychotherapy, as a dialogue between the physician and the family in which not only their specific questions regarding genetic risk, but also their wishes, fears, and hopes could be discussed and they could be helped to come to a reasonable conclusion. In the case of schizophrenia it was important within that framework to know whether more schizophrenic patients were marrying than had been the case at the time of the earlier study and whether they were having more children. Preliminary reports (176) by Erlenmeyer-Kimling, Rainer, and Kallmann on this study (which is still in progress) indeed indicated an increase in the marriage rate, in the divorce rate, and in the reproductivity rate among schizophrenic patients which is higher than that for the general population (see Table 7). Comparing a group of schizophrenic patients admitted in the mid-1930's with a group in the mid-1950's after modern treatment methods were instituted, the authors noted not

TABLE 7

REPRODUCTIVE RATES OF SCHIZOPHRENICS IN TWO SURVEY PERIODS AND COMPARISON WITH GENERAL POPULATION

| Survey Period | Number of Children Per 100 Persons | | | | Reproductivity of Schizophrenic Females Expressed as Per Cent of General Population |
| | Schizophrenics | | | General Population Females | |
	Both Sexes	Males	Females		
1934–36	60	50	70	120	58.3
1954–56	90	60	130	150	86.7

Adapted from data of Erlenmeyer-Kimling, Rainer, and Kallmann. Current reproductive trends in schizophrenia: A psychiatric-genetic survey. In P. H. Hoch & J. Zubin (Eds.) *Psychopathology of Schizophrenia*, New York: Grune & Stratton, 1966.

only this change in the marriage and fertility pattern but equally significant, an increase in the fertility rate in brothers and sisters of schizophrenic hospital patients. These findings were taken to indicate that any selective disadvantage which schizophrenia may have had in terms of its evolutionary history is now in the process of disappearing. In one of the last papers that Kallmann wrote (168) he described the developmental history of children born of two schizophrenic parents. Many of these children were found to be displaced from their homes for various periods of time during their formative years. Kallmann said that since any study, genetic or otherwise, indicated a poorer prognosis for these children, it was clearly indicated that "until the biological disciplines exploring one or the other facet of the complex etiology of schizophrenia come up with a reliable method for the prevention or treatment of this disorder, more attention should be given to the attainable goals of marriage and parenthood counseling in schizophrenic families requesting such guidance" (p. 145).

The second project (162), that on the deaf, had many clinical ramifications and led to outpatient and inpatient services for totally deaf psychiatric patients—as Kallmann phrased it, "a psychiatric genetic department in action." From the point of

TABLE 8

SCHIZOPHRENIC RISK DATA IN THE SIBLINGS
OF DEAF AND HEARING SCHIZOPHRENICS

	Number of Siblings		Corrected Frame of Reference	Crude Risk (%)	Corrected Risk (%)
	Surviving Age 15	Definitely Schizophrenic			
Of Deaf Index Cases:					
Hearing Siblings	303	25	223	8.3	11.2
Deaf Siblings*	28	3	19	10.7	15.8
Total	331	28	242	8.5	11.6†
Of Hearing Index Cases (Kallmann 1946):	2014	184	1288	9.14	14.3

* Includes seven cases with marked hearing loss.
† 14.1% if probable cases are included.
Adapted from Rainer, Altshuler, and Kallmann (Eds.) *Family and Mental Health Problems in a Deaf Population*, New York: New York State Psychiatric Institute, 1963, p. 211.

view of research, the study made some significant observations about the prevalence of schizophrenia among this severely deprived population. The best determination of the schizophrenia rate for the deaf in New York turned out to be 2.5 percent, a figure higher than the 1 percent figure for the general population, but not as high as that for any category of relative of a schizophrenic patient. A group of 138 deaf schizophrenic patients were taken as index cases and the schizophrenia rate among their sibs determined (see Table 8). The age-corrected schizophrenia rate for all the sibs of deaf schizophrenic patients was 11.6 percent. Most interesting was the absence of a statistically significant difference between the schizophrenia risks for hearing and deaf sibs; among the hearing sibs the corrected expectancy rate was 11.2 percent, among the deaf sibs 15.8 percent. All groups of sibs, the hearing as well as the deaf, and their combined total, had significantly greater risks for schizophrenia than the general population, risks which were the same order of magnitude as those computed in other family studies. In particular, they closely approximated the rate of 14.3 percent reported by Kallmann in 1946 for the sibs of schizophrenic index cases without a hearing loss. In this deafness study which was carried out by Drs. Altshuler and Sarlin, it therefore appeared from the data that

the severe and various stresses associated with early total deafness do little to increase the chance of developing clinical symptoms of schizophrenia.

Aside from these important statistical studies, Kallmann's vision in the last years turned toward the future goals and tasks of psychiatric-genetic research, and in so doing he dwelled again on the elucidation of the biology of schizophrenia. Having seen his work serve as the stimulus for much current pharmacological and biochemical research, he said in an unpublished progress report to the Scottish Rite Committee on Research in Schizophrenia: "There is a French proverb to the effect that people, as they grow older, tend to return to their first loves. If this saying is correct, you may be inclined to evaluate my report in terms of my advancing age." He went on to say that "over 30 years ago, while still working in pathological laboratories, I became interested in the function of the reticuloendothelial system as the system which is man's principle organ of defense. At that time we studied in laboratories the regulatory and defensive activities of cell elements in connection with artificially produced fever reactions, first in neurosyphilitics and later in schizophrenics. Ever since, I have had the nagging thought that some systematic work should be done along these lines in order to make it possible to have a connecting link between the psychodynamic and physiodynamic approaches to a pathological state that may be referred to in terms of lack of ego strength in coping with stress as well as in those of the organism's inability to maintain a state of adaptiveness in the presence of a noncontainable deficit in its biochemistry. Since I have always assumed that genes exert their effects through control of metabolism, although there is a long chain of reactions between the initial gene effects and its observable end products, I never thought of the genetic factor for schizophrenia as something that is static or fixed at birth. Instead we defined it as a specific, complex, and quite dynamic vulnerability factor that leads to adaptive incompetence only when the defense system collapses. Unfortunately, it took many years to obtain whatever statistical data were needed

123

to substantiate the theory that this collapse is more likely to occur in some people than in others. With this task accomplished, many fine clinicians had an incentive to search for the biological substrate of this presumably gene-specific metabolic deficiency while we finally got a chance to look again into the mysterious activity of reticuloendothelial cells." Kallmann went on to describe the function of monocytes, histiocytes, and phagocytes, the importance of studying such cell activity in potential schizophrenics prior to the manifestation of clinical symptoms, and the need to study therefore the offspring of two schizophrenic patients and the identical twins of persons with schizophrenic symptoms. Counting cellular elements in blister fluids, he observed tentatively a marked reduction in the total cell count and a rise in the percentage of lymphocytes. Kallmann soon established a cytogenetic laboratory in his department which began and continues now to investigate the phenomena, using modern tissue culture techniques.

If Kallmann were here, he would probably end his report to you by presenting his conception of the future of psychiatry in the perspective of genetics. He addressed himself to this theme in 1962 (146) at the meeting of the American Psychopathological Association where he outlined the new discoveries in human cytogenetics and molecular genetics and voiced his belief that genetic research at the molecular and chromosomal levels had the capacity of greatly enhancing our understanding of human behavior disorders. The length of time needed to achieve these ends, he said, could not be predicted because it depended upon our willingness to make heavier investments in terms of brain and manpower, laboratories, and above all, moral commitments. "If this stipulation can be met," he said, "no one among our junior colleagues should be even mildly astonished if much of the decoding of genetic elements in the etiology of puzzling psychiatric disorders is accomplished within his own lifetime" (p. 197). In another 1962 paper (151) he said, "the availability of precise experimental methods justifies the general conclusion that

exploration of quantitative, as well as qualitative, changes in the genetic components of personality organization is now well within our reach" (p. 89).

I can only add that I think that if Franz Kallmann had had the time, he would have tried to systematize his ideas. I know he planned, if he ever retired, to put on paper some of his broader philosophical and theoretical views. Meanwhile, always curious, always searching, always critical, he must have exasperated those of his friends of every psychiatric persuasion, who wanted him to endorse dogmatically their theories or positions; yet they remained his friends. His absorption in research did not prevent him from developing a wide variety of interests, ranging from a deep appreciation of music and art to travel and sports—and above all, human relations.

A particularly poignant glimpse into his character and style of mind came to light last week, when the night nurse who tended him during his last illness gave Mrs. Kallmann two notes he had written her a year ago. Mrs. Kallmann has given me permission to read them to you on this occasion. The first says, "Mrs. No Flashlight (what a pleasure). Must one make an early reservation if one wants to join a few old friends on Mt. Olympus, and how does one get there?" and the second, a few days later, "Since you did not give me the proper directions to Mt. Olympus, I unfortunately missed the boat today. Wann geht der Nächste Schwan? from the Lohengrin Clan."

I hope that tonight I have been able to give you something of a picture in historical form of Franz Kallmann's contributions as a psychiatrist interested in genetics to research in schizophrenia. Thank you.

REFERENCES

The following is a complete and definitive bibliography of Franz Josef Kallmann.

1. Kallmann, F. J. Accidental stab wounds as cause of death. *Ärztl. Sachverständingen Z¹schr.*, 1921, 22, 126. (German)
2. Kallmann, F. J. On the psychopathology of the superstitious criminal. *Mschr. Psychiat. Neurol.*, 1929, 72, 37. (German)
3. Kallmann, F. J. On the symptomatology of cerebral cysticercosis. *Mschr. Psychiat. Neurol.*, 1929, 72, 324. (German)

4. Kallmann, F. J., & Marcuse, H. Sulfosin therapy in general paresis and schizophrenia. *Nervenarzt*, 1929, 2, 149. (German)
5. Kallmann, F. J., & Salinger, F. Accident-conditioned metastasis in malignant tumors. *Ärztl. Sachverständigen Ztschr.*, 1929, 9, 1. (German)
6. Kallmann, F. J., & Salinger, F. Diagnostic and forensic aspects of cerebral cysticercosis. *Mschr. Psychiat. Neurol.*, 1930, 76, 38. (German)
7. Kallmann, F. J. The methods of fever treatment. *Hospitalstitende* 1932, 75, 1. (German)
8. Kallmann, F. J. The methods of fever treatment in neurosyphilis. *Mediz. Welt*, 1932, 43, 1. (German)
9. Kallmann, F. J. The results of fever treatment in the Herzberg Hospital. In K. Bonhoeffer, & P. Jossmann (Eds.), *Ergebnisse der Reiztherapie bei progressiver Paralyse*. Berlin: S. Karger, 1932. (German)
10. Kallmann, F. J. The fertility of schizophrenics. In H. Harmsen, & F. Lohse (Eds.), *Bevölkerungsfragen*, Munich: J. F. Lehmanns, 1936. (German)
11. Kallmann, F. J. Eugenic birth control in schizophrenic families. *J. Contracept.*, 1938, 3, 195.
12. Kallmann, F. J. *The genetics of schizophrenia*. New York: J. J. Augustin, 1938.
13. Kallmann, F. J. Heredity, reproduction and eugenic procedure in the field of schizophrenia. *Eugen. News*, 1938, 23, 105.
14. Kallmann, F. J. In memoriam: Dr. med. Wilhelm Weinberg. *J. nerv. ment. Dis.*, 1938, Vol. 87.
15. Kallmann, F. J. Informal discussion of "Sources of mental disease: Their amelioration and prevention." In F. R. Moulton, & P. O. Komora (Eds.) *Mental health*. Publication No. 9, American Association for the Advancement of Science, 1939.
16. Kallmann, F. J. Collaborator in *Psychiatric dictionary* (L. E. Hinsie, & J. Shatzky). New York: Oxford University Press, 1940.
17. Kallmann, F. J., Barrera, S. E., & Metzger, H. The association of hereditary microphthalmia with mental deficiency. *Amer. J. ment. Defic.*, 1940, 45, 25.
18. Kallmann,. F J. Editorial. *Amer. J. ment. Defic.* 1941, 46, 165.
19. Kallmann, F. J. Knowledge about the significance of psychopathology in family relations. *Marr. Fam. Living*, 1941, 3, 81.
20. Kallmann, F. J. The operation of genetic factors in the pathogenesis of mental disorders. *N. Y. S. J. Med.*, 1941, 41, 1352.
21. Kallmann, F. J., Barrera, S. E., Hoch, P. H., & Kelley, D. M. The role of mental deficiency in the incidence of schizophrenia. *Amer. J. ment. Defic.*, 1941, 45, 514.
22. Kallmann, F. J., & Barrera, S. E. The heredoconstitutional mechanisms of predis-

position and resistance to schizophrenia. *Am. J. Psychiat.*, 1942, 98, 544.
23. Kallmann, F. J. Genetic mechanisms in resistance to tuberculosis. *Psychiat. quart. Suppl.*, 1943, 17, 32.
24. Kallmann, F. J. Twin studies on genetic variations in resistance to tuberculosis. *J. Hered.*, 1943, 34, 269.
25. Kallmann, F. J., & Reisner, D. Twin studies on the significance of genetic factors in tuberculosis. *Amer. Rev. Tuberc.*, 1943, 47, 549.
26. Kallmann, F. J., & Schonfeld, W. A. Psychiatric problems in the treatment of eunuchoidism. *Amer. J. ment. Defic.*, 1943, 47, 386.
27. Kallmann, F. J. Review of psychiatric progress, 1943: Heredity and eugenics. *Amer. J. Psychiat.*, 1944, 100, 551.
28. Kallmann, F. J., Schonfeld, W. A., & Barrera, S. E. The genetic aspects of primary eunuchoidism. *Amer. J. ment. Defic.*, 1944, 48, 203.
29. Kallmann, F. J. Review of psychiatric progress, 1944: Heredity and eugenics. *Amer. J. Psychiat.*, 1945, 101, 536.
30. Kallmann, F. J. The genetic theory of schizophrenia. *Amer. J. Psychiat.*, 1946, 103, 309.
31. Kallmann, F. J. Review of psychiatric progress, 1945: Heredity and eugenics. *Amer. J. Psychiat.*, 1946, 102, 522.
32. Kallmann, F. J., & Anastasio, M. M. Twin studies on the psychopathology of suicide. *J. Hered.*, 1946, 37, 171.
33. Kallmann, F. J., & Mickey, J. S. The concept of induced insanity in family units. *J. nerv. ment. Dis.*, 1946, 104, 303.
34. Kallmann, F. J., & Mickey, J. S. Genetic concepts and folie à deux. *J. Hered.*, 1946, 37, 298.
35. Kallmann, F. J. Genetics in relation to mental disorders. *Eugen. News*, 1947, 32, 51.
36. Kallmann, F. J. Modern concepts of genetics in relation to mental health and abnormal personality development. *Psychiat. Quart.*, 1947, 21, 1.
37. Kallmann, F. J. Review of psychiatric progress, 1946: Heredity and eugenics. *Amer. J. Psychiat.*, 1947, 103, 513.
38. Kallmann, F. J., & Anastasio, M. M. Twin studies on the psychopathology of suicide. *J. nerv. ment. Dis.*, 1947, 105, 40.
39. Kallmann, F. J., & Sander, G. The genetics of epilepsy. In P. H. Hoch, & R. P. Knight (Eds.) *Epilepsy*. New York: Grune & Stratton, 1947.
40. Kallmann, F. J. Applicability of modern genetic concepts in the management of schizophrenia. *J. Hered.*, 1948, 39, 339.
41. Kallmann, F. J. Current trends in psychiatry and social medicine as observed at the International Conference of Physicians. *Psychiat. Quart. Suppl.*, 1948, 22, 326.
42. Kallmann, F. J. The genetic aspects of senes-

cence in the light of twin studies. *Mschr. Psychiat. Neurol.*, 1948, 116, 58. (German)
43. Kallmann, F. J. Genetics in relation to mental disorders. *J. ment. Sci.*, 1948, 94, 250.
44. Kallmann, F. J. The genetic theory of schizophrenia. In C. Kluckhohn, & H. A. Murray (Eds.), *Personality in nature, society, and culture.* New York: Alfred A. Knopf, 1948. (Same as no. 30)
45. Kallmann, F. J. Heredity and constitution in relation to the treatment of mental disorders. In P. H. Hoch (Ed.) *Failures in psychiatric treatment.* New York: Grune & Stratton 1948.
46. Kallmann, F. J. Review of psychiatric progress, 1947: Heredity and eugenics. *Amer. J. Psychiat.*, 1948, 104, 448.
47. Kallmann, F. J., & Sander, G. Twin studies on aging and longevity. *J. Hered.*, 1948, 39, 349.
48. Kallmann, F. J. Constitutional relationship between schizophrenia and tuberculosis. *De Paul J.*, 1949. Vol. 3, No. 8.
49. Kallmann, F. J. Medical genetics and eugenics in relation to mental health problems and senescence. *Eugen. News*, 1949, 33, 15.
50. Kallmann, F. J. On the frequency of suicide in twins and nontwins. *Mschr. Psychiat. Neurol.*, 1949, 117, 280. (German)
51. Kallmann, F. J. Review of psychiatric progress, 1948: Heredity and eugenics. *Amer. J. Psychiat.*, 1949, 105, 497.
52. Kallmann, F. J., De Porte, J., De Porte, E., & Feingold, L. Suicide in twins and only children. *Amer. J. hum. Genet.*, 1949, 1, 113.
53. Kallmann, F. J., & Feingold, L. Principles of human genetics in relation to insurance medicine and public health. *J. insur. Med.*, 1949, Vol. 4, No. 1.
54. Kallmann, F. J., & Planansky, K. Utilization of genetic data in insurance medicine. *J. insur. Med.*, 1949, Vol. 4, No. 4.
55. Kallmann, F. J., & Sander, G. Twin studies on senescence. *Amer. J. Psychiat.*, 1949, 106, 29.
56. Kallmann, F. J. The genetics of psychoses. In *Proceedings, First International Congress of Psychiatry, Sect. VI.* Paris: Hermann & Cie, 1950.
57. Kallmann, F. J. The genetics of psychoses. *Amer. J. hum. Genet.*, 1950, 2, 385.
58. Kallmann, F. J. Review of psychiatric progress, 1949: Heredity and eugenics. *Amer. J. Psychiat.*, 1950, 106, 501.
59. Kallmann, F. J., & Svendsen, B. B. Progress of genetics in relation to oligophrenia, epilepsy and other neurological disorders, 1939–1946. *Ztschr. ges. Neurol. Psychiat.*, 1950, 110, 1. (German)
60. Kallmann, F. J. Recent progress in relation to the genetic aspects of mental deficiency. *Amer. J. ment. Defic.*, 1951, 56, 375.
61. Kallmann, F. J. Relationship between schizophrenia and somatotype. *Mod. Med.*, 1951, 19, 140.

62. Kallmann, F. J. Review of psychiatric progress, 1950: Heredity and eugenics. *Amer. J. Psychiat.*, 1951, 107, 503.
63. Kallmann, F. J. Twin studies in relation to adjustive problems in man. *Trans. N. Y. Acad. Sci.*, 1951, 13, 270.
64. Kallmann, F. J., Feingold, L., & Bondy, E. Comparative adaptational, social, and psychometric data on the life histories of senescent twin pairs. *Amer. J. hum. Genet.*, 1951, 3, 65.
65. Kallmann, F. J. Comparative twin study on the genetic aspects of male homosexuality. *J. nerv. ment. Dis.*, 1952, 115, 283.
66. Kallmann, F. J. The genetic aspects of mental disorders in the aging. *J. Hered.*, 1952, 43, 89.
67. Kallmann, F. J. Genetic aspects of psychoses. In *The biology of mental health and disease.* New York: Paul B. Hoeber, 1952.
68. Kallmann, F. J. The genetics of psychoses. In *Proceedings, First International Congress of Psychiatry, Sect. VI.* Paris: Hermann & Cie, 1952.
69. Kallmann, F. J. Human genetics as a science, as a profession, and as a social-minded trend of orientation. *Amer. J. hum. Genet.*, 1952, 4, 237.
70. Kallmann, F. J. Introductory statement of moderator. Round table discussion on "Psychiatric guidance in problems of marriage and parenthood" (résumé). *Eugen. News*, 1952, 37, 55.
71. Kallmann, F. J. Review of psychiatric progress, 1951: Heredity and eugenics. *Amer. J. Psychiat.*, 1952, 108, 500.
72. Kallmann, F. J. Twin and sibship study of overt male homosexuality. *Amer. J. hum. Genet.*, 1952, 4, 136.
73. Kallmann, F. J., & Bondy, E. Applicability of the twin study method in the analysis of variations in mate selection and marital adjustment. *Amer. J. hum., Genet.* 1952, 4, 209.
74. Kallmann, F. J., & Sander, G. Twin studies of senescence. In R. G. Kuhlen, & G. G. Thompson (Eds.), *Psychological studies of human development.* New York: Appleton-Century-Crofts, 1952.
75. Aschner, B. M., Kallmann, F. J., & Roizin, L. Concurrence of Morgagni's syndrome, schizophrenia and adenomatous goiter in monozygotic twins. *Acta genet. med. gemellolog.*, 1953, 2, 431.
76. Kallmann, F. J. *Heredity in health and mental disorder.* New York: W. W. Norton, 1954.
77. Kallmann, F. J. Review of psychiatric progress, 1952: Heredity and eugenics. *Amer. J. Psychiat.*, 1953, 109, 491.
78. Kallmann, F. J. Genetic principles in manic-depressive psychosis. In P. H. Hoch, & J. Zubin (Eds.) *Depression.* New York: Grune & Stratton, 1954.
79. Kallmann, F. J. The genetics of psychotic

behavior patterns. In D. Hooker, & C. C.
Hare (Eds.) *Genetics and the inheritance
of integrated neurological and psychiatric
patterns*. Baltimore: Williams & Wilkins,
1954.

80. Kallmann, F. J. Heredity in health and mental disorder. In L. Gedda (Ed.) *Genetica
Medica*. Rome: Gregor Mendel Institute,
1954.
81. Kallmann, F. J. Review of psychiatric progress, 1953: Heredity and eugenics. *Amer.
J. Psychiat.*, 1954, 110, 489.
82. Kallmann, F. J. Twin data in the analysis
of mechanisms of inheritance. *Amer. J.
hum. Genet.*, 1954, 6, 157.
83. Allen, G., & Kallmann, F. J. Frequency and
types of mental retardation in twins. *Amer.
J. hum. Genet.*, 1955, 7, 15.
84. Kallmann, F. J. Review of psychiatric progress, 1954: Heredity and eugenics. *Amer.
J. Psychiat.*, 1955, 111, 502.
85. Kallmann, F. J., & Baroff, G. S. Abnormalities of behavior (in the light of psychogenetic studies). In C. P. Stone (Ed.)
Annual review of psychology, Vol. VI. Stanford: Annual Reviews, 1955
86. Kallmann, F. J. Genetic aspects of mental
disorders in later life. In O. J. Kaplan
(Ed.) *Mental disorders in later life*, (2nd
Ed.) Stanford: Stanford University Press,
1956.
87. Kallmann, F. J. The genetics of aging. *J.
chronic Dis.*, 1956, 4, 140.
88. Kallmann, F. J. The genetics of aging. In
J. E. Moore, H. H. Merritt, & R. J.
Masselink (Eds.) *The neurologic and psychiatric aspects of the disorders of aging*.
Baltimore: Williams & Wilkins, 1956.
89. Kallmann, F. J. The genetics of human behavior. *Amer. J. Psychiat.*, 1956, 113, 496.
90. Kallmann, F. J. Genetic variations in adjustment to aging. In J. E. Anderson (Ed.)
Psychological aspects of aging. Washington,
D. C., American Psychological Association,
1956.
91. Kallmann, F. J. Heredity in disturbed mentality; eugenic aspects. In *Enciclopedia
Medica Italiana, Vol. VIII*. Florence:
Sansoni Edizioni Scientifiche, 1956. (Italian)
92. Kallmann, F. J. Objectives of the mental
health project for the deaf. In *Proceedings,
37th Convention of American Instructors of
the Deaf*. Senate Document No. 99. Washington, D. C.: U. S. Government Printing
Office, 1956.
93. Kallmann, F. J. Psychiatric aspects of genetic counseling. *Amer. J. hum. Genet.*,
1956, 8, 97.
94. Kallmann, F. J. Review of psychiatric progress, 1955: Heredity and eugenics. *Amer.
J. Psychiat.*, 1956, 112, 510.
95. Kallmann, F. J., Aschner, B. M., & Falek,
A. Comparative data on longevity, adjustment to aging, and causes of death in a
senescent twin population. In L. Gedda
(Ed.) *Novant'anni delle Leggi Mendeliane*.
Rome: Gregor Mendel Institute, 1956.
96. Kallmann, F. J., & Roth, B. Genetic aspects
of preadolescent schizophrenia. *Amer. J.
Psychiat.*, 1956, 112, 599.
97. Sank, D., & Kallmann, F. J. Genetic and
eugenic aspects of early total deafness.
Eugen. Quart. 1956, 3, 69.
98. Allen, G., & Kallmann, F. J. Mongolism in
twin sibships. *Acta Genet. Stat. Med.*, 1957,
7, 385.
99. Jarvik, L. F., Kallmann, F. J., Falek, A., &
Klaber, M. M. Changing intellectual functions in senescent twins. *Acta Genet. Stat.
Med.*, 1957, 7, 421.
100. Jungeblut, C. W., Kallmann, F. J., Roth, B.,
& Goodman, H. O. Preliminary twin data
on the salivary excretion of a receptordestroying enzyme. *Acta Genet. Stat. Med.*,
1957, 7, 191.
101. Kallmann, F. J. Heredity and aging. *Newsl.
Geront. Soc.*, 1957, 4, 5.
102. Kallmann, F. J. Medical Arts Congress of
Turin: With International Symposium of
Medical Genetics. *Eugen. News.*, 1957, 4, 162.
103. Kallmann, F. J. Review of psychiatric progress, 1956: Heredity and eugenics. *Amer.
J. Psychiat.*, 1957, 113, 595.
104. Kallmann, F. J. The role of genetics in psychiatry. *Amer. J. Psychother.*, 1957, 11, 885.
105. Kallmann, F. J. Twin data on the genetics of
aging. In G. E. W. Wolstenholme, & C. M.
O'Connor (Eds.) *Methodology of the study
of aging*. Ciba Foundation Colloquia
on Ageing, Vol. III. London: J. & A.
Churchill, 1957.
106. Kallmann, F. J., & Baroff, G. S. Heredity
and variations in human behavior patterns.
Acta Genet. Stat. Med., 1957, 7, 410.
107. Rainer, J. D., & Kallmann, F. J. Behavior
disorder patterns in a deaf population.
U.S.P.H.S. Rep., 1957, 72, 585.
108. Kallmann, F. J. An appraisal of psychogenetic twin data. *Dis. nerv. Syst. Suppl.*
1958, 19, 9.
109. Kallmann, F. J. Comments on eugenic abortion from the viewpoint of psychiatric
genetics. *Med. Klin.*, 1958, 53, 2064. (German)
110. Kallmann, F. J. Genetic aspects of schizophrenia. *Med. Hyg.*, 1958, No. 393, 173.
(French)
111. Kallmann, F. J. The genetic viewpoint of the
etiology of mental illness. In *Proceedings,
Joint Commission on Mental Health*. Boston,
JCMH, 1958.
112. Kallmann, F. J. In memoriam: Bruno Schulz,
1890–1958. *Arch. Psychiat. Ztschr. ges.
Neurol.*, 1958, 197, 121.
113. Kallmann, F. J. Review of psychiatric progress, 1957: Heredity and eugenics. *Amer.
J. Psychiat.*, 1958, 114, 586.

127

114. Kallmann, F. J. Types of advice given by heredity counselors. *Eugen. Quart.*, 1958, 5, 48.
115. Kallmann, F. J. The use of genetics in psychiatry. *J. ment. Sci.*, 1958, 104, 542.
116. Kallmann, F. J., & Jarvik, L. F. Twin data on genetic variations in resistance to tuberculosis. In L. Gedda (Ed.) *Genetica della Tubercolosi e dei Tumori.* Rome: Gregor Mendel Institute, 1958.
117. Kallmann, F. J., & Sank, D. Genetics, eugenics and psychohygiene. In H. Meng (Ed.) *Psychohygienische Vorlesungen.* Basel: Benno Schwabe, 1958. (German)
118. Rainer, J. D., & Kallmann, F. J. Constructive psychiatric program for a deaf population. In *Proceedings, 38th Convention of American Instructors of the Deaf.* Senate Document No. 66. Washington, D. C.: U. S. Government Printing Office, 1958.
119. Rainer, J. D., & Kallmann, F. J. The role of genetics in psychiatry. *J. nerv. ment. Dis.*, 1958, 126, 403.
120. Kallmann, F. J. Genetic aspects of schizophrenia. In *Proceedings, Second International Congress for Psychiatry, Vol. IV.* Zurich: Orell Füssli Arts Graphiques, 1959.
121. Kallmann, F. J. The genetics of mental illness. In S. Arieti (Ed.) *American handbook of psychiatry.* New York: Basic Books, 1959.
122. Kallmann, F. J. Psychogenetic studies of twins. In S. Koch (Ed.) *Psychology: A study of a science, Vol. III.* New York: McGraw-Hill, 1959.
123. Kallmann, F. J. Review of psychiatric progress, 1958: Heredity and eugenics. *Amer. J. Psychiat.*, 1959, 115, 586.
124. Kallmann, F. J. Types of advice given by heredity counselors. In H. G. Hammons (Ed.) *Heredity counseling.* New York: Paul B. Hoeber, 1959.
125. Kallmann, F. J., & Jarvik, L. F. Individual differences in constitution and genetic background. In J. E. Birren (Ed.) *Handbook of aging and the individual. Psychological and biological aspects.* Chicago: University of Chicago Press, 1959.
126. Kallmann, F. J., & Rainer, J. D. Genetics and demography. In P. M. Hauser, & O. D. Duncan (Eds.) *The study of population.* Chicago: University of Chicago Press, 1959.
127. Rainer, J. D., & Kallmann, Genetic F. J. and demographic aspects of disordered behavior patterns in a deaf population. In B. Pasamanick (Ed.) *Epidemiology of mental disorder.* Publication No. 60. Washington, D. C.: American Association for the Advancement of Science, 1959.
128. Rainer, J. D., & Kallmann, F. J. Observations, facts and recommendations derived from a mental health project for the deaf. *Trans. Amer. Acad. Ophth. Otolar.* 1959, 63, 179.
129. Falek, A., Kallmann, F. J., Lorge, I., &

Jarvik, L. F. Longevity and intellectual variation in a senescent twin population. *J. Geront.*, 1960, 15, 305.
130. Jarvik, L. F., Falek, A., Kallmann, F. J., & Lorge, I. Survival trends in a senescent twin population. *Amer. J. hum. Genet.*, 1960, 12, 170.
131. Kallmann, F. J. Important events in genetics. *A. M. A. Arch. Neurol.*, 1960, 2, 363.
132. Kallmann, F. J. Review of psychiatric progress, 1959: Heredity and eugenics. *Amer. J. Psychiat.*, 1960, 116, 577.
133. Kallmann, F. J. Twin studies (human genetics). In W. H. Crouse (Ed.) *Encyclopedia of science and technology, Vol. VI.* New York: McGraw-Hill, 1960.
134. Kallmann, F. J. Discussion of "Defining the unit of study in field investigations in the mental disorders." In J. Zubin (Ed.) *Field studies in the mental disorders.* New York: Grune & Stratton, 1961.
135. Kallmann, F. J. Discussion of two psychiatric twin studies. *Amer. J. Psychiat.*, 1961, 117, 804.
136. Kallmann, F. J. Genetic factors in aging: Comparative and longitudinal observations on a senescent twin population. In P. H. Hoch, & J. Zubin (Eds.) *Psychopathology of aging.* New York: Grune & Stratton, 1961.
137. Kallmann, F. J. Genetic factors in the etiology of mental disorders. *Amer. J. Orthopsychiat.*, 1961, 31, 445.
138. Kallmann, F. J. Heredity in the etiology of disordered behavior. In P. H. Hoch, & J. Zubin (Eds.) *Comparative epidemiology of the mental disorders.* New York: Grune & Stratton, 1962.
139. Kallmann, F. J. New goals and perspectives in human genetics. *Acta genet. med. gemellolog.*, 1961, 10, 377.
140. Kallmann, F. J. Review of psychiatric progress, 1960: Heredity and eugenics. *Amer. J. Psychiat*, 1961, 117, 577.
141. Jarvik, L. F., Kallmann, F. J., & Falek, A. Intellectual changes in aged twins. *J. Geront*, 1962, 17, 289.
142. Jarvik, L. F., Kallmann, F. J., & Falek, A. Psychiatric genetics and aging. *Gerontologist*, 1962, 2, 164.
143. Jarvik, L. F., Kallmann, F. J., Lorge, I., & Falek, A. Longitudinal study of intellectual changes in senescent twins. In C. Tibbits, & W. Donahue (Eds.) *Social and psychological aspects of aging.* New York: Columbia University Press, 1962.
144. Kallmann, F. J. Discussion of "Somatic chromosomes in mongolism". In L. C. Kolb, R. L. Masland, & R. E. Cooke (Eds.) *Mental retardation.* Williams & Wilkins, Baltimore, 1962.
145. Kallmann, F. J. (Ed.). *Expanding goals of genetics in psychiatry.* New York: Grune & Stratton, 1962.
146. Kallmann, F. J. The future of psychiatry in

the perspective of genetics. In P. H. Hoch, & J. Zubin (Eds.) *The future of psychiatry.* New York: Grune & Stratton, 1962.

147. Kallmann, F. J. Genetic factors in relation to psychiatric diagnosis. *Dis. nerv. Syst.*, 1962, 23, 594.

148. Kallmann, F. J. Genetic research and counseling in the mental health field, present and future. In F. J. Kallmann (Ed.) *Expanding goals of genetics in psychiatry.* New York: Grune & Stratton, 1962.

149. Kallmann, F. J. The hybrid speciality of psychiatric genetics. *Acta genet. med. gemellolog.*, 1962, 11, 317.

150. Kallmann, F. J. Introduction, research in genetics. In R. M. Steinhilber, & G. A. Ulett (Eds.) *Psychiatric research in public service.* Psychiatric Research Report No. 15. Washington, D. C.: American Psychiatric Association, 1962.

151. Kallmann, F. J. New genetic approaches to psychiatric disorders. In T. T. Tourlentes, S. L. Pollack, & H. E. Himwich (Eds.) *Research approaches to psychiatric problems.* New York: Grune & Stratton, 1962.

152. Kallmann, F. J. Recent cytogenetic advances in psychiatry. In *Proceedings, Third World Congress of Psychiatry, Vol. 1.* Toronto: University of Toronto Press, 1962.

153. Kallmann, F. J. The William Allan Memorial Award for outstanding work in human genetics. *Amer. J. hum. Genet.*, 1962, 14, 95.

154. Kallmann, F. J., Baroff, G. S., & Sank, D. Etiology of mental subnormality in twins. In F. J. Kallmann (Ed) *Expanding goals of genetics in psychiatry.* New York: Grune & Stratton, 1962.

155. Kallmann, F. J., & Glanville, E. V. Review of psychiatric progress, 1961: Heredity and eugenics. *Amer. J. Psychiat.*, 1962, 118, 577.

156. Rainer, J. D., & Kallmann, F. J. The role of genetics in thyroid disease. In S. C. Werner (Ed.) *The thyroid*, (2nd ed.) New York: Hoeber, Harper & Row, 1962.

157. Kallmann, F. J. Genetic aspects of sex determination and sexual maturation potentials in man. In G. Winokur (Ed). *Determinants of human sexual behavior.* Springfield, Ill: Charles C Thomas, 1963.

158. Kallmann, F. J. Specialized psychiatric services for the deaf. In G. M. L. Smith (Ed.) *The psychiatric problems of deaf children and adolescents.* London: The National Deaf Children's Society, 1963.

159. Kallmann, F. J., & Glanville, E. V. Review of psychiatric progress: Heredity and eugenics. *Amer. J. Psychiat.*, 1963, 119, 601.

160. Kallmann, F. J., & Rainer, J. D. Psychotherapeutically oriented counseling techniques in the setting of a medical genetics department. In B. Stokvis (Ed.) *Proceedings, Fifth International Congress of Psychotherapy, Vol. IV. Topical problems in psychotherapy.* Basel: S. Karger, 1963.

161. Rainer, J. D., Altshuler, K. Z., & Kallmann, F. J. Psychotherapy for the deaf. In B. Stokvis (Ed.) *Proceedings, Fifth International Congress of Psychotherapy, Vol. III. Advances in psychosomatic medicine.* Basel: S. Karger, 1963.

162. Rainer, J. D., Altshuler, K. Z., & Kallmann, F. J. (Eds.) *Family and mental health problems in a deaf population.* New York: New York State Psychiatric Institute, 1963.

163. Kallmann, F. J. Main findings and some projections. In J. D. Rainer, K. Z. Altshuler, & F. J. Kallmann (Eds.) *Family and mental health problems in a deaf population.* New York: New York State Psychiatric Institute, 1963.

164. Rainer, J. D., Altshuler, K. Z., & Kallmann, F. J. Psychotherapy for the deaf. In J. D. Rainer, K. Z. Altshuler, & F. J. Kallmann (Eds.) *Family and mental health problems in a deaf population.* New York: New York State Psychiatric Institute, 1963.

165. Rainer, J. D., & Kallmann, F. J. Preventive mental health planning. In J. D. Rainer, K. Z. Altshuler, & F. J. Kallmann (Eds.) *Family and mental health problems in a deaf population.* New York: New York State Psychiatric Institute, 1963.

166. Sank, D., & Kallmann, F. J. The role of heredity in early total deafness. *Volta Rev.*, 1963, 65, 461.

167. Kallmann, F. J. Some genetic aspects of deafness and their implications for family counseling. In *Proceedings, International Congress on Education of the Deaf.* Senate Document No. 106. Washington, D. C.: U. S. Government Printing Office, 1964.

168. Kallmann, F. J., Falek, A., Hurzeler, M., & Erlenmeyer-Kimling, L. The developmental aspects of children with two schizophrenic parents. In P. Solomon, & B. C. Glueck, Jr. (Eds.) *Recent research on schizophrenia.* Psychiatric Research Report No. 19, Washington, D. C.: American Psychiatric Association, 1964.

169. Kallmann, F. J., & Goldfarb, C. Review of psychiatric progress, 1963: Heredity and eugenics. *Amer. J. Psychiat.*, 1964, 120, 625.

170. Kallmann, F. J., & Rainer, J. D. The genetic approach to schizophrenia: Clinical, demographic and family guidance problems. In L. C. Kolb, F. J. Kallmann, & P. Polatin (Eds.) *Schizophrenia.* International Psychiatry Clinics, Vol. I, No. 4. Boston: Little, Brown, 1964.

171. Kolb, L. C., Kallmann, F. J., & Polatin, P. (Eds.) *Schizophrenia.* International Psychiatry Clinics, Vol. I, No. 4. Boston: Little, Brown, 1964.

172. Kallmann, F. J. Contributor to *Aging and levels of biological organization* (A. M. Brues, & G. A. Sacher, Eds.) Chicago: University of Chicago Press, 1965.

173. Kallmann, F. J. The genetic theory of schizophrenia. In R. C. Teevan, & R. C. Birney

(Eds.) *Readings for introductory psychology*. New York: Harcourt, Brace & World, 1965. (Same as No. 30)

174. Kallmann, F. J. Review of psychiatric progress, 1964: Heredity and eugenics. *Amer. J. Psychiat.*, 1965, 121, 628.

175. Kallmann, F. J. Some aspects of genetic counseling. In J. V. Neel, M. W. Shaw, & W. J. Schull (Eds.) *Genetics and the epidemiology of chronic diseases*. Public Health Service Publication No. 1163. Washington, D. C.: U. S. Government Printing Office, 1965.

176. Erlenmeyer-Kimling, L., Rainer, J. D., & Kallmann, F. J. Current reproductive trends in schizophrenia: A psychiatric-genetic survey. In P. H. Hoch, & J. Zubin (Eds.) *Psychopathology of Schizophrenia* New York: Grune & Stratton, 1966.

Book Reviews

1. *Zwillinge und Schule*, by H. Graewe. *Psychol. Bull.*, 1939.
2. *Multiple human births*, by H. H. Newman. *Ment. Hyg.*, 1941.
3. *Tall men have their problems too*, by F. B. Riggs. *Ment. Hyg.*, 1944.
4. *The dice of destiny. An introduction to human heredity and racial variations*, by D. C. Rife. *Ment. Hyg.*, 1946.
5. *The biology of schizophrenia*, by R. G. Hoskins. *Ment. Hyg.*, 1947.
6. *Le granulo-diagnostic de la tuberculose*, by R. Benda. *Quart. Rev. Biol.*, 1948.
7. *A guide for the tuberculous patient*, by G. S. Erwin. *Quart. Rev. Biol.*, 1948.
8. *Méthode génétique et tuberculose pulmonaire*, by J. Troisier and J. Van Der Stegen. *Quart. Rev. Biol.*, 1948.
9. *The Papworth families. A 25 years' survey*, by E. M. Brieger. *Quart. Rev. Biol.*, 1948.
10. *Pulmonary tuberculosis. A handbook for students and practitioners*, by R. V. Keers, & B. G. Rigden. *Quart. Rev. Biol.*, 1948.
11. *Studies on the morphogenesis of the brain in Hyracoidea, Ungulata, Carnivora and Pinnipedia*, by K. H. Krabbe. *Amer. J. Psychiat.*, 1948.
12. *Tuberculosis. A discussion of phthisiogenesis, immunology, pathologic physiology, diagnosis, and treatment*, by F. M. Pottenger. *Quart. Rev. Biol.*, 1948.
13. *L'allergie tuberculeuse chez l'homme*, by G. Canetti. *Quart. Rev. Biol.*, 1950.
14. *The chemotherapy of tuberculosis. The experimental approach*, ed. by R. W. Miner, W. Briggs, & G. Rake, *Quart. Rev. Biol.*, 1950.
15. *Microphthalmos and anophthalmos with or without coincident oligophrenia: A clinical and genetic-statistical study*, by T. Sjögren, & T. Larsson. *Amer. J. Psychiat.*, 1950.
16. *Principles of human genetics*, by C. Stern. *J. nerv. ment. Dis.*, 1950.

17. *Tuberculosis: A global study in social pathology*, by J. B. McDougall. *Quart. Rev. Biol.*, 1950.
18. *Tuberculosis in history: From the 17th century to our own times*, by S. L. Cummins. *Quart. Rev. Biol.*, 1950.
19. *Principles of human genetics*, by C. Stern. *Amer. J. Psychiat.*, 1951.
20. *A study of epilepsy in its clinical, social and genetic aspects*, by C. H. Alström. *J. Hered.*, 1951. (with B. Aschner)
21. *L'Hérédité des prédispositions morbides*, by R. Turpin. *Quart. Rev. Biol.*, 1952.
22. *Die nachkommen geisteskranker Elternpaare: Der Einfluss endogener Elternpsychosen auf die Psychosen, Charaktere und Lebensschicksale ihrer Kinder*, by G. Elsässer. *N. England J. Med.*, 1953.
23. *Twins: A study of three pairs of identical twins*, by D. Burlingham. *Quart. J. child Behav.*, 1953.
24. *Frontal lobes and schizophrenia*, ed. by M. Greenblatt, & H. C. Solomon. *Quart. Rev. Biol.*, 1954.
25. *Höchstbegabung: Ihre Erbverhältnisse sowie ihre Beziehungen zu psychischen Anomalien*, by A. Juda. *Amer. J. Psychiat.*, 1954 (with G. Allen).
26. *Höchstbegabung: Ihre Erbverhältnisse sowie ihre Beziehungen zu psychischen Anomalien*, by A. Juda. *Psychosom. Med.*, 1954 (with G. S. Baroff).
27. *Some antecedent factors in the family histories of 392 schizophrenics*, by C. W. Wahl. *Amer. J. Psychiat.*, 1954.
28. *A study in manic-depressive psychosis. Clinical, social and genetic investigations*, by A. Stenstedt. *Quart. Rev. Biol.*, 1954.
29. *Über eine eigenartige hereditär-familiäre Erkrankung des Zentralnervensystems*, by A. von Braunmühl. *Arch. Psychiat.*, 1954.
30. *The concept of schizophrenia*, by W. F. McAuley. *Quart. Rev. Biol.*, 1955.
31. *Genetics and the inheritance of integrated neurological and psychiatric patterns*, ed. by D. Hooker, & C. C. Hare. *Amer. J. Psychiat.*, 1955 (with E. Jensen).
32. *Wirksame Faktoren im Leben des Menschen*, by O. F. von Verschuer. *J. Hered.*, 1955 (with W. Haberlandt).
33. *Culture and mental disorders: A comparative study of the Hutterites and other populations*, by J. W. Eaton, & R. J. Weil. *Contemp. Psychol.*, 1956 (with B. Roth).
34. *The evolution of human nature*, by C. J. Herrick. *Amer. J. hum. Genet.*, 1956 (with M. M. Klaber).
35. *L'hérédité en médecine. Caractères, maladies, correlations*, by A. Touraine. *Eugen. Quart.*, 1956 (with W. Haberlandt).
36. *Induced abortion on psychiatric grounds: A follow-up study of 479 women*, by M. Ekblad. *Amer. J. hum. Genet.*, 1956 (with J. D. Rainer). •

37. *La progénèse. Facteurs préconceptionnels du developpement de l'enfant*, ed. by R. Turpin. *Eugen. Quart.*, 1956 (with W. Haberlandt).

38. *Clinico-genetic study of hereditary disorders of the nervous system*, by U. Murakami. *Psychosom. Med.*, 1958 (with K. Z. Altshuler).

39. *Biochemistry of human genetics*, ed. by G. E. W. Wolstenholme, & C. M. O'Connor. *Amer. J. Psychiat.*, 1961.

40. *Principles of human genetics* (2nd ed.), by C. Stern. *Amer. J. Psychiat.*, 1961.

41. *Lehrbuch der Allgemeinen Humangenetik*, by F. Vogel. *Amer. J. hum. Genet.*, 1962. (with E. V. Glanville)

42. *Medical genetics 1958–1960*, by V. A. McKusick. *Amer. Scientist*, 1962 (with E. V. Glanville).

43. *Monozygotic twins brought up apart and brought up together*, by J. Shields. *Amer. J. Psychiat.*, 1963 (with L. A. Hurst).

44. *Monozygotic twins brought up apart and brought up together*, by J. Shields. *Amer. J. hum. Genet.*, 1963 (with D. Sank).

45. *Progress in medical genetics, Vol. II*, ed. by A. G. Steinberg, & A. G. Bearn. *Amer. J. Psychiat.*, 1963.

46. *Senile dementia: A clinical, sociomedical and genetic study*, by T. Larsson, T. Sjögren, & G. Jacobson. *Ment. Hyg.*, 1963 (with L. F. Jarvik).

47. *Progress in medical genetics, Vol. III*, ed. by A. G. Steinberg, & A. G. Bearn. *Amer. J. Psychiat.*, 1964.

48. *Senile dementia: A clinical, sociomedical and genetic study*, by T. Larsson, T. Sjögren, & G. Jacobson. *Quart. Rev. Biol.*, 1964.

49. *Genetics and metabolism* (2nd ed.), by R. P. Wagner, & H. K. Mitchell. *Clin. Med.*, 1965 (with L. F. Jarvik).

(Manuscript received May 26, 1966)

cᴧᴕ

131

1967 DEAN RESEARCH AWARD

Introduction To The Garmezy And Rodnick Papers

The Duke Studies in Schizophrenia spanned the decade 1950-1960. At the end of that period Dr. Rodnick and Dr. Garmezy both departed for other academic climes — one to take over direction of the Clinical Training Program at UCLA, the other to perform a similar task at the newly-formed Center for Personality Research of the University of Minnesota. Thus, when the Stanley Dean Award was made in 1967 for studies conducted at Duke during the preceding decade, it came at a time when their collaboration had ended and each had begun 'independent' programs of investigation. Over the years they planned recurrently to write a paper, recapitulating the studies and, hopefully, extending their implications, but the project never came to fruition. The reasons were not at all complicated. Problems of space and time obviously intervened. But of greater importance was the fact that their research interests had slowly begun to turn towards areas that, although clearly derived from the Duke studies, differed from the earlier investigations both in orientation and focus. Initially, both had continued to study performance factors in the adult schizophrenic patient. Thus, at UCLA Rodnick supervised a number of related dissertations: one stressed the quality of the patient's performance under several conditions, including the critical one of having the patient's mother serve as the informant for correctness or error following each successive trial of a discrimination task (Stoller, 1964); another studied the defensive and adaptive behavior of process and reactive schizophrenic patients in response to anxiety-evoking words (Hunting, 1966); still another project involved ratings by good and poor premorbid patients of words and photographs representing parental punishment, rejection, love and affection (Nathanson, 1967). Later, studies of the effects of phenothiazine medication on the schizophrenic patient's psychophysiological and psychological functioning were initiated (Goldstein, Judd, Rodnick & LaPolla, 1968).

At Minnesota other dissertations, too, were conducted in the previous tradition. Bradford (1965) engaged in an investigation of the perceptions of mothers and maternal roles of drug and drug-free good and poor premorbid schizophrenic patients and their normal siblings as well as those of normal controls and their siblings, using a number of scales, the semantic differential, and experimental-laboratory procedures. Wright (1970) compared impairment of abstract conceptualization in parents of poor premorbid schizophrenic patients and normal controls; still other studies focused on patterns related to good and poor premorbidity, including the attribution of traits assigned by patients to mother, father and self (Katz, 1963), MMPI test patterns (Shaeffer, 1965) and drug effects on discrimination behavior (Garmezy, et al., 1969).

Thus, both of them at their new posts retained clear evidence of the tie to the Duke studies through a continuing focus on several independent and dependent variables: maternal and paternal relations in schizophrenia; the effect of premorbid competence on performance; avoidance and adaptive behaviors in drug and drug-free patients; and the personality attributes of good and poor premorbid schizophrenic subjects.

But these studies began to be displaced by a newly emergent concern: their independently-derived decisions to study the adaptation of vulnerable children. At UCLA, Rodnick joined with Goldstein and Judd to initiate a program of research on disturbed adolescents and their parents who were being seen in a departmental clinic. Their program of research actively integrated both clinic and laboratory in studying the twin problems of adaptation and outcome in these disturbed families. At both the Universities of Minnesota and Rochester, Garmezy joined other colleagues in studying children who were at risk for the subsequent development of psychopathology, including schizophrenia, using a paradigm developed by Mednick & Schulsinger, but elaborated to define other forms of risk in addition to children born to schizophrenic mothers. In these studies, subject groups included children born to depressive mothers and (like the UCLA investigators) clinic children who were being treated for acting-out, over-inhibited, and highly anxious behaviors (Achenbach, 1966; Weintraub, 1968, Rolf, 1969, Marcus, 1970; Garmezy, 1970).

In the two articles that follow, the relationship of the Duke studies to these more recent programs of research with vulnerable children are described. Garmezy's paper is an effort to update six areas of investigation reflected in the Duke project with some peripheral commentary provided on their implications for ongoing studies of vulnerable children. His is not intended as a definitive review of the relevant literature but rather as a preliminary appraisal of the contemporary status of those central variables that made up the core of the Duke studies. For a more specific statement of some perceived relationships between the Minnesota studies and the Duke project, the reader is referred to several recent papers (Garmezy, 1967; 1970, 1973, in press). Rodnick focuses on his collaborative project with Goldstein & Judd, providing in the course of his description substantive bridges to the earlier studies of schizophrenia. Two of his previous papers (Rodnick, 1967a; 1967b) provide even more explicit statements of the interrelationships between the Duke studies and his current investigations of disturbed adolescents.

N. Garmezy   E.H. Rodnick
University of Minnesota   University of California
University of Rochester   Los Angeles

REFERENCES

Achenbach, T.M. The classification of children's psychiatric symptoms: A factor analytic study. *Psychological Monographs*, 1966, 80, 6, 37 pages.

Bradford, N. Comparative perceptions of mothers and maternal roles by schizophrenic patients and their normal siblings. Unpublished Ph.D. dissertation. University of Minnesota, 1965.

Garmezy, N. Contributions of experimental psychology to understanding the origins of schizophrenia. In Romano, J. (Ed.) The origins of schizophrenia. *Excerpta Medica International*, 1967.

Garmezy, N. Vulnerable children: Implications derived from studies of an internalizing-externalizing symptom dimension. In *The Psychopathology of Adolescence*. Zubin, J., & Freedman, A.M. (Eds.) Grune & Stratton, 1970, Pp. 212-239.

Garmezy, N. Vulnerability research and the issue of primary prevention. *American Journal of Orthopsychiatry*, 1971, 41 (1), 101-116.

Garmezy, N. Models of etiology for the study of children who are at risk for schizophrenia. In *Life History Research in Psychopathology*, Vol. II. M. Rolf, L. Robins, and M.M. Pollack, Eds. Minneapolis: University of Minnesota Press. In Press.

Garmezy, N. Research strategies for the study of children who are at risk for schizophrenia. In *Schizophrenia: Implications of Research Findings for Treatment and Teaching*.

Garmezy, N., Weintraub, S.A., Wright, D.M., Tredici, L., & Schiele, B.C. Effects of censure and chlorpromazine on visual discrimination behavior of schizophrenic and alcoholic patients. *Proceedings of the 77th Annual APA Convention*, 1969.

Goldstein, M.J., Judd, L.L., Rodnick, E.H., & LaPolla, A. Psychophysiological and behavioral effects of phenothiazine administration in acute schizophrenics as a function of premorbid status. *Journal of Psychiatric Research*, 1969, 6, 271-287.

Hunting, W.H. Differences in the perceptual recognition responses of good and poor premorbid schizophrenics to anxiety and neutral words. Unpublished doctoral dissertation. University of California (Los Angeles), 1966.

Katz, S.E. Trait attributes assigned to mother, father, and self by schizophrenic and normal subjects. Summa cum laude thesis. University of Minnesota, 1965.

Marcus, L. Attention, set and risk-taking in disturbed, vulnerable and normal children. Ph.D. dissertation proposal. Mimeographed, University of Minnesota. Project Competence, 1971.

Nathanson, I.A. A semantic differential analysis of parent-son relationships in schizophrenia. *Journal of Abnormal Psychology*, 1967, 72, 277-281.

Rodnick, E.H. Cognitive and perceptual response set in schizophrenics. In *Cognition, Personality & Clinical Psychology*. R. Jessor and S. Feshbach (Eds.). San Francisco: Jossey-Bass, 1967, 173-209.

Rodnick, E.H. The psychopathology of development: Investigating the etiology of schizophrenia. *American Journal of Orthopsychiatry*, 1968, 38, 784-798.

Rolf, J.E. The academic and social competence of school children vulnerable to behavior pathology. Unpublished Ph.D. dissertation. University of Minnesota, 1969.

Schaefer, S.M.J. MMPI profiles of good and poor premorbid schizophrenic patients. Summa cum laude thesis. University of Minnesota, 1965.

Stoller, F.H. The effect of maternal evaluation on schizophrenics and their siblings. Unpublished doctoral dissertation. University of California (Los Angeles), 1964.

Weintraub, S.A. Cognitive and behavioral impulsivity in internalizing-externalizing and normal children. Unpublished Ph.D. dissertation, University of Minnesota, 1968.

Wright, D.M. Impairment in abstract conceptualization in the parents of poor-premorbid male schizophrenics. Unpublished Ph.D. dissertation, University of Minnesota, 1970.

After receiving his Ph.D. in Psychology at Yale University, **ELIOT H. RODNICK** *joined an interdisciplinary research staff at Worcester State Hospital where he undertook research on schizophrenia. In 1946, he succeeded David Shakow as Director of Psychological Research and as Chief Psychologist, while also serving as a consultant to the Worcester Foundation for Experimental Psychology and on the graduate faculty at Clark University. He was next appointed Professor of Psychology at Duke University, where he became chairman of the department in 1951. Since 1961 he has been on the faculty of the psychology department at U.C.L.A. where he is also Director of Clinical Psychology Training. During the past he has been a visiting faculty member at several universities, including Harvard, Colorado, and Mt. Holyoke College. His other professional duties have included consulting for the Veterans Administration since 1949, serving on the editorial boards of several scientific journals, and on the advisory committees of the National Institute of Mental Health.*

ANTECEDENTS AND CONTINUITIES IN SCHIZOPHRENIFORM BEHAVIOR[1]

Eliot H. Rodnick

Introduction

Several lines of research in recent years consistently and empirically support the view that the conditions underlying schizophrenic behavior clearly implicate interpersonal relations within the family (Mishler & Waxler, 1968; Rodnick, 1968). Even though the identification of factors etiologically significant for schizophrenia, as they may be ultimately delineated, probably will involve the interplay of many conditions not necessarily independent of one another, it is very likely that the familial environment will be found to be of prime importance in eliciting schizophrenic behavior. Yet such a statement is too non-specific to have much use for mapping the factors contributing to the etiology of schizophrenia. We are still at the stage of identifying and elaborating the conditions that appear to have some reasonable probability of contributing to its development. Systematically exploring some of the variables and the conditions surrounding them in any particular investigation need not necessarily imply that more than a limited portion of the variance is being investigated. At this stage of development of our knowledge about schizophrenia, wise strategy still favors the systematic parametric exploration, in some depth, of quite disparate domains of variables, for which there is both empirical evidence and theory to indicate their probable involvement in the underlying mechanisms. The investigator, in following up a particular strategy of empirical inquiry, may choose to avoid conceptual overload by temporarily ignoring other variables for which evidence exists that they also may be important, but which would greatly complicate the research if they were prematurely brought into a research plan which is poorly designed for those variables. In other words, a research strategy which prematurely seeks to explain too much, may end up accounting for too little.

---

[1]The research on which this paper is based was supported by NIMH Grants MH-08744 and MH-13512. The substance of this paper was read at a symposium held May 8, 1971, at the National Institute of Mental Health, in honor of David Shakow.

This paper is concerned with describing aspects of
a research strategy which seeks to identify some factors
which may be related to the development of schizophrenia.
From the standpoint of empirical evidence, it is at
present perhaps premature and presumptuous to discuss
the actual significance of such factors for the etiology
of schizophrenia. We are merely seeking to identify
some consistent regularities in the interpersonal environment of schizophrenics which appear to covary with the
incidence of the condition and to its outcome. Whether
they are causally related will depend on the evidence
from other studies which are specifically designed for
that purpose. If factors can be identified in the
interpersonal, familial environment of the premorbid
phase of adult schizophrenics, which are consistently
found to relate to the occurrence of schizophrenic behavior, we can then seek to delineate the attributes of
those adolescents who are exposed to comparable intrafamilial environments. Is there similarity in the
behavior of both groups? Does the behavior of such
adolescents or young adults appear to be prodromal for
schizophrenia? Such a strategy, if workable, could
serve as a step toward identifying attributes of adolescents who may be high risk for schizophrenia as they move
into adulthood. There are problems, however, with this
strategy. There are too many difficulties involved in
gaining access to the privacy of the intrafamilial
environments of families, particularly those which may
resemble the familial attributes reported for adult
schizophrenics.

An alternative is to investigate aspects of the intrafamilial environment of adolescents who are already
showing sufficient difficulty in adjustment to warrant
referral to a clinic for help. We can then investigate
the relationship between the patterns of the interpersonal environment of this sample of families and the
type of disturbance the adolescent shows. Are there
consistent similarities or systematic differences in
familial relations for the various patterns of adolescent
disturbance? For those who show behavioral attributes
which bear some similarity to those of schizophrenics,
how comparable are the intrafamilial environments? Do
these adolescents constitute a group which is high risk —
or vulnerable — for schizophrenia later on as they move
into adulthood? What if they were to be followed over
a period of years? One advantage of investigating a
relatively random sample of adolescents seen in a clinic
is that we have controls already at hand who can be
studied as intensively as those who may be showing
schizophreniform behavior. Our controls can be contrasting intrafamilial environments, or contrasting adolescent
behavior.

Our group at UCLA took as a starting point the evidence
from a variety of sources, such as those reported by
Lidz, Fleck, & Cornelison (1965), Wynne & Singer (1963),
and Garmezy & Rodnick (1959), which indicates that the
intrafamilial environment of schizophrenics is probably
discriminably different from that of other psychopathological conditions, and that the specific attributes of
this intrafamilial environment are probably antecedent
to the development of schizophrenic behavior. The basic
model we were elaborating was that if this intrafamilial
environment is a precondition for the occurrence of at
least some forms of schizophrenia, it should be found to
occur in adolescents with a high risk for schizophreniform behavior. Not all children with such intrafamilial
environment need necessarily develop schizophrenia, since
vulnerability for schizophrenia is a function of many
attributes ranging from genetic liability, biochemical
and physiological dysfunctions, early experiences, through
any pattern of circumstances which may shape the development of social competence. We were merely seeking to
establish at an empirical level whether those adolescents
with behavior that bears some similarity to that of the
prodromal schizophrenic have characteristic intrafamilial
environments comparable to those reported for schizophrenic patients.

The research described here is the work of a group at
UCLA associated with Michael Goldstein and myself. For
the early phases of this work we were joined by Drs.
Lewis Judd, Edward Gould, and Armand Alkire. The group
at present includes Drs. Jerome Evans, Sigrid McPherson,
Kathryn West and several graduate students.

Research Design

We decided at first to study adolescents between the ages
of 13 and 18 in interaction with their parents under
standardized and controlled conditions which would assure
reasonable comparability across subjects. The adolescents
were a random sample of clients referred to the Psychology
Department Clinic. Most were self-referrals by their
parents because of difficulties in school, behavioral
maladjustment within the family, or because of pressure
from the juvenile court and probation authorities. The
only restriction on the sample was that the family be
intact and that the adolescent and both parents come
together to the clinic for at least 5 to 6 sessions for
an assessment period, after which recommendations for
referral or treatment would be discussed with them.

We were aware of the risks of bias in this sample and
its probable nonrepresentativeness of disturbed adolescents in the community. We decided nevertheless to
accept the bias, with its restrictions on the subject

141

sample. The requirement of intactness of family, and the
cooperation of the parents and adolescent involved in
coming together for a series of sessions, probably results
in selecting a sample which favors more passive adolescents and more involved parents. We hoped to compensate
for the bias, by comparing one segment of the sample with
another, using as the independent variable the pattern of
behavioral disturbance or particular patterns of parent-
child interaction. At first our intent was to use
4-person families: parents, target child and a comparison sibling, but postponed doing so until the procedures
were developed, pretested, and found to be sufficiently
productive to warrant the additional complexities introduced by adding the sibling as a within-family control
for the target child in the particular set of techniques
we were employing. The first 50 families were hence
3-person families, but we are now expanding the design
to permit us to study 4-person and in selected cases even
5-person families.

We decided to explore the interaction within the family
by having the members interact with one another in role-
playing their actual spontaneous responses to problems
which both child and parent had identified as significant
issues for either or both of them. In addition, they
were important enough to be closely related to the
reasons for their having come to the clinic for assistance.

The heart of the procedure, which covers Sessions 2
through 5, involves an identical interview given to each
person separately, parents as well as child, covering
some eight areas of child-parent interaction which might
provide a basis of conflict between them. The objective
was to elicit idiosyncratic conflicts which were characteristic of the child and his parents, intense enough to
evoke defensive coping behavior, and yet under sufficient
control to keep them in the situation with little regulation by the investigators. The conditions for eliciting
the material were standardized, and in a form which
permitted objective assessment of the attributes of the
interaction. The areas of interaction tapped by the
interview were achievement, sociability, responsibility,
communication with parents, response to frustration,
autonomy, sex and dating, and overall family tone. During
each area of the interview, the interviewer probes for
conflicts specific to each family. Once a specific
problem has been identified for the area, the parent or
child, as the case may be, is instructed to role-play a
specific instance of this problem with the intent of
attempting to influence the other family member. That is,
he addresses the other person, as if he were present,
and as the problem existed at that particular moment. These
cue statements are recorded and serve as the stimuli to
which the other family member is subsequently asked to

142

respond. We also obtain from the subject the actual words he expects the other person to use in response to his own remarks. A comparison with the actual remarks which the responder makes later provides a measure of how well parent and child know one another, as well as of compliance and yielding under conflict.

These recorded cue statements and expectancies of each directed toward the other provide the materials for the following session. At that time, the edited cue statements are played to the appropriate member of the family. As he hears the problem over the speaker, in the actual voice of the member of his family directing remarks to him, his task is to respond as if the situation were an actual one, with the other person present. His responses are recorded, both before and after he hears what the other person expected him to say.

This array of cue statements, responses, and expectancies provides the basis for a family interaction in a free modification of the revealed difference technique in which the various members of the family are brought together in dyads and a triad to hear cue statements and responses relevant to the dyad. They are instructed to discuss for a maximum of 5 minutes the simulated interaction they had just heard, and in a discussion with each other to indicate why each said what he did and how he feels about it. They are then to initiate a discussion of how to resolve the problem issues in a mutually satisfactory manner. Since we elicit and record a number of problem situations involving each member of the family, we are able to use different problems in each dyad and in the triad which are relevant to the particular family members concerned. Since each tape segment contains material that one of the members of the dyad has not heard before, this confrontation interaction has a considerable amount of spontaneity and novelty. The confrontations are videotaped, and provide the material for the next session, when the members of the family view the videotaped interactions of the session. At that time they rate one another in segments of the dyads and triads as they appear on the videotape of the previous confrontation session. The rating instrument used is one developed by our colleagues Kaswan and Love (Kaswan, Love & Rodnick, 1971) as an extensive modification of the Osgood semantic differential.

The conditions for making the ratings also serve to introduce a guided discussion period which follows when they discuss the behavior of each person on the video screen in objective terms by avoiding the use of personal pronouns. Each, in turn, must talk about what he observes about himself (but as "That child," "That woman," etc.), then about each of the others. Finally, each discusses what he would like changed in himself, and in each of the others.

In essence, then, the procedure is designed to bring
into the laboratory samples of personalized conflictful
interaction among members of the family, under the same
conditions of eliciting the conflict and with a suitable
balancing of roles of initiator and responder for each
member of the family. We hoped that this design would
permit a comparison of mother and father in the role they
played in relating to the child in this sample interaction. We also hoped that we would be able to assess
the comparative strengths of the child's relationship to
each parent. One aspect of the design appeared very
important to us. We wished to minimize as much as
possible the appearance that we were allies of the
parents against the adolescent — from his viewpoint
perhaps allies of the aggressor. We therefore took
special pains to ensure that parents were subjected to
the same interview as the adolescent, and that he had as
much of an opportunity as his parents to be the initiator
of cue statements. On the basis of the degree of cooperation we have enjoyed from our adolescents, we believe
that we were reasonably successful.

Attributes of the Disturbed Adolescents and Their Parents

Since the objective was to explore the specificity of the
interaction between parents and adolescents for various
patterns of adolescent pathology — particularly of those
who might show schizophreniform behavior — the design
was dependent upon some method for characterizing the
adolescent sample in terms of subgroups.

In order to avoid preconceived biases regarding a suitable
nosology for characterizing adolescent psychopathology,
which might force too heavy a reliance on a formal mental
status examination which could bias the research conditions,
we decided to be crassly empirical. Each parent was asked
at the time of admission to write down briefly and
succinctly in a paragraph, his perception of the child's
problem which brought him and the adolescent to the clinic.
We found that these statements could be sorted into four
groups with satisfactorily high reliability. For relatively few of the cases was there sufficient ambiguity
in making the sort to force arbitrary group assignments.

Some of the emerging findings for the first 24 to 30
families have been reported in a series of papers on
social power and influence, galvanic skin responses in
the confrontation, analysis of TAT's, and family distantiation and closeness in the triadic interaction
(Goldstein, Judd, Rodnick, Alkire, & Gould, 1968; Goldstein, Rodnick et al., 1970; McPherson, 1970; Alkire,
Goldstein et al., 1971). We have found significant discrimination for a variety of characteristics among these
four symptom groups of adolescents comprising our research

sample. Based on an overall impression from the parents'
description of the child's problem, the four groups were:

Group I — Aggressive, antisocial, characterized by
poorly controlled, impulsive and acting out behavior
toward authority in the community.

Group II — Active family conflict, characterized by
a defiant, disrespectful stance toward the parents.

Group III — Passive-negative adolescents, characterized by negativism, sullenness and indirect forms of
hostility toward parents or school authority.

Group IV — Withdrawn, passive, isolated adolescents
— characterized by marked social isolation, general
uncommunicativeness, and excessive dependence on one or
both parents.

This last group comes closest to the poor premorbid
schizophrenic, as identified by the Phillips Scale, even
though most of the cases were clearly free of overt
psychotic signs at the time they were seen. Since the
clinic is a non-medically oriented clinic, clients with
florid psychotic or somatic symptoms are unlikely to be
referred to or accepted by the clinic. In other respects
the cases are fairly typical of the usual run-of-the-mill
community clinic. Since it is housed on a university
campus some distance from low-income areas, there tends
to be a bias toward a middle-class clientele, despite
efforts to reduce the bias.

James Armstrong, Dr. Kathryn West and I have recently
analyzed in considerable detail statements of the problem
descriptions for the first 50 families. It is clear that
the discrete phrases comprising the statements can be
readily classified, with high reliability into the four
sets of child attributes, which at first had been classified on an overall general impression. When the
phrases were sorted out for the descriptive information
conveyed, these short paragraphs could be classified
into child attributes (as reported by the parent) and
parent attributes as each parent may have commented on
his role in the child's problem. We were prepared for
the likelihood that a fine-combed analysis of the statements would even more sharply distinguish among the four
groups of children. The attributes as reported by the
parents of each of the four groups could be used as a
checklist, and then integrated to arrive at an overall
description of each of the adolescent groups. We were
not prepared, however, for the amount of information
these brief problem statements conveyed about the parents.
We found that a comparable checklist of parent attributes
could be developed which was derived solely from the
terse problem-description paragraph which appeared to

145

differentiate the adolescents into the four groups. It
is particularly relevant that these statements of the
parents regarding themselves, and their relation to the
child's problem are entirely spontaneous and gratuitous.
They were merely asked to write a brief description of
the child's problem which brought them to the clinic.

Some of the flavor of the correspondence between the child
attributes and the parental attributes for each of the
four groups is indicated by the categories into which the
phrases could be sorted for both child and parent. The
summary of the problem description statements for each
of the four adolescent groups with an actual example
follows.

Group I

CHILD ATTRIBUTES   PARENTAL ATTRIBUTES

Core quality is one of   Core quality is one of dis-
externalizing and acting out;   tantiation of relation-
this may be expressed in any   ship between parent and
of six ways: child; this is expressed in
                                    three areas:

Ic1 Opposition to and/or   Ip1 Parents lack the role-
     rejection of authority   appropriate techniques
     in general, including   for controlling the
     parents.   child; they have no
                                    sense of parenting.

Ic2 Rejection of and   Ip2 Parents report a total,
     avoidance of parents,   rather than partial,
     specifically.   absence of meaningful
                                    communications and/or
                                    interactions among the
                                    members of the family;
                                    tension in the home in
                                    general.

Ic3 Antisocial (illegal) be- Ip3 Parents externalize
     havior; inability to   responsibility for
     follow rules of social   problems; correction
     conduct.   is expected to come
                                    from an external
                                    agency; the suggestion
                                    that causality may lie
                                    within the family is
                                    not the idea of the
                                    parent, but is sug-
                                    gested to him by an
                                    external agent; if the
                                    parent calls for help
                                    it is to solve his
                                    problem rather than to

                                        abet his serving as
                                        a change agent for
                                        the child.

Ic4   General truculence and
      hostility; initiated
      aggression; impulsive
      and/or unmodifiable
      behavior, with lack of
      concern for consequences;
      self-concept of the
      "born loser."

Ic5   Inability to accept
      responsibility.

Ic6   Drug taking as part of
      an anti-social syndrome.

                    Example of Group I

Family 07 (Father - Son)

"Serious indications of my son, ..., who, while having
excellent potentials, seems to be rebelling or has little
respect for that which we consider proper — that is —
respect for law, order, proper authority, school, church,
parents, etc. Feels rules and regulations do not apply
to him."

"I would like to have his thinking and attitude readjusted
so that he can become a worthwhile citizen and reach his
capabilities, rather than see him get progressively worse
which we have told will occur unless corrections are
made."

                        Group II

CHILD ATTRIBUTES   PARENTAL ATTRIBUTES

Core quality is one of   Core quality is the expres-
rebelliousness and op-   sion of affiliational ties
position to parental   between parent and child;
controls or regulation   psychological mindedness;
(and perhaps to school),   empathy; concern for child;
with active struggle for   sense of personal respon-
independence, and concern   sibility; this is expressed
for the dissonance created   in seven areas:
by the struggle; this is
expressed in four ways:

                          147

IIc1 Overt acts of rebel-
liousness and opposi-
tion to parents; turbu-
lence in home between
parents and child.

IIp1 Recognition that child
has personal problem
to solve.

IIc2 Requests and/or demands
that parent give (or
permit) more freedom.

IIp2 Expression of desire to
help child solve his
problem for his own
sake.

IIc3 Indications of child's
concern about family
discord.

IIp3 Recognition that as
parent he is causal or
contributory to the
child's problem; self-
critical as parent.

IIc4 Variability in the
child's expression of
love or warmth toward
the parent.

IIp4 Expression of desire
to receive help per-
sonally in order to be
able to help child.

IIp5 Recognition of parental
responsibility for
tutelage and direction,
and to control the
child with under-
standing.

IIp6 Expression of concern
over difficulty in
communicating with
child.

IIp7 Expression of desire
for increased close-
ness as a family.

Example of Group II

Family 04 (Mother - Son)

"... is not happy. He is insecure and unhappy at home and
in school. He feels that his parents are very overbearing
and tend to treat him like a baby. He doesn't exhibit
maturity enough for independence but feels he should be
completely free of parents. We want to find out what we
are doing wrong as parents. We also feel ... has deep
psychological problems which we hope can be uncovered.
We feel ... needs a great deal of help and that we as
parents may also need a great deal."

CHILD ATTRIBUTES	PARENTAL ATTRIBUTES
Core feature is opposi- tional behavior in school and/or home:	Core feature is one of trying to control the child, to manipulate him, entitled by right of parenthood:

IIIc1 Oppositional tendencies, including non-
cooperation and mani-
pulative behavior,
outside the home,
primarily in school.

IIIp1 Parental effort to
control child is
through manipulation
or material rewards
and the effort fails;
parental role is
viewed in legalistic
manner rather than
with empathic qualities.

IIIc2 Oppositional tendencies,
including non-coopera-
tion and manipulative
behavior in home; may
include overt anger or
temper display.

IIIp2 Outside agents (school,
clinic, drugs) seen as
responsible for either
causing child's diffi-
culty or correcting it;
parents are not seen
as responsible.

IIIc3 Antisocial behavior
occurs only if entirely
a function of drug-
taking.

IIIp3 Parents feel un-
appreciated.

Example of Group III

Family 11 (Father - Son)

"I feel that our son should be doing better in school
subjects; that he should be able to stay away from
marijuana peddlers at school; and to keep out of trouble
from his instructors at school — I can't seem to improve
his study habits; work habits; my efforts to control him
just don't seem to work."

Group IV

CHILD ATTRIBUTES	PARENTAL ATTRIBUTES
The core features are with- drawal and passivity:	Core feature is parallelism between parents and between parent and child, rather than direct interaction between parent and child; expressed along main dimensions:

IVc1 Withdrawal is expressed by asociality and isolation, especially from peers and from members of the opposite sex; withdrawal may manifest itself within the home by child isolating himself from family.

IVp1 Parents view their role as agent for solving child's problem but not themselves as part of the problem; they seek assistance in finding the reason or explanation of the child's problem; allusions to other parent impersonal (e.g. his mother, rather than my wife and I).

IVc2 Secondary to withdrawal, child seems preoccupied with and/or devaluing of self; he is reported as insecure or unhappy, within the context of being passive and dependent.

IVp2 Parent's attitude toward child is one of infantalizing him; they describe or judge him to be grossly immature.

IVc3 Secondary to withdrawal, child behaves eccentrically and/or expresses concern over loss of control (insanity).

IVp3 Parent alludes to own history in reference to child.

IVc4 Passivity is expressed by non-involvement or severely limited involvement, by low level of energy, or by distractibility and lack of persistence.

IVc5 Passivity extends to participating in school, but through refusal to attend school rather than active rebellious behavior about school.

IVc6 Child is source of unhappiness and "pain" experienced by other family members; parents report that their efforts are rejected or unappreciated.

150

Example of Group IV

Family 06 (Father - Daughter)

"Our daughter is withdrawn and unable to actively relate
to her peers socially. She has worked hard to overcome
this but seems only to reap rebuffs and heartache. She
has no real friends, social life or close relationships
at all with the opposite sex. Our desire is to locate
the roots of her problem to free her and allow her to
relax into a more nearly normal life."

There are consistent differences among the allusions to
parental behavior — the underparenting and distantiation
of Group I; for Group II the expressed parental concerns
for closeness and affective involvement with the child
in their day to day relationships, while being troubled
by what they consider to be premature efforts at independence striving of the child; the stress on control and
manipulation of Group III; and the special quality of
blandness of affectivity in the interaction of parent-child
in Group IV, combined with a criticalness towards the
immaturity of the child.

In order to simplify the discussion of the issues, this
discussion will concentrate primarily on Groups II and IV.
Comparing parental attributes of these two groups, we
find some striking differences: when the parents of Group
II refer to themselves, they tend to stress the existence
of and need for affiliation ties between themselves and
their child. There is some recognition of their parental
responsibility, and that they may be causal or contributory to the child's problem. In contrast, implicit in
the statements of Group IV parents is a parallelism rather
than direct interaction with the child. They do not
recognize themselves as part of the problem, but rather
see themselves as the agent to solve the child's problem
by calling attention to some explanation of the child's
behavior, or some intellectualized causal factor. Though
both are concerned with the child's immaturity, this
concern is expressed quite differently. In Group II,
the parents feel the child is not ready to be granted the
independence he is demanding; in Group IV, they are often
critical of the child for not being more mature, yet they
continue to infantilize him and to keep him dependent.

These differences among the parents of the four groups
which are reflected even in these inadvertent mini-
phrases which slip into the description of the dominant
attributes of their children, come through consistently
in various interactions in the sessions themselves.
Three quite separate analyses which have been reported
elsewhere corroborate this finding of differences between
Group II and Group IV families.

In order to keep the contrasts among the various patterns
of adolescent disturbance in focus for the purposes of
this paper, the comparison will be restricted primarily
to Group II and IV families although consistent differences have been found among the four groups. For both
groups the presenting problem tends to center in the
home situation, rather than as rebelliousness or hostile
behavior in school or with the juvenile authorities.

In a report on the TAT stories of the parents and child
of the first 24 families (Goldstein, Gould, Alkire,
Rodnick, & Judd, 1970) we commented:

> "Parents of the active family conflict [Group II]
> ... adolescents appear willing to see a family
> unit, but they see it full of both negative and
> positive involvements. This suggests that a high
> degree of emotional involvement is perceived among
> the family members, but one which may be ambivalent
> and conflictual...

> "The withdrawn children [Group IV] were willing to
> perceive family relationships on the cards but
> indicated that the familial involvements they saw
> were almost invariably harmful and detrimental.
> These two characteristics did set them apart from
> the other groups of adolescents. Their parents
> similarly saw the involvement between the characters
> on the cards as being universally negative. The
> perceptions by the fathers and mothers of the with-
> drawn adolescents were quite different even though
> each parent projected relationships in which one
> family member was excluded. In their stories, the
> fathers often left out the child, while the mothers
> often eliminated the fathers. This struggle on the
> level of a projective test to see unilateral
> alliances within the family is certainly compatible
> with clinical studies on families of schizophrenics
> ... This suggests that familial conflicts over
> alliances may stimulate the child to use withdrawal
> as a means of coping with this type of family
> conflict [p. 363]."

In another report (Alkire et al., 1971) on the analysis
of social influence and control methods used in the cue
statements and responses in the role playing phase of
the research, we commented:

> "Parents of adolescents whose problems are manifest
> primarily in the home setting [Groups II and IV]
> avoided power-assertive techniques, and relied
> primarily on the indirectness of informational power
> ... Active family conflict adolescents do not
> discriminate between parents and expect neither

parent to yield to him.... The most striking discrepancy is in the withdrawn group in which the
adolescents expect their fathers to be quite weak
but that their mothers will be quite resistant to
compromise.... The maternal social influence style
in the latter group involves pervasive restrictive
questions, a more covert style of control which
in turn is less apt to lead to direct confrontation by the child... The pattern for the withdrawn group is particularly interesting by virtue
of the resemblance to the subtle maternal domination and paternal passivity noted so frequently in
studies of [poor premorbid] schizophrenics... In
the active family conflict group, the child is
confronted with subtle maternal power in the form
of restrictive questions similar to those received
by the withdrawn child. However, unlike the latter,
the father seems to ally with the mother and both
parents fail to yield. It is this non-yielding by
the father which distinguishes this group from
that of the withdrawn child ... [We commented at
that time that] it is interesting to note that both
of the within-home groups (active family conflict
and withdrawn groups) are characterized by maternal
use of restrictive questions which in essence
forces the adolescent to justify his behavior. It
raises the question of whether this style may not
be a condition for increasing guilt and ultimate
internalization of conflict [pp. 39-41]."

[This heavy use of questions has been reported by others
for the families of schizophrenics (Lennard, Beaulieu, &
Embrey, 1965)].

Finally, McPherson (1970), in her analysis for the first
28 families of the "intents" toward each other expressed
in the statements of the triadic interactions during the
confrontation session, found that:

Group II Father: Controlling and hostile toward
child but not toward mother

Mother: Critical and hostile toward child,
but combined with little distantiation and disengagement from
child

Child: High controlling behavior toward
both father and mother

Group IV Father: Weak and yielding, with absence of
controlling and hostile behavior
toward mother

Controlling and covertly depre-
ciating toward child

153

<pre>
Mother: Controlling, but not hostile
          toward child; controlling and
          covertly depreciating toward
          father and child

Child: Low controlling and hostile be-
          havior toward both father and
          mother

          High yielding to father

          Much distantiation from mother
</pre>

She also found that in Group II families both parents consistently accepted and shared the parental role, even though the child may have tended to communicate more commonly with one parent. In Group IV, however, the mothers covertly depreciated their husbands by speaking to them with questioning and domineering intents at a rate far exceeding that found with mothers in the other problem groups.

The Group I and III families differed both from Group II and IV, as well as from each other. The emphasis of parental control and acceptance of parental responsibility which was most prevalent in Group II families seemed to go along with the adolescent's coping style of confining his acting out behavior to the home. For the Group IV families, the most striking characteristic was the covert depreciation of fathers by their wives in the triadic interaction and the persistent domination of both toward the child.

Relation between Group IV Adolescents and Poor Premorbid Schizophrenics

The Group IV adolescents, as indicated earlier, are comparable in pattern of social adjustment to the poor premorbid schizophrenics as defined by the Phillips Scale. This limited sampling of illustrative findings indicates that the pattern of parental-child interaction may possess some similarity to that reported in the Duke studies on premorbidity in schizophrenia, on which Garmezy and Rodnick and their associates (e.g., Rodnick & Garmezy, 1957; Garmezy & Rodnick, 1959) had reported some years ago. Especially noteworthy are the findings of maternal domination for the poor premorbid patient and paternal domination for the good premorbid schizophrenics (e.g. Farina, 1960) and the yielding and conformity acquiescence reported by Clark (1964) for poor premorbid schizophrenics.

What is missing so far in this report is any evidence that the Group IV adolescents are prodromal, high risk,

or highly vulnerable for schizophrenia. The selection
of the adolescents tended to preclude actively psychotic
adolescents, although two showed borderline psychotic,
or at least possible prodromal evidence of a schizophrenic
break. The difficulties involved in assessing borderline,
incipient or prodromal signs of schizophrenia in adolescents with adequate validity and objectivity are severe.
We decided therefore to avoid this issue at the time the
adolescents and their families were seen in the clinic.
In fact, we wanted to avoid studying a family interaction
containing an active psychotic child, since the interaction could be dominated by the psychosis rather than
being indicative of basic interpersonal dynamics. We
chose to rely instead on the follow-up of the adolescents several years later when the occurrence of pathology could be evaluated more objectively in terms of the
usual incidence criteria — namely through behavioral
disturbance sufficiently severe for some treatment agency
to be seen, and by indications of actual psychotic
behavior as reported by members of the family, or as
elicited in an evaluative and diagnostic interview with
the young adult. We also obtained an MMPI at the time
of this interview.

Our research plan includes the regular follow-up of the
adolescents seen on the project, which now includes the
first twenty-five adolescents five years after they were
originally seen in the clinic. Three and possibly four
may have had a psychotic-like break, or currently show
signs of borderline psychotic behavior depending on the
criteria used. Considering that these patients have not
yet entered the period of highest risk, the base-rate
seems higher than would be expected on a random basis.
This is not the place to comment on this finding, beyond
indicating that the adolescents of greatest vulnerability
are probably in Group IV, followed by Group II. Until we
have more cases and the data analyzed more thoroughly,
this should probably be given no more credence than
hearsay evidence.

Another source of data which bridges the findings for
our disturbed adolescents and those of adult schizophrenics is provided by a second thrust of our research
program. We are following up acute schizophrenics seen
in a nearby mental health center for short periods of
hospitalization. We chose a small county, geographically
isolated from Los Angeles, and with few population
centers, which was covered by a central mental health
center. The follow-up includes periodic interviews with
them and with members of their families in order to identify
possible relationships between post-hospitalization social
adjustment of the schizophrenic and premorbid behavior. In
addition, we are exploring factors in the post hospitalization

familial environment which may be related to the continuing clinical condition, and the role which phenothiazine therapy may play in this process. This follow-up
investigation of the post-hospitalization phase of acute
schizophrenia affords the opportunity to compare the
social adjustment of diagnosable schizophrenics with the
follow-up of the disturbed adolescents seen in the family
project.

The findings of this research, some of which have been
reported (Goldstein, Judd, Rodnick, & LaPolla, 1969;
Goldstein, 1970), are interesting and germane to this
discussion. We found further strong support for the
utility of the Phillips premorbid scale for controlling
for the heterogeneity of the response of schizophrenics
to phenothiazine therapy. For example, in a controlled
double-blind drug-placebo study of acute schizophrenics,
the good premorbids remained in the hospital for a mean
of 63 days in contrast to a mean of 100 days for the
poor premorbid patients. This represents about a 1/3
shorter hospitalization for the good premorbid patients.
This merely confirms a number of other reports of the
predictive significance of the Phillips Scale for hospital
remissions. A more surprising finding is that at the end
of the first 28 days of hospitalization (the first point
at which these research patients could be considered for
discharge) of those patients considered by the ward staff
to be ready for discharge from the hospital, 61% of the
good premorbid but only 14% of the poor premorbid patients
were in the placebo group (p < .05). This finding raises
the question whether phenothiazines might be an indicated
therapy primarily for the poor premorbid patients.
Despite the fact that there appear to be no readily
discriminable differences in pattern or amount of schizophrenic symptoms between the two groups at the time of
admission, by the time of discharge from the hospital the
ward team (which ignored premorbid data) recommended
phenothiazine medication for only 26% of the good premorbid
patients in contrast to the recommendation of drug therapy
for 88% of the poor premorbid group (p < .01). This
provides firm evidence that the good premorbid patients
not only clear up rapidly from the more obvious psychiatric symptoms which brought them to the hospital initially, but that the two groups are probably at different
levels of remission at the time of discharge. The staff
considers the good premorbid patients as less in need of
phenothiazine medication, the poor premorbid patients are
being sent home while still in need of active therapy.

These data serve to highlight the importance of considering
the characteristics of social competence in the premorbid
history of schizophrenics as significantly related to the
course of the schizophrenic disorder, the responsivity to
phenothiazine medication, and the character of the post-

hospital social adjustment. Any attribute of the pre-
psychotic adjustment such as level of social competence
prior to the overt display of schizophrenic symptoms,
which carries this much information regarding remission
potential, duration of hospitalization, and even responsivity to phenothiazine medication merits intensive
scrutiny and systematic research inquiry.

We have decided to concentrate on the chronological dimension. Hospitalized schizophrenics are being followed
through the period of post-hospital adjustment in order
to look at close hand at the relation between social
competence and rehospitalization. In the other direction
we are following a group of adolescents who may be high
risk for schizophreniform as well as other varieties of
maladjustment to see whether there is any consistent
relation between characteristics of the intrafamilial
environment and both particular patterns of disturbed
adolescent behavior and attributes of adult schizophrenic
psychosis.

A more direct linkage between the disturbed adolescent
and the adult schizophrenic is provided by some initial
data of interviews of parents of our post-hospitalized
schizophrenics regarding the premorbid adjustment of
their schizophrenic child during the adolescent period,
long before the occurrence of overt psychotic behavior.
The interview schedule we are using provides a direct
comparison with data being obtained with the disturbed
adolescent group.

One of the weaknesses of the simplified Phillips Scale is
that the scale lends itself readily to assessing the premorbid heterosexual and peer relations of males, but is
insensitive for women, since marriage and heterosexual
relationships are not adequate discriminators of premorbid
level for women. Susan Sturzenberger of our group is
finding that peer relationships during adolescence,
however, are a good marker variable for women when treated
as comparable to the heterosexual and peer relations
attributes used for male patients. Using these criteria
the same relation is found for both men and women between
premorbidity, prognosis and phenothiazine medication. No
differences were found in behavior in the adolescent period
between men and women.

The following significant differences were found by Sturzenberger between 18 good and 16 poor premorbid schizophrenics at the time they were adolescents.

Q14. As a teenager what jobs did your child hold?

Good	Poor	P
2.56	1.67	.01

Q70. How many close friends did your child have?

Good   Poor   P

2.28 (many)   3.00 (few)   .05

Q76. Was he a leader?

Good   Poor   P

3.00 (occasionally)4.31 (rarely)   .01

Q57. Arguing with parents

Good   Poor   P

3.25   2.25   .10

Q5. Lack of school motivation (rebellious)

Good   Poor   P

3.39 (unconcerned) 2.56 (concerned) .05

Thus, the poor premorbid schizophrenics at the time they were adolescents, look suspiciously like Group IV problem adolescents, while the good premorbid patients have strong resemblances to Group II.

Significant differences are found between the good and poor premorbid groups in social withdrawal, lack of ambition, being a follower, and fear of leaving home. These are all characteristics of our Group IV adolescents. The other differences, such as holding jobs, argumentativeness with parents, very poor motivation in school, are higher for the good premorbid patients, and tend to characterize the Group II adolescents.

These findings, if they continue to be confirmed and further corroborated by other data, may provide a basis for identifying in adolescence potential schizophrenics who even at that time show the distinctive pattern of premorbid adjustment, which serves as such an important marker variable in research with adult schizophrenics. The findings which are emerging from our work with the families of problem adolescents provide evidence that the premorbidity differences may in turn be related to consistent differences in the interpersonal environment within the home of the adolescent. In time we may begin to identify the data needed to describe the mechanisms involved in integrating factors in gene pool, early experiences, and psycho-social transmission of parental, and hence familial styles of thinking and coping, which increase the vulnerability for inadequate social competence and schizophrenic modes of adaptive functioning.

It is already clear that these disturbed adolescents, particularly those of Group II and IV should be studied systematically, to see whether they show other response attributes of schizophrenia, such as the response to stimulus overload, autonomic arousal patterns, the development of segmental sets, the presence of incipient schizophreniform cognitive styles, etc., as part of a systematic inquiry into prodromal indicators of schizophrenia.

REFERENCES

REFERENCES

Alkire, A.A., Goldstein, M.J., Rodnick, E.H., & Judd, L.L. Social influence and counterinfluence within families of four types of disturbed adolescents. Journal of Abnormal Psychology, 1971, 77, 32-41.

Clarke, A.R. Conformity behavior of schizophrenic subjects with maternal figures. Journal of Abnormal and Social Psychology, 1964, 68, 45-53.

Farina, A. Patterns of role dominance and conflict in parents of schizophrenic subjects. Journal of Abnormal and Social Psychology, 1960, 61, 31-38.

Garmezy, N., & Rodnick, E.H. Premorbid adjustment and performance in schizophrenia: Implications for interpreting heterogeneity in schizophrenia. Journal of Nervous and Mental Disease, 1959, 129, 450-466.

Goldstein, M.J. Premorbid adjustment, paranoid status, and patterns of response to phenothiazine in acute schizophrenia. Schizophrenia Bulletin, 1970, 3, 34-37.

Goldstein, M.J., Gould, E., Alkire, A., Rodnick, E.H., & Judd, L.L. Interpersonal themes in the thematic apperception test stories of families of disturbed adolescents. Journal of Nervous and Mental Disease, 1970, 150, 354-365.

Goldstein, M.J., Judd, L.L., Rodnick, E.H., Alkire, A., & Gould, E. A method for studying social influence and coping patterns within families of disturbed adolescents. Journal of Nervous and Mental Disease, 1968, 147, 233-251.

Goldstein, M.J., Judd, L.L., Rodnick, E.H., & LaPolla, A. Psychophysiological and behavioral effects of phenothiazine administration in acute schizophrenics as a function of premorbid status. Journal of Psychiatric Research, 1969, 6, 271-287.

Goldstein, M.J., Rodnick, E.H., Judd, L.L., & Gould, E. Galvanic skin reactivity among family groups containing disturbed adolescents. Journal of Abnormal Psychology, 1970, 75, 57-67.

Kaswan, J.W., Love, L.R., & Rodnick, E.H. Information feedback as a method of clinical intervention and consultation. In C. Spielberger (Ed.), Current topics in clinical and community psychology. Vol. 3. New York: Academic Press, 1971.

Lennard, H.L., Beaulieu, M.R., & Embrey, N.G. Interaction in families with a schizophrenic child. Archives of General Psychiatry, 1965, 12, 166-183.

Lidz, T., Fleck, S., & Cornelison, A. Schizophrenia and the family. New York: International Universities Press, 1965.

McPherson, S. Communication of intents among parents and their disturbed adolescent child. Journal of Abnormal Psychology, 1970, 76, 98-105.

Mishler, E.G., & Waxler, N. Family progress and schizophrenia. New York: Science House, 1968.

Rodnick, E.H. The psychopathology of development: Investigating the etiology of schizophrenia. American Journal of Orthopsychiatry, 1968, 38, 784-798.

Rodnick, E.H., & Garmezy, N. An experimental approach to the study of motivation in schizophrenia. In M.R. Jones (Ed.), Nebraska Symposium on Motivation. Lincoln: University of Nebraska Press, 1957.

Wynne, L.C., & Singer, M.T. Thought disorder and family relations of schizophrenics: I. A research strategy. Archives of General Psychiatry, 1963, 9, 191-198.

NORMAN GARMEZY is a "clinical psychologist by training and an experimental psychopathologist by predilection. " Over the past 25 years his research interest has been exclusively in behavioral studies of schizophrenia. Currently he holds appointments at the University of Minnesota where he is Professor of Psychology and at the University of Rochester School of Medicine where he is Clinical Professor of Psychiatry (Psychology). At both institutions Dr. Garmezy is engaged in programmatic research on children vulnerable to schizophrenia. After graduation from the City College of New York he went on to graduate study at Columbia University and the State University of Iowa where he received his Ph.D. degree in 1950. Dr. Garmezy is the recipient of a life-time Research Career Award from the National Institute of Mental Health which enables him to pursue his research on children at risk.

Competence and Adaptation in

Adult Schizophrenic Patients and Children at Risk

Norman Garmezy, Ph.D.

The preparation of this paper was supported by a Research Career Award MH-K6-14, 914, a grant from the Supreme Council 330, A.A. Scottish Rite, Northern Masonic Jurisdiction, and USPHS Contract No. PH 43-68-1313.

INTRODUCTION

Two decades have passed since the inception of the Duke
studies in schizophrenia. The passage of time provides
a vantage point from which to evaluate that ten year
period of research, and to record, in the light of subsequent investigations, the extent to which the findings of
that project can be viewed as stable or unreliable.

Two articles, descriptive of the program, appeared toward
the close of the 50's (Rodnick & Garmezy, 1957; Garmezy
& Rodnick, 1959) and contained descriptions of a set of
experiments that broadly encompassed six areas of research
relevant to schizophrenia:

1)   The first, and undoubtedly the most significant,
transcended any individual experiment and came to serve
as the basic framework for subject selection. This was
the effort to test the experimental consequences of
differentiating patients along a continuum of good to
poor premorbid competence;

2)   Within that context of patient selection, emphasis
was placed upon the creation of experimental-laboratory
analogues that made use of constructs that were concep-
tually significant in psychodynamic formulations of the
development of schizophrenia;

3)   Specifically, the stimulus focus became the depiction
of early family relationships that emphasized the power
and punishment aspects of the mother-child and, to a
lesser extent, the father-child relationship. Later in
the program ways were sought to test variations in such
patient-parent relationships at a function of the premorbid interpersonal competence of the patient;

4)   Interest in the reinforcing properties of punishment
led to studies designed more broadly to examine the
effects of censure per se on the level of performance of
schizophrenic patients in comparison with normal control
subjects;

5)   The study of such effects suggested an ubiquitous
pattern of avoidance responding that appeared to characterize patients exposed to censure stress,

6)   Finally, when the so-called "tranquilizers" began
to assume therapeutic ascendancy in the mid and late 50's,
preliminary assessments were begun on the influence of
the phenothiazines on the patient's avoidance response
systems under conditions of stress.

The Duke Studies: A Retrospective Appraisal

What is the current status of these six areas of research? To what extent have the early studies proven contributory and to what extent have they been found wanting? In the section that follows, a brief (and hopefully) unbiased summary will be presented. In a number of instances, such as those related to the role of premorbid competence and the effects of punishment, the summary statements are based upon determinate reviews. In other cases, however, the judgment reflects opinion that is rooted in less searching reviews of the literature.

1. Schizophrenic Performance and the Continuum of Premorbid Competence

The Phillips Scale of Premorbid Adjustment in Schizophrenia (Phillips, 1953) early became the instrument by which we sought to distinguish behavioral differences between "poor" and "good" premorbid schizophrenic patients. This dimension of early interpersonal competence we recognized to be isomorphic with earlier distinctions that had been espoused in the clinical study of schizophrenia: dementia-praecox-schizophrenia; process-reactive; typical-atypical; chronic-episodic; evolutionary-reactive; true-schizophreniform. Although cognizance of this basic dichotomy was clearly evident in clinical appraisals of schizophrenia, the distinction had not been systematically applied to experimental data prior to the Duke program. In the course of that research program, the Phillips Scale clearly demonstrated its power for reducing the highly variable group data that was inevitably provided by acutely disturbed schizophrenic patients.

Surveying the current investigations of schizophrenia, one must conclude that of the six areas studied by the Duke group, the demonstration of the power of this poor-good premorbid dichotomy for reducing data variance has been the most significant and lasting contribution. Today the use of the distinction is widely accepted and the Phillips Scale has become a stable aspect of design considerations in the experimental study of schizophrenia. The power of the variable is attested to by evaluations that have appeared recently in a number of review articles and books (Garmezy, 1968; 1970; Higgins, 1964, 1966, 1969; Kantor & Harron, 1966; Phillips, 1968).

2. Experimental Analogues of Parent-Child Relationships in Schizophrenia

Experimental analogues in the Duke studies took two different directions: one group of studies required patients and controls to cope with stimuli designed to serve as symbolic cues for deviant parent-child relationships. In a second group, censuring signals ("Wrong") were used to provide information to the schizophrenic patient of his inadequate performance on tasks involving learning, perception, discrimination and judgment.

An aside seems desirable here. Our use of such content-laden analogues did not constitute espousal of a psychogenic theory of schizophrenia. Others, however, came to perceive us as advocates of a psychological model of etiology. In truth, our research orientation was far simpler and infinitely less presumptuous. We asked merely what would be the behavioral consequences for the schizophrenic patient were we to bring successfully into the laboratory symbolizations of the type of early family stressors that had been suggested in the formulations of a number of distinguished clinical investigators, including Fromm-Reichman, Lidz, Bateson, Jackson and others. We never failed to appreciate the possibility that the patient's performance with regard to these symbolic cues could reflect his disorder and not necessarily the presence of a significant pre-illness antecedent.

Looking back to these earlier studies, one perceives their simplicity and not in an entirely favorable light. To study the complexities that inhere in family relationships demands a reasonable approximation to such complexity in the laboratory. Were this not to be achieved, it is unlikely that the experimental domain could provide a meaningful test of the role played by the family in the development of the patient's psychopathology. Reviewing the adequacy of the stimulus materials used to depict maternal scolding in the studies of Dunn (1954) or Harris (1957) or the family problems that demanded resolution by parents of schizophrenic patients in the research conducted by Farina (1960) and Farina & Dunham (1963), it is evident that the themes are universal, the stimulus contents simple. A line drawing suffices to illustrate scolding; a briefly expressed problem understates a theme of parent-child conflict. The contrast with the more elaborate methods used by Rodnick, Goldstein, Judd and their colleagues to study the interpersonal, familial environment of disturbed adolescents is striking (See Rodnick's paper in this volume). "Real" parents now become the object of scrutiny, and the cue representations of disturbing events within the family are made intensely personal and immediate by the use of contents derived directly from clinical interviews with parent and child. The description by Goldstein et al (1968) of the decision to focus on themes that are idiosyncratic in content, albeit universal in context, bears repetition:

167

... each of the three family members (mother,
father, child) separately experiences a structured, standardized interview which covers seven
general areas of adolescent behavior, selected
for the high likelihood of conflict between the
adolescent and his parents. The interview is
designed to pinpoint a specific problem between
parent and child in each of the following areas:
achivement, sociability, responsibility, communication (with parents), response to frustration,
autonomy, and sex and dating.

During each area of the interview, the interviewer
probes for conflicts, specific to each family.
Originally, it was hoped to use a common set of
standard problems for each area to elicit emotionally meaningful interactions between parents and
children. However, pilot data with this type of
problem were very disappointing, and it was found
that idiosyncratic expressions of general problems
were more effective in stimulating family interaction. In many families much of the emotional
charge of a broad problem area becomes focused
around a specific conflict situation and this
conflict is chosen as the symbolic battleground
for a more general principle. (p. 236)

It is these situations that subsequently become the
significant cue stimuli for subjects used in the Rodnick-
Goldstein-Judd project. And, if one cannot help but
contrast the greater richness and meaningfulness of
such situations to the earlier ones used in the Duke
studies, it is appropriate to observe that a procedure
not unlike one of successive approximations produced
the shift to this heightened experimental reality. Thus
the line of succession begins with line drawings of
mother-child interactions (Dunn, Harris), moves to taped
recordings of hypothetical parent-child interactions
that demand resolution (Farina), proceeds to more
dramatic tapes of pseudomothers describing child-rearing
practices (Clarke, 1964) which, in turn, leads to the
introduction of real mother directly into the experimental
situations (Stoller, 1964), and, finally, uses actual
clinical content and the family members involved in
those family exchanges as the basis for the selection
of cue stimuli and subject matter (Goldstein et al).
Science often moves with measured tread and this sequence
of a growing sophistication in method reflects such a
trend.

Note too the shift from retrospective inquiry to concurrent examination of significant familial events
that are here-and-now concerns. To have patient and
parent retrace the past on the basis of a faith in their

retrospective recall is to insure conclusions that are fraught with potential error (Yarrow et al, 1970; Haggard, et al, 1960). Thus, a decision to focus on the child predisposed to disorder but not yet actively caught up in consequences resulting from patienthood that irrevocably distort the past seems the wiser course of inquiry. Consideration of this position has been treated in an earlier paper (Garmezy, In Press).

But what of the stability of the findings derived from these earlier experimental analogues? I would render several judgments. First, the contribution would appear to derive less from the specific findings and more from the demonstration of the power of the laboratory analogue in research in schizophrenia. In the 1957 Nebraska Symposium volume, Marshall R. Jones, editor of the series, ventured to predict with reference to the Duke project that "we will see a whole new crop of Ph.D. dissertations in this area." It is indeed the case that the laboratory study of schizophrenia has become a significant domain of psychology and a fruitful content area for dissertation research in psychopathology.

Second, on the substantive side, the empirical data with regard to familial patterning in schizophrenia is more equivocal. Sensitivity to maternal cues on the part of poor premorbid patients finds both refutation (Cicchetti et al, 1967) and support (Stoller, 1964). With regard to the issue of method, it may be the more sophisticated experimental treatment of the latter study that may account for the positive findings. Stoller used the patient's mother as the direct conveyor of criticism of poor performance. Using a procedure not too dissimilar to one used earlier (Garmezy, 1952), the patient was first presented information as to the accuracy of his perceptual judgments through the use of "Right" and "Wrong" signals. In a third condition, however, the mother was in the room with the subject; upon a coded signal from the experimenter, which could not be seen by the patient, she informed the patient whether he was wrong or right on a particular trial. In addition, the mother predicted aloud whether she thought her son would be correct or incorrect on the following trial. Under this condition, poor premorbid patients, unlike their nonschizophrenic siblings or good premorbid counterparts, showed a significant increase in stimulus generalization, confirming a differential reactivity to mother's criticism. Furthermore, unlike the good premorbid's mother, the poor premorbid patient's mother significantly overestimated the performance of her psychotic son who, in turn, produced more errors following her predictions, whether these expressed her belief in his success or his failure.

As for the presumed differential sensitivity of good
premorbids to paternal cues and poor premorbids to
maternal cues [despite Goodman's (1964) supportive
findings], this has been refuted with sufficient
frequency (Nathanson, 1967) to suggest the unreliabil-
ity of that specific formulation. Farina, whose early
research, in part, provided the basis for the hypothesis,
has reported a failure to replicate his earlier findings
(Farina & Holzberg, 1968), although some of the prior
data on dominance and conflict relationships in schizophrenic families have been reaffirmed.

3. Censure and Performance in Schizophrenia

There are two questions associated with the effect of
censure on task performance of schizophrenic patients.
How powerful are the effects of punishment? Does
punishment invariably induce performance deficits as
suggested in the 1957 paper? The answer to the first
question is "Powerful, indeed!" The answer to the second
a resounding negative.

With regard to the second question, it may be helpful to
position prominently our original formulation which, in
the light of more than 150 studies, has proved to be
grievously incorrect. The following quotation contained
the critical initial statement:

> "We shall try to demonstrate that schizophrenic
> patients can and do respond adaptively in tasks
> of considerable complexity and difficulty provided
> that these tasks have been made sufficiently
> interesting to insure the cooperation of the
> patient. This adaptability, however, is a tenuous
> one which can be disturbed by the introduction of
> minimal censure into an experiment. Under these
> conditions the deficit behaviors which have been
> described as characteristic of the schizophrenic
> patient appear." (Rodnick & Garmezy, 1957, p.116)

There appears to be no reason for retreat from the first
sentence of the above paragraph. Complex experiments
demonstrably can involve schizophrenic patients, provided
experimenters approach the construction of their studies
with innovativeness and creativity. The problem lies
with the latter part of the paragraph; the hypothesized
censure-deficit formulation proved to be incorrect,
primarily because we failed to analyze the response demands of our experiments in relation to the ubiquitous
and powerful avoidance response systems that the schizophrenic patients exhibited following the censure experiences.

In a major paper on psychological deficit in schizophrenia, Buss & Lang (1965) appropriately observed:

170

"The thesis that punishment invariably disrupts performance is clearly not tenable. Both a negative evaluation and specific verbal or physical punishment for errors can lead to significant improvement in performance rather than further deficit." (p. 11)

The authors, however, then proceed to assign, as the basis for such improvement, the factor of the greater amount of information that is provided by punishment.

"The fact that this improvement occurs in both the presence and absence of socially or personally punitive conditions suggests that the significant factor is information about inadequate responses rather than the interpersonal context.

Knowledge of results is important to any task in which improvement is expected with practice, and in general the normal subject recognizes the correctness or wrongness of a response as soon as it occurs, and no assistance is required. However, schizophrenics seem to be less able to instruct themselves and less able to maintain and usefully alter a response set. Furthermore, studies of incidental learning reveal that relative to normals, schizophrenics fail to observe objects or relationships towards which their attention has not been specifically directed. Thus, informational cues introduced by the experimenter have greater importance for the psychotic subject in certain tasks." (pp.11-12)

Since it is clear from existent data that deficits or increments in performance can follow in the wake of censure, the more fundamental question to be asked is what mechanism, if any, operates to explain these divergences. An explanation based upon greater informational cues cannot suffice and is clearly refuted by other studies in the literature. (Contrast, for example, Stoller's three conditions involving information when correct, information for extreme error and information provided by mother on every trial. The poorer performance of patients under the last named condition would suggest that the number of informational cues alone cannot predict enhancement of a patient's performance.)

Elsewhere I have detailed in a review of the literature of punishment (Garmezy, 1966) a mechanism that may help to explain the findings of a diverse number of studies. Unfortunately the review has not received wide circulation, and, as a result, investigators continue to ascribe to both Rodnick and to me continued advocacy of the 1957 censure-deficit formulation.

171

Within the experiments conducted by the Duke researchers, as well as by others, there were recurrent and marked indications of the pervasive nature of patients' avoidance tendencies - responses that were as evident in the laboratory as they were in clinical practice. But the analysis of the congruence or noncongruence of this type of response pattern in relation to the response demands of the experimental task was not attempted until there was clear evidence of the shortcomings of the earlier formulation (e.g. Cavanaugh, 1958; Leventhal, 1959; Atkinson & Robinson, 1961). The suggested interaction of these two variables — the patient's disposition to avoid and the demands of the task — can be set forth by quoting from the 1966 review:

"In the light of these clinical hypotheses, it seems reasonable to conclude that the use of censure in laboratory tasks should heighten the evocation of withdrawal behavior in schizophrenic patients. Thus, responses elicited in experimental tasks that are followed by some signal suggesting criticism or disparagement should undergo a marked reduction in response strength. Although we can predict a modification of responsiveness on the basis of censure, we cannot predict the adequacy of the patient's performance on a task without knowledge of the response alternatives that are available to him. Alternative choices may be one or many, structured or unstructured.

In terms of available alternatives, we can define those situations that are most and least evocative of performance deficits.

1. The likelihood of behavior decrements will be heightened if the experimental procedures provide simply for a general devaluation of the patient's performance at some point in the experimental sequence; such decrements will be accentuated if the task permits a multiplicity of response alternatives. Since the criticism is nonspecific with regard to the inappropriateness of the subject's previous responses, the schizophrenic patient can be expected to become either less responsive or more grossly inappropriate in his behavior as the experiment proceeds. Compounding the effect of punishment will be the oft-noted difficulty of the patient in maintaining a mental set and his propensity for discontinuing task-oriented activity.

* * *

172

2. In many studies, the experimental procedures that have been employed have involved a punishing signal that is administered immediately following an experimenter-designated, incorrect response. As we have seen, such a signal, in some studies, takes the form of a noxious (pain) stimulus that is terminated only when S makes the appropriate response. This probably constitutes the optimal condition for behavior improvement since the stimulus literally forces the patient to respond correctly — a situation that doesn't readily permit irrelevant response sets to be retained.

However, in other studies, censure (rather than a physically noxious stimulus) has been used in the form of a "Wrong" signal following an error in responding; but the termination of such psychologically noxious event is not made dependent upon the subject's choice of the correct alternative... in such paradigms the effectiveness of the censure is best revealed on the trial that follows the one on which the patient's response has been punished. Given the simplest situation in which there are two highly structured response alternatives (such as those requiring simple motor movements), one of which is followed by a punishing signal, we can predict that the schizophrenic patient will show more frequent responding with the alternative response that avoids the censure.

If this is a highly probably consequence, the prediction of deficit or incremental behavior in schizophrenia becomes a rather straightforward one: if the response alternative that permits avoidance of the censuring signal is a task-congruent response, behavior facilitation should follow; if the response alternative is noncongruent, performance deficits should ensue." (Garmezy, 1966, pp. 136-139)

The remainder of the earlier paper was devoted to a consideration of the power of the formulation in terms of a reanalysis of a number of empirical studies, seeking to test its efficacy by applying the hypothesis to findings of published studies.

Finally, what about the broader issue of the presumed motivational power of punishment relative to reward that the Duke research group asserted was a characteristic of the schizophrenic patient? Countless studies of the differential effects of these two classes of reinforcers on the behavior of schizophrenic patients have appeared in the psychological literature. In 1968 in a seminar on Experimental Psychopathology at Minnesota,

173

one of the student participants, Raymond Knight,[1] set
out to analyze statistically 91 studies dealing with
the effects of punishment on the performance of schizophrenic patients. Unfortunately, his definitive review
is still unpublished, althought Knight intends to
revise the monograph for publication. `His review
encompassed the majority of studies that had appeared
through 1967 — studies that he found to be "riddled
with sampling problems, lack of proper controls, inadequate statistics and the confounding of variables."

Knight's procedural review was as follows: First he
coded and punched on Unisort cards the reinforcement
contingencies, subject samples, types of tasks, situa-
tional variables and results for each of the studies.
His defined reinforcement conditions included: 1)
positive reinforcement in which a response or a
response class was followed by a reward; 2) punishment
in which responses were followed by an aversive
stimulus; 3) negative reinforcement in which a correct
response terminated an aversive stimulus; and 4) mixed
reinforcement involving a reward that followed a
correct response and a punishment that was presented
after an incorrect response.

Results were coded into four categories: 1) positive (+),
when the subject's performance was improved by the reinforcer; 2) negative (-), when it was impaired; 3) zero
(0), when it had no statistically significant effect
(p> .05); and 4) questionable (?), when the reinforcement
effect could not be analyzed because of an absence of a
control group or as a result of inadequate data analysis.
Coded studies were then sorted into different combinations to calculate the frequency of occurrence of the
various results. X^2 analyses were used to test whether
different combinations of independent variables produced
significantly different distributions of results across
studies.

With Dr. Knight's permission I quote at length from the
concluding section of his monograph, for it provides a
thorough appraisal of a very complication and not
always 'rewarding' literature:

"Through the review and analysis some tentative...
relationships were revealed and several sugges-
tions for future research emerged. In general,
schizophrenics were found to be more reactive
to punishment than to reward, remaining unchanged
in their performance in fewer instances when
punished than when rewarded. Also, negative
reinforcement was found to be the most successful
reinforcer for schizophrenics, producing far more

[1]Dr. Knight is now Assistant Professor of Psychology,
Brandeis University.

174

positive and fewer negative results than any
other reinforcer.

An examination of sampling problems led to the
suggestion that the variety of control groups
employed be increased, and that the various
samples of subjects be stratified across certain
dimensions to reduce their heterogeneity and
eliminate error due to the response of opposing
subgroups cancelling each other out. It was also
hypothesized that the good-poor premorbid distinction, which seems to be a promising mode for
stratification, has elicited contradictory
results because it has often been confounded
with the acute-chronic dimension. The separation
of the effects of these two means of dichotomizing
samples may clear up some of the confusion extant
in the literature.

Schizophrenics seemed to be more able to take
advantage of the motivation increments afforded
by both reward and punishment when the task
was simpler than when the task was more complicated. More difficult tasks produced more differential responding among groups of schizophrenics,
with the less intact groups being more disrupted
by punishment than the more intact groups. Finally,
a statistical analysis of the effects of the four
most prevalent tasks (paired-associate learning,
concept formation, reaction time, and rote simple
tasks) suggested that punishment might cause more
differential results among various tasks than
reward.

Although the studies dealing with the effects of
social variables on the performance of schizophrenics had somewhat perplexing and contradictory
results, some tentative generalizations worthy of
investigation became evident. It was found that:

1)   schizophrenics, especially acutes, tended to
have more difficulty with tasks involving social
rather than neutral stimuli;

2)   schizophrenics were more sensitive to stimuli
representing censure than normals, but the hypothesis that poor and good premorbid schizophrenics
are differentially sensitive to maternal and
paternal censure was not consistently supported;

3)   the experimenter was an aversive stimulus for
the schizophrenic subject, even in reward conditions;

4) strong social praise produced more negative results than weak social praise, suggesting along with the previous finding that a warmer more positive attitude of an experimenter aroused interpersonal anxiety in schizophrenics;

5) social reward occasioned fewer positive and more negative results in schizophrenics than in normals, and in schizophrenics it produced more zero and fewer positive results than social punishment;

6) schizophrenics tended to be more reactive to social censure than normals, having fewer zero results and more negative and slightly more positive results under this condition;

7) nonsocial punishment was a less effective motivation (had more negative and fewer zero outcomes) than nonsocial reward;

8) the social-nonsocial findings seemed to be more the result of the presence or absence of the experimenter rather than due to the verbal element in the censure."

Knight also reported that contingency and information feedback were important in determining the quality of performance of schizophrenics. Thus, both contingent punishment and reward led to more positive results and fewer negative ones than did noncontingent reinforcement, but only the differences for punishment proved to be statistically significant.

For normals, contingent and noncontingent conditions produced equivalent results. Information feedback was less powerful than the contingency of the reinforcement. For the schizophrenic patients, no information produced more negative and fewer positive results (a difference which approached significance) in comparison with test conditions in which information was provided about performance. By contrast, normal subjects were less dependent on feedback regarding their performance.

Dr. Knight concludes that no single experiment can determine the effect on the schizophrenic patient's performance of the many complex variables suggested by his review. He believes that only through a program of carefully delineated experiments will it be possible to arrive at definitive generalizations of the effect of punishment on performance. Knight's review thus provides a glimpse into the complexity of the problem and raises anew the question of the ultimate viability of any encompassing formulation of the relationship of punishment to performance, including the more extensive 1966 statement quoted earlier.

The Influence of Phenothiazines on Avoidance Behavior

The advent of the phenothiazines as a major therapeutic weapon against schizophrenia occurred at the midpoint of the Duke studies. Undoubtedly, some portion of later failures to replicate earlier findings may be related to the fact that it is now difficult to find drug-free patients who are not long-term chronic, "burned-out" schizophrenics. This critical lack of control in experiments clearly freighted with motivational variables can be expected to be a telling one. To suggest that the effect of the drug variable is attenuated because good and poor premorbid patients do not differ in the dosage level received (Klein et al, 1967), or that the "main effects of all phenothiazine drugs are essentially the same" (Klein et al, 1967) or that "all drugs belonging to the phenothiazine family are about equally effective in alleviating psychotic symptoms" (Cicchetti, 1967) is to fail to ask the critical and far more penetrating question: Do the effects of such drugs differentially affect response systems relevant to performance in good and poor premorbid patients? Earlier studies gave evidence that experimental effects were attenuated in the drug schizophrenic groups in comparison with nondrug patients (Engelhardt, 1959; Alvarez, 1957; Bradford, 1965) in ways meaningful to an interpretation of differential deficit functioning in goods and poors. More recently, Goldstein et al (1969; 1970) has reported a comparison of a fixed dosage of phenothiazine and a matched placebo on a variety of performance measures for a sample of 38 acute, newly admitted male schizophrenics divided into good (N - 22) and poor (N - 16) premorbid subgroups. The drug and placebo conditions were run for a period of 7 to 21 days, following a "drying out" placebo period extending 7 days after admission.

Marked differences were found between the two groups of patients under the drug and placebo regimens. For the poor premorbid schizophrenic patients three weeks of phenothiazine medication produced a marked reduction in behaviors that reflect disorganization — a finding that did not hold for the placebo group. Drug poors showed a lowered level of general arousal, reduced psychophysiological reactivity to stimuli, more comprehension of ongoing events, "less avoidance behavior to potentially anxiety-arousing words, fewer remote associations and lower self-rated anxiety" (p. 283, italics ours). Good premorbid patients on extended phenothiazine medication showed seemingly paradoxical effects that included "greater psychophysiological reactivity, more avoidance behavior to verbal anxiety stimuli, less of a decrease in distant associations and more autistic associations" than the good premorbid placebo group.

177

The authors conclude that the phenothiazines affect good and poor premorbid schizophrenics differently:

"In the goods, the general reduction in arousal is associated with greater responsivity to specific changes in the environment and avoidance behavior to threat. In the poors, the same reduction in arousal is associated with lessened responsivity to the environment and vigilance for threat. If we consider that good and poor premorbid patients were probably differentially responsive to their environments prior to their psychotic episodes, it may be that phenothiazine medication returns each type of patient to his premorbid style of coping, permitting relatively more appropriate behavior to reappear." (p. 284)

Such data are congruent with several of the later studies in the Duke program in which goods and poors had been separated into drug and nondrug cases in an effort to compare avoidance patterns under censure within each subgroup. Avoidance proved to be most characteristic of drug-free poor premorbid patients. However, the confounding effects of acuteness are present in these early studies, since such patients were more likely to receive drug therapy (Garmezy, 1966).

It is obvious that there is a need for carefully controlled investigations to specify the action of ataractic drugs on specific response parameters in good and poor premorbid schizophrenic patients. Until such data are forthcoming, interpretations of differences among studies comparing patient groups on behaviors that clearly implicate motivational systems should only be advanced with marked caution.

In the section that follows, I turn from adult schizophrenia to my current research interest in studying the adaptation of children who are at risk for the disorder. The conceptual tie between the earlier Duke program and the research on vulnerability now underway at the University of Minnesota and the University of Rochester is to be found in the unifying theme of competence. In the Duke program competence was the explicit criterion for determining a patient's status as a "good premorbid" or "poor premorbid" patient. In the studies of risk the criterion for competence is broadened but its function is the same — to delineate the adaptive potential of risk children not as a measure of their prognosis for recovery from disorder but rather as an index of their resistance to its emergence.

Competence and the Study of Children at Risk

The study of premorbid competence has not only helped
to resolve the riddle of recovery from schizophrenia,
but has been instrumental in delineating qualities of
the 'healthy personality'. Freud's twin criteria of
lieben und arbeiten couples with an aphorism attributed
to Whitehorn by Grinker (1968):

> Concerning mental health and the absence of a
> concept of positive mental health, I would like
> to give you a kind of cookbook definition deve-
> loped by John Whitehorn, although it is not a
> complete statement. What I frequently tell my
> students is that people who are mentally healthy
> usually work well, play well, love well and
> expect well. I think that 'expect well' is the
> most important in that there is an anticipation
> that the future will have something of value to
> them. (p. 23)

To work, play and love "well" foretells recovery from
mental disorder. The designation of good premorbid
and poor premorbid schizophrenic patient which became
the central independent variable in the Duke studies,
summarized the attributes of low and high scorers on
the Phillips Scale of Premorbid Adjustment in Schizophrenia (Phillips, 1953). That this differentiation
appears to be isomorphic with the process-reactive
dimension simply enhances the power of the experimental
correlates that accompany the dichotomy (Garmezy, 1968,
1970). The Phillips Scale emphasizes the form and
quality of the patient's patterns of love and play
during the period preceding the onset of his disorder:
adjustment in the areas of sex and interpersonal relations, social aspects of sexuality during adolescence
and adulthood, and his history of personal relations
from childhood onward. This emphasis primarily upon
sex and friendship patterns can predict recovery from
schizophrenia because the process-type schizophrenic,
typically, is characterized by a tragically low ceiling
of premorbid adaptation. However, to broaden the base
of prediction to include recovery from more diverse
forms of psychopathology, or to apply the concept of
competence to both normal and other psychiatric populations requires that the criteria for effective functioning be extended to include level of intellectual development and cognitive functioning, achieved occupational
and educational status, regularity of employment, participation in community organizations and constructive use
of leisure time. In the volume, Human Adaptation and Its
Failures, Phillips (1968) discusses this extension of
the criteria that define the nature of competence:

In our view adaptation implies two divergent
yet complementary forms of response to the human
environment. The first is to accept and respond
effectively to those societal expectations that
confront each person according to his sex and
age. Included here, for example, are entering
school and mastering its subject matter, the
forming of friendships, and later, dating, court-
ship, and marriage. In this first sense, adaptation implies a conformity to society's expectations
for behavior. In another sense, however, adaptation
means more than a simple acceptance of societal
norms. It implies a flexibility and effectiveness
in meeting novel and potentially disruptive conditions and of imposing one's own direction on
the course of events. In this sense, adaptation
implies that the person makes use of opportunities
to fulfill internally established goals, values,
and aspirations. These may include any of a
universe of activities as, for example, the choice
of a mate, the construction of a house, or the
assumption of leadership in an organization. The
essential quality common to all such activities is
the element of decision-making, of taking the
initiative in the determination of what one's
future shall include. (p. 2)

This broadened set of criteria, when joined by measures
of "normal development" that incorporated such factors
as "accountability, obligation and reciprocity" in
personal relationships, forms a nexus with Whitehorn's
definition with its emphasis on effectiveness in work,
love and play. If the criterion "to expect well" has
not been mapped by Phillips, it is likely because it
is essentially derivative; "to expect well" speaks to
issues of self-esteem and a positive self-concept and
these are founded on skills which are reflections of
economic, social and sexual adequacy.

Although it is not possible within the limits of this
brief paper to review the literature relevant to the
self-concept, the derivative nature of Whitehorn's
fourth criterion can be seen in studies of the antecedents of self-esteem. Coopersmith (1967), on the basis
of his studies of middle-class preadolescents, locates
the antecedents for esteem in parental acceptance,
opportunities for individual expression and successful
academic performance. Wenar (1971) parallels these
observations with a commentary in which the growth of
self-esteem in adolescents is made dependent upon how
"love-worthy" the child is to his parents, the extent
to which he is "respect-worthy" to his peers, and the
"grade-worthy" quality of his performance in school.
To "expect well", thus, is to anticipate the regard of

parents and peers, and to be able to approach problems with the expectation that success and rewards will be forthcoming — qualities that can only be stabilized by a history of prior achievement. White (1965), who has contributed so substantially to an analysis of effectance motivation, expresses the relationship of competence to self-esteem in this manner:

> It is important ... to make allowance for the child's action upon his environment, of the extent to which this action is apt to be successful, and consequently of the confidence he builds up that he can influence his surroundings in desired ways. I use the term sense of competence to describe this, and I think that one's sense of competence is an exceedingly important aspect of self-esteem. (p. 201)

In his paper on the experience of efficacy in schizophrenia, White writes of the schizophrenic patient's major liability — the manner in which he is victimized by ineffective actions, and his lack of initiative and persistence in problem-solving — a liability that extends back to a period that long antedates the disorder:

> ... weak action on the environment has very great generality in schizophrenic behavior. Poor direction of attention and action, poor mastery of cognitive experience, weak assertiveness in interpersonal relations, low feelings of efficacy and competence, a restricted sense of agency in leading one's life — all these crop out in almost every aspect of the schizophrenic disorder.

> I should like now to entertain the hypothesis that this ineffectiveness in action is central not only in the picture of the schizophrenic's ultimately disordered behavior but also throughout his whole course of development — that from the start it is the future schizophrenic's major liability. It characterizes his behavior from an early point in life, and it leads to a precarious development in all the spheres I have discussed, including interpersonal competence and self-esteem. (p. 202)

It is this last paragraph that forms the bridge between the disturbed adult caught up in a network of schizophrenic pathology and the study of children who are at risk for that malignant disorder.

Children at Risk

The study of risk has assumed the proportions of a movement, but limitations of space do not allow me to chronicle that growth. Suffice to say that the constraints placed by retrospective data upon theorizing about the antecedents of schizophrenia have led a number of investigators here and abroad to study the developmental course of those who may be predisposed to the disorder. One critical problem is the identification of such vulnerable persons. Predisposition and the heightened probability of later disorder have begun to be defined in terms that largely reflect the etiological models that dominate the study of schizophrenia: biogenesis, family disorganization, socio-cultural deviance, and early neglect and deprivation, e.g. birth and pregnancy defect, poor prenatal care, nutritional deficiency, etc. (Garmezy, in Press)

Studies of children at risk typically are longitudinal in design — a method that inevitably imposes logistical and conceptual problems of great complexity. Obviously, these studies share the common goal of attempting to predict disorder by relating deviant outcomes in the adult to earlier patterns of behavior observed in childhood. But two factors militate against the exclusive reliance on such long-term ultimate outcomes in prediction. First, the Ns in these studies tend to be small, as is the proportion of anticipated adult deviance. Viewed from the standpoint of empirical probabilities, investigators who study vulnerability in children born of schizophrenic parentage can anticipate that the morbidity risk for their subjects will approximate 10% (Rosenthal, 1970; p. 114), but this figure presumably would have to be projected through a risk period extending to age 45. Children who are truly at high risk, faced with the unfortunate circumstance of having been born to parents both of whom have been schizophrenic, show a fourfold increase in morbidity risk that rises to a figure approximately 35 percent (Rosenthal, 1970; p. 117).

Were one to broaden the concept of risk to include other forms of maladaptation, the proportions of assumed deviance in children clearly would rise. But in either case, variability in outcome must be anticipated and planned for in the design of risk experiments. This projection of a heightened variability in outcomes is not inherently disadvantageous. It is as important to study risk children who escape disorder as it is to evaluate those who fall victim to it. But the context for doing so may be better served by more circumscribed short-term, longitudinal-prospective studies which are designed to measure the efficiency with which specific behavioral and biological variables differentiate not only high-risk from low-risk children but also separate within the high-risk group those children who show patterns of incompetence and maladaptation from others who appear to be proceeding toward adulthood along paths of mastery and adaptation.

The study of competence vs. incompetence in childhood emphasizes the utility of intermediate outcomes, and must be distinguished from research oriented to predictions of an ultimate outcome of disorder vs. normality in adulthood. But, if studies of intermediate outcomes are to prove meaningful to risk researchers, one must be able to demonstrate, at some point, that there exists a continuity to competence that extends from childhood into adulthood. Phillips (1968) has stated the issue in this form:

> The key to the prediction of future effectiveness in society lies in asking: 'How well has this person met, and how well does he now meet, the expectations implicitly set by society for individuals of his age and sex group?' What we need to learn is the person's relative potential for coping with the tasks set by society, compared to others of his age and sex status. Expected patterns of behavior change with the person's age. Presumably, relative potential for meeting these expectations remains far more stable. Thus, to the extent that an individual's relative standing in adaptive potential remains constant, we should, in principle, be able to predict his future effectiveness in adaptation to society. The pragmatic question in need of resolution is the extent to which relative adaptive potential does, in fact, remain constant. Only to this extent are we in a position to predict the person's future. (p. 3)

We may as well ready ourselves for the prediction errors that will follow. MacFarlane's (1964; MacFarlane & Clausen, 1971) observations made in the course of the famed longitudinal study of children conducted by the staff of the Institute of Human Development of the University of California, Berkeley, suggest this likelihood. Her subjects are now moving into their 40's. It is evident that many competent children have indeed become competent adults, but others characterized by early academic failure and patterns of social isolation and withdrawal have become outstanding adults, while still others who clearly gave evidence of mastery during the years of childhood are now unhappy adults puzzled by their manifest failure to sustain the pattern of their earlier achievements.

Nevertheless, it is probabilities that we deal with — and the probabilities stand in favor of the continuity

of competence. I would, therefore, suggest that a
tenable first stage in risk research is to explore the
correlation between the behaviors of children presumed
to be vulnerable to psychopathology against a criterion
of their qualities of competence.

A Four Stage Strategy for Risk Research

Reflecting on the many methodological problems in risk
research, I believe it appropriate to think in terms
of a four stage strategy. Basically we are engaged in
a search for specific behavioral and biological differ-
entiators that will separate risk from non-risk children.
But the differentiating power of any parameter in the
study of predisposition must, as I have indicated, meet
an even more stringent criterion of discriminating the
competent from the incompetent children who are at risk.
It may not be possible to achieve this goal over the
entire age range of childhood since adaptive insufficiency within the high risk group will grow more
apparent as children reach toward the more stressful
years of middle childhood and adolescence. However,
this search for predictor variables assumes that external
criteria of success or failure in adaptation are available to the investigator.

Stage 1 If these criteria are not available, then the
first priority in risk research must be to provide age-
related indices of competence. This is necessary to
cope with a disorder characterized by low incidence
rates and a lengthy time period before the appearance
of illness. Were individuals to become the victims of
schizophrenia with a rapid and inexplicable urgency
in which there was an absence of precursor signs,
investigators could lean more heavily on the ultimate
criterion of presence or absence of disorder. Fortunately, schizophrenia typically does not follow such
an unpredictable course, and the more malignant form of
the disorder shows clear prodromal indicators. This
fact, based upon an extensive empirical literature,
justifies the use of intermediate outcomes as a strate-
gically viable procedure for inferring successful or
unsuccessful adaptation in later life, although one's
predictions, as has been suggested, will be subject to
considerable error.

There arises the question as to which aspects of com-
petence/incompetence are most appropriate to study.
Listings of the qualities of the healthy personality
have never been in short supply in our literature, but
a more stringent screening is necessary. I believe that
the most effective screen is to study the qualities of
stress-resistant children — the "invulnerables" of our
society — on the assumption that these children approx-

184

imate more closely the competent child at risk. This
method, to be described in the section to follow, has
been the procedure used by our Minnesota group.

Stage 2 Once developmental measures of competence-in-
competence have been identified, the selection of
response parameters that can successfully differentiate
between and within risk and control groups becomes the
focus of the second stage of research. Such Stage 2
studies, I assume, will include variables that have
proved to have significant predictive power in the study
of adult schizophrenia (Garmezy, in Press, 1971, 1972). Thus
studies of psychophysiological responsiveness, attention
deployment, and cognitive efficiency are examples of the
type of variables that would meet this definitional
criterion for Stage 2 variables. But other variables
may be suggested by developmental studies of children
on the assumption that developmental lags may forecast
maladaptation. A further requirement must be added to
all Stage 2 studies; a Stage 1 (competence) variable
must be incorporated in order to test the power of a
Stage 2 differentiator to segregate subjects who differ
in levels of achieved competence.

Stage 3 The third stage in risk research would then
involve the selection of several powerful differen-
tiators for use in short-term prospective studies comparing adaptation in children at risk with appropriate
control groups. Elsewhere I have suggested that the
convergence technique espoused by Bell (1953) and
successfully utilized by Schaie & Strother (1968) in
a study of age changes in cognitive behavior be applied
in these circumscribed longitudinal investigations.
This method involves the use of cross-sectional groups
of different ages studied over a sufficient period of
time to allow each age group to brook into the next,
hopefully to permit inferences to be made about the
developmental nature of the variables under study.

Stage 4 The final stage in risk research would involve
intervention efforts cast into a non-traditional format.
For the critical element in such Stage 4 studies would
be the use of experimental-clinical techniques designed
initially to modify performance on Stage 2 factors with
later evaluations designed to test the effects of such
behavioral changes on Stage 1 competence factors.
Example: if attention deployment is faulty in the risk
child, can operant procedures be used to enhance attentional focusing? Assuming that such intervention proves
successful and that the behavior can be maintained and .
transferred beyond the laboratory, does it result in
positive shifts in competence in the child?

I do not suggest that these four stages be viewed as a rigid sequence of priorities. A flexible project, hopefully, would move comfortably among these various stages to test new hypotheses and to introduce and elaborate other variables on the basis of new data inputs.

Studies Illustrating the Four-Stage Sequence

Stage 1: Competence Indices

The investigator of risk can often turn, with gain, to the work of other researchers who have studied age-related indices of competence. Some illustrative examples: Bruner's ethological-toned research on the development of various types of skills in infancy; Wenar's (1964) studies of competence at age 1 — high "intensity" of behavior, "self-sufficiency", social curiosity and an orientation to complexity; Burton White's (1971) elaborate program for studying the pattern of human competence relevant to the first six years of life.

This last named project is particularly significant for students of risk. White's investigation, ethological and anthropological in orientation and intensity, and determinately empirical in context, illustrates the difficult task of developing competence criteria for any given age period:

> Initially, we selected as broad an array of types of preschool children as we could. Our original sample consisted of some 400 three-, four-, and five-year-old children living in eastern Massachusetts. We reached the children through 17 preschool institutions (kindergarten and nursery schools). These children varied in at least the following dimensions: (1) residence — from rural to suburban and urban, (2) SES (socio-economic status) - lower-lower to lower-upper class, (3) ethnicity - Irish, Italian, Jewish, English, Portuguese, Chinese and several other types. On the basis of extensive, independent observations by 15 staff members and the teachers of these children, and also on the basis of their performance on objective tests such as the Wechsler and tests of motor and sensory capacities we isolated 51 children. Half were judged to be very high on overall competence, able to cope consistently in superior fashion with anything they met. The other half were judged to be free from gross pathology but generally of very low competence. We then proceeded to observe these children each week for a period of eight months.

We gathered some 1,100 protocols on the typical
moment-to-moment activities of these children,
mostly in the institutions, but also in their
homes. At the end of the observation period we
selected the 13 most talented and 13 least
talented children. Through intensive discussions by our staff of 20 people, we compiled a
list of abilities that seemed to distinguish
the two groups. (p. 74)

Social and non-social abilities dominate the list, whereas
sensory-motor capacities proved to be ineffective discriminators. Relevant social abilities reflective of
competence include the following: attention-seeking
from adults in socially acceptable ways; the ability
to express affection and hostility to adults and to
use them effectively as resources; the ability to
behave similarly with peers, to compete with them and
to assume positions both of leadership and followership;
to show pride in accomplishment; and to express a desire
to grow up, as evidenced, in part, by involvement in
"adult-role play behavior."

Non-social abilities include linguistic and intellectual
competence, attentional ability, and "executive abilities" of the type involved in planning multi-step
activities and effectively using environmental resources.

The Minnesota Studies of Competence

At Minnesota, we have focused on competence indices that
may be applicable both to the middle years of childhood
and early adolescence. Our approach initially was to
search extensively the literature of the healthy personality to catalogue as many indices of adaptive functioning as could be found. Such listings typically lack an
empirical base and readily reveal their armchair
origins. We, therefore, used two requirements in
selecting our basic criteria: 1) frequency of occurrence in the literature (which meant simply that many
had occupied the same armchair); and 2) satisfactory
application of a more stringent and meaningful standard.
To meet the latter, we generated another literature
review — one which emphasized empirical studies of competence in children who could also be considered to be
at risk. Using socio-cultural disadvantage as the risk
component (a choice made necessary by the lack of a
substantive literature available on able children
exposed to genetic risk, early neglect or familial disorganization), Nuechterlein (1970) reviewed a largely
unpublished literature contained in the studies and
documents to be found in ERIC (Educational Resources
Information Center). Nuechterlein's summa thesis, The
Competence Disadvantaged Child: A Review of Research,

provided us with competence indicators in selected
groups of children exposed to poverty. We used these
indicators as a basis for narrowing the wide-ranging
list of attributes assigned to the healthy personality,
reasoning that children who had mastered environments
weighted with stress and strain were an appropriate
criterion group against which to study children vulnerable to psychopathology.

Applying the findings of Nuechterlein's review of
the ERIC literature, we selected six indices of competence for use in our risk project, believing these
to be the most relevant for adaptation during the
period of middle childhood and early adolescence.

The Six Competence Criteria are these:

1. Effectiveness in work, play and love; satisfactory educational and occupational progress;
   peer regard and friendships; behavior;

2. Healthy expectancies and the belief that
   'good outcomes' will follow from the imposi-
   tion of effort and initiative; an orientation
   to success rather than the anticipation of
   failure in performing tasks; a realistic
   level of aspiration unbeclouded by unrealis-
   tically high or low goal-setting behavior;

3. Self-esteem, feelings of personal worthiness,
   a proper evaluative set toward self and a
   sense of 'fate control', i.e. the belief
   that one can control events in one's environment rather than being a passive victim of
   them (an internal as opposed to external
   locus of control);

4. Self-discipline, as revealed by the ability to
   delay gratification and to maintain a future-
   orientedness;

5. Control and regulation of impulsive drives;
   the ability to adopt a reflective as opposed
   to an impulsive style in coping with problem
   situations;

6. The ability to think abstractly; to approach
   new situations flexibly and to be able to
   attempt alternate solutions to a problem.

To reduce these criteria to ratable proportions, our
research group has devised a graphic Competence Rating

Scale for Teachers.* The scale was designed for teachers
for several reasons: teachers provide a common base for
observations of target and control children; the schools
have been very cooperative in allowing us access to
records and classroom (with informal consent from parents); the children we observe share a common arena for
observation of their competence qualities. Two items
from the scale may provide an indication of its format.

A. Relationship of achievement to ability level: The
   extent to which the child's performance is consonant
   with his ability level. The level of performance can
   be high, moderate or low; rate only its consistency
   with ability level.

```
                              ┌─ Consistent maximum
                              │  achievement in relation
                              │  to ability
Utilizes abilities            │
well - typically works ───────┤
close to potential            │
                              │  Achievement tends to
                              └─ approximate ability level
                                 with occasional under-
                                 achievement

Often fails to work    ───────┐
up to level of ability        │
                              └─ Markedly underachieving
```

Incident: (teacher's description of incidence)

B. Control of aggression with peers: Two factors are
   involved; the intensity of the child's anger and the
   appropriateness of it in terms of external events.

```
                              ┌─ A bully; often cruel;
                              │  threatens others without
                              │  provocation
Overly aggressive; at         │
times may fight or be  ───────┤
verbally abusive with         │
little provocation            │
                              │  Generally even-tempered;
                              └─ on occasion may overact
                                 with aggression but
                                 regains control quickly

                              ┌─
Usually well-controlled;      │
can be provoked but    ───────┤
rarely gets angry with-       │
out cause                     │  Rarely antagonistic;
                              └─ anger, when shown, is
                                 justified.
```

Incident:

*Members of Project Competence who have been instrumental
in the development of the Competence Rating Scale for
Teachers include Beverly Kaemmer, Roger Lazoff, Lee Marcus,
Keith Nuechterlein, Paul Sanders, and Susan Sanger.

Stage 1 Study: <u>Social and Academic Competence of Children</u>
<u>Vulnerable to Schizophrenia and Other</u>
<u>Behavior Pathologies</u> (Jon E. Rolf)*

We place a high valuation on the first criterion of competence:

"Effectiveness in work, play and love; satisfactory educational and occupational progress; peer regard and friendships;"

It is rooted in the literature of prognosis in schizophrenia, socialization in childhood and studies of competence amidst poverty.

Contained within this first criterion is the important constellation described earlier — economic (or academic), social, and sexual competence. This factor became the initial study of Project Competence** in which Rolf (1969, In Press) sought to measure the academic and social competence of six groups of elementary school children: Four of these groups shared in common a potential vulnerability to divergent forms of psychopathology. One consisted of children whose mothers had had a previous history of hospitalization for schizophrenia (N - 31); another had mothers whose prior history included hospitalization for depression (N - 26); a third group was comprised of children who were being seen in psychiatric clinics for externalizing (acting-out) symptoms (N - 36), while a fourth group of clinic children presented internalizing (phobic, withdrawn) symptoms (N - 27). As far as could be determined by an appraisal of case histories, these clinic children did not have mentally ill parents. These four groups of target children, when located, were attending 37 schools and were in 113 different classrooms of a city public school system. Within each classroom, Rolf read all the cumulative records of the pupils to select two control children who in the opinion of principal, teacher or social worker were behaving competently. These two children and the

---

* Dr. Rolf is currently Assistant Professor of Psychology, University of Vermont.

**The project title has undergone a series of changes designed largely to underplay our concern with the child at risk. Originally titled <u>Vulnerable Children</u>, the research program is now identified as <u>Project Competence</u>. The change in title is not simply opportunistic, since we have begun to formulate studies of "invulnerable children" concurrent with ongoing studies of children at risk. (Garmezy & Nuechterlein, 1972).

target child comprised a triad consisting of a child
at risk, a competent child matched in terms of his or
her comparability to the target child on such factors
as age, sex, grade, social class, intactness of the
home, school achievement, and IQ (when available),
and a competent, random control child of the same sex
and grade but unmatched on the other demographic
variables. Thus, the total number of subjects that
comprised Rolf's triads was 360 (targets N - 120;
matched controls, N - 120; random controls N - 120).

Measures of social competency were derived from the
ratings of peers and teachers. Sociometric ratings
built around Bower's (1969) "Class Play" were based
on the judgments of some 3400 children who participated
in the project. (Every child in each of the 113 classrooms successfully joined in the study.) The typecast
assignments given to the members of the triad by their
peers was the basis for determining peer approval or
disapproval. Teachers completed rating scales designed
to reflect positive academic behavior, emotional stability and maturity, social agreeableness and positive
social extroversion. Academic competence was also
analyzed by a thorough-going appraisal of the children's
cumulative records and included an application of Watt
et al's (1970) method for quantifying dimensional
attributes derived from qualitative descriptions of
the children written by teachers over successive years.
This last analysis is still in progress and cannot be
reported in detail here. To date, the variables of
yearly grade reports, health status, standardized
achievement and intelligence test scores, grade reports,
notations of absences and tardiness, socioeconomic
status of the family and the frequency of address
changes per academic year have been abstracted and
readied for computer analysis. Overall grade averages
for the most recent academic years do indicate that the
sons of schizophrenic mothers appear to be significantly
less achieving than their respective controls. Rolf
further plans to subject the teachers' descriptive
comments to a computerized analysis that will provide
sketches of the modal personality profiles of each
target group as well as to catalogue the traits of its
individual members.

The study of social competence as adduced from peer and
teacher ratings has undergone more extensive analysis,
and provides partial confirmation of some of the negative social correlates of risk status. Since peer
regard is a powerful predictor of adaptation (Lippitt
& Gold, 1959; Teele et al, 1966; Hartup, 1970), Rolf's
findings are of particular interest.

Summarizing the results of his study, Rolf (In Press)
writes:

191

At the triad level, the prediction was generally supported that the target groups, in comparison with their respective control groups, obtained lower competence scores. At the target group level, the trend of peer-rated competence score ranks indicated that for both males and females the externalizing children were lowest, followed in order of ascending competence by the children with schizophrenic mothers, the internalizing children, and by the children whose mothers had internalizing symptoms. This order was also obtained for the teacher-rated competence scores, but only for the girls and not the boys. In the latter case, teachers rated externalizers lowest, and internalizers next lowest, but teachers generally did not discriminate, with certain exceptions, between the two male target groups with mentally ill mothers and their respective control groups.

Stage 2 Studies: Performance Variables in Relation to Competence

The study of attentional factors in children at risk holds promise for evaluating precursor signs of deficit functioning. In the long history of experimental research with schizophrenic patients, the area of attention and preparatory set as measured by reaction time has repeatedly been shown to differentiate reliably patients from control subjects (Shakow, 1963). This suggests that the study of such attentional factors in children at risk could hold promise as a precursor sign to deficit functioning. To link such attentional components to independent indices of competence would satisfy the structure demanded of Stage 2 studies. An ongoing experiment by Marcus (1971) using the basic design of Rolf's study with its four different groups of target children and two groups of matched and random controls exemplifies the strategy. Three studies constitute the core of Marcus' dissertation research: 1) attention and set are studied as a function of varying preparatory intervals presented in a simple reaction time procedure using regular and irregular RT sequences. [This study essentially replicates the classical RT study of Rodnick & Shakow (1940) and those of Shakow and his associates (e.g., Zahn, et al, 1961, 1963)]. A second study of attentional mechanisms uses the reaction time procedure with irregular preparatory intervals but with pretrial information given to reduce temporal uncertainty. The third study also utilizes the basic reaction time task, but modified to focus on decision-making and choice behavior of the children under conditions of risk-taking in which the probability of positive and negative outcomes is varied by experimenter.

192

The purpose of the latter study is to provide pilot data regarding behavior relevant to several competence criteria including success vs. failure orientation, impulsive vs. reflective cognitive styles, and internal vs. external locus of control.

The Marcus study provides an example of the Minnesota strategy.* Reaction time is essentially a Stage 2 variable; it has demonstable significance as a measure of attentional deficit in schizophrenia and may provide in similar fashion a measure of task set in children. But it is necessary that a Stage 1 variable also be incorporated into the study to provide a measure of competence that can be correlated with RT performance. Such a proviso has been made in three ways: 1) formal evaluation of the children's cumulative school records; 2) teachers' ratings on the Competence Rating Scale; 3) the creation within the experiment of a risk-taking component to measure level of aspiration, locus of control, and cognitive style.

Verbal Associative Behavior of Children Varying in Vulnerability to Psychopathology: The Effect of Reward and Censure

In a study now getting underway,** we are attempting to test an observation by Mednick & Schulsinger (1968, Mednick, 1970) that children who are at risk for schizophrenia tend, in a continuous word association test, to show evidence of associative "drift". Thus instead of maintaining a task set that generates sequential, relevant associations to the original stimulus word, such risk individuals, it is reported, tend to associate to their own previous responses so that subsequent response chains that appear bear no direct and evident relationship to the original stimulus word. Such findings are relevant to the successful maintenance of a task set, association deficits and subtle manifestations of cognitive deviance. As such, they accentuate the potential relevance of data derived from the association procedure as a Stage 2 variable in the study of adaptation in children at risk.

---

* Preliminary evidence from the Marcus study indicates that difficulty in maintaining a task set falls to the children born to schizophrenic mothers and clinic children manifesting externalizing behaviors. These findings parallel Rolf's data on social competence. Since there is overlap in the subjects within the risk groups, these results suggest the viability of the Stage 1-Stage 2 strategy.

** Coparticipants in the research include Roger Lazoff, Paul Sanders, Susan Sanger and Keith Nuechterlein.

The present experiment is more than a cross-validating effort. It provides for a test of the hypothesis using carefully matched groups of words which, prior to the continuous association procedure, are exposed to exper- imental manipulations designed to arouse in the subjects positive and negative affects specific to each group of words. The methods for testing for drift involve, on the one hand, quantitative scores based upon the use of existent standard lists of the word associations provided by American children and, on the other, clin- ically sensitive methods designed to elicit the pattern of drift, if it occurs. The competence measures employed in Marcus' study will also be applied to the investigation of associative drift, with responsiveness to the stress imposed by success and failure experiences constituting an additional criterion of adaptation.

Stage 3 Studies: Short-Term Longitudinal Studies

For a description of a program of risk research centering on a relatively short-term prospective design, it is necessary that I turn toward research that is now underway in the Department of Psychiatry at the University of Rochester Medical School. Under the coordinating leadership of Lyman Wynne more than 20 professional staff have gathered, drawn from four major universities (Rochester, Cornell, Berkeley, Minnesota) and a diversity of disciplines that include psychiatry, clinical psycho- logy, developmental psychology, experimental psycho- pathology, epidemiology, sociology and statistics.

The program focus, rooted in the study of children and family members who are at risk for schizophrenia, is comprised of three subprograms, all interrelated and all central to an understanding of the problem of predis- position. One set of studies focuses on children and siblings born to schizophrenic and depressive mothers as defining the samples at risk;· another core is oriented to studies of the families and the parents of these children with an emphasis on family organization, modes of intrafamilial communication and significant aspects of parenting patterns; a third group of studies is epidemiological in orientation and utilizes as instrument uniquely advantageous to epidemiological research — the Psychiatric Case Register for Monroe County, which is housed in the department's Division of Preventive and Social Psychiatry. (Miles and Gardner, 1966; Babigian, in Press)

The program incorporates both a cross-sectional and a short-term longitudinal-prospective strategy which, in combination, may produce within a span of six years a projected developmental picture of the vulnerable child ranging from infancy to early adolescence. Hopefully, this can be achieved through the convergence procedure

to which reference has been made earlier. This strategy
involves the use of groups of children at ages 1,* 4, 7
and 10 who will be followed initially over a span of
four years thus providing for retesting of subgroups of
children at the convergence age points of 4, 7, 10. If
the project warrants extension to seven years, it would
be possible to strengthen the Ns at each convergence
point and to extend the group's observations on these
children into the period of puberty and beyond.

The variables to be studied are numerous and embrace
such diverse components of adaptation as cognitive and
social development employing a Piagetian framework,
modes of information processing and sensory integration,
psychophysiological studies of children and parents,
learning efficiency under censure and praise, quality
of school functioning, formal diagnostic assessment of
children and parents, modes of parenting, patterns of
communication within the family, mother-child play
interaction, styles of conflict resolution, follow-up
studies of disturbed adolescents, and the role of birth
complications in risk. Since the components of competence have been made an integral part of the research
program, the relevance of adaptation to the range of
dependent variables to be studied may indicate whether
such a relatively short-term longitudinal-developmental
program can suggest the pattern of outcomes in groups of
vulnerable children.

Stage 4 - Intervention

There is little to be said about this final stage of
risk research, for no data have been brought to bear
on the important problem of intervention. What, indeed,
can one say about intervention when there exists such
restricted information about the etiology of schizophrenia? On the island of Mauritius Mednick & Schulsinger (see this volume) are readying a program of preschool training with children whose risk status is
revealed not by the psychiatric status of parents but
by the pre-schoolers' "deviant" psychophysiology. The
investigators indicate that they hope to provide specific
training for the children in learning to cope with frustration, to develop approach rather than avoidant behaviors in the face of environmental stress, and to
encourage active play participation with peers. Such an
orientation fulfills the specific function I have assigned
to Stage 4 studies.

---

* The one-year-olds are children who are being seen in an
infant risk project under the direction of Professors
Arnold Sameroff and Melvin Zax of the University of
Rochester, with the collaboration of Professor Harouton
Babigian.

A closer approximation to the projected intervention strategy and one whose power has been empirically demonstrated has been provided by one of my Rochester colleagues, Michael Chandler (1971). Reared in a developmental-Piagetian framework and tempered by clinical training at the Menninger Foundation, Chandler has been interested in problems of egocentricism and role playing as significant manifestations of adaptation within delinquent and abandoned-neglected children. The ability to demonstrate perspective or role-taking skills Chandler sees as a dispositional attribute of the maturing organism. Children with tenuous adaptive qualities presumably would show a lessened skill to assay the role of another and to perceive a self-other differentiation. Devising and adapting a variety of assessment procedures for measuring egocentricism, Chandler applied his procedures to the study of 75 normal public school children between the ages of six and thirteen. Other groups consisted of children with 'long histories of social and interpersonal failures' including 50 children from 8-13 years of age who were institutionalized for emotional disturbance and 50 chronically delinquent boys. The disturbed children showed a significant deficit in role-taking skills. Most normal children by age 10 can adopt the orientation of another, but many disturbed children had difficulty in doing so and failed to show the maturing of such skills between the ages of six and ten. Chandler reports that the typical disturbed child at 13 was more egocentric than the average seven-year-old normal child. But variability prevailed in the disturbed group. Non-egocentricity characterized those children who had been brutalized and were 'hyperalert to and suspicious of the motives of others'.

Chandler's intervention strategy exemplifies best the Stage 4 principle. In effect, he asked: 'What would be the consequence of training these disturbed children in role-taking skills? His procedure was. to take 50 chronically delinquent boys between the ages of 11 and 13 and to divide them into three groups on the basis of their prior egocentricism scores. One group remained untreated and was retested after ten weeks. Remaining subjects were seen in groups of five for a total of 30 hours over a ten week period. Half of these Ss were involved in making documentary films during the intervention period. Chandler's (1971) comments on the experiences given the remaining half of the Ss warrants description:

> '"Having noted the presence of substantial developmental delays in the role-taking abilities of various populations of disturbed children, an effort was made to formulate and test a program of remedial training intended as a means of testing the modifiability of these observed deficiencies.

There is little information in the
research literature that provides useful
clues as to how a curriculum for improving
faulty role taking skills might be devised.
What seemed required was some vehicle for
transporting the subjects into the perspectives of others and for encouraging and
facilitating their efforts to adopt roles
other than their own. Efforts to satisfy
these task requirements led to the development of a storefront video film and actors
workshop where delinquent adolescents were
provided closed-circuit television recording equipment and encouraged to make films
about their own role taking efforts. They
were helped to develop skits or short plays
about persons their own age and required to
replay and review these skits until each
participant had occupied every role in the
plot.'"

What, then, were the consequences of this training effort
to get subjects to relinquish their egocentric biases and
take on the more mature social skills commensurate with
their age? The documentary film-making group and the no
treatment group, together with the role-playing groups,
were all administered equivalent forms of the pre-test
role-taking test. Only the group trained in role-taking
showed substantial improvement on the tests.

A broader question, of course, relates to the daily real-
life adaptation of children exposed to such a specific
regimen of social skills training. Chandler, in response
to my direct inquiry on this important point, wrote me of
a group of delinquent and a group of abandoned and neglected
children with whom he and his associates have worked:

"In both instances the Ss were selected on
the grounds that they were egocentric beyond
their years and were enrolled in a three month
long intervention effort which relied on the
making of videotape movies of dramatic productions
as a training vehicle. With the delinquent
sample, behavioral ratings were made both before
and after the termination of the treatment effort
and the delinquent histories of the group members were examined through a search of police
and court records. This record search was
carried out at the outset of the program and
at 6-12- and 18 months intervals after the
program's termination. Program participants,
in contrast to control Ss, did show some minor
reduction in the level of their post-program
delinquent involvement. The population of in-

stitutionalized abandoned and neglected children
were rated by teachers and custodial staff
before and after the intervention project. In
addition to changing in more manifest behavioral
ways, these observed changes were generally in
the direction of increased social competence
and comfort in social situations."

Despite my enthusiasm for research of this type, I must con-
fess to a concern regarding this fourth stage of a total
research strategy. Can piecemeal treatment via skills
training provide for the development of those higher skills
necessary for adaptation in our complex society? I am torn
between the search for a form of precise intervention and
an awareness that the future environmental demands that
children must face, whatever their degree of vulnerability
to psychopathology, are so great that a broader program of
intervention seems necessary. As Bruner (1970) has indicated, the development of skill and competence occurs
by small accretions on a day-to-day basis throughout infancy and childhood. Such skills lead to new mastery, which,
in turn, encourages the development of other skills that
generate an in-depth competence that effectively inoculates
an individual against the ravaging effects of disorder.
But this pattern of skill acquisition requires a view of
intervention that must be broad-gauged. Bruner's appraisal
of the problem of intervention with disadvantaged children
provides a fitting final statement to the citical problem
of reducing the risk potential of vulnerable children:

"... little can be done for a human
being with a 'one-shot' intervention. One
has to work at it. Head Start alone does
not work, if afterward the child is dumped
into a punishing school experience. When
we build an expectancy, build a skill, we
incur a responsibility for nurturing it. It
may, in some instances, be a compounding
of evils to open the child's vulnerabilities
and then disappoint or dump him. If we are
to be effective in helping disadvantaged
children cope better, it is their life
cycle that must be dealt with not their
preschool or their nursery or their street
life. That is why we need diverse forms of
care and can hardly tolerate quarrels about
this form vs. that form on ideological
grounds rather than evidence .... The important thing is to get going. We must
surely praise the attitude that though the
first programs may not happen to be our
preferred ones, nonetheless, we try to make
them as good as possible knowing that we
shall surely go on from there." (pp. 115-116)

REFERENCES

Alvarez, R.R. A comparison of the preferences of schizophrenic and normal subjects for rewarded and punished
stimuli. Unpublished Ph.D. dissertation, Duke University, 1957.

Atkinson, Rita L. & Robinson, Nancy M. Paired associate
learning by schizophrenic and normal subjects under
conditions of personal and impersonal reward and punishment. J. abnorm. soc. Psychol., 1961, 62, 322-326.

Babigian, H.M. Schizophrenia in Monroe County. In
Schizophrenia: Implications of research findings for
treatment and teaching. By M.M. Katz, A. Littlestone,
L. Mosher, M.S. Roath., A.H. Tuma (Eds.). In Press.

Bell, R.Q. Convergence: an accelerated longitudinal
approach. Child Development, 1953, 24, 142-145.

Bower, E.M. Early Identification of Emotionally Handicapped Children in School. Springfield, Illinois,
Charles C. Thomas, 2nd ed., 1969.

Bradford, N. Comparative perceptions of mothers and
maternal roles by schizophrenic patients and their
normal siblings. Unpublished Ph.D. dissertation.
University of Minnesota, 1965.

Bruner, J.S. Discussion: Infant education as viewed by
a psychologist. In Education of the Infant and Young
Child. V.H. Denenberg (Ed.). New York Academic Press,
1970. pp. 109-116.

Buss, A.H. & Lang, P.J. Psychological deficit in schizophrenia. I. Affect, reinforcement, and concept attainment. J. abnorm. Psychol., 1965, 70, 2-24.

Canvanaugh, D.K. Improvement in the performance of
schizophrenics on concept formation tasks as a function
of motivational change. J. abnorm. soc. Psychol.,
1958, 57, 8-12.

Chandler, M.J. Egocentricism in normal and pathological
child development. Paper presented at the First
Symposium of the International Society for the Study
of Behavioral Development. Nijmegen, Holland, 1971.

Cicchetti, D.V. Reported family dynamics and psychopathology, J. abnorm. Psychol., 1967, 72, 282-289.

Clarke, A.R. Conformity behavior of schizophrenic subjects with maternal figures, J. abnorm. soc. Psychol., 1964, 68, 45-53.

Coopersmith, S. The Antecedents of Self-Esteem, San Francisco, W.H. Freeman Co., 1967.

Dunn, W.L. Jr. Visual discrimination of schizophrenic subjects as a function of stimulus meaning. J. Pers., 1954, 23, 48-64.

Engelhardt, R.S. Semantic correlates of interpersonal concepts and parental attributes in schizophrenia. Unpublished Ph.D. dissertation. Duke University, 1959.

Farina, A. Patterns of role dominance and conflict in parents of schizophrenic patients. J. abnorm. soc. Psychol., 1960, 61, 31-38.

Farina, A. & Dunham, R.M. Measurement of family relationships and their effects. Archives of gen. Psychiatry, 1963, 9, 64-73.

Farina, A. & Holzberg, J.D. Interaction patterns of parents and hospitalized sons diagnosed as schizophrenic or non-schizophrenic. J. abnorm. Psychol., 1968, 73, 114-118.

Garmezy, N. Approach and avoidance behavior of schizophrenic and normal subjects under conditions of reward and punishment. J. Pers., 1952, 20, 253-276.

Garmezy, N. Prediction of performance in schizophrenia. In Psychopathology of Schizophrenia, P. Hoch, & J. Zubin (Eds.) New York: Grune & Stratton, 1966, Pp. 129-181.

Garmezy, N. Process and reactive schizophrenia: Some conceptions and issues. In Katz, M. & Cole, J. (Eds.) The Role and Methodology of Classification in Psychiatry and Psychopathology. U.S. Department of HEW, Government Printing Office. Reprinted (with addendum) in Schizophrenia Bulletin, Washington, D.C., NIMH, Vol. 1, A 2, 1970, Pp. 30-74.

Garmezy, N. Commentary, J. nerv. Ment. Dis., 1971, 153, 317-322.

Garmezy, N. Research strategies for the study of children who are at risk for schizophrenia. In Schizophrenia: Implications of Research Findings for Treatment and Teaching. M.M. Katz, R. Littlestone, L. Mosher, M.S. Roath, & A.H. Tuma, Eds. In Press.

Garmezy, N. Models of etiology for the study of children who are at risk for schizophrenia. In Life History Research in Psychopathology, Vol. II. M. Rolf, L. Robins, and M.M. Pollack, Eds. Minneapolis: University of Minnesota Press. In Press.

Garmezy, N. & Nuechterlein, K.H. Vulnerable and invulnerable children: The fact and fiction of competence and disadvantage. Amer. J. Orthopsychiat., (abstract) 77, 1972.

Garmezy, N. & Rodnick, E.H. Premorbid adjustment and performance in schizophrenia: Implications for interpreting heterogeneity in schizophrenia. J. Nerv. Ment. Dis., 1959, 129, 450-466.

Goldstein, M.J. Premorbid adjustment, paranoid status, and patterns of response to phenothiazine in acute schizophrenia. Washington, D.C. NIMH Schizophrenia Bulletin, No. 3, Winter, 1970.

Goldstein, M.J., Judd, L.L., Rodnick, E.H., Alkire, A., & Gould, E. A method for studying influence and coping patterns within families of disturbed adolescents. J. nerv. ment. Dis., 1968, 147, 233-251.

Goldstein, M.J., Judd, L.L., Rodnick, E.H., & LaPolla, A. Psychophysiological and behavioral effects of phenothiazine administration in acute schizophrenics as a function of premorbid status. Journal of Psychiatric Research, 1969, 6, 271-287.

Goodman, D. Performance of good and poor premorbid male schizophrenics as a function of paternal vs. maternal censure. J. abnorm. soc. Psychol., 1964, 69, 550-555.

Grinker, R.R. Psychiatry and our dangerous world. In Psychiatric Research in Our Changing World. Proceedings of an International Symposium. Montreal, 1968, Excerpta Medica International Congress Series, No. 187.

Haggard, E.A., Brekstad, A., & Skard, A. On the reliability of the anamnestic interview. J. abnorm. soc. Psychol., 1960, 61, 311-318.

Harris, J.E. Size estimation of pictures as a function of thematic content for schizophrenic and normal subjects. J. Pers., 1957, 25, 651-671.

Hartup, W.W. Peer interaction and social organization. In Manual of Child Psychology, 3rd Ed. P.H. Mussen (Ed.) New York: John Wiley & Sons, 1970, Pp. 361-456.

Higgins, J. The concept of process-reactive schizophrenia: Criteria and related research. J. nerv. Ment. Dis., 1964, 138, 9-25.

Higgins, J. Process reactive schizophrenia: Recent developments. J. nerv. Ment. Dis., 1969, 149, 450-472.

Higgins, J. & Peterson, J.C. Concept of process-reactive schizophrenia: a critique. Psychol. Bull., 1966, 66, 201-206.

Kantor, R.E. and Herron, W.G. Reactive and Process Schizophrenia. Palo Alto, Calif: Science & Behavior Books, 1966.

Klein, E.B., Cicchetti, D.V., & Spohn, H.E. A test of the censure-deficit model and its relation to pre-morbidity in the performance of schizophrenics. J. abnorm. Psychol., 1967, 72, 174-181.

Knight, R. Effect of punishment on performance of schizophrenics: a review of the literature. University of Minnesota. Mimeographed, 1968. 116 pp.

Leventhal, A.M. The effects of diagnostic category and reinforcer on learning and awareness. J. abnorm. soc. Psychol., 1959, 59, 162-166.

Lippitt, R. & Gold, M. Classroom social structure as a mental health problem. J. soc. Issues. 1959, 15, 40-49.

MacFarlane, J.W. Perspectives on personal consistency and change: the guidance study. Vita Humana, 1964, 115-126.

MacFarlane, J.W. & Clausen, J.A. Childhood influences upon intelligence, personality and mental health. In The Mental Health of the Child. J. Segal (Ed.) Rockville, Maryland, National Institute of Mental Health. 1971, pp. 131-154.

Marcus, L. Attention, set and risk-taking in disturbed, vulnerable and normal children. Ph.D. dissertation proposal. Mimeographed University of Minnesota Project Competence, 1971.

Mednick, S. Breakdown in individuals at high risk for schizophrenia: possible predispositional perinatal factors. Ment. Hygiene, 1970, 54, 50-63.

Mednick, S.A., & Schulsinger, F. Some premorbid characteristics related to breakdown in children with schizophrenic mothers. In The Transmission of Schizo-phrenia. D. Rosenthal & S.S. Kety (Eds.) Oxford: Pergamon Press, 1968, pp. 267-291.

Miles, H.C. & Gardner, E.A. A psychiatric case register. Archives of Gen. Psychiatry, 1966, 14, 571-580.

Nathanson, I.A. A semantic differential analysis of parent-son relationships in schizophrenia. J. abnorm. Psychol., 1967, 72, 277-281.

Nuechterlein, K.H. Competent disadvantaged children: A review of research. Summa cum laude Thesis. University of Minnesota, 1970.

Phillips, L. Case history data and prognosis in schizophrenia. J. nerv. ment. Dis., 1953, 117, 515-525.

Phillips, L. Human Adaptation and Its Failures, New York: Academic Press, 1968.

Rodnick, E.H. & Garmezy, N. An experimental approach to the study of motivation in schizophrenia. Nebraska Symposium on Motivation. M.R. Jones (Ed.) Lincoln, Nebraska: University of Nebraska Press, 1957, pp. 109-184.

Rodnick, E.H. & Shakow, D. Set in the schizophrenic as measured by a composite reaction time index. Amer. J. Psychiat., 1940, 97, 214-225.

Rolf, J.E. The academic and social competence of school children vulnerable to behavior pathology. Unpublished Ph.D. dissertation. University of Minnesota, 1969.

Rolf, J.E. The academic and social competence of children vulnerable to schizophrenia and other behavior pathologies. J. abnorm. Psychol. In Press.

Rosenthal, D. Genetic Theory and Abnormal Behavior. New York: McGraw-Hill Book Co., 1970.

Schaie, K.W., & Strother, C.R. A cross-sequential study of age changes in cognitive behavior. Psychol. Bull., 1968, 70, 671-680.

Shakow, D. Psychological deficit in schizophrenia. Behavioral Science, 1963, 8, 275-305.

Stoller, F.H. The effect of maternal evaluation on schizophrenics and their siblings. Unpublished doctoral dissertation. University of California (Los Angeles), 1964.

Teele, J.E., Schleifer, M.J., Corman, L., & Larson, K. Teacher ratings, sociometric status, and choice-reciprocity of anti-social and normal boys. Group Psychotherapy, 1966, 19 (3-4), 183-197.

Watt, N.F., Stolorow, R.D., Lubensky, Amy W., & McClelland, D.C. School adjustment and behavior of children hospitalized for schizophrenia as adults. Amer. J. Orthopsychiat., 1970, 40, 637-657.

Wenar, C. Competence at one. Merrill Palmer Quarterly, 1964, 10, 329-342.

Wenar, C. Personality Development. Boston: Houghton Mifflin Co., 1971.

White, B.L. An analysis of excellent early educational practices: Preliminary report. Interchange, 1971, 2, 71-88.

White, R.W. The experience of efficacy in schizophrenia. Psychiatry, 1965, 28, 199-211.

Yarrow, Marian R., Campbell, J.D., & Burton, R.W. Recollections of childhood: A study of the retrospective method. Monographs of the Society for Research in Child Development, 1970, 35, #5, 83 pp.

Zahn, T.P., Rosenthal, D., & Shakow, D. Effects of irregular preparatory intervals on reaction time in schizophrenics. J. abnorm. soc. Psychol., 1963, 67, 44-52.

Zahn, T.P., Rosenthal, D., & Shakow, D. Reaction time in schizophrenic and normal subjects in relation to the sequence of series of regular preparatory intervals. J. abnorm. soc. Psychol., 1961, 63, 161-168.

1968 DEAN RESEARCH AWARD

GABRIEL LANGFELDT *("Schizophrenia: Diagnosis and Prognosis"), recipient of the seventh annual Stanley R. Dean Research Award for his work in establishing diagnostic criteria for schizophrenia, is a member of the Norwegian Academy of Science. Interested in forensic as well as clinical psychiatry, Dr. Langfeldt is author of many books, including* The Jealousy Syndrome. *His most recent work, published in 1961, is* A Study of the Philosophy and Life of Albert Schweitzer. *Dr. Langfeldt is director of the Psychiatric Clinic at the University of Oslo, where he has been a professor of psychiatry since 1930.*

SCHIZOPHRENIA: DIAGNOSIS AND PROGNOSIS

by Gabriel Langfeldt

ᏯᎧᎽ

MY interest in a clearcut and circumscribed diagnosis of schizophrenia disorders began during the years 1923–26, when I was studying the effect of these illnesses (called "dementia praecox" at that time in Norway) on the functioning of the endocrine and vegetative systems. With methods at that time considered the best available for the detection of endocrine anomalies and functional disturbances of the vegetative nervous system, I investigated forty cases with a typical clinical symptomatology. The methods at hand were a general clinical investigation, which included x-ray examination of the Sella turcica (the depression in the skull containing the pituitary gland) and the epiphyses (the cartilaginous lines at which growth occurs in the long bones of the young) and determination of the blood picture and basal metabolism as well as a study of subcutaneous adrenalin injection and peroral administration of sexual gland extracts and thyroid tablets upon basal metabolic levels, which are abnormally low in some schizophrenics. In all cases an examination of the carbohydrate metabolism was also performed. The autonomic nervous system was examined clinically as well as with intravenously applied adrenalin, atropine, and pilocarpin.

INITIAL FINDINGS

Although I found none of the well-known endocrine disorders, I did find, as a result of my examinations, metabolic anomalies well known to the endocrine clinic. A leading idea in my procedure was that possible physiological anomalies should be correlated not only with the type of schizophrenic disorder in question, but also with the dominating mental picture and stage of development. The results of my findings were collected in a monograph entitled "The endocrine glands and autonomic system in dementia praecox."

In my opinion the most interesting result of this study was the conclusion that Kraepelin's three types of dementia praecox—catatonic, hebephrenic, and paranoid—were characterized by different physiological anomalies, varying, in addition, with whether the stage of development was quiescent or chronic. While there is no point in my dwelling on my 1926 findings here, I merely mention that I showed, then, for the first time that one distinction between catatonic cases, on the one hand, and hebephrenic and paranoid cases, on the other, was that the former were, at times, immune to intravenously injected adrenalin, in that no elevation of blood pressure was demonstrated. Because some normal persons, as I also discovered then, show a similar negative reaction to adrenalin, I could not use this test to help diagnose schizophrenia, or to differentiate between catatonic and other types of the disorder.

Another observation was that basal metabolism is reduced predominately in acute, withdrawn cases of catatonia (in 6 out of 8 cases). Of 13 cases of hebephrenia, only one was characterized by a reduction in basal metabolism—about 22 percent. I also found that such reduced basal metabolism could not be raised by the administration of thyroid hormone and that there were essential differences in the blood picture and the condition of the autonomic nervous systems, especially between the catatonic and hebephrenic cases. These led me to feel strongly that future research on schizophrenia needed to correlate possible somatic findings, type of disorder, and stage of development with the actual symptomatology.

SCHIZOPHRENIA: DEFINITION

I would like to cite the following lines from my 1926 monograph: "On the basis of these [1926] studies, it must be emphasized here that the tendency which at present prevails among a great number of psychiatrists to let the whole dementia praecox idea be absorbed by the collective designation 'schizophrenia,' is extremely detrimental to the further progress of psychiatry. 'Schizophrenia' is a symptom complex, not a diagnosis. On the other hand, when we speak of catatonia, every psychiatrist and most physicians know what picture of disease we have before us. The same is the case with hebephrenia, which—we have learned from our experiments—is also somatically well correlated." As is well known, since my investigation with the rather simple methods of 45 years ago, intensive research has taken place for the purpose of detecting somatic and psychological factors related to the etiology of schizophrenia. Imposing work has been performed with the help of methods from the natural sciences, experimental and clinical psychology, psychoanalysis, and even existential philosophy. However, in spite of the thousands of investigations, thus far no conclusion has been borne to the point of universal authority by further investigation. This circumstance is, in part, due to the fact that there is no agreement on the characteristics of the schizophrenic disorders.

During the last 25 years I have been visiting many psychiatric hospitals and clinics in Scandinavia, Germany, Austria, Switzerland, Great Britain, and the United States, discussing, among other things, the concept of schizophrenia. The diagnostic term "schizophrenia" differs, unfortunately, not only from country to country, but even from hospital to hospital within a country. While in some places the term was reserved for a group with a quite typical history, symptomatology, and course, this term was in other places a rather comprehensive one including psychoses with a widely varying symptomatology. If researchers on schizophrenia, in reporting their findings, had always indicated the special type and mental state of the disorder instead of merely using the term "schizophrenia," the progress in research on these sorts of disorders would probably have been much greater.

The prognosis for dementia praecox was viewed differently from today in the years before Bleuler proposed, that "dementia praecox" be replaced by "schizophrenia," at the same time extending the latter term to include psychoses of a widely varying origin. At the time of Kraepelin, psychiatrists were interested in follow-up investigations of dementia praecox cases. Researchers of the day were in agreement that the prognosis of this disorder was poor, and the results of follow-up investigations corresponded fairly well to the reports of Kraepelin: in long-term studies, 12.6 percent of the group diagnosed as dementia praecox recovered immediately. Because most of these suffered a relapse within two or three years, the number of *lasting* recoveries amounted to only 2.6 percent. While 17 percent showed a social remission, the rest deteriorated. (Kraepelin cites in his textbook several reports from other experienced psychiatrists who, like Albrecht, Mattouschech, Schmidt, Stern, and Zabloha, had achieved similar results.)

If the percentage of recovery varied a little, it was generally felt before the time of the appearance of the schizophrenia concept that a real cure for dementia praecox was an exception. Most research workers reported that 30–40 percent of the socialized group were more or less able to work, while the rest steadily deteriorated to a degree which made permanent hospitalization or other support necessary. The content of the schizophrenia group, as described by

Bleuler, is in no way identical with that of the dementia praecox group. The latter—and many other psychoses which we now consider to have quite another etiology and symptomatology—were described by Bleuler as belonging to the schizophrenia group. Thus he writes that "in the term 'schizophrenia' are included atypical melancholias and manias of other schools, most of the hallucinatoric confusions, a great deal of what other psychiatrists diagnose as amentia, some types of psychoses described as acute delirium, Wernickes disease, the primary and secondary dementias without any typical picture, most cases of paranoia from other schools, and almost all cases of hypocondriasis with poor prognosis as well as certain nervous, obsessional, and compulsive neuroses. In addition, the diseases described as juvenile and masturbatory as well as the great number of psychoses described by Magnan as degenerative psychoses associated with puberty are included."

Little by little the term "schizophrenia" replaced the term "dementia praecox" all over the world. Because of the diffuse description of its content, however, it is no wonder that the diagnosis has differed tremendously from hospital to hospital. Consequently since 1911, when the term was introduced, most researchers have found the prognosis for schizophrenia to be better than that for dementia praecox. Bellak, for instance, discovered that before shock treatment, improvement rates ranged from 8.8 to 44 percent. Subsequently, Sakel found an 88 percent rate of improvement in cases of schizophrenia treated with insulin comas. There can be no doubt that one of the principal causes of the difference between the course of dementia praecox cases, on the one hand, and the schizophrenias, on the other, is that the schizophrenia group included different syndromes. The reasons for this difference are many, and I shall return to them later.

SCHIZOPHRENIFORM PSYCHOSES

I became more interested in the diagnosis and prognosis of schizophrenia when Sakel announced in 1935 that, through the use of insulin-coma therapy, he had been able to bring about a satisfactory social remission in 88 percent of what, at the Vienna clinic, had been diagnosed as schizophrenia. I was at that time senior psychiatrist at the University Psychiatric Clinic of Oslo. I had the opportunity to make a trip to Vienna, where I was able to study the records of many of the patients treated. From this inspection I concluded rather quickly that a large proportion of the patients who were "schizophrenic" in Vienna would, in Norway, have been diagnosed under other categories: psychogenic psychoses, reactive psychoses, toxic and infective reaction types, as well as psychoses in individuals with organic brain disorders. I also noticed that while patients with such psychoses—which since 1937 I have grouped as "schizophreniform"—as a rule reacted favorably to the treatment, the cases which did not improve corresponded to the cases which at the Oslo clinic were diagnosed as true schizophrenias. Meduna, at the same time, drew a similar conclusion: cases which reacted favorably to metrazole treatment did not belong to the dementia praecox group. I decided upon my return to Oslo to treat ten cases of typical schizophrenia of short duration with insulin-coma therapy in the manner of Sakel. Two of these had a brief remission but relapsed, and all of them had to be transferred to a mental hospital. Follow-up investigation indicated that all had deteriorated severely.

During the following years, the results of more and more investigations of the treatment of schizophrenia with metrazole and insulin shock appeared. All of them, however, had two essential drawbacks: they merely used the term "schizophrenia," without indicating type, symptomatology, or phase of disorder. As a rule, control material was also completely lacking. Thus, I became more and more convinced that most of the cases which recovered after such treatment were those which had a tendency to spontaneous remission, and that they could be helped by other, less dangerous therapy. To prove this, it was necessary, in the first place to get a thorough knowledge of the spontaneous course of the psychoses diagnosed as schizophrenic. As I've said, by then there was a rather comprehensive body of knowledge indicating the course of dementia praecox cases, but statistics relating to the more extensive group of the schizophrenias were rather scanty. Certainly, some interest in this question had been shown, but most of the statistics presented were based only on written reports from either the patients themselves or their relatives. In my book *The Prognosis of Schizophrenia and the Course of the Disease* (1937), I showed how unreliable such reports can be. Comparison of a report like this with a follow-up study of the patient would indicate often that the patient was, for example, severely demented even though according to the report he was well-adjusted. There is not necessarily any contradiction here: the patient's adjustment in the nonstressful home situation may have been adequate or his "queerness" may have become accepted by the family and not noticed by them. In the years after that, therefore, I considered determination of the spontaneous course of those psychoses usually diagnosed as schizophrenic, including individual follow-up investigation, to be an important topic for research. Only with such material at hand would it be possible to estimate, among other things, the value of the different types of shock treatment.

Next, my experiences with the highly variable content of the concept of schizophrenia had made it quite clear to me that the enormous number of papers on the effects of treatment could never be helpful in deciding the question of whether the real schizophrenic disorder had been influenced by the treatment. Conditions seemed to indicate that a therapist who had included many of the typical dementia praecox cases in his concept of schizophrenia would get far fewer remissions than would his colleague whose concept consisted mainly of schizophrenia-like cases belonging to other groups of psychoses regularly connected with a tendency to spontaneous remission. In my opinion, then, this is the principal cause of an 85 percent variation in remission rates: from 3–4 percent to 50–60 percent (as mentioned by Sakel), and on up to as much as 88 percent.

THE DICHOTOMY

It would have been an easy matter to determine the effect of the shock treatment on the true schizophrenias if, at that time— 34 years ago—generally accepted diagnostic criteria of the genuine schizophrenias had existed. But this was not the case. On the contrary, the different psychiatric schools defined schizophrenia in very different ways, a fact which was the natural consequence of Bleuler's broad concept of the psychic pictures included in the term. As already mentioned, in later decades researchers have searched eagerly for a specific cause of schizophrenia and for clues to its diagnosis and prognosis. Thousands of investigations have been performed with methods from the fields of genetics, biochemistry, immunology physiology, and others. Also, experimental psychology and experiments with model psychoses as well as psychoanalytic and existential philosophical approaches have been directed to the establishment of valid diagnostic criteria. There can be no doubt that some of these investigations have led to interesting results. We must, however, bear in mind that these findings, no matter how interesting, have not yet been adequately verified.

In addition, we must also remember that there has not been agreement as to whether the results mentioned are primarily connected with the schizophrenic disorder as such, or if they can be explained more reasonably as secondary or parallel to emotional or other psychic disturbances. One must also assume that if schizophrenia is not a single disease but a conglomerate of different psychotic disorders, it is not reasonable that a single cause of the disorder will be detected. Although the great body of data on the schizophrenic disorders is most interesting, it is impossible to consider it here. Let me, on this point, merely conclude that it is at present of little practical significance to the task of providing clues to diagnosis and prognosis which might be easy to teach medical students and could also be useful in international comparative psychiatry. We must never forget that a principal aim of psychiatric research is to produce information about the psychiatric disorders which will help the practicing physician as well as the psychiatric specialist. I assume that, among other things, psychoanalytical and existential philosophical con-

210

cepts revolving about this question are of more theoretical than practical significance. It would be hopeless, for example, to diagnose schizophrenia on the basis of "the way of life" of the patient. Neither can the capacity for social adjustment be helpful. On the whole, a single aspect of behavior or a single symptom is not a usable basis for diagnosis or prognosis. Most psychiatrists, I assume, now agree that schizophrenia is a multiform disorder in which individually varying, inborn, and exogenic psychic and somatic factors play roles in the production of symptoms and final outcome of the disorder.

Since my somatic studies of schizophrenia in the twenties, I have stressed the significance of restricting the diagnosis of schizophrenia to the group of disorders which, as proven by individual follow-up investigations, have a poor prognosis. The initial advantage of such a diagnostic method is that in reports on schizophrenia research we can compare the same type of disorder internationally. It is also easy to teach students the symptoms related to this diagnosis. By reserving the diagnosis of schizophrenia to the cases which empirically are connected with a poor prognosis, we will, I believe also have much greater chances of detecting possible metabolic and psychological changes characteristic of the group. My proposal in 1937 was that this central group should be termed typical or genuine schizophrenias, while psychoses whose relation to the group was doubtful should be termed schizophreniform psychoses. This dichotomy embraced the advantages outlined above.

CONTRIBUTIONS

I should like now to summarize my own contributions to the diagnosis and prognosis of schizophrenia as well as some comparable, individual follow-up investigations. I had a good starting point because two sorts of "schizophrenia" had already been distinguished at the University Psychiatric Clinic of Oslo, when it opened in 1926. The great influence in Scandinavia of the Kraepelin school led Dr. Vogt, the director of the Oslo Clinic at that time, to stress whether or not a case of schizophrenia belonged to the central dementia praecox group. If so, the diagnosis at discharge was "schizophrenia." If at discharge there was any doubt, one, two, or three question marks were added to the diagnosis. (The more doubt, the more question marks.) In addition, the type of disorder (hebephrenic, catatonic, paranoid) was noted as a subdiagnosis. In the cases with question marks, the other possible diagnoses were added: paranoid-hallucinatory psychosis in an alcoholic, sensitive self-reference psychosis, or confusional psychosis in a feebleminded personality, for example.

Following the course of spontaneous remission

To produce material illustrating the spontaneous course of schizophrenia, I decided, in 1936, to follow up each of 200 schizophrenics who had been hospitalized during the years 1926–29—that is, during a period before shock treatment. One hundred of these had at their discharge been diagnosed as schizophrenias belonging to the central dementia praecox group, while the other hundred had received one or more question marks. These last cases, which in a 1937 monograph I described as schizophreniform psychoses, were—because they involved hallucinations, delusions, and special personality traits, among other things—reminiscent of the true schizophrenias, even though they lacked the central, primary symptoms typical of the classic dementia praecox cases. Many interesting facts were revealed through my follow-up investigations in 1936, a comparison of diagnosis at discharge with information about the mental status of the patient gained at his home, 7–10 years later. Sixty-six of the cases diagnosed as typical schizophrenics at discharge were unchanged or worse, while 17 had completely recovered, and 17 others were improved.

Because a change in the concept of the content of schizophrenic disorders had taken place during the seven to ten years which elapsed between the hospitalization of these patients and re-examination in 1936, I decided to revise the diagnosis of the cases followed up. After such revision it became apparent that out of the 100 cases considered schizophrenia at discharge in 1926–29, 13 were lacking the symptoms which I considered essential to this group in 1936. The final result of this follow-up of the typical schizophrenias—then consisting of 87 cases —was that by 1936, only 6 had recovered completely, while 11 of the 13 cases which were considered schizophreniform had recovered completely, and 2 had improved. Of the group of 100 schizophrenics considered doubtful at discharge in 1926–29, 32 cases had recovered at the follow-up in 1936. Twenty-five had improved, and 43 were unchanged or worse. After the later revision of the diagnosis, however, it appeared that of the 100 schizophrenia-like or schizophreniform psychoses, 45 had revealed a history and symptomatology which—in 1936—was considered characteristic of the central group. Of these 45 cases only one had recovered and 8 improved by the follow-up in 1936. Of the 55 schizophreniform cases still diagnosed as such at the re-examination, 31 had recovered and 17 improved, while only 7 were unchanged or worse.

If we summarize the outcome of the total number of psychoses, we find—taking into account the diagnosis at the follow-up in 1936—that of 132 typical cases of schizophrenia, 102 had remained unchanged or worse, 7 had recovered, and the remainder, 23, had improved. On the other hand, of the total number of schizophreniform psychoses —68 cases—only 17 were worse or unchanged, while 42 had recovered and 19 had improved. These results seem to indicate convincingly that by dividing the large schizophrenia group into typical and schizophreniform cases, we had succeeded in differentiating between two prognostically widely varying groups of the psychotic disorders regularly diagnosed as schizophrenia. We can learn from this follow-up that the best clue to a valid prognostication is a demonstration of the presence of central symptoms which empirically indicate a poor prognosis. If such symptoms are not present in the initial stages, the course cannot be predicted with the same accuracy.

In this connection I must mention, however, what Stromgren has stressed in a special paper on the schizophreniform psychoses, that although the term "schizophreniform" has now certainly been widespread through the literature, different meanings have been assigned to it. The term "schizophreniform psychoses" should only indicate that we have to do with a psychosis which is characterized by a schizophrenia-like picture, but without such symptoms of schizophrenia as regularly are connected with a poor prognosis. In the early stages of such psychoses it may be difficult to detect the typical schizophrenic symptoms, and as a consequence of this several cases of schizophreniform psychoses may develop in the direction of schizophrenic deterioration. Most cases of schizophreniform psychoses, however, belong to other types of psychoses. This term does not represent—as some writers assume—a distinct diagnostic entity.

It need only be added that from my studies it emerged that in addition to the symptomatology in the initial stages, several other factors—such as bodily constitution and temperament type, age of outbreak and duration of the psychosis from outbreak until admission to the hospital, precipitating external factors, and whether there was acute or gradual onset—might in the single case have some prognostic significance. It was proven statistically that acute onset and external precipitating factors were prognostically favorable factors, but in the single case it is the constellation of the different signs and symptoms which indicates the further course.

Diagnosis

Initial changes in the personality and the acute mental symptomatology are, in my experience, the most general and best clues to a diagnosis of the genuine schizophrenic type regularly connected with a poor prognosis. Changes in the personality, which are rather characteristic in many of the typical cases of schizophrenia, manifest themselves as a special type of emotional blunting followed by lack of initiative and altered, frequently peculiar behavior. In hebephrenia especially these changes are quite characteristic and are a principal clue to the diagnosis. The changes which take place are frequently more difficult to describe than to recognize, but the experienced psychiatrist regularly feels intuitively that he is confronted with a morbid personality of the genuine schizophrenic type. In catatonic types, the history as well as the typical signs in periods of restlessness and stupor (with negativism, oily facies, catalepsy, special vegetative symptoms, and so on) are frequently so characteristic that no doubt can exist that the case belongs to the typical schizophrenia type.

The greatest difficulty arises in connection with the diagnosis of paranoid cases of schizophrenia. Especially as described by Retterstol in his monograph on paranoid and paranoiac psychoses, the paranoid syndrome appears in most types of psychoses, and—as a whole—the prognosis for these disorders does not seem to be unfavorable. Consequently, it is important in the initial stages of a paranoid disorder to be able to decide whether it is a case belonging to the prognostically unfavorable central group of schizophrenias, or whether it is a psychosis with a more favorable course. Even in recent times, a psychosis characterized by paranoid ideas and hallucinations is in many hospitals diagnosed as schizophrenia, even if none of the symptoms which indicate a progressive course with deterioration are present. In my follow-up investigations, it was proved that the paranoid psychoses which regularly were associated with a poor prognosis were characterized by essential symptoms of split personality (or "depersonalization symptoms") and a loss of reality feeling ("derealization symptoms"). In addition, Kraepelin's cases of dementia praecox characterized by primary—in contrast to secondary—delusions had an unfavorable course. I cannot here describe in detail the symptoms characteristic of the depersonalization and derealization states. I shall only stress the fact that for the typical signs of schizophrenia it is not enough that the patient talk about being influenced by forces from the outer world, or that he entertain strange ideas about his surroundings. He must—as stressed by Mauz—really experience these influences. It should be emphasized that mild depersonalization and derealization symptoms may occur as transient symptoms in neuroses and in some psychoses, especially those connected with confusional states. If no sign of organic brain disorder, infection, or intoxication can be demonstrated, however, a mental picture dominated by what I have described as depersonalization and derealization is characteristic of the genuine cases of paranoid schizophrenia associated with a poor prognosis.

Thus, the significant clues to a diagnosis of the genuine types of schizophrenic disorder are a typical break in personality development, emotional blunting, and catatonic restlessness and stupor, as well as the symptoms of depersonalization and derealization. If we restrict the diagnosis "schizophrenia" to these groups, we can, with high probability, predict an unfavorable course. According to my proposal all psychoses which—because they involve hallucinations and delusions—may have a superficial similarity with the genuine schizophrenias but are lacking the essential symptoms of these, should be diagnosed as schizophreniform psychoses. The question of confusional or emotionally abnormal states and many paranoid psychoses will be important here. Many psychoses in feebleminded, hysterical, obsessional, and hypersensitive individuals are characterized by delusions and hallucinations, but they lack other symptoms of the true schizophrenias as defined above. In international literature, cases which should be considered belonging to the group of schizophreniform psychoses have different names such as oneirophrenia, schizoaffective states, acute confusional states, ambulatoric schizophrenia, sensitive delusions, pseudoneurotic or pseudopsychopatic schizophrenias, and others. The reason these cases are often diagnosed as schizophrenia is probably that the personality types in question contribute to the subjective symptomatology. Some features—schizoid traits, emotional flattening, ideas of reference, for example—can resemble genuine schizophrenic symptoms. The further course of these cases, however, have been proven by many researchers to be much more favorable than are true cases of genuine schizophrenia.

Second follow-up: The course of spontaneous remission

I arrived at the above conclusions by studying the spontaneous course of cases of schizophrenia which had been submitted to only the usual types of therapy during the years 1926–29. As it was of interest to make

213

a similar follow-up of cases treated with one or another type of shock treatment, or with lobotomy, my senior psychiatrists, L. Eitinger and C. L. Laane at the University Psychiatric Clinic of Oslo, and I agreed to carry out such a comparison. The follow-up was carried through the year 1955. It dealt with 783 patients hospitalized during the years 1940–49. Every patient was re-examined by questionnaire, and also 154 of these patients were re-examined individually by Drs. Eitinger and Laane. In my discussion here I shall limit my remarks only to the 154 individually examined patients. My assistants and I had agreed that in this follow-up I would confine myself to diagnosis and prediction on the basis of the records of hospitalization, while they would actually travel around and perform the re-examinations. Thus, I made up my mind as to whether the case should be considered a typical schizophrenia or a schizophreniform psychosis and, at the same time, indicated whether recovery, improvement, or lack of change was the most probable outcome. After the cases were followed up, my prognostication was compared to the actual results 5 to 15 years after discharge had taken place.

We found that for those treated with electrical shock, insulin coma, or lobotomy, the outcome was much better in the schizophreniform cases than in the genuine schizophrenias. The correspondence between my prognostication and the real facts as determined independently by my assistants was good. Of the 110 cases diagnosed by me as typical schizophrenias, 105 had, according to the statements of my assistants, developed as such—101 of them had deteriorated, while 4 had recovered or were improved. On the other hand, of 39 schizophreniform psychoses, 14 were essentially unchanged, while the rest had recovered or were much improved. It seems reasonable, therefore, to draw the conclusion that cases of typical schizophrenia treated differently in the long run do not have a more favorable course than untreated cases. On the other hand, many schizophreniform psychoses seem to recover after different treatment.

CORROBORATING RESEARCH

Little by little, the dichotomy into genuine schizophrenias and schizophreniform psy-

choses attracted interest, especially among Scandinavian psychiatrists. Several papers and some monographs have been published in which the results of different kinds of therapy and follow-up investigations have been related to the two groups. In a 1962 monograph by Astrup, Fossum, and Holmboe, the result of a follow-up of 1,102 patients during the years 1955–60 is reported. The patients had been hospitalized during the years 1938–50 and had been subjected to the usual shock treatment. From this publication I would like to quote the following: "Whereas the primary symptoms of Bleuler are rather vaguely defined, the process-symptoms of Langfeldt are as a rule so clear-cut that they can be established when present. In our previous publication we could show, like Langfeldt, that when process-symptoms are not present, the risk of a schizophrenic deterioration is very small. One could therefore agree with Langfeldt that psychoses without process symptoms should not be diagnosed as schizophrenias. When process symptoms were present, there was always a considerable risk of schizophrenic deterioration." In this study, of the schizophreniform cases without classical schizophrenic symptoms, 78 percent recovered, while of the nuclear group of schizophrenia, only 13 to 20 percent recovered.

Retterstol (1966), reporting his follow-up of different types of psychoses, has stated that only in two out of 31 cases of schizophrenia was the diagnosis changed. He concluded therefore that on the basis of the process-symptoms it should be possible to differentiate between process-schizophrenia and schizophreniform psychoses 90 to 95 percent of the time.

In 1961 Achte published a monograph on the course of schizophrenia and the schizophreniform psychoses from Lapinlahti Hospital in Finland. His population consisted of 100 patients who had been hospitalized in 1930 and 100 patients hospitalized in 1950. During the years 1950–60 he followed up on the 132 cases which could at that time be traced. He writes that "The criteria conform by and large to Langfeldt's [1953] concept of the primary symptoms of schizophrenia. On the other hand, if the patient had displayed none of them, the case is regarded as schizophreniform psychosis." It is further stated that the classification was carried out by relying upon the entries in the case records and without any knowledge of the post-hospital progress of the patient. According to the classification, 70 percent of the 1930 patients belonged to the group of schizophrenias; the corresponding figure for the 1950 material was 54 percent.

I cannot go into the details of the result of the follow-up of these cases four years after the discharge, but Achte states: "If account is taken of all the patients who had social remissions within four years, on the one hand, the prognosis of the patients with schizophreniform disease pictures was significantly better (0.1 percent) than the diagnosis of those affected by typical schizophrenias. This holds good for the materials of both decades." And further: "It can accordingly be concluded that typical schizophrenia is rarely cured even by methods which are in use at our clinic today." The author adds, however, that if the typical signs of schizophrenia are not present in the initial stages of the disorder, it is difficult to make a dependable prognosis regarding the course of the psychosis in question.

Eva Johanson (1958) has carried through a similar follow-up investigation in Sweden of 100 cases of typical schizophrenias, 27 patients with uncertain schizophrenias, and 11 cases in which the psychoses had not been considered as schizophrenic at all. The prognosis of the typical cases was highly unfavorable, for only one case could be considered "recovered" and eight additional cases were considered predominantly favorable. The prognosis in the uncertain or schizophreniform psychoses was significantly better, and the author concludes that the differences between the two groups are so large that "there seems to be good reason for a separation."

Stromgren and Welner have described in a 1958 paper a genetic and clinical study of a benign group of schizophreniform psychoses differentiated from the main group of more or less malignant schizophrenias by means of clinical criteria. Seventy-two patients carefully diagnosed as schizophreniform psychoses were observed from 1.5 to 20 years, 8.8 years on the average. The follow-up showed that the cases were either cured or suffered from nonschizophrenic psychopathology. The conclusion of this study is that "the family picture indicates that the psychoses concerned are not manifestations of a specific genetic factor. From a genetic point of view, there seems, therefore, to be good reason to keep the typical schizophrenias in a separate group."

Finally, it should be pointed out that in England a comprehensive follow-up investigation of schizophrenic and schizophreniform psychoses has been carried through by Roth and his associates. Over three years they followed up 1,100 cases classified as schizophrenic and 72 as schizophreniform psychoses: "In a survey of the results of treatment in all patients admitted to hospitals in the northeast of England, it was found that schizophreniform psychoses, differentiated by criteria similar to those of Langfeldt, responded to some forms of treatment including a combination of *ECT* and tranquilizing drugs more favorable than schizophrenic cases, as judged by status on discharge and length of span in hospital. Readmission rates were also substantially lower for schizophreniform cases, although the differences are not statistically significant."

CONCLUSION

Psychiatrists in different countries have been able to differentiate between the typical or genuine schizophrenias and the schizophrenia-like psychoses I have called schizophreniform. Researchers have arrived at the conclusion that the typical schizophrenias have a much poorer prognosis, with or without treatments, than is the case with schizophreniform psychoses. I am personally convinced that if researchers in the field of psychiatry, in the teaching of students, in research, and in practical clinical psychiatry would always adhere to the dichotomy I proposed, psychiatry would profit much from it. In all types of schizophrenia research the findings must be correlated with the special symptomatology in the two groups, schizophrenia and schizophreniform psychoses.

To avoid misunderstandings, I would like to close by stressing that the poor prognosis of typical cases of schizophrenia should not result in a pessimistic attitude toward the possibility of rehabilitation and a better social adjustment for these patients. Occupational therapy, psychotherapy, and pharmacotherapy are certainly useful in this regard. Scientific evidence that the basic schizophrenic disorders can be effectively and lastingly cured is still lacking, however. The great hope is that metabolic disorders, possibly different in various types of genuine schizophrenia, will be detected and that treatment of these disorders will return the patient to complete health.

REFERENCES

Achte, K. A. Der Verlauf der Schizophrenien und der Schizopreniformen Psychosen. *Acta psych. Scand.*, Suppl. 155, 1961.

Astrup C., Fossum, A., & Holmboe, R. *Prognosis in functional psychosis. Clinical, social and genetic aspects.* Springfield, Ill.: Charles C Thomas, 1962.

Bellak, L. *Schizophrenia.* New York: Logos Press, 1958.

Johanson, Eva. A study of schizophrenia in the male. A psychiatric and social study based on 138 cases with follow-up. *Acta psych. Scand.*, Suppl. 125, 1958.

Langfeldt, G. The endocrine glands and the autonomic systems in dementia praecox. Bergen, Norway: J. W. Eide, 1926.

Langfeldt, G. Clinical and experimental investigations on the relation between internal secretions and dem. praecox. *Acta medica Scand.* Suppl. XVI, 1926.

Langfeldt, G. Die Insulin-Schockbehandlung der Schizophrenie Psych-Neurol. Wochenschrift. nr. 38, 1936.

Langfeldt, G. The prognosis in schizophrenia and the factors influencing the course of the disease. Monograph. London: Humphrey Melford, 1937.

Langfeldt, G. Neue Gesichtspunkte zur Bewertung der Insulinschock Therapie bei Schizophrenie. Monatschr. fur Psych. und Neurol. Ed. 98. P. 352, 1938.

Langfeldt, G. The schizophreniform states. Monograph. London: Humphrey Melford, 1939.

Langfeldt, G. Zur Frage der spontanen Remissionen der Schizophreniformen Psychosen mit besonderer Berücksichtigung der Frage nach der Dauer dieser Remissionen. Zeitschr. f. d. g. Neurol. und Psych. 164 Bd. 4 H, 1939.

Langfeldt, G. The clinical subdivision of the schizophrenia group. Premiér Congrès mondial de Psychiatrie. Compt. rendues des séances. Paris: Hermann & Cie, 1950.

Langfeldt, G. The diagnosis of schizophrenia. *Americ. J. Psych.*, 1951, 108.

Langfeldt, G. Modern viewpoints on the symptomatology and diagnostics of schizophrenia. *Acta Psych. et Neurol. Scand.*, Suppl. 80, 1953.

Langfeldt, G., Ford, L., Mazzitelli, Helen, Rohan, Anne Marie. Comparative diagnostic considerations and prognostic evaluations of electro-shock and insulin coma treatments. A Norwegian-American psychiatric-psychological teamwork. *Amer. J. Psych.*, 1955.

Langfeldt, G. La portée d'une dichotomie du groupe des schizophrénies. L'Evolution Psychiatrique No. 2, 1966.

Retterstöl, N. *Paranoid and paranoiac psychoses.* Springfield, Ill.: Charles C Thomas, 1966.

Strömgren, E. Schizophreniform psychoses. Celebration volume for Gabriel Langfeldt. *Act. Psych. Scand.* Vol. 41, fasc. 3, 1965.

Welner, J., & Strömgren, E. Clinical and genetic studies on benign schizophreniform psychoses based on a follow-up. *Act. Psych. Scand.* 33, 377–399, 1958.

1969 DEAN RESEARCH AWARD

MANFRED EUGEN BLEULER *is currently Professor of Psychiatry at the University of Zurich and Director of the University Psychiatric Clinic. Son of Eugen Bleuler, the specialist who first defined schizophrenia, Dr. Bleuler attended the University of Geneva and the University of Zurich. He also studied in the United States, where he held positions at the Boston Psychotherapic Hospital, Boston City Hospital, and the Westchester Division of New York Hospital. During his prestigious career in research on and treatment of schizophrenia, Dr. Bleuler has served as Chief Psychiatric Physician at Heilanstalt, St. Pirmingsberg, and at the University Clinic at Basel. In the United States, he also served as guest lecturer at Cornell University. His most recent publications include* **Die Schizophrenen Geisteskrankenheiten im Lichte Langer Kranken und Ehmiliengeschickten,** *1970, and* **Eugen Bleuler, Lerbuch der Psychiatrie** *(11th Edition: 1968).*

SOME RESULTS OF RESEARCH IN SCHIZOPHRENIA

by Manfred Bleuler

∽

It would be quite inappropriate for me to give you an over-all presentation of the problems of schizophrenia on such an occasion. Rather, I should like to discuss some of the results of the research carried out by myself and others at Burghölzli.

RESEARCH AIMS

Our research has been directed towards three important areas. We have followed the history of the psychosis and the life-history of patients as well as the life histories of their close relatives over long periods, mainly, decades. We have tested various influences on the course of the psychosis, particularly that of the therapy, but also the effect from other sources, such as the loss of relatives, long periods of hospitalization, and so on. The main work within these boundaries has been a study of 208 schizophrenics who were admitted to the Burghölzli Clinic in 1942–43. All of these patients, as well as their parents, siblings, spouses, and offspring, were followed until 1963–64, or until death.

We have investigated how essential a role physical damage plays in the genesis of schizophrenia. Because I wanted to know how frequently and to what degree schizophrenic or similar complications arose in somatic patients, I examined the sequelae of the most varying physical dis-turbances. If somatic damage is important in the genesis of schizophrenia, then schizophrenic or similar psychoses could be expected to occur among physical patients. I have been particularly interested in the psychopathology of all kinds of endocrine illnesses.

SPECIFIC STUDIES

Throughout my career, I have felt that one knows the patient he has personally treated best, and so the great majority of schizophrenics in my research have been my own personal patients. From these, I have selected a few who I think merit attention here. These consist mainly of the 208 schizophrenics and their families mentioned above. I shall discuss schizophrenic psychoses which endured for decades, their therapy, research on their etiology, and the fate of the schizophrenic's offspring. But I shall not here document these with specific figures: all the correlations and exact citations appear in my writings and I refer the interested to those sources.[1]

Diagnosis

We should not speak of the course of schizophrenia without commenting on diag-

[1] A selected bibliography of Dr. Bleuler's research may be found on p. 218.

nosis. As you are well aware, the term "schizophrenia" is frequently misused: there are still some who use this diagnosis only for the most severe, incurable, and deteriorating psychoses. Others use it in such a wide sense that almost all of us could be called schizophrenic. In Europe, at least, it is becoming more and more usual to call a politician schizophrenic when one does not agree with him.

The diagnosis of schizophrenia must be reserved for real psychoses. It entails an extremely severe alteration of the personality, at least temporarily. If we judge from our own everyday experience and that of our healthy fellowmen, we cannot understand the thoughts, feelings, and behavior of a psychotic. This does not exclude the possibility of an understanding during careful psychiatric treatment. People who are well-characterized, so-called originals, schizoids, psychopaths, nervous subjects, and so on are not included in my diagnosis of schizophrenia.

Criteria. What kinds of psychoses do we then acknowledge as being schizophrenias? Most important for diagnosis is the double life in the schizophrenic: behind or beside psychotic phenomena, signs of a normal intellectual and emotional life can be discovered. Furthermore, I have made the diagnosis of schizophrenia only if at least three of the following signs were present: (a) typical schizophrenic dissociation of thought; (b) typical alterations of emotional expressions; (c) catatonic symptoms; and (d) delusions or hallucinations of the sort usual in schizophrenia. Psychoses with amnesic symptoms, with thought disorders of the organic type, or with somnolence are never considered to be schizophrenic. Conjectures as to the course and prognosis should not be considered when the diagnosis is being made. Much more could be said with regard to diagnosis. It is sufficient to state here that, with the above mentioned diagnostic criteria in mind, a large majority of psychiatrists agree concerning the diagnosis "schizophrenia" in a large proportion of patients.

Course

Schizophrenia used to be considered a disease that was, generally speaking, progressive in nature. However, such an assumption was based mainly on the observation of hospitalized, chronic patients. My own investigations give quite another picture. They have been carried out on unselected patients, and they have also included all the patients who were discharged after hospitalization. *On an average the psychosis shows no change for the worse after a duration of five years.* Twenty, 25, and more years after the onset of psychosis, the proportion of recovered to improved and to unimproved patients remains the same as five years after onset. This statement is just as valid if we take hospitalization, earning capacity, or general psychiatric findings as a criterion. After the fifth year of the psychosis, about one-fourth of the schizophrenics are always still hospitalized and three-fourths are not. It is important to add that the one-fourth who remain hospitalized does not always consist of the same patients. Many patients are hospitalized for a certain time, discharged, and later readmitted. What remains stable is only the proportion of hospitalized as compared to nonhospitalized patients.

I shall select only two figures from my statistics in regard to the social condition of schizophrenics decades after the onset of the disease: after the fifth year, about half the former patients live outside the hospital without special care or treatment; only about 10 percent live permanently in hospital wards for severe and moderately severe cases. It is not always the same patients who are hospitalized. These figures are valid at least for Switzerland in the middle of this century.

Of more general value is the evaluation of the course on the basis of an over-all psychiatric assessment. More than a quarter of the patients still develop acute episodes 20 to 40 years after the onset of the psychosis, and they improve or again recover from these. Such patients never attain any long-standing stable condition; however, more than half—perhaps even three-quarters—do attain stability some years after onset: between a fourth and a third of these are definite recoveries. It should be added, however, that no chronic schizophrenic conditions are entirely stable. If we observe old schizophrenics carefully, we always see fluctuations of their conditions. What is surprising and unexpected is a further observation: late changes in the condition of old schizophrenics are more frequently improvements than deteriorations. Improvements in chronic schizophrenics 20, 30, and more years after onset of the psychosis are frequent, and in rare cases we even see late recoveries.

Careful observation also shows that even decades after onset, schizophrenics quite frequently show reactions to environmental changes which make psychological sense. I shall mention only one pertinent example which impressed me very much. After the death of a near relative, the psychotic condition of a schizophrenic is often altered. Whether the condition is improved or impaired depends upon the type of relationship the patient had to the decreased: if the patient was dependent upon the decreased in an infantile manner and if he did not fight against his dependence, the death of the protective person is usually followed by impairment. This is not the case if the patient had a highly ambivalent and painful relationship to the deceased, if he fought against his dependence, if he sought protection and at the same time hated the protection and the protector. In such a case, the death of a relative can be followed by the improvement of a chronic schizophrenic.

All these findings together give us the modern picture of schizophrenic psychoses. The general, average course of the disease during decades is not toward progressive deterioration, not toward petrification, not toward dementia, not toward the loss of all human qualities and a mere vegetative existence. On the contrary, whereas it was formerly thought that the outcome of real schizophrenia would always be complete deterioration if the patient lived long enough, today we have reason to hope, rather, that all schizophrenics could recover if they lived long enough. Research on the clinical course of the illness confirms what clinicians realized long ago: in the schizophrenic, the healthy human is hidden and remains hidden, even if the psychosis last long. The healthy life of schizophrenics is never extinguished. How different such an observation is from what we see in patients with chronic brain diseases!

Therapy

If we survey the successes and the failures of most therapies, not only some months or years afterwards, but also two and more decades later, we can no longer believe that in one specific therapeutic procedure is the correct one. We rather see that any procedure may either succeed or fail. Each therapeutic technique may be successful if it accomplishes one or more of the following results: (a) helps to introduce the patient to an active community; (b) confronts him suddenly with new responsibilities or severe dangers; or (c) helps him to quiet down and relax. These aims must be striven for. It is of secondary importance what technique in the service of these aims is chosen.

(a) An active community may be built up in very different ways: in many cases, initially during the personal psychotherapy, and then later in group psychotherapy with a physician or an occupational therapist as leader. Life in a ward of the hospital should in itself be group therapy. Sometimes the family of the patient can be a good therapeutic community, for instance if the members work together in agriculture or in a family business. In other cases, a first contact between the patient, his nurses, and his doctors might best be initiated during somatic therapy.

(b) Confrontation with a new and threatening situation even in the healthy mobilizes emotional and somatic defensive forces. The effects of electroshock and of other shock therapies probably arise mainly from such a mobilization. Even more important than somatic shock is sudden confrontation with a new and surprising social situation demanding action: giving the patient unexpected responsibilities, early discharge from the hospital, sudden change of hospitals, and so on. Surprising and appropriate interpretation in direct psychotherapeutic analysis can have the same effect.

(c) Quiet and orderly surroundings as well as regularity in the day's schedule have a tranquilizing influence. The way in which physicians, nurses, and relatives speak with the patient and react to his morbid behavior is of great importance. They have to be natural and must behave as they actually are and as they feel, but at the same time, they must feel and must show a stable and mature kind of sympathy. Their personalities must enable them to remain calm and benevolent when confronted with wild outbursts and resistance.

Every measure which results in introducing a schizophrenic to an active community, in shaking him out of his autism, or in calming down his excitation may be helpful. Choice of special therapeutic techniques and of their sequence has to be adapted to the most personal needs and to the momentary condition of the patient.

RESULTS

I have compared the outcome of the 208 schizophrenic patients from my main studies to the outcome of other patients who had fallen ill some decades earlier. The resultant statistics enable us to compare the efficiencies of former and more recent treatments. The result of such a comparison corresponds to the impression of most clinicians. It seems certain that:

1. The most severe forms of schizophrenia can be prevented by appropriate therapy. I refer to the psychoses which start early in life with an acute episode, followed without improvement by a life-long chronic condition. This form of psychosis, which used to be frequent at the beginning of the century, is less common now.
2. All schizophrenic conditions can at least be improved and alleviated by therapy.
3. With the help of therapy, episodic courses with good intermissions are becoming more frequent, and chronic psychoses with constant hospitalization, rarer.
These are encouraging statements. Two further statements are less so:
4. My statistics do not indicate that the number of permanent, full recoveries has increased since the improvement of therapeutic methods.
5. The statistics do not show that the number of severe chronic psychoses is diminished by therapy.

Such a lack of statistical evidence does not exclude the possibility that in some cases therapy results in permanent full recovery of otherwise chronic patients. These fortunate results, however, are not frequent enough to be visible in statistics.

Nobody denies that the introduction of neuroleptic drugs was an important step in the progress of schizophrenic therapy. Reliable statistics demonstrate that the prognosis of the disease some months or even some years after its onset is best if the patients have been put on neuroleptics after admission to hospital. On the other hand I should like to point out that none of my 208 patients took neuroleptics for long periods. Despite the lack of longstanding medication, the percentage of steady recoveries is great. If we consider such an observation and if we also consider the many dangers of neuroleptic medication for long periods, we shall be cautious in its application. We can dispense with permanent administration of drugs more frequently than usual. However, there are some patients in whom new acute attacks can only be prevented by medication lasting many years. In other instances a chronic psychosis can only be kept under a certain control with permanent medication.

THE GENESIS AND NATURE OF SCHIZOPHRENIA

A good deal of my clinical work has been devoted to investigating the conditions under which schizophrenia develops. Like most clinicians, I have abandoned the idea that one single cause of the disease can be discovered. There must be a combination of many different conditions in the background of schizophrenia.

Clinical experience compels me first to make a negative statement: I have studied very carefully the endocrinological functions of schizophrenics and the psychopathology of endocrine patients. Clinical experience can easily be summarized in the statement: Endocrine patients are not schizophrenics and schizophrenics are not endocrine patients. We studied not only the psychopathology of endocrine patients but also the psychopathology of many other severe acute somatic patients in general hospital practice. If they became mentally disturbed, it was not, as a rule, in the same way schizophrenics did.

Genesis

One of the most profound experiences a physician can have is to plunge into the study of the lives of schizophrenics and their relatives. He feels as if he were caught up in a fatal destiny, in a tragedy which follows logical lines. Frequently, the person who later became a patient was a problem child of problem parents. We can follow step-by-step how the child influenced his parents, and how the parents affected their child, in unhealthy ways. As he grows, the child becomes more difficult, more afflicted, more dependent, and more insecure. Growing up as a harmonious personality becomes more and more impossible for the child, and being a good parent becomes more and more impossible for the parents. If new demands are made on the unity and harmony of the personality, on the constancy and harmony of the ego, the psychosis breaks out in a way that seems to be fatal. Many clinicians have had the same impression. It has frequently and carefully been described in the psychoanalytical and phenomenological literature.

I suffer doubts when I consider critically my impression that the disease develops clearly as the consequence of the actions and reactions of the patient's personality to his human environment. Can we explain such a tremendous disaster as becoming schizophrenic by simple psychological conclusions, just as we explain everyday experiences with our healthy acquaintances? Similar doubts lead many physicians to refuse to consider that schizophrenia could be psychogenic. Jaspers comes to the conclusion that it is not from philosophic considerations. I know that these same doubts do not play the same dominant role in American psychiatry.

As the physician of a schizophrenic whom I have studied carefully, I am tormented again and again with this great question: Have I discovered the actual etiology or have I imagined it? Can I deduce the causes of the psychosis from psychological principles? Is an apparent psychodynamic explanation the right one? Confronted with these questions, I feel myself compelled to look for answers in every possible way.

Statistical considerations are important to the study of the problem. I investigated the frequencies of many kinds of psychological stress in the life histories of schizophrenics and compared them to their frequencies in the life histories of other patients and of healthy people. I could not find an outstanding specific stress situation in the history of all schizophrenics which was not also common in the history of many other people. Certainly misery of any kind is more frequent in the premorbid lives of schizophrenics than in the general population, but not more frequent than in the lives of patients with neurotic or psychopathic development, or with drug or alcohol problems. Widespread inquiries, including the questioning of 3,355 persons, showed, for instance, that a broken home is on the average not more common in the histories of schizophrenics than in the population as a whole.

In spite of all this, the search for statistical correlations with possible psychogenic bases for the illness has not been useless. If the correlations failed to explain schizophrenia clearly and simply as a psychological problem, they have confirmed, nevertheless, that at least some psychological reactions in many cases have some significance for its etiology. My statistics showed, for instance, that many types of worry about a loved person have different incidences in schizophrenic men from schizophrenic women. Early loss of a parent which increased tension in the relationship with the remaining parent during childhood, and education by schizophrenic parents or by foster parents are more frequent in female than in male schizophrenics. The pathogenic significance of emotional stresses in the parental family is further demonstrated by another observation: among schizophrenics who have schizophrenic siblings, there are more women than men. We must conclude that familial worries during childhood are more important for the genesis of the psychosis in girls than in boys (or only important in girls). A similar observation can be made after onset of the disease: dramatic alterations of the psychotic condition after the death of the father, the mother, the husband, or a loved one are more frequent in women than in men.

All this seems to indicate that disturbed relationships with the family members are significant for the development of schizophrenia in women. Statistics demonstrate that causal relationships do exist. In schizophrenic men the relationships to other men, to managers, and to subordinates probably play a similar role.

Statistics up to now do not prove that

schizophrenia is a psychogenetic disease. They only suggest that some psychological developments participate in the genesis of the psychosis. This is not much, but it is an encouragement when we are meditating and pondering over a life history and when we are trying to identify ourselves with our schizophrenic patient.

Hereditary predisposition

It is not possible in all cases to trace a convincing story of psychological dynamics. Most resistant to any psychological explanation are the benign, acute, phasic forms of schizophrenia. We are frequently quite perplexed when we try to discover the psychodynamics of a sudden acute new episode which arises in a seemingly recovered patient. These phasic schizophrenic psychoses frequently lack a convincing psychological background which often characterizes manic-depressive psychoses. There are also reasons to assume that hereditary predispositions are more decisive for these forms of illness.

It is impossible to find in the life history of schizophrenics any psychotraumatic situation to which only schizophrenics and not also many non-schizophrenic people were exposed. Nobody has been successful in discovering a specific psychotraumatic situation in the background of schizophrenia. Psychological and environmental reasons and psychodynamics are, therefore, not sufficient in themselves to explain schizophrenia. We must postulate other dispositions and we cannot find any others but personal sensibilities due to hereditary predispositions.

I cannot discuss here in detail the hereditary background of schizophrenia but should only like to point out that it should be considered differently from the way it was viewed during the last half century. The view that schizophrenia is transmitted from one generation to the next through a pathogenic gene, according to Mendel's law, has become quite improbable. Family histories and the number of schizophrenics among relatives of schizophrenics do not support such an assumption. A further important argument against the Men-

delian theory of schizophrenia is found in the fact that schizophrenics are much less fertile in comparison to the general population. I was able to confirm this finding of earlier authors. Diminished fertility in a disease of the frequency of schizophrenia, if it resulted from one or two pathogenic genes, would presuppose a much higher mutation rate than has ever been observed. We can exclude the possibility that the essential background of schizophrenia consists in one or a few pathogenic genes which influence the brain by an error of metabolism.

On the contrary, however, there is much evidence for the assumption that the hereditary background of schizophrenia is given by many genes. These might not be pathogenic in themselves. The hereditary predisposition might rather consist of a lack of harmony among different inborn dispositions, an incompatibility of certain constellations of genes.

On the basis of what we know and leaving out speculations, we can summarize our present knowledge about the nature and genesis of schizophrenia: the background of schizophrenia consists in both dysharmonic, contradictory inborn dispositions in the development of the personality, and dysharmonic, contradictory human relationships. An unsound human environment reinforces the contradictions in the personality and the unsound personality creates contradictory attitudes towards the later patient. He gets sick when confronted with severe demands. Therapeutic experience confirms this theory: the same influences which help the schizophrenic, develop a strong and resistant personality in the healthy: being a member of a community, in which we can use hands and brains, at times confrontation with difficulties and dangers and enough time to calm down and relax.

THE CHILDREN OF SCHIZOPHRENICS

An important part of my interest and of my research has been devoted to the children of schizophrenics. Their expectation of health and happiness, according to other authors, is poor. Kallman, for instance, found that 15 percent of them were destined to become schizophrenic, many of them schizoid, and psychopathic, while only about one-third could be expected to be normal.

In my own experience, 9 percent of the children of schizophrenics themselves become schizophrenic, if they grow to maturity. Some other authors agree. On the other hand, I found many more healthy children and fewer psychopathic children than did most other authors. Nearly three quarters of the children of my schizophrenics are healthy. It is interesting to look for the reasons behind such a tremendous difference between the findings of most other authors and myself. The main reason is to be found, I believe, in the way I became acquainted with these children, which was quite different from that of the other authors. I was the physician responsible for treating the schizophrenics and often also their children. I knew the life history and the living conditions of these children. Other authors who have investigated the children of schizophrenics have carefully collected information with regard to unsound personality traits. The result of the two types of observation must be different: a collection of unhappy personality types easily gives the picture of a psychopathic personality— if one does not consider the terrible living conditions to which these personality types were a reaction. A timid, retiring, and moody child might be called a psychopath, but not if one knows that his paranoid mother has isolated this child from any contact with other children and other people, that she even keeps him away from school, and warns him all day long against delusional persecutors. I admire the love of these children for their sick mothers and fathers, their endeavors to help them, and their fight for a suitable position in life in spite of the tremendous restraints and sufferings conferred upon them by their parents' psychoses. Compared to these healthy aspects of their personality, the unhealthy ones have often seemed to me to be insignificant.

The further life history of these children frequently demonstrates that, when the immediate influence of the schizophrenic parent had ceased, they developed into healthy and able adults. They had not been psychopathic, but had shown a quite natural reaction to a terrifying stress situation, and were able after it was over to overcome their difficulties.

We must esteem the great energy with which most children of schizophrenics fight their way toward a good social position in life, in spite of tremendous difficulties. The large majority of the children of my schizophrenics who have grown up have achieved what can be expected from their schooling and professional training, and have reached the social standard of their parents or have even surpassed it. Some of them seem to have been hardened and to have developed strong personalities because of the hardships of their childhood.

Until recently, the interest in the children of schizophrenics has been concentrated upon their mental health. Their suffering in itself, however, has not been described and considered enough. Their care and education are often neglected to an unbelievable degree. It is true that many schizophrenic parents can love their children and be very kind to them, but it is also true that many others maltreat their children, both physically and morally. The children suffer even more from the ambivalent attitude of their parents than from their constant cruelty. Many healthy parents are not able to protect their children from ill treatment at the hands of psychotics. The children of schizophrenics are also frequently cared for by foster parents who are not equal to the task. As a rule the grief of these children remains concealed. They do not complain themselves. Their parents have distorted memories of what they have done to their children and they deny maltreating them. The foster parents remain silent on the subject of their incompetence.

If one considers the sad childhood of many children of schizophrenics, one is astonished that many more than half of them are healthy personalities. However, the grief even of many of the healthy children exists, and it is never quite extinguished. It overshadows their life. They feel humiliated by misery and inferior to happier people. I have heard many of them say: "If anybody has suffered as I have because of my mother, he can never laugh and be happy as anyone else." They often feel uncertain in erotic partnership. They feel that a happier boy or girl would not want to have anything to do with them. They are also afraid of the danger that they or their children could become psychotic. Some of them do not marry. Others feel that they only deserve an inferior partner—a dangerous attitude for the prognosis of marriage. Social care for children is well organized in Switzerland. However, many children of schizophrenics do not get the help they are in need of. I have collected similar reports from six different countries with different welfare organizations. Nowhere is sufficient assistance given to children of schizophrenics. So many times they would need psychiatric advice, consolation and friendship, and they do not get it.

As we all know, schizophrenics themselves need much more help than is given to them in many hospitals all over the world. But we should also bear in mind the grief of the children of our patients. It is great enough for us to do everything we can do to allay it.

So I've summarized in the short time available to me the major findings in various aspects of schizophrenia, of the lifetime of research of myself and my colleagues who were closely associated with me. Given an opportunity for a longer presentation I would be able to provide both qualitative and quantitative observations to document them.

MANFRED BLEULER: SELECTED BIBLIOGRAPHY

Vererbungsprobleme bei Schizophrenen. *Z. ges. Neurol. Psychiat.* 127, 321–388, 1930; Eng. trans. in *J. nerv. ment. Dis.* 74, 1931.

Schizophrenia. Review of the work of Prof. Eugen Bleuler. *Arch. Neurol. Psychiat*, 26, 610–627, 1931.

Psychotische Belastung von körperlich Kranken. *Z. ges. Neurol. Psychiat.* 146, 780–810, 1932.

Der Rorschach-Vejrsuch als Unterscheidungsmittel von Konstitution und Prozess. *Z. ges. Neurol. Psychiat.* 151, 571–578, 1934.

Erblichkeit und Erbprognose: Durchschnittsbevölkerung, Schizophrenie, manisch-depressives Irresein, Epilepsie, 1933–1936. *Fortschr. Neurol. Psychiat.* 9, 250–664, 1937.

Erblichkeit und Erbprognose: Schizophrenie, manisch-depressives Irresein, Epilepsie, Durchschnittsbevölkerung. *Fortschr. Neurol. Psychiat.* 10, 392–403, 1938.

Erblichkeit und Erbprognose: Schizophrenie, manisch-depressives Irresein, Epilepsie, Durchschnittsbevölkerung. *Fortschr. Neurol. Psychiat.* 11, 287–302, 1939.

Erblichkeit und Erbprognose: Schizophrenie, manisch-depressives Irresein, Epilepsie, Durchschnittsbevölkerung (1939–1940). *Fortschr. Neurol. Psychiat.* 13, 49–63, 1941.

Krankheitsverlauf, Persönlichkeit und Verwandtschaft Schizophrener und ihre gegenseitigen Beziehungen. Leipzig: Thieme, 1941.

Das Wesen der Schizophrenieremission nach Schockbehandlung. *Z. gen. Neurol. Psychiat.* 173, 553–597, 1941.

Die späтschizophrenen Krankheitsbilder. *Fortschr. Neurol. Psychiat.* 15, 259, 1943.

Schizophrenes und endokrines Krankheitsgeschehen. *Arch. Klaus-Stift. Vererb.-Forsch.* 18, 403, 1943.

Die Prognose der Psychosen, insbesondere der Schizophrenie. *Periodische Mitteilungen der Schweiz. Lebensversicherungs-Ges.* 1946, 175–186.

Forschungen zur Schizophreniefrage. *Wien. Z. Nervenheilk.* 1, 129–148, 1948.

Bedingte Einheitlichkeit im Erbgang—eine überwundene Schwierigkeit in der Konstitutionsforschung am Menschen. *Arch. Klaus-Stift. Vererb.-Forsch.* 24, 355–364, 1949.

Endokrinologie in Beziehung zur Psychiatrie (Uebersichtsreferat). *Zbl. ges. Neurol. Psychiat.* 110, 225, 1950.

Forschungen und Begriffswandlungen in der Schizophrenielehre 1941–1950. *Fortschr. Neurol. Psychiat.* 19, 385–456, 1951.

Biologie und Entwicklungslehre der Personlichkeit. *Verh. schweiz. naturforsch. Ges. Bern*, 1956, 66–43.

Gedanken zur heutigen Schizophrenielehre—am Beispiel der Konstitutionspathologie erläutert. *Wien. Z. Nervenheilk.* 7, 255–270, 1953.

Endokrinologische Psychiatrie. Stuttgart: Thieme, 1954.

Zur Psychotherapie der Schizophrenie. *Dtsch. med. Wschr.* 79, 841–842, 1954.

Das Wesen der Serpasil-Behandlung an Schizophrenen. In: Das zweite Serpasil-Symposium in der psychiatrischen Universitätsklinik Burghölzli, Zürich. *Schweiz. med. Wschr.* 85, 439–444, 1955.

Familial and personal background of chronic alcoholics. In: O. Diethelm: *Etiology of chronic alcoholism.* Springfield, Ill.: Charles C Thomas 1955, Pp. 110–166.

A comparative study of the constitution of Swiss and American alcoholic patients. In: O. Diethelm: *Etiology of chronic alcoholism.*

Springfield, Ill.: Charles C Thomas, 1955, Pp. 167–178.

Research and changes in concepts in the study of schizophrenia, 1941–1950. *Bull. Isaac Ray Med. Lib.*, 3, 1–132, 1955.

Psychiatrische Irrtümer in der Serotoninforschung. *Dtsch. med. Wschr.* 81, 1078–1081, 1956.

Comparaison entre les effets de la Chlorpromazine et de la Réserpine en psychiatrie. *Encéphale*, 45, 334–338, 1956.

Comparaison entre les effets de la Chlorpromazine et de la Réserpine en psychiatrie. *Encéphale*, 45, 334–338, 1956.

Eugen Bleuler. Die Begründung der Schizophrenielehre. In: *Gestalter unserer Zeit. Bd. 4: Erforscher des Lebens*. Oldenburg: Gerhard Stalling Verlag, 1956.

Aspects secrets de la psychiatrie. *Evolut. Psychiatr.* 1956/I, 45–50.

Die Problematik der Schizophrenien als Arbeitsprogramm des II. Internationalen Kongresses für Psychiatrie. *Nervenarzt* 28, 529–533, 1957.

Scopo e tema del nostro congresso. *Pisani* 71/3, 481–491, 1957.

Aims and topic of our congress. Hamdard, *Medical Digest* (Karachi), May 1958.

International cooperation in research on schizophrenia. *Bull. Menninger Clinic* 22, 43–49, 1958.

Endokrinologische Behandlungsverfahren bei psychischen Störungen. In: *Therapeutische Fortschritte in der Neurologie und Psychia-*

trie, hgg. v. H. Hoff; Urban und Schwarzenberg, Wien-Innsbruck 1960, Pp. 294–305.

Entwicklungslinien psychiatrischer Praxis und Forschung. *Schweiz. med. Wschr.* 91, 1549, 1961.

Early Swiss sources of Adolf Meyers concepts. *Amer. J. Psychiat.* 11973, 193–196, 1962.

Schizophrenieartige Psychosen und Aetiologie der Schizophrenie. *Schweiz. med. Wschr.* 92, 1641–1647, 1962.

Conception of schizophrenia within the last fifty years and today. *Proc. roy. Soc. Med.* 56, 945–952, 1963.

Endokrinologische Psychiatrie. In: *Psychiatrie der Gegenwart—Forschung und Praxis*. Band I/1b; Teil B, S. 161–252. Springer, Berlin-Gottingen-Heidelberg 1964.

Ursache und Wesen der schizophrenen Geistesstörungen. *Dtsch. med. Wschr.* 89, 40 & 41, 1865–1870 und 1947–1952, 1964.

Neue Therapiemöglichkeiten im Vergleich zu alten in der Psychiatrie. *Dtsch. med. Wschr.* 89, 501–505, 1964.

Significato della ricerca psicoterapeutica per la teoria sulla schizofrenia e per il paziente schizofrenico. *Arch. Psicol. Neurol. Psichiat.* 27/4–5, 353–368, 1966.

Neue Entwicklung des Schizophrenieproblems. *Praxis* (Bern) 56/10, 326–331, 1967.

A 23-year longitudinal study of 208 schizophrenics and impressions in regard to the nature of schizophrenia. In: *The transmission of schizophrenia*, D. Rosenthal & S. S. Kety, (Eds.) Pergamon Press, Oxford 1968, Pp. 3–12.

1970 DEAN RESEARCH AWARD

DAVID ROSENTHAL *was born in Harlem and grew up in Brooklyn. After receiving his B.A. at the University of Akron prior to World War II, he joined the Army and worked in a psychiatric ward. Following the war, he took his M.S. and did research on group psychotherapy with chronic schizophrenics. At the University of Chicago, he earned his Ph.D., married, and later went to Johns Hopkins, where he served as psychologist for the Phipps Clinic for four and a half years. He was then invited to join the Laboratory of Psychology to undertake full time research on schizophrenia. He is now chief of the Laboratory, and, as he states, "I am still trying to find out what this disorder is all about."*

A PROGRAM OF RESEARCH ON HEREDITY IN SCHIZOPHRENIA

by David Rosenthal

Laboratory of Psychology, National Institute of Mental Health, Bethesda, Maryland

ᑦᘏᓺ

INTRODUCTION AND BACKGROUND

FOR GOOD and various reasons, though not compelling ones, American behavioral scientists have long shown a remarkable indifference to the possible role of heredity in the etiology of behavioral disorders. The reasons included: a healthy skepticism regarding the validity and reliability of assessing traditionally defined diagnostic categories, such as schizophrenia, manic-depressive psychosis, psychoneurosis, psychopathy, and others; the association of fallacious, hereditary theories with the political ideology of the Nazis; the fact that genetic research has sometimes been linked to the suppression of black people; the repugnance to Americans of any theory that implied a genetic determination of behavior, even in part, in that it threatened to delimit our concept of personal freedom as well as our subjective or collective consciousness of such freedom; the fact that so-called genetic research has often been cavalier in its disregard of basic, accepted methodological practices, such as the use of a control group, or making assessments while blind with respect to the relationship between a subject and the index case in a given study; the popular but mistaken belief that if a disorder had a genetic basis, it was ipso facto untreatable; the absorption of psychologists in psychodynamic explanations of psychopathology and in principles of learning left little room for an ego-alien notion such as genetics in their conceptualization of behavioral disorder; and the fact that none of the behavioral disorders followed any clear Mendelian distribution.

Nevertheless, during the past fifty years, evidence for an hereditary contribution to the psychopathologies had been gathering steadily in Europe, and to a lesser extent in the United States. The evidence might have been fallible because of methodological insufficiencies, but its accumulating weight began to demand attention here. The evidence was based essentially on two kinds of studies:

1. Consanguinity Studies. Here the assumption was that if a disorder occurred more frequently in the relatives of an affected individual than in the population at large, this finding provided evidence for an hereditary contribution to that disorder. Moreover, if the frequency of the disorder was greater in first degree relatives as compared to second or third degree relatives, this finding reinforced the evidence for an hereditary contribution. However, investigators who made these assumptions were ignoring the possibility that nongenetic factors could also have accounted for such

distributions of the disorder. Such nongenetic factors could be psychological, such as parental behavior that has been described as attention-fragmenting, chaotic, or double-binding, to name a few of the terms used by psychodynamic environmentalists, or these factors could be sociocultural, so that a trait such as poverty might show the same patterns of correlation between degree of consanguinity and degree of poverty that one might find with various forms of psychopathology.

2. Twin Studies. The classical twin study design is based on the fact that monozygotic twins have exactly the same heredity whereas dizygotic twins have only about half their genes in common. Therefore, it has been assumed that if pairs of monozygotic twins are concordant—i.e., have the same psychopathology—more often than pairs of dizygotic twins, then such a finding constitutes evidence of a genetic contribution to the disorder. This inference is based on the assumption that intrapair environmental factors are the same for both monozygotic and dizygotic twins. Usually the environmental factors that have been considered most relevant involved a common rearing in the same home. Since both members of the monozygotic and the dizygotic pairs were reared together, then the assumption of equal intrapair environmental variance across groups was considered to have been met.

However, psychological factors unique to monozygotic twins, especially that of shared identity, have been described vividly by several investigators who maintain therefore that the equal environment assumption is ill-founded, that solely on psychological grounds one would predict a higher concordance rate for monozygotic twins, and that the inference of a genetic contribution to the disorder is not warranted based on such findings alone. We should note too that the classical twin study design invokes a unidirectional hypothesis; the prediction is always that there will be greater intrapair similarity for monozygotic twins, But there is almost never any reason to predict greater intrapair similarity for dizygotic twins, whether for genetic or for environmental reasons. Therefore, the traditional twin studies of psychopathology have been suggestive but not conclusive. Studies of twins reared apart could be helpful in that the problems associated with shared identity cannot arise in separated twins. However, it is difficult to obtain representative samples of separated twins, and the happenstance case by case reporting of such twins might involve selective bias.

For these reasons, Dr. Seymour Kety and I began a series of conversations about ten years ago in which we decided to embark on a different research strategy in attempting to resolve the old controversies. We planned to use naturally occurring adoptions to tease apart the hereditary and environmental factors that were thought to be implicated in most forms of psychopathology. Not long afterward we were joined by Dr. Paul Wender who had had the same idea. The psychopathology that we chose for our investigations was the one called schizophrenia. Most of the previous genetic research by far had been devoted to this disorder, and it was the one of greatest concern to the mental health professions and to the population at large. The environmental variable we chose to work on involved type of rearing, which many psychiatrists, psychologists, and laymen felt was the primary etiologic agent in the schizophrenic disorders. Since rearing involves a huge subset of variables, we chose to focus more specifically on rearing by or with a schizophrenic relative.

Of course, the idea of using adoption to separate the genetic and rearing variables is not new. Psychologists have employed this research strategy liberally in the study of intelligence (Burks, 1928; Honzik, 1957; Skeels, 1936; Skodak, 1939; Skodak & Skeels, 1949). One adoption study has been carried out with respect to alcoholism (Roe, 1945) and one with respect to antisocial behavior (zur Nieden, 1951). However, considering the potential value of such research, the adoption strategy has been used very sparsely. There were good reasons for this apparent neglect. Adoption agencies and the courts have been zealous in their desire to protect all parties to the adoption, the biological parents, the adopting parents, and the child, and the agencies have usually been unwilling to divulge any information about them to outsiders. Without the agencies' cooperation, it becomes extremely difficult to mount any adoption study at all, although we have generated one research strategy that circumvents this problem. Nevertheless, to carry out our studies in the way we wanted, we eventually felt obliged to go abroad, where cooperation was possible. Perhaps in the future there will be some liberalization of American agencies' rules with respect to information released to researchers. The researchers, in turn, will have to commit themselves to prescribed practices and constraints that must be acceptable to the agencies.

Although the adoption strategy is not new, Dr. Kety, Dr. Wender and I have developed research designs that build upon and amplify the potential usefulness of this strategy. We did not have all these designs in mind when we started, but as happens often in research, once we were enmeshed in the work itself, new findings and problems that arose suggested new methodological approaches. In this presentation, I will focus on these research designs rather than on the details of our research findings. However, I will touch briefly upon the findings, where they are available, using them primarily to indicate the power of the designs and the nature of the information they yield. Through all these designs, we treat heredity as though it were an independent variable, just like any other independent variable in a well carried out laboratory experiment.

EXPERIMENTAL DESIGNS

The first group of studies that I will discuss was carried out in Denmark under the excellent supervision of Dr. Fini Schulsinger. In the first of these studies (Kety, Rosenthal, Wender, & Schulsinger, 1968), we were interested in the incidence of schizophrenic disorders in the biological and adoptive relatives of schizophrenics and nonschizophrenics, respectively. The design of the study is shown in Figure 1. Because the focus of the study is the relatives of the adoptees rather than the adoptees themselves, we may call it the Adoptees' Families Design. In this study we are testing two op-

RELATIVES

Probands	Biological	Adoptive
Schizophrenic		
Control (nonschizophrenic)		

FIGURE 1. Adoptees' Families Design.

posed hypotheses. (1) If schizophrenic disorders are heritable, we should find a higher prevalence of such disorders among the biological relatives of our schizophrenic index cases than among the biological relatives of the matched controls. (2) If schizophrenic disorders are transmitted behaviorally, and at least in good part by rearing parents whose own behavior is confused, disorganized, erratic or chaotic, to mention some of the terms cited in the literature, we should expect that the index cases would have a greater number of adoptive relatives with schizophrenic disorders than would be found in the adoptive relatives of the controls.

To carry out this design, we began by collecting identifying information on all persons who had formally been given up for nonfamily adoption at an early age in the greater Copenhagen area between 1923 and 1947. There were almost 5,500 such adoptions. From the records we learned the name and birthdate of the adoptee, and the names and other identifying information of the adopting and biological parents. From the Psychiatric Register, we found out which of the approximately 5,500 adoptees had been admitted to a psychiatric facility. The hospital records for each admitted adoptee were examined by two Danish psychiatrists, and the main information provided by one psychiatrist was sent to the American investigators. All five made their own independent diagnoses. By this procedure, we were able to select 33 index cases. Of these, 16 were chronic or process schizophrenics; 7 were acute schizophrenic reactions of the schizophreniform, schizo-affective or paranoid type, and 10 were cases of borderline schizophrenia.

We selected from among the remaining adoptees in the total pool a control group

233

who did not have a file in the Psychiatric Register and who were matched individually to the index cases with respect to sex, age, pretransfer history, and socioeconomic status of the rearing family.

In determining the rates of schizophrenic disorders among the relatives of our 66 probands, we did not examine the relatives personally. Instead, we first identified each biological or adoptive relative who was either a parent, sib or half-sib of a proband, and we then identified each one of these relatives who had a known psychiatric history. These histories were abstracted from records by a Danish psychiatrist who did not know if the individual case he was abstracting was the biological or adoptive relative of an index case or a control. The psychiatric abstract was then sent to the U. S. investigators who independently made their own diagnoses while they were similarly blind regarding the relationship of the relative to the proband. Diagnostic differences among the four major investigators were settled by discussions based on more complete data from the records before we broke the relationship code.

At this point, I would like to call to your attention two important features of our research. The first is that, wherever possible, we keep all examiners blind with respect to the index or control status of the subject under examination. We are almost always successful in this respect. This procedure insures against the possibility of bias either for or against any preferred hypothesis that the examiner may hold. The second feature has to do with the fact that we have included a broad spectrum of disorders in the ones I am calling schizophrenic. These include not only the classical chronic, process types of cases, but patients called doubtful schizophrenic, reactive, schizo-affective, borderline or pseudoneurotic schizophrenic, or schizoid or paranoid. If we dealt only with hardcore schizophrenia, our ns would be too small to make any of these studies meaningful. However, a more positive reason for including the spectrum of disorders is that in the process, we hope to be able to determine whether any or all of these disorders, which phenotypically have strong resemblances to hardcore

schizophrenia, are genetically related to it as well (Rosenthal, 1970).

With respect to Figure 1, the major finding was that we obtained the highest concentration of schizophrenic spectrum disorders among the biological relatives of the schizophrenic index cases. The rates for such disorders did not differ appreciably in the other three cells. Thus, this finding provides strong evidence for an hereditary contribution to such disorders. However, I want to point out that Figure 1 does not comprise a true fourfold table. That is why a double line is drawn to separate the biological and adoptive halves. The reasons for this are practical rather than theoretical. I will mention just the major reason. It is important to understand that both the adopting and biological parents of our adoptees represent screened populations. The screening with respect to adopting parents is well-known, since adoption agencies have long taken the view that mentally ill people do not make the kinds of parents that serve the best interests of the child. But biological parents are also screened in that if they are known to be schizophrenic, adoption agencies may be reluctant to place their children for formal adoption. Instead, the children may be reared in foster homes or in institutions. Moreover, at least in Denmark, schizophrenic women, or women with schizophrenia in their families, may request and have legal abortions. Thus, fewer such children are born and cannot come into the pool of probands in Figure 1. We do not know the extent of screening in the biological and adopting families, but the screening may be unequal. This fact limits the possible range of differences that might otherwise be found in this type of study, but it does not invalidate the procedure. It also means that we can compare the two groups of biological relatives, and the two groups of adoptive relatives, but we cannot now make valid comparisons between biological and adoptive relatives.

The second model (Rosenthal, Wender, Kety, Schulsinger, Welner, & Östergaard, 1968) is shown in Figure 2. We call it the Adoptees Study Design because the focus of study is the adoptees themselves rather than

Schizophrenic	Nonschizophrenic
1	1'
2	2'
3	3'
4	4'
⋮	⋮
n	n'

ADOPTEES

FIG. 2. Adoptees Study Design.

their relatives. The design asks the question: What is the fate of offspring of schizophrenic parents when these offspring are reared adoptively? In this study, the starting point is the approximately 10,000 biological parents of our pool of adoptees. A search was conducted to see who among these parents had a file in the Psychiatric Register. The hospital records of each such parent were reviewed in detail by a psychiatrist who completed a prescribed form which was reviewed independently by the American investigators. If we agreed that the parent's diagnosis belonged in our spectrum of schizophrenic disorders, or was a clearcut or possible case of manic-depressive psychosis, the adopted-away child of that parent was chosen as an index case. From among the remaining adoptees, we chose as controls those whose both biological parents had no known psychiatric history, i.e., neither parent had a file in the Psychiatric Register. Controls were matched to the index cases for sex, age, age at transfer to the adopting family, and the socioeconomic status of the adopting family.

The index and control subjects were invited to participate in a study of the relationship between environment and health. We were able to achieve almost 80 percent cooperation, an acceptable figure, and the two groups did not differ in this respect. At this time, we are able to report on 76 index cases and 67 controls. The subjects were given a semi-structured psychiatric interview by Dr. Joseph Welner that lasted from 3 to 5 hours. Each subject also had one and a half days of psychological testing, but we will not be able to present the test findings now. The examinations of all subjects spanned a period of four years.

The main finding of this study is that there is a significantly greater number of schizophrenic spectrum disorders among the index cases than among the controls. Three cases were called clearcut schizophrenia by Dr. Welner. All three were index cases. However, only one of these had been hospitalized for the disorder. As a matter of fact, the rate for hospitalized schizophrenia and for diagnosed schizophrenia tends to be appreciably lower than the rates usually found in Scandinavia for the nonadopted offspring of schizophrenics. Therefore, this study leads us to the twofold conclusion that heredity contributes significantly to the development of schizophrenic spectrum disorder, and that adoptive rearing may contribute to the reduced expressivity of such disorder. In both studies presented, evidence is accumulating that the disorders in our spectrum are genetically related, with the probable exception of reactive schizophrenia, which may have to be excluded from the spectrum.

Now I would like to show you a research model that is based on an experimental design that has been used in the past by behavioral geneticists (Ginsburg & Allee, 1942; Fredericson, 1952; Broadhurst, 1961; Ressler, 1963). It has generally been referred to as a cross-fostering or reciprocal fostering model. To review briefly the essentials of this model, let us assume that the experimenter is interested in learning whether he can breed in a trait such as social dominance. He would first decide on a test or criterion for the trait. He would then run his starting pool of animals through this test and separate those who test high (called dominant) and those who test low (called submissive). He would then inbreed the dominant animals and inbreed the submissive animals, and repeat the test with the next generation. This procedure is continued as long as the respective inbreedings continue to increase the test discrimination between the dominant and submissive groups. Let us say that at the nth generation, the experimenter decides that he can no longer increase the discrimination. At this point, he must ask himself whether he has successfully bred in the trait or whether each generation had become more dominant or more submissive because it had, in turn, been reared with successively more dominant or more submissive parent populations. Therefore, he checks this possibility with the $n + 1$ generation. He does this by transposing the $n + 1$ dominant animals to be reared by submissive dams, and $n + 1$ submissives to be reared by dominant dams. Then he runs the $n + 1$ adult generation through his test to see what effect the transposed rearing may have with respect to the test performance.

We cannot control human breeding, but we can follow the model somewhat by thinking of our pool of adoptees as an $n + 1$ generation. The design is shown in Figure 3. We begin with the biological parent generation. From among them we select those who are schizophrenic and who are presumably breeding the trait. Among their adult offspring, we select those who were reared by adoptive parents who had had no schizophrenic disorder, as far as we can tell. These offspring constitute one testing group. Then we select from among those biological parents who had had no schizophrenic disorder, as far as we can tell, those whose offspring had been reared by an adopting parent who did have some schizophrenic disorder. These offspring comprise our second testing group. The two groups of offspring are then compared with respect to the trait in question. Although we have not yet analyzed the data in this study, a preliminary look at the data suggests that the incidence of schizophrenic spectrum disorders tends to be about equal for the two cross-fostered groups. Should this tentative observation prove true, it would not mean that heredity is irrelevant, but rather that rearing by a schizophrenically disordered parent may also be influential in the development of spectrum disorders.

Although the cross-fostering design has its own built-in elegance, what it does in effect is to pit two competing hypotheses against one another. However, we also want to know in more detail the effect of each independent variable considered separately. Now that some statistical evidence is accumulating to the effect that rearing by a schizophrenic parent may itself produce spectrum disorders in offspring, it is important that we have a research model that provides a clean test of this hypothesis. This model is shown in Figure 4.

In this model, we begin with biological parents who do not have any schizophrenic spectrum disorder, as far as we can tell. This is done to insure to the maximal extent possible that the offspring under study are as free of genetic contamination as we can make them. Preferably, all biological parents should be examined personally and in depth to make the determination of no spectrum disorder, but we have not as yet been able to do this. Now we ask the question: When there is minimal or no genetic predisposition in the child, will rearing by a schizophrenic parent induce spectrum disorders in the child? Thus, we have two groups of adoptees. The first or index group are reared by a schizophrenic spectrum parent, the second or control group by rearing parents who are free of spectrum disorder. The second group, which is matched to the first group for various relevant variables, constitutes as ideal a control group as we can find in that both their biological and rearing parents are free of spectrum disorders. Any psychopathology that we find in these offspring should arise

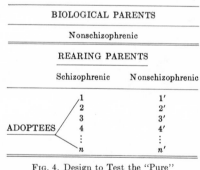

FIG. 4. Design to Test the "Pure" Environmentalist Hypothesis.

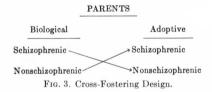

FIG. 3. Cross-Fostering Design.

from other factors. Any psychopathology in the index group in excess of that occurring in this idealized control group represents the contribution of rearing by a schizophrenic parent. We cannot at this time report any findings on this study, but will do so in the future.

We must be alert to another alternative. It may be that rearing by a schizophrenic parent is insufficient per se to induce spectrum disorders in offspring, but that such rearing could raise havoc with genetically predisposed individuals. To test this possibility, we require a research model such as that shown in Figure 5.

This design is exactly like that of the previous design, with one important exception: this time all subjects must have a biological parent who has schizophrenic spectrum disorder. Thus, from a genetic standpoint, the amount of hereditary predisposition for such disorder should be the same for our two groups, and it should be considerable. Again the difference between the groups occurs in the rearing variable. Actually, it is not possible to carry out such a design in pure form, at least not in Denmark, since this would require that both groups of subjects should be adoptees. However, the likelihood of generating a sample in which the subjects have a biological parent who is schizophrenic and are then given up for adoption to a rearing parent who is also schizophrenic is, fortunately, very small. Thus, to carry out the intent of the design, we have had to substitute for adoptees a

---

BIOLOGICAL PARENTS
Schizophrenic

REARING PARENTS

	Schizophrenic	Nonschizophrenic
	1	1'
	2	2'
	3	3'
ADOPTEES	4	4'
	⋮	⋮
	n	n'

Fig. 5. Design to Test the Effects of the Hypothesized Environmental Variable Coacting with the Genetic Variable.

---

group of subjects who had a schizophrenic parent and who were reared in the parental home at least during their first fifteen years of life. This represents the group in which the hypothesized genetic and rearing factors would be truly coacting to produce the schizophrenic phenotype. The comparison group of adoptees provides a baseline that represents only the genetic contribution, without the superimposition of rearing by a schizophrenic parent. Any difference between the two groups should represent the coaction or true interaction effect. We have collected a matched sample of nonadoptees to carry out this design, but the research material has not yet been subjected to analysis.

We are now in a position to bring together several of the samples of subjects we have collected and arrange them in a fourfold table that represents the various combinations of genetic and rearing variables, as shown in Figure 6.

Thus, we have two types of rearing variables, schizophrenic and nonschizophrenic, and two types of genetic variables, schizophrenic and nonschizophrenic. Three of the four cells contain adoptees. Two diagonal cells represent subjects in the cross-fostering design. The adoptees in the lower right cell are obtained from the control group in the adoptees study design. The upper left cell, unfortunately, has to be represented by the nonadoptees obtained in the previous design, and that is why it is represented by a double line. Thus, in one cell the factor of adoption does not hold and we do not know to what extent this fact invalidates the findings of this otherwise neat design. Nevertheless, we may carry out such an analysis if we have reason to think it will be worthwhile.

The next study I want to present was carried out in Bethesda (Wender, Rosenthal, & Kety, 1968). It represents the kind of study that can be done without requiring the cooperation of adoption agencies. The design is based on the following rationale. Many investigators have maintained that a child develops a schizophrenic disorder because his parents have subjected him to various kinds of noxious rearing. In accounting for the elevated incidence of schizophrenia

237

Genetic Background	SCHIZOPHRENIC	NONSCHIZOPHRENIC
Schizophrenic	Nonadoptees	Cross Fostering
Nonschizophrenic	Cross Fostering	Controls

Fig. 6. Modified Design to Test for Statistical Interaction Between the Hypothesized Genetic and Environmental Variables.

among the parents of schizophrenics, they point out that such parents are more likely than normal parents to emit these noxious behaviors in regard to their children and that, therefore, the elevated incidence of schizophrenia among parents of schizophrenics is to be expected on rearing grounds alone. Alanen, Rekola, Stewen, Takala, and Touvinen (1966) reported that parents of schizophrenics had a higher rate of severe psychopathology than did the parents of neurotics, and inferred that the correlation between parents and children regarding severity of psychopathology represented evidence for behavioral transmission. However, such findings could equally well imply that the elevated rates of schizophrenia and severe psychopathology in the parents represent genetic factors that are transmitted to offspring who in turn manifest schizophrenic disorder. To test these alternative hypotheses, we invoke the design shown in Figure 7.

In this design, we are concerned with the parents of schizophrenics. Since in the type of study done by Alanen and other investigators the genetic and rearing variables are confounded in the same parents, we again resort to adoption to separate the two variables. We begin by finding young adult schizophrenics who had been given up for adoption early in life. This can best be done by interviewing all new admissions to mental hospitals, and their parents. It is a tedious job, but it is feasible. From among other schizophrenic admissions who were home reared, we find a group that is matched to the adopted schizophrenics with respect to the variables deemed most relevant. The third group in the design shown is used to control for the factor of adoption. However, this group of adoptees is free of schizophrenic disorder. The subjects studied are not the offspring, but the parents. The particular focus of the study is the adoptive parents of the schizophrenics. Our reasoning goes like this: If the schizophrenia in the children represents primarily genetic influences, the degree of psychopathology in their adoptive parents should not be severe, as Alanen had reported, and should be less than that of the biological parents of schizophrenics. If the schizophrenia in the children represents the effects of noxious behavioral influences, the degree of psychopathology among the adoptive parents should be the same as that found in the biological parents.

Our findings indicated that the degree of psychopathology in the adoptive parents of schizophrenics was significantly less than that of the biological parents of schizo-

DIAGNOSIS OF PROBANDS

	Schizophrenic	Schizophrenic	Nonschizophrenic
REARING PARENTS	Adoptive	Biological	Adoptive

Fig. 7. The Adoptive Parents Study Design.

phrenics but significantly greater than that of the adoptive parents of normal subjects. Thus, it is possible to have schizophrenia in offspring who are not subjected to the noxious influences associated with severe psychopathology in the rearing parents. The finding of a difference in degree of psychopathology between the adoptive parents of schizophrenics and the adoptive parents of normals could have any of several explanations which I will not take the time to discuss here. It is interesting that on a word association test, the biological parents of schizophrenics produced more unusual responses than did the adoptive parents of schizophrenics.

To carry out the last design that I shall present, I went to Israel. This study was done without the collaboration of my two brilliant colleagues, Dr. Kety and Dr. Wender. As noted earlier, our attempts to generate a clean fourfold-table design by using adoption fell short of our goals. However, we can forego the advantages conferred by adoption if we can specify two different environments that bear on the kinds of rearing we have been talking about. Israel provided two such environments, the kibbutz and the nuclear family types of rearing. The reasoning underlying the study is: In the typical nuclear family, if a parent—let us say the mother—is schizophrenic, the child is likely to endure the following psychological hazards: the mother may be too autistic to attend or to be responsive to the child's needs and she may program reinforcements haphazardly and unpredictably, thus impairing the child's cognitive training and her affective and motivational integration; during the times she is not hospitalized, she is likely to be the only person in the child's environment during most of each day, so that during the greater part of the time that he is awake, the child has no other model with whom to identify during his formative years; sometimes the parent undergoes successive hospitalizations, so that the child may suffer increased insecurity each time he loses her, and he may develop a deep sense of mistrust of the world around him; sometimes the home will be broken, the child may be reared by relatives or friends, in institutions, or he may be shuttled back and forth in various combinations of such rearing; he may be isolated from other children; if he has siblings, they are likely to be similarly influenced and they may tend to influence each other noxiously in turn.

Although kibbutzim vary among themselves in a number of ways, in the main they may provide greater protection for the child who has a schizophrenic parent. For example, the child grows up in children's houses under the guidance of trained caretakers. During the greater part of each day, he receives the same tutelage and training as do other children. During evenings and holidays when the children and parents visit together, the child will visit with both the well parent and the sick parent, and the well parent may help to neutralize any noxious impact of the sick parent. Usually, the child is well-known to other adults in the kibbutz and they may serve as parent surrogates. If the sick parent requires hospitalization, the child suffers minimal disruption of his life. He remains in the same children's house with the same caretakers, teachers, and friends. He lives in the same community, and he can still visit with the well parent during the evenings and holidays.

The design for this study is shown in Figure 8.

This study was carried out under the supervision of Dr. Shmuel Nagler and Dr. Sol Kugelmass. The key cell is in the upper lefthand corner. We had to find children who

PARENTAGE	TYPE OF REARING	
	Kibbutz	Nuclear Family
Schizophrenic	25	25
Nonschizophrenic	25	25

Source	df
Parentage	1
Rearing	1
Parentage × Rearing	1
Error	96
Total	99

Fig. 8. Generalized Design for Estimating the Relative Contributions of Heredity, Environment, and Heredity-Environment Interactions.

were born and reared in a kibbutz and who had a schizophrenic parent. We were able to find 25 such cases. We then found 25 matched cases who lived in the usual nuclear family situation and who also had a schizophrenic parent. For kibbutz controls, we selected a group of children who were reared in the same children's houses as the index cases, but whose parents had no spectrum disorder, and for nuclear family controls we selected children from the same neighborhood and classroom, but without a schizophrenic parent. The children had two days of examination. They were brought in pairs, each index case and his control, but all examiners were kept blind as to which child was which. Thus, we had the rare opportunity to observe and test both the index and control subjects in the same situation. The children ranged in age from 8 to 14. Our major dependent variables involve the degree and type of psychopathology found in the four groups of subjects. With respect to each variable, we can apportion the amount of variance contributed by genetic background or parentage, the amount contributed by type of rearing environment, and the amount contributed by the genetic-rearing interaction. At this time, data are being analyzed. We hope to begin reporting our findings in the next year. It is worth noting that this is a generalized design that avoids the problems confronting us in adoption studies, and that can be applied whenever the investigator can specify two contrasting types of environment, whether they have to do with rearing or with other kinds of environmental or experiential phenomena. The latter can be conceptualized narrowly or broadly, depending on the investigator's theoretical predilection.

OUTLOOK

In closing, I would like to say that only a decade ago there existed a widespread air of pessimism about the possibility of ever unraveling the hereditary and environmental factors involved in the etiology of the behavioral disorders. Today, the outlook is completely opposite. During the seventies we should see a marked acceleration in the accumulation of knowledge in this important field.

REFERENCES

Alanen, Y. O., Rekola, J. K., Stewen, A., Takala, K., & Tuovinen, M. The family in the pathogenesis of schizophrenic and neurotic disorders, *Acta psychiat. Scand., Copenhagen,* Suppl. 189, 42, 1966.

Broadhurst, P. L. Analysis of maternal effects in the inheritance of behavior. *Anim. Behav.,* 1961, 9, 129–141.

Burks, B. S. The relative influence of nature and nurture upon mental developments. A comparative study of foster parent-foster child resemblance and true parent-true child resemblance. *27th yearbook of the national society for the study of education,* 1928, Pt. 1, 219–316.

Fredericson, E. Reciprocal fostering of two inbred mouse strains and its effect on the modification of aggressive behavior. *Amer. Psychologist,* 1952, 7, 241–242 (Abstract).

Ginsburg, B. E., & Allee, W. C. Some effects of conditioning on social dominance and subordination in inbred strains of mice. *Physiol. Zoology,* 1942, 15, 485–506.

Honzik, M. P. Developmental studies of parent-child resemblance in intelligence. *Child Develpm.,* 1957, 28, 215–228.

Kety, S. S., Rosenthal, D., Wender, P. H., & Schulsinger, F. The types and prevalence of mental illness in the biological and adoptive families of adopted schizophrenics. In D. Rosenthal & S. S. Kety (Eds.), *The transmission of schizophrenia.* London: Pergamon Press, 1968, Pp. 345–362.

Ressler, R. H. Genotype-correlated parental influences in two strains of mice. *J. comp. physiol. Psychol.,* 1963, 56, 882–886.

Roe, A. Children of alcoholic parentage raised in foster homes. In *Alcoholism, Science, and society,* published by Quarterly Journal of Studies on Alcohol, 1945, Pp. 115–127.

Rosenthal, D. *Genetic theory and abnormal behavior.* New York: McGraw-Hill, 1970.

Rosenthal, D., Wender, P. H., Kety, S. S., Schulsinger, F., Welner, J., & Östergaard, L. Schizophrenics' offspring reared in adoptive homes. In D. Rosenthal & S. S. Kety (Eds.), *The transmission of schizophrenia.* London: Pergamon Press, 1968, Pp. 377–391.

Skeels, H. M. Mental development of children in foster homes. *J. genet. Psychol.,* 1936, 49, 91–106.

Skodak, M. Children in foster homes: A study of mental development. *University of Iowa Studies of Child Welfare,* 1939, 16, No. 1.

Skodak, M. & Skeels, H. M. A final follow-up study of one hundred adopted children. *J. genet. Psychol.,* 1949, 75, 85–125.

Wender, P. H., Rosenthal, D., & Kety, S. S. A psychiatric assessment of the adoptive parents of schizophrenics. In D. Rosenthal & S. S. Kety (Eds.), *The transmission of schizophrenia*. London: Pergamon Press, 1968, Pp. 235–250.

zur Nieden, M. The influence of constitution and environment upon the development of adopted children. *J. Psychol.*, 1951, 31, 91–95.

1971 DEAN RESEARCH AWARD

Currently on the Graduate Faculty of Political and Social Science at the New School for Social Research, **SARNOFF A. MEDNICK** has taught at the University of Michigan, the University of Copenhagen, and Harvard University as well. He has also served as the Director of the Psykologisk Institut at the Kommunehospitalet in Copenhagen since 1968. Dr. Mednick attended City College, Columbia University, and Northwestern, where he received his Ph.D. in 1954, and has devoted his career in research to the study of schizophrenia.

President of the Danish Psychiatric Association since 1972, **FINI SCHULSINGER** was born in Copenhagen in 1923. After receiving his M.D. at the University of Copenhagen and earning a citation as "Specialist in Psychiatry" from the National Health Administration, Dr. Schulsinger served as the resident psychiatrist at the Psychopathic Detention Institution in Nykøbing Sjaelland and at the Kommunehospitalet in Copenhagen, where he has held the post of Director of the psychiatry department since 1960. He also worked in private practice from 1955-1962 and as consultant to the Danish Parole and Probation Society during the same period. Along with his other current duties, Dr. Schulsinger is professor and chairman of the psychiatry department at the University of Copenhagen Medical School.

ACKNOWLEDGEMENTS

We would first like to acknowledge 14 years of research support from the Scottish Rite Committee for Research in Schizophrenia. Dr. William Malamud and Dr. George Gardner encouraged us when others expressed the opinion that "high-risk" research was impractical. We have also had generous support from USPHS currently via NIMH grant No. 19225. We wish to thank Professor Fritz Fuchs, Obstetrics Department, Cornell University Medical School; Professor Preben Plum, University of Copenhagen, Faculty of Medicine; Dr. Bengt Zacchau-Christiansen, Rigshospitalet, Copenhagen for their help and advice in our work on perinatal factors. The City of Copenhagen has provided the setting and facilities for all this work.

Studies of Children at High Risk for Schizophrenia[1]

Sarnoff A. Mednick

&

Fini Schulsinger

The heart of this talk will be a description of a longitudinal, prospective study of children at high risk
for developing schizophrenia. These are children with
schizophrenic mothers. Some interaction of genetic
predisposition and environmental strain will probably
cause almost half of these high risk children to
evidence some form of social deviance; 15% will probably
become schizophrenic (Heston, 1966; Kallmann, 1938).

When we began this project 10 years ago, it was our
intention to follow these children until they had gone
through the major risk period for schizophrenia. Then,
when sufficient numbers had suffered psychiatric breakdown we planned to look back to the original assessment
procedures to see how the experiences and characteristics
of those subjects who suffered breakdown differed premorbid-
ly from those who did not break down.

Figure 1* represents our design schematically. It can be
conceptualized as developing at 3 levels or stages. At
the first level we have a crossectional comparison of
200 children at high risk from schizophrenia and 100
matched low risk children. At level 2, we can estimate
that about 50% of the high-risk children will suffer
social or psychiatric breakdown. This includes criminality, personality disorders of varying severity and
quality as well as schizophrenia. Rather good comparison
subjects for these deviants are the non-deviant children
with schizophrenic mothers as well as low risk controls.

---

[1] We have few illusions about this study. It is premature; our interventions will most likely not be
effective. But perhaps daily exercise, vitamins,
safety belts, not smoking, and acts of kindness such
as you have bestowed upon us today will enable us to
live long enough to do a better project next time.

* Figures 1 to 12, and Tables 1 to 8 are attached at
the end of this article.

At the 3rd level we can estimate that perhaps 30 of the 100 high risk deviants will be diagnosed schizophrenic. A rather interesting group of controls for these schizophrenics are the remaining 70 high risk deviants, the 100 non-deviant high-risk children and the low risk controls. We should parenthetically point out that the design lends itself to the study of the origins of other human conditions, both positive and negative. Some students working with us have begun to consider the project as a long term study of the effects of pregnancy and delivery complications. Others are interested in the etiology of criminality.

We are quite concerned about the reliability of our findings. Twenty-five year longitudinal studies are not readily replicated. Even if others are attracted to the same research design they may choose to study other variables. In view of this, a form of replication was built in.

At level 2, the 100 eventually-deviant individuals may be conceived of as suffering breakdown in 5 waves of 20 subjects each. This gives us 4 potential replications of the data analysis on the first wave of 20 breakdowns. The precision of the replications will, of course, be attenuated to the extent that the subsequent breakdown waves differ in age at breakdown or in diagnosis. The 30 schizophrenics can be conceived of as suffering breakdown in two waves of 15 subjects each.

When we compare this research methodology with the typical study which observes characteristics of patients already schizophrenic, we find certain advantages in the high risk design.

1. When they are first examined in the study, the high risk children typically have not yet experienced such aspects of the schizophrenic life as hospitalization or drugs. These factors do not color their reactions to the test procedures.

2. Since, at the time of the examination, no one knows which of the high risk subjects might become schizophrenic, this relieves the data of much of the tester bias.

3. The information we gather in such research tends to be current and not exclusively retrospective.

4. The data are uniformly and systematically obtained. A more complete statement of the retionale of the high risk design may be found in Mednick & McNeil (1968).

Having presented the rationale of this design, we will now briefly describe the manner in which the 1962 project was conducted. We selected children who had mothers whose schizophrenia was typical and severe and would be agreed upon as being typical and severe both in Europe and the United States. Low risk controls had had no member of their immediate family hospitalized for mental illness for three generations. This was determined by reference to the National Psychiatric Register which maintains a central file for every psychiatric hospitalization in the Kingdom of Denmark going back to 1916.

Table 1 presents the matching characteristics of the High and Low Risk samples. Note that we attempted to match for their having been reared in a children's home. Note also that the average age of the samples was 15.1 years. They range from 9-20 years of age. Studies of 3-year old and 10-year old high risk samples are currently underway.

Figure 2 presents a list of the procedures and examinations which all subjects experienced. During the examination, the examiners did not know whether a subject was a High Risk or Low Risk individual.

Almost all of these measures were selected in accordance with a theory of schizophrenia proposed by Mednick in 1958. In the course of the paper we will briefly describe some salient aspects of this theory. Because of its importance in what will follow we will take time to briefly describe the psychophysiological procedures. We measured the psychophysiological response of the subjects in conditions of rest, and in response to nine very loud and irritating noises. We measured their ease of conditioning and stimulus generalization. After the conditioned reponse was established we measured their rapidity of extinction and ease of habituation. For each response we measured its latency, amplitude, rate of recovery and prerespose basal level.

RESULTS

The initial assessment of these children took place in 1962. To save time we will entirely omit any description of differences between the entire High and Low Risk groups.

In 1967 when the project had reached its 5th year, 20 of the High Risk children had suffered severe psychiatric breakdown. These 20 individuals constituted the first of the five breakdown waves mentioned earlier. Having identified this wave we turned to the 1962 assessment to determine how these 20 differed from those who did not break down. Any such distinguishing characteristics or experiences could have been predispositional to their breakdown. We will call these 20 individuals the Sick Group. Fifteen have been admitted to psychiatric hospitals with many diagnoses including schizophrenia. The 5 not admitted include some who we feel are clearly schizophrenic. A brief description of the Sick subjects is presented in Figure 3.

To each of these 20 Sick individuals we matched a well-functioning High-Risk subject of the same age, sex, social class, and institutional-rearing status. This matched High-Risk control group we call the Well Group. Note that both the 20 Sick and 20 Well subjects come from the group of 207 High Risk subjects. In addition, we matched the Sick and Well Groups for their 1962 level-of-adjustment rating as judged by the interviewing psychiatrist. We tried as much as possible to select individuals for the Well Group who, since 1962, had shown some improvement in level of adjustment. Also 20 Controls were matched from the 104 Low Risk subjects for comparison purposes.

This yielded two rather well matched groups of 20 High-Risk subjects each, the Sick Group and the Well Group. In 1962, both were judged by an experienced psychiatrist to be equal in level of adjustment. Yet since 1962 one group has improved in level of mental health; the other group has suffered severe psychiatric breakdown. Why? Part of the answer could lie with the characteristics measure in 1962 at the time of the intensive examination.

We now go back to our 1962 assessment and ask if there were any characteristics in that assessment which distinctively differentiated the Sick Group. I report only the more outstanding, statistically reliable differences.

The most important characteristics distinguishing the Sick Group from the Well and the Control Groups were:

1. Separation from mother. The Sick Group lost contact with their mother much earlier in their lives than did the other two groups. These mothers were, of course, schizophrenic and the reason for which they lost contact with their children was their psychiatric hospitalization. Table 2 presents the percentage of the Sick, Well and Control Groups for whom the mother was completely absent during a specified period in the child's life. As can be seen, by the age period 5-10 years the Sick Group greatly exceeds the Well and Controls in absence of their mother from the home. On the average the Sick Group lost their mothers to psychiatric hospitalization at the age of 4.0 years while the Well and Control groups on the

average lost their mothers at the age of 8.25 years.

For the Sick and Well Groups the absence of the mother from the home was in every case occasioned by psychiatric hospitalization. On the basis of the length of hospitalization, degree of recovery between hospitalizations, and treatment received, the illness of the mother of the Sick or Well subject was rated as Very Severe or Moderately Severe. Of the Sick Group mothers, 75% were rated as Very Severe; only 33% of the Well Group mothers were rated as Very Severe ($\overline{X^2}$= 6.35, 1 df, p .05). As might be expected, the mothers who were very severely ill left their home for hospitalization at a time when the child was significantly younger. (Mednick, B., Mednick, S. & Schulsinger, F., 1972).

2. Teacher's report. The teacher's report indicates that the subject tended to be highly disturbing to the class. The Sick subjects were disciplinary problems, domineering, aggressive, created conflicts and disrupted the class with their talking. This was true of 53% of the Sick Group, 18% of the Well Group, and 11% of the Control Group. ($\underline{X}^2$ = 10.59, 2 df, p < .01).

3. Continual Association Test. The Sick Group evidenced two distinctive patterns on the Continual Association Test in which the subject was asked to give, in one minute, as many single-word associations as he could, to a stimulus word.

A. They had a strong tendency to rattle off a whole series of interrelated but contextually, somewhat irrelevant words ("Opremsning" in Danish). The mean Opremsning scores (corrected for total number of responses) for the Sick, Well and Control Groups were 1.33, 0.11, 0.33, respectively ($\underline{F}$ = 4.33, 2.51 df, p < .05). The Sick versus Well Group differences were also significant ($\underline{t}$ = 2.30, 36 df, p < .05).

B. Also on the Continual Association Test, the associations of the Sick Group tended to "Drift" away from the stimulus word. Each of the Sick and Well Group sets of associations to each of the 30 stimulus words were rated on a scale from 1 (no Drifting) to 3 (much Drifting). The Sick Group had a mean Drifting score of 1.72, the Well Group 1.33 ($\underline{t}$ = 2.10, 38 df, p < .05). Perhaps here we were seeing the beginning of the thought disorder many of these Sick subjects eventually manifested.

4. Psychophysiology. Some of the variables most sharply differentiating the Sick Group from the Well and Control

Groups were the galvanic skin response measures taken during the psychophysiological testing. The anomalies observed seemed to be best characterized as a failure of control mechanisms either of the ANS or hormonal systems or both.

I will describe analyses of 4 measures of the GSR, basal level, latency of response, amplitude of response and rate of recovery from the response.

BASAL CONDUCTANCE LEVEL

There were no significant differences among the three groups in log conductance basal level at any point in the examination.

LATENCY

A summary of the latency data may be found in Figure 4. As you can see, the latencies of the Sick subjects tended to be considerably faster than those of the Well subjects. The mean latencies across all stress trials for the Sick, Well and Control groups, respectively, were 1.57, 1.77, 2.47 seconds (F = 8.63, 2.52 $\underline{df}$, $p < 0.005$). If we can focus on the 9 stress trials in Figure 4, on which the subject was exposed to a very loud and irritating noise, one other interesting thing concerning the latency shows itself. The Sick Group did not show any signs of habituation of latency. If you look at the responses of the Control and Well Groups you will note that they tend to evidence progressive increase of their response latencies from the first to the last of the stress trials. The latencies of the Sick Group progressively decrease suggesting a negative habituation or even increasing irritability. We have never before observed this pattern. Moving from the first to the last UCS, 69% of the Well Group exhibits the expected slowing of response latency, (habituation); 75% of the Sick Group actually increase the speed of their responses across these 9 trials.

RESPONSIVENESS

As can be seen from Table 3 the responsiveness of the Sick Group was far above the levels of the Well or Control Groups. These differences were significant in almost all the 9 stress trials. The differences were also consistently significant during the extinction testing. For the data in Table 3 the significance of differences was tested by an analysis of covariance with the basal level just preceding the response as the covariance control. Figure 5 presents evidence that the Sick Group was responding well above the other groups in level of generalization. The generalization test trials took

252

place under extinction conditions, consequently it is also possible to interpret the responsiveness on these trials as indicants of rapidity of extinction. The Well and Control Groups evidenced very rapid extinction. That is, they responded to only one or two of the 9 extinction trials. The Sick Group exhibited great resistance to extinction, in many cases responding with tenacity under the very end of the extinction period. This failure to extinguish the GSR response may also be viewed as another aspect of the failure of habituation which was observed in the latency findings.

RECOVERY

After a response occurs it tends to return to its pre-stimulus level. We measured the rate of this recovery by calculating the number of ohms recovered per second. The mean ohms recovered per second is reported in Table 4. UCS Trial 1 is omitted from the Table inasmuch as most subjects did not succeed in recovering half their response on this Trial before the onset of UCS 2. The overlap between the Sick and Control Groups distributions for this variable was not very large. On many trials we find 80% of the Sick Group and 20% of the Control Group above the median of the pooled distributions. On UCS Trial 6 all but one of the Sick subjects and only two of the Controls were above the median of the pooled distributions. The pooled Sick and Well distributions typically found 70% of the Sick Group and 30% of the Well Group above the median.

5. Midwife's report. We had no hypotheses or expectations regarding the midwife's reports. We simply gathered them because they were there. We were lucky. They appear to be critical. Seventy percent of the members of the Sick Group had suffered one or more serious pregnancy or birth complications (or PBCs). This contrasted with 15% of the Well Group and 33% of the Control Group. (Our scheme for judging severity of complication from the Midwife Report is presented in Table 5). The PBC's included anoxia, prematurity, prolonged labor, placental difficulties, umbilical cord complications, mother's illness during pregnancy, multiple births and breech presentations.

A summary of all of these findings is listed in Table 6. I would like to point out, in passing, with minimal comment, some interesting, perhaps coincidental, similarities in the behavioral consequences of surgically inflicted hippocampal damage in rats (see Table 7) and the behavior of our Sick subjects with perinatal casualty. The hippocampus is an area of the brain selectively vulnerable to perinatal casualty (Blackwood, et al, 1967; Spector, 1965). In a recent paper Mednick (1970)

has developed the speculative notion that perhaps perinatal hippocampal damage in combination with genetic
predisposition plays some role in the etiology of schizophrenia. Note, in Tables 6 and 7 that both the Sick
subjects with pregnancy and birth complications (PBC's)
and the hippocampal rats evidence fast response latency,
very poor habituation and poor extinction of a conditioned response. We can also tentatively link the
hyperactivity of the hippocampal rats to the unruly
classroom behavior of our Sick subjects. Two points
that do not immediately relate to each other are the
fast avoidance conditioning of the hippocampal rats and
the fast GSR recovery of the Sick Group with PBC's. The
linking of fast autonomic recovery with fast avoidance
conditioning contains the essence of our explanation of
how one becomes schizophrenic.

Let us pause a moment and consider avoidance learning
in a relatively simple case, the rat in the shuttlebox.
Why does the rat learn to avoid? One critical reason
is that when the rat runs out of the shock compartment
and into the safe compartment his fear is reduced. This
reduction of fear serves as a reinforcement for his
avoidance response. Now the value of a reinforcement is
directly related to its speed of delivery and its magnitude. The faster and greater the reduction of fear the
greater the reinforcement value. The rate at which this
fear is reduced depends in large part on the rate at
which the autonomic nervous system recovers from a state
of agitation to a normal level. The faster the rate of
recovery, the faster the delivery of the reinforcement
and the greater the reinforcement. If the rat recovers
very slowly the difference between the shock compartment
and the safe compartment will be minimized as will the
reinforcement value of his avoidance response. If the
rat has abnormally fast autonomic recovery his reinforcement will come abnormally quickly; he will learn
the avoidance response abnormally quickly. The fast
autonomic recovery then functions as an aptitude for
learning avoidance responses just as nimble fingers and
absolute pitch provide an aptitude for learning to play
the violin.

In earlier papers Mednick (1958, 1962) has attempted to
formulate specifically how this pattern of avoidance
could result in some of the common symptoms of schizophrenia. If fast recovery does constitute such an
aptitude, one would expect that those subjects in the
High Risk Group who manifested a fast rate of recovery
will have, in the course of their lives, learned a
large number of avoidance responses. As a test of this
hypothesis Mednick, Schulsinger & Lampasso (1971) determined the individual rate of GSR recovery for the Sick
& Well subjects and correlated this with a score for

avoidant associates ("Chaining" Score from the Continuous Association Test, Diderichsen, 1967). The two scores correlated positively (r = .48, 25 df, p < .05). As predicted, those subjects who have a faster rate of recovery had learned more avoidant associates.

This formulation would also predict that the schizophrenic would perform well in a situation where an avoidant response is functional or correct. For example, such a response might avoid noxious stimulation or punishment. In general, censure or punishment produces marked deterioration in schizophrenic's performance (Rodnick and Garmezy, 1957). If, however, the situation is constructed so that the schizophrenic can learn to avoid the censure (response-contingent censure) his performance improves disproportionately. (Cavanaugh, 1958; Losen, 1961; Johannesen, 1964; McCarthy, 1963). Unlike normal subjects, schizophrenics learn faster when their response can avoid punishment than when their response merely produces reward (Atkinson & Robinson, 1961).

This formulation would also predict that schizophrenics would perform better than normals in eyelid conditioning. Their task here is to learn to close their eyelid to a warning signal in order to avoid the noxious effects of a puff of air on the eyeball. Spain (1964) demonstrated that schizophrenics learned this avoidance response faster than normals. In addition, those schizophrenics that evidenced most withdrawn ward behavior manifested the fastest avoidance conditioning in this situation!

Since within this learning theory orientation, learned avoidant associates are the essence of the schizophrenic disorder, the aptitude of fast recovery must be interpreted as a crucial factor predisposing to schizophrenia. Empirically, we would expect to find this aptitude in schizophrenic patients. Stimulated by our reports of fast recovery in the Sick subjects, Al Ax (1971) reanalyzed psychophysiological data on schizophrenics in order to score their recovery rates. His results support our findings. Schizophrenics evidence markedly faster GSR recovery rates than do controls. Gruzelier & Venables (1971) conducted two new studies with schizophrenics, studying their GSR behavior. Their data replicate ours very well in almost all details including the crucial recovery variable. Lidsky, Hakerem and Sutton (1967), observed unusually fast recovery from contraction of pupils (redilation) of their psychiatric patient population (mainly schizophrenic) in comparison to controls. This study is interesting since it involves another response modality sensitive to autonomic influences.

Our theory suggests that the combination of:

1. an autonomic nervous system that responds too quickly and too much,

2. an inability to habituate to mild stress,

3. an abnormally fast rate of recovery,

provide an aptitude for learning avoidance responses. These ANS variables may be profitably classified into two categories, those that can produce ANS distress (fast latency, exaggerated response amplitude and lack of habituation) and the variable (fast recovery) that helps resolve the distress by providing an aptitude for learning to avoid distressing stimuli. If an individual is to become schizophrenic he must possess both of the types of ANS characteristics. If an individual is rapidly, exaggeratedly, and untiringly emotionally reactive he may become anxious or psychotic but won't tend to learn schizophrenia unless his rate of recovery tends to be very fast. It also seems likely that an extraordinarily reactive ANS will only require moderately fast recovery while an extraordinarily fast recovery will only require moderate reactivity. Both very high reactivity and very fast recovery will result in a very heavy predisposition for schizophrenia.

The greater the autonomic responsiveness and lack of habituation, the more protective avoidance will be necessary to fend off potentially distressing internal and external stimuli. The ultimate protection is perhaps the almost totally avoidant thought pattern and behavior or the truly chronic schizophrenic. In this case, thoughts and behavior are almost totally dominated by avoidant associative and motor responses. If from among the chronic schizophrenics we select those who evidence a pattern of most extreme withdrawal, we should find these withdrawn chronics to be characterized by perhaps the most responsive ANS. This is precisely what has been found (Fowles, Watt & Maher, 1970; Venables, 1966; Venables & Wing, 1962). It also follows that chronic schizophrenics should exhibit a lack of ANS habituation, as indeed Zahn et al, (1964) & Milstein, et al, (1969) have found.

One final point. We have stressed the importance of the physiological predispositions. But the hypothesized ANS predispositions will only result in distress in response to unpleasant environments or noxious thoughts. An individual who is treated kindly is far less likely to evidence distressing ANS overexcitement and will have relatively little provocation to learn a massive pattern of avoidant responses. The development of schizophrenia depends then on an interaction of reactive, sensitive and quickly recovering autonomic nervous systems and unkind environments. Let us turn now to a consideration of the relationship between unkind environments and the ANS variables.

Speculations and data on the origins of ANS abnormalities.

The ANS variables play a crucial role in our theoretical constructions concerning the etiology of schizophrenia and were distinctive, empirically, in differentiating the Sick Group. It was consequently inevitable that our interest turned to exploring the possible origins of this autonomic deviance. There was evidence that some aspects of the GSR can be influenced by genetic factors and that schizophrenia has a genetic component (Kety, Rosenthal, Wender & Schulsinger, 1968). It seemed clear that genetic factors could not be excluded as possible origins of the ANS deviance in the Sick Group. On the other hand, it seemed a good bet that early environmental stress could also produce chronic autonomic aberrations. This genetic factor also had to be considered. Finally the autonomic variables studies have proven to be relatively independent of one another. (The correlation between log conductance response and the rate of recovery from that response hovers around .10). Consequently, it seemed very possible that some autonomic factors could be influenced by genetic and some by environmental variables. We could tentatively explore the genetic factors in a rather imprecise way by comparing our High and Low Risk groups which differ in their familial loading for schizophrenia.

Parental separation and ANS factor. We looked for an important, reliable way of dividing the subjects on the factor of environmental stress. Many of the children were separated from their parents quite early in life in both the High & Low Risk groups. In view of the pervasive stressful influence of such separation we chose parental separation as an environmental stress whose chronic effect on GSR we would explore. In Western society, a young child lacking a special adult who will love, protect and educate him has a relatively elevated probability of leading a difficult early life. There are implications for almost every aspect of his existence from his nourishment to his intellectual competence. Our goal in this next study was to compare risk, separation and their interaction as possible determinants of autonomic deviance, and thus possibly as predispositional to schizophrenia. The study involved groups varying in risk but "equated" for separation, and groups varying in separation but "equated" for risk. Thus, we had the opportunity to observe the effects of separation with the influence of psychiatric familial background greatly reduced or eliminated. It is in such a situation, where genetic variance is restricted, that environmental

variance such as parental separation can have an opportunity to show its influence. Parenthetically, we might
mention that it is likely that the lack of such genetic
control in the parental-separation literature may be in
part responsible for the conflicting findings in that
area. This parental-separation study is being conducted
as a doctoral dissertation by Mrs. Edna Herrmann, a
graduate student working with Mednick at the New School.
She is making use of the data from the 1962 high-risk
study.

Mrs. Herrmann developed several scales relating to the
quantity and continuity of parent or substitute-parent
contact in the first five years of life. These several
scales proved to intercorrelate so highly that she
expressed them as one scale score ... the Separation
Scale. This scale gives a score indicating the degree
to which a child has been free of, or deprived of, the
direct and individual care of a parent or parent substitute in the first 5 years of life. The children with
high scores have led rather chaotic lives. High Separation and Low Separation groups were chosen from both the
High and Low Risk groups. All four groups were matched,
individual for individual, for sex, age, social class,
and years of education. The High and Low Risk, High
Separation groups were matched for Separation Scale
scores as were the High and Low Risk, Low Separation
groups. With all this careful matching, Mrs. Herrmann's
N's have come down to 30, each, in the Low and High-
Separated, High Risk group and 15, each, in the Low and
High-Separated, Low Risk group.

Results of Risk-Separation Study. The High Risk group evidenced markedly poorer mental health than the Low Risk
group on a series of items based on teacher's judgment
and interviewing psychiatrist's judgment (F = 18.39,
1/87 df, df, p .01). Note that this was true with
amount of separation equated. The poorer mental health
of the High Risk group probably could not be ascribed to
aspects of their life experiences related to separation
from their parents. It would seem possible here to
attribute their adjustment difficulties to genetic
factors. However, in the groups differing in Separation,
but "equated" for genetic background, the Separation
Scale proved equally effective in predicting to level of
mental health (see Figure 6). Poorer mental health was
associated with more separation (F = 16.33, 1/87 df ,
p < .01). It is difficult, however, to postulate a
direction of causality. Were these children separated
because they manifested poor mental health and perhaps
were irritating to care for? Did they develop the poor
mental health because of the separation? (or was it some
spiralling combination of these circumstances?)

258

There is another possible interpretation of the effectiveness of separation. The mothers of the High Separated
group may differ in some specific heritable characteristic which is related to separation. The children of the
High Separation mothers might have inherited this specific
characteristic which might have given them some predisposition to poor mental health. We are currently checking
severity of illness of the High Risk mothers and some
limited information we have on pre-separation characteristics of the children in order to evaluate these
alternate interpretations.

But in any case these very well-matched groups enable us
to assess the relationship between psychophysiology and
separation while holding risk constant, and between risk
and psychophysiology while holding separation constant.
Figure 7 presents the latency of the GSR as a function
of separation and risk. Both High Risk and High Separation produce a significantly faster latency [F (risk) =
7.25, 1/87 $\underline{df}$, $\underline{p} < .01$; F (separation) = 3.51, 1/87 $\underline{df}$,
$\underline{p} < .03$, one-tail test], (a significant statistical inter-
action was not observed). The effect of separation does
seem a bit greater in the Low Risk group but it should
be recalled that the latency of the High Risk group is
working against a physiological limit. The mean GSR
latency of 1.81 sec. for the High Risk, High Separation
group is rather fast. What we can conclude from this is
that even when the High and Low Risk groups are equated
for separation, large differences still exist in latency
of the GSR. We might permit ourselves the speculation
that this finding represents a genetic effect. Likewise
where the risk variable is controlled (implying some
genetic control) separation also proves to be a powerful
variable influencing latency. Granting some of the
cautions we have mentioned above, we might consider that
this finding represents an environmental effect. These
two variables having independently demonstrated effectiveness in influencing latency, produce a clear additive
effect. That is, if you have been separated from your
parents you will have an unusually fast GSR latency; if
you also happen to be born to a schizophrenic woman your
latency will be that much quicker.

The same pattern is observed in amplitude (Figure 8).
Both the risk and separation variables are again inde-
pendently significant [F (risk) = 9.82, 1/87 $\underline{df}$, $\underline{p} < .01$;
F (separation) = 3.35, 1/87 $\underline{df}$, $\underline{p} < .03$, one-tail test).
The interaction of the two is not statistically signif-
icant. But again these variables are additive in their
effect. Having been both born to a schizophrenic mother
and having also been separated from her produces an
extremely highly reactive autonomic nervous system.

The pattern for recovery is different. Here (Figure 9)

while the risk variable is highly significant (F = 9.32, 1/87 ', $\underline{df}$, $\underline{p}$ < .003), the separation variable is not at all so ($\overline{F}$ = .02, 1/87 , $\underline{df}$, n.s.), nor is the interaction of the two significant. This pattern suggests that we have in recovery a variable that is not sensitive to the type of environmental stress implied in the separation variable. You will recall that the recovery variable separated the Sick, Well and Control Groups better than any of the other measures in our test battery. The recovery variable occupies a central position in our speculations concerning the development of the clinical behavioral pattern called schizophrenia. There is a reasonable possibility that important, uncontrolled, environmental variables, correlated with risk status and unrelated to genetics, produced the rate of recovery effects in the children with schizophrenic mothers. It is tempting,however, to speculate that (being the only ANS variable uninfluenced by the environmental variables related to early parental separation) recovery may be an important part of the genetic pattern passed on to the child by the schizophrenic parent.

From these analyses we concluded that the aspects of autonomic functioning which are sensitive to and associated with distress can be chronically influenced by the early environmental stress of separation from parents Recovery was no so influenced. ln continuing our search for the origins of the observed pattern of autonomic deviance we turned next to the perinatal data.

Perinatal complications and ANS factors. As noted above, the Sick Group had suffered considerably more pregnancy and birth complications (PBCs) than the Well and Control Group. Perusing the midwife data for the Sick Group we noted a very marked correspondence between presence of PBCs and the deviant ANS behavior. In fact, much of the GSR differences between the Sick and Well Groups as well as the Control Group could be explained by the PBCs in the Sick Group. In the Control Group the PBCs were not as strongly associated with these extreme GSR effects. The PBCs in the Sick Group seem to trigger some characteristic which may be genetically predisposed. We determined to explore the PBC-NAS relationship in the entire High and Low Risk Groups. This data analysis is currently being conducted by Miss Nina Kassen, a graduate student at the New School, working on her doctorate with Mednick. We can report some of her findings. She has submitted these data to a Stepwise Multiple Regression Analysis (MR) with the autonomic measures as her dependent variable and risk and degree of PBC as her independent variables. She has modelled her analysis along the lines suggested by Cohen (1968). We wish to acknowledge Dr. Cohen's invaluable advice in this analysis. When PBCs were analysed, the constant was the mean of the group with no PBCs. When interaction effects

were analysed the constant was the Low Risk group with
no PBCs. Variables were forced into the regression
equation so as to test the hypothesis that severity of
PBCs would predict the autonomic variables.

Figure 10 presents the data for GSR latency as a function
of risk and PBCs. The PBCs are ineffective in influencing the GSR latencies of the Low Risk subjects but
have a significant effect in the High Risk Group. This
matches our findings for the Sick, Well and Control
Groups. The interaction term is significant (F = 20.67,
1/241 df, p < .001). Figure 11 presents the data for
GSR amplitude as a function of risk and PBCs. The PBCs,
in this case, produce highly significant effects in both
the High and Low Risk Groups. There is no interactive
effect as there was in the Sick, Well and Control Groups.
As is the case with the separation data, the effect
seems to be additive. Having a schizophrenic mother is
associated with elevated responsiveness of the ANS; if
in addition the individual has suffered PBCs his
autonomic responsiveness will be even more exaggerated.
The effects of PBCs were significant (F = 9.07, 1/241
df, p < .01) as were the effects of the risk variable
(F = 13.49, 1/241 df, p < .01).

Much the same picture is seen with recovery (see Figure
12). Both the risk and the PBC variables are related
to significant changes in the recovery rate of the GSR
[F (risk) = 7.67, 1, 241 df, p < .01; F (PBC) = 11.97,
1, 241 df, p < .01). The High Risk subjects with severe
PBCs recover at a mean rate of 1054 ohms per second in
the stress trials. This puts them well up into the
range of recovery rates observed in the Sick Group.

It is difficult to compare magnitude of PBC effects
across the variables of latency, recovery and amplitude
because different units of measurements are involved
and different physiological ceiling effects are doubtless
operating. However, visual inspection of the three
figures suggests that amplitude (graphed in log units)
was most strongly affected by PBCs. Miss Kassen ranked
the pooled High and Low Risk distribution of amplitudes
and divided this pooled distribution into Large, Medium
and Small Responders. She then looked to see which PBCs
were associated with being a Large Responder. Especially
strongly associated were: dry birth, use of ether during
labor, severe prolonged labor, use of quinine during
labor, intrauterine asphyxia, and umbilical cord complications. Most of these complications tend to occur
together, and would very likely result in fetal anoxia
and/or mechanical damage (pressure) of brain tissue.
This type of analysis might suggest hypotheses regarding
the mechanisms by which PBCs might affect autonomic
functioning.

At this point we hasten to add two cautions. First, it is possible to suggest that it is not the PBCs that are causing the autonomic deviance. It could be argued that genetically determined, autonomic deviance in the fetus was in some unknown way responsible for provoking the PBCs. Maternal stress during pregnancy might also be responsible for autonomic deviance in the fetus (Sontag, 1944) and also for the delivery complications. Secondly, we find the results of these more detailed exploratory attempts quite exciting and suggestive. However, they are based on midwife reports whose reliability we will discuss below. Until these findings are replicated we would urge that your attention be drawn more to the problems and methods than to the individual results.

Summary: possible factors etiologically related to autonomic deviance. To sum up, this exploration of some possible etiological factors related to autonomic deviance, we can tentatively put forth the following assertions:

1. High risk, separation from parents, and perinatal disturbance are associated with deviance in autonomic functioning.

2. Amplitude of response seems to be most heavily influenced by PBCs and separation. There is some hint that delivery difficulties which could have produced fetal anoxia were the instrumental PBC variables.

3. Rate of recovery was not at all influenced by separation but was affected by PBCs. Rate of recovery was consistently faster for the group with schizophrenic mothers. We were tempted to speculate that this variable is, in part, related to genetic factors.

4. Early separation from parents produced a quick GSR latency in both risk groups; PBCs and risk had an interactive effect on latency. The latencies of the Low Risk group were unaffected by the PBCs; PBCs in the High Risk group, however, related to significantly enhanced speed of autonomic response.

This interaction is reminiscent of the interactive effect of risk and PBCs found in the Sick-Well-Control comparisons. Perhaps, in the vulnerable High Risk children the PBCs were triggering or exacerbating some genetically determined sensitivity of the ANS. This finding attracted our attention; we turned to see if we could find parallels in the genetics literature and discovered that this type of perinatal-genetic interaction was not unknown.

Fraser & Fainstat (1951) subjected pregnant mice to a heavy dose of cortisone and in a <u>genetically vulnerable strain</u> radically increased the frequency of cleft palates. Joffe (1969) subjected a group of pregnant rats to repeated, severe, and inescapable electric shocks. In comparison to controls, the resultant pups demonstrated significantly faster response latency and interestingly enough faster avoidance conditioning. These results are startlingly similar to those of the hippocampal rats and our PBC-Sick subjects. Again these effects of gestational stress varied markedly as a function of rat genetic strain. Ingalls, Avis, Curley and Temin (1953) reduced atmospheric pressure in the environment of mice 9 days pregnant and differentially caused an increase in sternum malformations in the litters of genetically predisposed strains. A genetic predisposition could very well be exacerbated by perinatal complications. Research by Kalter suggests "that the factors controlling PBC susceptibility... involve both the maternal and fetal genotypes." (1954, p. 195).

We stopped to consider our position at this point. The perinatal data were exciting but suffered from limitations:

1. The midwife is an adequate but not ideal recorder of the pregnancy and delivery;

2. She did not produce her records for purposes of research.

Danish investigators working with midwife records have noted that the midwife would tend to err in the direction of omitting mention of some difficulties. If she did record complications we could be sure they had occurred.

In view of these limitations of our data and in view of our perception of the importance of the problem, we determined to launch a new longitudinal study of children of schizophrenic parents. We were lucky enough to be able to contact children who were part of a massive Danish perinatal study of 9006 consecutive deliveries at the University Hospital in Copenhagen from 1959-1961; excellent pregnancy and delivery information is available for them. As controls we have selected from this same perinatal-study population, children with normal parents, and children with parents who have suffered non-schizophrenic psychiatric disorders. These children are currently being brought in for intensive assessment. Because of the high quality of the perinatal data these groups give us an excellent opportunity to attempt to replicate and extend our earlier PBC findings.

At this point, I can very briefly sketch for you the
course of the pregnancy, delivery and first year of
development of these high-risk children. Greater detail
may be found in Mednick, Mura, Schulsinger and Mednick
(1971). It was our hypothesis that while there would be
no differences between the three groups in the amount of
pregnancy or delivery complications, we would observe
a genetic-perinatal casualty interaction. That is, the
same level of perinatal difficulties would have a more
pronounced effect in the Schizophrenic group than in
other groups.

The subjects had been examined during pregnancy and
delivery, immediately after birth, and at one year of
age. The Schizophrenic Parents, Psychiatric Controls
and Normal Controls were matched, individual for individual, for the following factors (in order of importance): Sex of ill parent, Sex of child, Race, Multiple
birth (twins), Pregnancy number, Mother's age, Mother's
height, Father's age. In Table 8 you can see the success
of our matching.

We devised several scoring systems for the pregnancy and
delivery. The different scoring systems intercorrelate
very highly. I will present results for the simplest
system - a count of the number of complications of pregnancy - a count for delivery - a count of the number of
neurological and physical disorders in the neonatal and
in the one year exams and a count of developmental
anomalies in the one year exam. In this simple system
more serious complications or conditions get more points
because their effects are more widespread. For example,
severely low birth weight would receive only one point
but it would get additional points for use of incubator,
associated difficulties of the fetus in beginning to
breathe, various signs of prematurity, and disturbances
in heart-beat.

Results. There were no impressive differences in the
progression of the pregnancies and deliveries of the
Schizophrenic, Psychiatric Control, and Normal Control
groups. In the neonatal examination both the Psychiatric and Schizophrenic group children evinced more
abnormalities. The abnormalities for the children of
schizophrenics tended to come in the absence or weakness
of their motor reflexes. These results agree well with
those reported by Fish and Alpert (1963). Most remarkable
in the one year examination was the retarded motor development of the children of schizophrenics. In almost
every item they are retarded in the age of attainment of
motor milestones.

The relationship between the pregnancy and delivery complications and the neonatal and one year examination

scale scores was explored by intercorrelating these
scores. In this manner, high scores on the birth factors
indicating complications and high scores on the postnatal examinations indicating abnormalities should tend
to go together and yield positive correlations. As
expected, almost all correlations were positive. Difficulties in pregnancy and delivery, however, showed no
significant correlations with neonatal status for any
of the groups except the schizophrenics. For the children of schizophrenics, both pregnancy and delivery scales
correlated positively and significantly with the child's
appearance at the time of the neonatal examination.

Low birth weight was consistently related to difficulties
in the neonatal examination for all groups. For all
groups but the Schizophrenics it proved to be unrelated
to the status of the child at the one year exam. Exclusively in the case of the schizophrenics, and especially
so in the case where the mother was schizophrenic, birth
weights below 3000 grams were associated with retarded
development during the first year.

The Schizophrenic Group suffered levels of PBCs which
were quite similar to those of the two control groups.
Despite this, the effect of these PBCs was much greater
for the Schizophrenic Group in the neonatal and one year
examinations. This result may be considered support for
the hypothesized PBC-genetic interaction.

All of the 10-12 year old children described in this
study are currently being brought into our Institute in
Copenhagen for intensive examination. An important
purpose of this new longitudinal study is to seek out
the details of the PBC-genetic interaction. To further
this aim a new control group is being gathered. This
group with normal parents will be matched to the Schizophrenic Group for the nine matching variables listed
earlier. In addition, they will be matched individual
for individual for the course of their pregnancy and
delivery. Each pattern of abnormality noted in the
pregnancy or delivery of a Schizophrenic Group subject
will be found in a normal mother from the pool of 9006
deliveries. This group of children will also be brought
in for examination. The new Control Group will thus be
matched to the Schizophrenic Group for a rather impressive list of factors. The great difference between the
two groups of children will be the schizophrenia in their
mother or father. This group will further enable us to
assess the result of "identical" perinatal difficulties
in two groups of children differing in genetic background.

Perinatal factors and prevention

If the importance of perinatal factors in schizophrenia

is confirmed this will suggest a course of prevention involving perinatal care for high-risk mothers. Prevention, along with understanding, has been an important goal of our research program from its inception. This is, in part, because of the theory guiding this research. Learned avoidance responses are difficult to change. Every time the avoidance response is made, the relief it brings reinforces the avoidance. It is thus self-reinforcing. In the shuttle box the rat's avoidance response can be extinguished by closing the door to the safe compartment and not delivering any shocks. By physically preventing the response it can be extinguished This method is useless in the case of avoidant thoughts. But because the theory suggests that treatment will be unrewarding, our effort has been directed toward the goal of prevention. It is for this reason we developed the high risk method; one of the important products of this method is the identification of measures to identify children at high risk. Such children might then be helped by preventive efforts aimed at the anomalies for which the children were selected. In the case of our research, the psychophysiological measures, the word association measures, classroom behavior and extensive parental separation could be seen as potential premorbid, identifying characteristics. If one wanted to work in prevention with very young children, however, the classroom behavior, associations and parental separation might not be useful. In that case one just might choose to identify high risk children by means of their psychophysiology.

We are, in association with Abdul Raman and Peter Venables attempting to launch a WHO-sponsored research project on prevention making use of psychophysiological characteristics to choose high risk, three year old children.

On the island of Mauritius, off the east coast of Africa, we will examine 2000 three year old children psychophysiologically. We will select high risk children from among those whose characteristics match those of our Sick subjects. These high risk children and controls will be brought into two nursery schools. One group of high risk children and controls will not be admitted to the nursery schools but will be kept as controls for the nursery school experience.

Our interventive procedures will be administered in a very strictly maintained factorial design. The evaluation of change as a function of intervention will be made by outside observers uninformed as to the children's risk status or treatment group. The interventive procedures have not been selected as yet. In view of the extensive research on the damping effect of some classes of drugs on autonomic nervous system activity such agents are tempting to consider. It is also possible to try operant training techniques such as those reported by Neal Miller (1969). To change avoidant behavior that may already have begun we may lean heavily on behavior conditioning techniques. Where the child is separated from parental care we may attempt to provide some substitute parent. Since neither of us is a pediatrician or pharmacologist we are seeking the advice of an international panel via a WHO technical experts conference on the question of preventive procedures. In view of the factorial nature of the design we hope to be able to evaluate the effects of the interventions as well as the interactions.

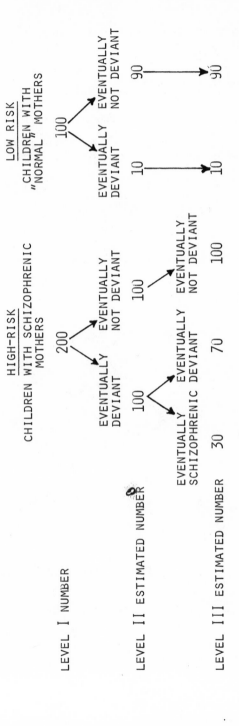

FIGURE I

EXAMPLE OF DESIGN OF
STUDY OF HIGH-RISK SAMPLES

FIGURE 2

LIST OF EXPERIMENTAL MEASURES

1962 HIGH RISK ASSESSMENT

1. PSYCHOPHYSIOLOGY
   A. CONDITIONING-EXTINCTION-GENERALIZATION
   B. RESPONSE TO MILD AND LOUD SOUNDS
2. WECHSLER INTELLIGENCE SCALE FOR CHILDREN (DANISH ADAPTATION)
3. PERSONALITY INVENTORY
4. WORD ASSOCIATION TEST
5. CONTINUOUS ASSOCIATION TEST
   A. 30 WORDS
   B. ONE MINUTE OF ASSOCIATING TO EACH WORD
6. ADJECTIVE CHECK LIST
   USED BY EXAMINERS TO DESCRIBE SUBJECTS
7. PSYCHIATRIC INTERVIEW
8. INTERVIEW WITH PARENT OR REARING AGENT
9. SCHOOL REPORT FROM TEACHER
10. MIDWIFE'S REPORT ON SUBJECT'S PREGNANCY AND DELIVERY

FIGURE 3

DESCRIPTIONS OF CONDITIONS OF SICK GROUP

Male, born 16 March 1953. Extremely withdrawn, no close
contacts, 2 months' psychiatric admission following
theft, currently in institution for boys with behavior
difficulties, still performing petty thieveries.

Female, born 19 January 1943. Married, one child,
extremely withdrawn, nervous. Evidence of delusional
thinking, pulls her hair out, has large bald area.

Female, born 29 March 1946. Promiscuous, highly unstable
in work, no close contacts, confused and unrealistic,
psychiatric admission for diagnostic reasons, recent
abortion, some evidence of thought disorder.

Male, born 1 July 1946. Under minor provocation had
semi-psychotic breakdown in Army, expresses strange
distortions of his body image, thought processes vague,
immature.

Male, born 2 May 1944. Severe difficulties in concentrating, cannot complete tasks, marked schizoid
character, marginally adjusted.

Male, born 3 June 1947. Lonely in the extreme, spends
all spare time at home. Manages at home only by virtue
of extremely compulsive routines. No heterosexual
activity, marked schizoid character.

Male, born 1 October 1953. No close contact with peers,
attends class for retarded children, abuses younger
children, recently took a little boy out in the forest,
undressed him, urinated on him and his clothes, and sent
him home.

Male, born 17 January 1954. Has history of convulsions,
constantly takes antiseizure drug (Dilanthin), nervous,
confabulating, unhappy, sees frightening "nightmares"
during the day, afraid to go to sleep because of nightmares and fear that people are watching through the
window, feels teacher punishes him unjustly.

Female, born 18 March 1944. Nervous, quick mood changes,
body image distortions, passive, resigned. Psychiatric
admission, paranoid tendencies revealed, vague train of
thought.

270

Figure 3 (2)

Male, born 14 March 1952. Arrested for involvement in
theft of motorbike. Extremely withdrawn, difficulties
in concentration, passive, disinterested, father objected
to his being institutionalized, consequently he is now
out under psychiatric supervision.

Male, born 19 October 1947. Level of intellectual performance in apprenticeship decreasing, private life
extremely disorderly, abreacts through alcoholism.

Male, born 20 January 1944. Severe schizoid character,
no heterosexual activity, lives an immature, shy,
anhedonic life, thought disturbances revealed in TAT.

Female, born 25 May 1947. Psychiatric admission, abortion, hospital report suspect pseudoneurotic or early
schizophrenia, association test betrays thought disturbance, tense, guarded, ambivalent. Current difficulties
somewhat precipitated by sudden death of boy friend.

Male, born 13 August 1950. Sensitive, negativistic,
unrealistic. Recently stopped working and was referred
to a youth guidance clinic for evaluation. Is now
under regular supervision of a psychologist.

Male, born 28 May 1947. History of car stealing,
unstable, drifting, unemployed, sensitive, easily hurt,
one year institutionalization in a reformatory for the
worst delinquents in Denmark.

Female, born 1 June 1945. Psychotic episode, one year of
hospitalization. Diagnoses from 2 hospitals: (1) schizophrenia, (2) manic psychosis.

Male, born 3 September 1946. Severe schizoid character,
psychotic breakdown in Army, preceded by arrest for car
thievery. Now hospitalized.

Male, born 28 January 1953. Perhaps borderline retarded.
Psychiatric admission for diagnostic reasons, spells of
uncontrolled behavior.

Male, born 23 June 1948. Repeatedly apprehended for
stealing, severe mood swings, sensitive, restless,
unrealistic, fired from job because of financial irregularities.

Female, born 5 July 1941. Highly intelligent girl with
mystical interests. Very much afflicted by mother's
schizophrenia. TAT reveals thought disorder. Receiving
psychotherapy.

271

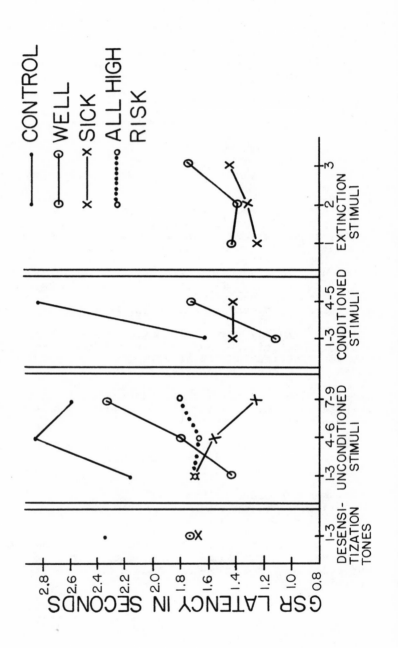

FIGURE 4

FIGURE 5

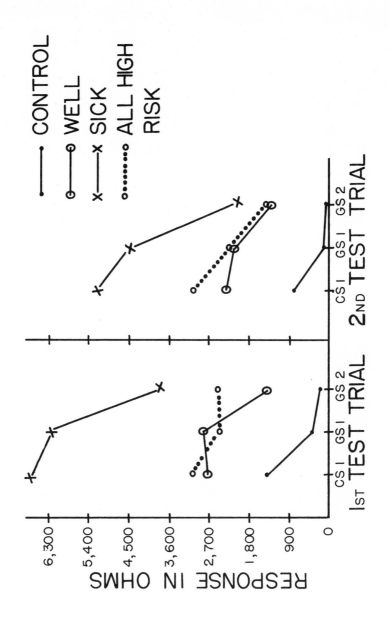

FIGURE 6

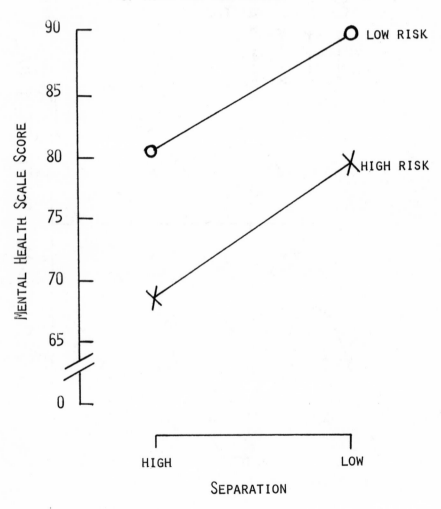

Mental Health Score As a Function
of Risk and Separation

FIGURE 7

LATENCY OF GSR AND DEGREE OF SEPARATION FROM PARENTS
(STRESS STIMULUS TRIALS)

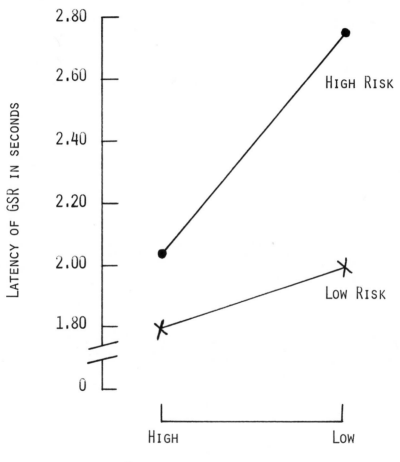

FIGURE 8

AMPLITUDE OF GSR & DEGREE OF SEPARATION FROM PARENTS

(STRESS STIMULUS TRIALS)

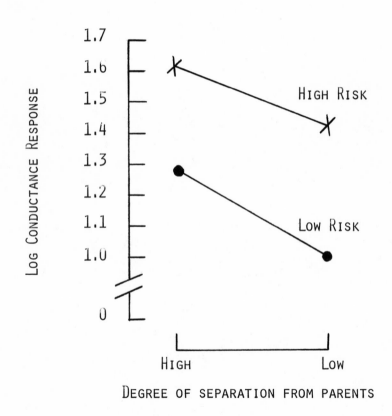

FIGURE 9

Rate of Recovery of GSR and Degree of Separation from Parents (stress-stimulus trials)

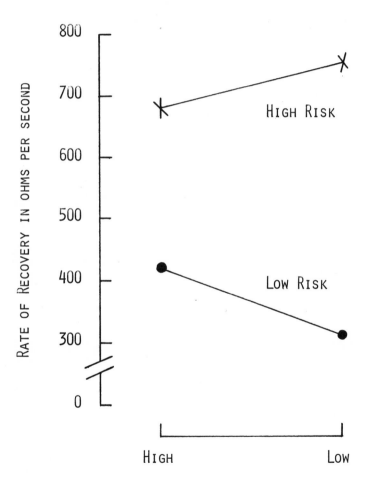

DEGREE OF SEPARATION FROM PARENTS

FIGURE 10

LATENCY OF GSR AND SEVERITY OF BIRTH COMPLICATIONS

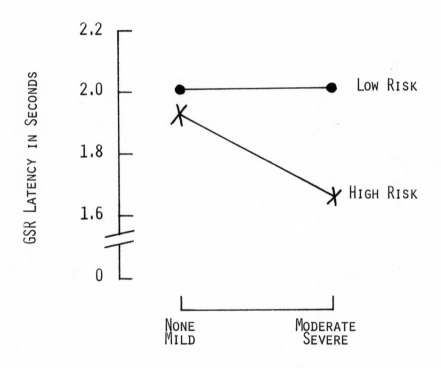

SEVERITY OF PREGNANCY AND BIRTH COMPLICATIONS

FIGURE 11

AMPLITUDE OF GSR AND SEVERITY OF BIRTH COMPLICATIONS

(STRESS-STIMULUS TRIALS)

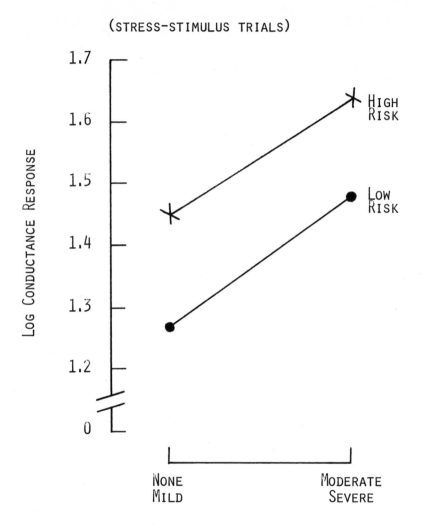

SEVERITY OF PREGNANCY AND BIRTH COMPLICATIONS

FIGURE 12

RATE OF RECOVERY OF GSR AND SEVERITY

OF BIRTH COMPLICATIONS

(STRESS-STIMULUS TRIALS)

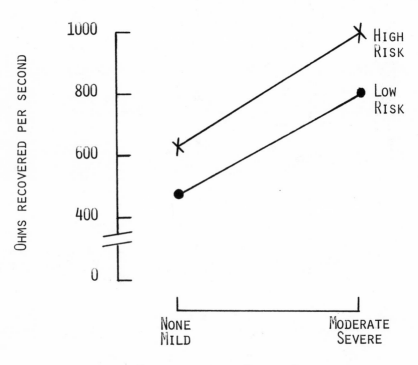

TABLE 1

CHARACTERISTICS OF THE EXPERIMENTAL & CONTROL SAMPLES

	Control	Experimental
Number of cases	104	207
Number of boys	59	121
Number of girls	45	86
Mean age*	15.1	15.1
Mean social class**	2.3	2.2
Mean years education	7.3	7.0
Per cent of group in children's homes (5 years or more)#	14%	16%
Mean number of years in children's homes (5 years or more)#	8.5	9.4
Per cent of group with rural residence@	22%	26%

* Defined as age to the nearest whole year.

** The scale runs from 0 (low) to 6 (high) and was adapted from Svalastoga (1959).

We only considered experience in children's homes of 5 years or greater duration. Many of the Experimental children had been to children's homes for brief periods while their mothers were hospitalized. These experiences were seen as quite different from the experience of children who actually had to make a children's home their home until they could go out and earn their own living.

@ A rural residence was defined as living in a town with a population of 2500 persons or fewer.

TABLE 2

PER CENT OF GROUP WITH MOTHER COMPLETELY ABSENT FROM HOME DURING SPECIFIED PERIODS IN THE CHILD'S LIFE

CHILD'S AGE IN YEARS	SICK	WELL	CONTROL	CHI SQUARE	P
0-1	7	5	0		N.S.
1-2	11	5	5		N.S.
3-5	30	10	10		N.S.
5-10	65	15	30	20.6	<0.01
11-13	81	40	35	15.1	<0.01
14-17	85	42	46	11.8	<0.05

TABLE 3

MEAN AMPLITUDE OF GSR TO STRESS STIMULI

(SICK, WELL AND CONTROL GROUPS)

MEAN GSR IN OHMS

CS-UCS TRIALS	SICK	WELL	CONTROL	P
I	25,859	17,194	9, 238	<0.01
II	14,467	10,472	6,583	<0.05
III	11,128	8,167	4,133	<0.01
IV	10,823	11,567	5,365	N.S.
V	10,759	6,859	4,900	<0.05
VI	10,900	5,494	3,606	<0.05
VII	8,778	6,728	2,922	N.S.
VIII	10,983	5,761	4,241	<0.05
IX	9,682	7,217	3,244	<0.05

TABLE 4

RATE OF RECOVERY OF GSR RESPONSE

TO STRESS STIMULI

UCS Trial	MEAN OHMS RECOVERED PER SEC.		
	SICK GROUP	WELL GROUP	CONTROL GROUP
2	1607	634	521
3	1538	651	595
4	1386	764	394
5	1230	615	582
6	1282	606	331
7	1816	749	401
8	1490	884	392
9	1406	691	590

TABLE 5

MIDWIFE PBC SCALE

Pregnancy Complications

Mild:

one infarct in the placenta

other placental and membrane difficulties (for example:
    placenta retained, placental insufficiency, detached
    placenta, ruptured placenta)

Rh immunization : titre 2-32

mother ill during pregnancy (for example: gonorrhea,
    syphilis, tuberculosos, mild circulatory disturbance)

mother's age: 15 years old or less
               35 years old or more

inferred emotional difficulties or stress during
    pregnancy (for example: mother abandoned during
    pregnancy by putative father, mother unmarried,
    divorced, separated or widowed)

previous fetal loss (miscarriage or abortion)

prematurity: (1) more than 2500 grams but not full term
                 (2-3 weeks early and not fully developed
                 with at least 2 signs of prematurity
                 (red skin, thin legs, soft nails,
                 wrinkled face)

             (2) less than 2500 grams but full term and
                 no signs of prematurity

Moderate:

two or more infarcts in the placenta

Rh immunization (titre not recorded)

twin birth

prematurity: 1501 to 2500 grams (including 2500 grams)
    or 33-36 weeks

Table 5 (2)

mother ill during pregnancy (for example: anemia,
    pyelitis or kidney inflammation, adipositas or
    grossly overweight, cancer, tumor, hypertension,
    pre-eclampsia, controlled epilepsy)

addiction to narcotics (heroin), amphatamines or
    barbituates during pregnancy

Severe:

triplets

Rh immunization (titre more than 32)

mother ill during pregnancy (for example: diabetes
    mellitus, eclampsia, toxemia of pregnancy, uncontrolled
    epilepsy)

prematurity: 1000 to 1500 grams or 29-32 weeks

Delivery Complications

Mild:

weak labor

narrow pelvis

tearing of the perineum

episiotomy required

suture of rift required

bleeding after birth

birth weight of child more than 4000 grams

drugs used during labor: ether, morphine, quinine,
    stimulation of labor with drugs (pituitrin, methergin,
    ergometrin)

premature rupture of membrane (up to but not including
    6 hours prior to labor)

viginal exploration required during labor

birth occurred before midwife or doctor arrived

child is first or fifth (or more) born

Table 5 (3)

Moderate:

narrow pelvis causing noteworthy deformity of child's head

extreme lack of muscle one during labor (atoni)

premature rupture of membrane (dry birth): 6 to 12 hours
    prior to labor

bleeding during pregnancy

precipitous birth (length of labor less than 2 hours)

fetal position problem: breech, forehead, face, foot,
    breech-foot

umbilical cord complications: cord loosely tied around
    neck

instruments used during delivery: forceps

caesarian section

prolonged labor: for multipara -- 16 to 24 hours
                 for primipara -- 24 to 36 hours

Severe:

premature rupture of membrane (dry birth): more than 12
    hours prior to labor

umbilical cord complication: prolapse of cord

prolonged labor: for multipara -- more than 24 hours
                 for primipara -- more than 36 hours

asphyxia (intrauterine)

bleeding immediately before labor

convulsions during labor

instruments used during delivery: breech extraction
    instruments

TABLE 6

DISTINGUISHING CHARACTERISTICS OF THE SICK GROUP

1. Lost mother to psychiatric hospitalization early in life.

2. Teacher reports disturbing, aggressive behavior in school.

3. Evidence associative drift.

4. Psychophysiological anomalies:

    A. Markedly fast latency of response

    B. Response latency evidenced no sign of habituation

    C. Great resistance to experimental extinction of conditioned GSR

    D. Remarkably fast rate of recovery following response peak

5. 70% of the Sick Group suffered serious pregnancy or birth complications.

TABLE 7

RELEVANT CHARACTERISTICS OF HIPPOCAMPECTOMIZED RATS

1.   Fast latency of response

2.   Poor habituation of response latency

3.   Great resistance to experimental extinction
      of conditioned responses

4.   Hyperactivity

5.   Fast acquisition of shuttle-box avoidance
      responses

TABLE 8

IDENTIFYING CHARACTERISTICS FOR ENTIRE SAMPLE
SCHIZOPHRENIC, CHARACTER DISORDER, AND NORMAL PARENTS

GROUP	ENTIRE SAMPLE	SCHIZO-PHRENIC	CHARACTER DISORDER	NORMAL
NUMBER	9006	83	83	83
MALES	4696	42	42	42
FEMALES	4486	41	41	41
NUMBER OF TWINS	170	3	3	3
MEAN PREGNANCY NUMBER	1.96	1.86	1.90	1.87
MEAN SOCIAL CLASS	3.45	3.58	3.54	3.53
MEAN MOTHER'S AGE	26.0	26.6	26.7	26.6
MEAN MOTHER'S HEIGHT IN CM.	163.9	163.8	164.5	164.0
MEAN FATHER'S AGE	28.4	30.8	31.2	30.6

REFERENCES

Atkinson, R.L., & Robinson, N.M. Paired-associate
learning by schizophrenic and normal subjects under
conditions of personal and impersonal reward and punishment. Journal of Abnormal and Social Psychology, 1961,
62, 322-326.

Ax, A.F. & Banford, J.L. The GSR recovery limb in
chronic schizophrenics. Psychophysiology, 1970, 7,
145-147.

Blackwood, W., McMenemy, W.H., Meyer, A., Norman, R.L.
& Russel, D.S. Greenfield's Neuropathology. Baltimore:
Williams and Wilkins, 1967.

Cavanaugh, D.K. Improvement in the performance of
schizophrenics on concept formation tasks as a function
of motivational change. Journal of Abnormal and Social
Psychology, 1958, 57, 8-12.

Cohen, J. Multiple regression as a general data-analytic
system. Psychological Bulletin, 1968, 70, 426-433.

Diderichsen, B. Formelle Karakteristika ved Associationsforløbet hos en gruppe børn med høj risiko for schizophreni, Københavns Universitet, 1967.

Fish, B. & Alpert, M. Patterns of neurological development in infants born to schizophrenic mothers, Recent
Advances in Biological Psychiatry, Vol. 5, New York,
1963.

Fowkes,D.C., Watt, N.F., & Maher, B.A. Autonomic
arousal in good and poor premorbid schizophrenics.
British Journal of Social and Clinical Psychology, 1970,
9, 135-147.

Fraser, F.C., & Fainstat, T.D. Production of congenital
defects in the offspring of pregnant mice treated with
cortisone. Pediatrics, 1951, 8, 527-533.

Gruzelier, J. & Venables, P. Paper presented at British
Psychological Association, London, 1971.

Heston, L.L. Psychiatric disorders in foster home
reared children of schizophrenic mothers. British
Journal of Psychiatry, 1966, 112, 819-825.

Ingalls, T.H., Avis, F.R., Curley, F.J., Temin, H.M.
Genetic determinants of hypoxia-induced congenital
anomalies. Journal of Heredity, 1953, 44, 185-194.

Joffe, J.M. Prenatal Determinants of Behavior. London: Pergamon Press, 1969.

Johannesen, W.J. Motivation in schizophrenic perform-ance: A Review. Psychological Reports, 1964, 15`, 839-870.

Kallmann, F.J. The genetic theory of schizophrenia. American Journal of Psychiatry, 1946, 103, 309-322.

Kalter, H. The inheritance of susceptibility to teratogenic action of cortisone in mice. Genetics, 1954, 39, 185-196.

Kety, S.S., Rosenthal, D., Wender, P.H. & Schulsinger, F. The types and prevalence of mental illness in the biological and adoptive families of schizophrenics. Journal of Psychiatric Research, 1968, 6 (supplement 1), 345-362.

Lidsky, A. Hakerem, G. & Sutton, S. Psychopathological patterns of pupillary response to light. Paper presented at Fifth Pupil Colloquium, University of Pennsylvania, May, 1967.

Losen, S.M. The differential effects of censure on the problem solving behavior of schizophrenic and normal subjects. Journal of Personality, 1961, 29, 258-272.

McCarthy, J.F. The differential effects of praise and censure upon the verbal responses of schizophrenics. Unpublished doctoral dissertation, The Catholic University of America, 1963.

Mednick, S.A. A learning theory approach to research in schizophrenia. Psychological Bulletin, 1958, 55, 316-327.

Mednick, S.A. Schizophrenia: a learned thought disorder. in G. Nielsen (Ed.). Clinical Psychology, Proceedings of the XIV International Congress of Applied Psychology, Copenhagen, Munksgaard, 1962.

Mednick, S.A. Breakdown in children at high risk for schizophrenia: Behavioral and autonomic characteristics and possible role of perinatal complications. Mental Hygiene, 1970, 54, 50-63.

Mednick, B., Mednick, S., & Schulsinger, F. Breakdown in high risk subjects: familial and early environmental factors, 1972, unpublished manuscript.

Mednick, S.A. and McNeil, T.F. Current methodology in research on the etiology of schizophrenia. Psychological Bulletin, 1968, 70, 681-693.

Mednick, S.A., Mura, E., Schulsinger, F., & Mednick, B. Perinatal conditions and infant development in children with schizophrenic parents. Social Biology, 1971, 18, 103-113.

Mednick, S.A., Schulsinger, F. & Lampasso, A. Rate of GSR recovery and avoidant associations, unpublished manuscript, 1971.

Miller, N.E. Learning of visceral and glandular responses, Science, 1969, 163, 434-445.

Milstein, V., Stevens, J., & Sachdev, K. Habituation of the alpha attentuation response in children and adults with psychiatric disorders. Electroencephalography and Clinical Neurophysiology, 1969, 26, 12-18.

Rodnick, E. & Garmezy, N. An experimental approach to the study of motivation in schizophrenia. In Jones, M.R. (Ed.): Nebraska Symposium on Motivation. Lincoln: University of Nebraska Press, 1957, 109-184.

Royce, J.R. and Covington, Genetic differences in the avoidance conditioning of mice. Journal of Comparative and Physiological Psychology, 1960, 53, 197-200.

Sontag, L.W. Differences in modifiability of fetal behavior and physiology. Psychosomatic Medicine, 1944, 6, 151-154.

Spain, B. Eyelid conditioning and arousal in schizophrenic and normal subjects. Journal of Abnormal Psychology, 1966, 71, 260-266.

Spector, R.G. Enzyme chemistry of anoxic brain injury. In C.W.M. Adams (Ed.). Neurohistochemistry, New York: Elsevier, 1965.

Venables, P.H. Psychophysiological aspects of schizophrenia. British Journal of Medical Psychology, 1966, 39, 289-297.

Venables, P.H. & Wing, J.K. Level of arousal and the sub-classification of schizophrenia. Archives of General Psychiatry, 1962, 7, 114-121.

Zahn, T.P., Rosenthal, D., Lawlor, W.G. Electrodermal and heart-rate orienting reactions in chronic schizophrenia. Journal of Psychiatric Research, 1968, 6, 117-134.

BIBLIOGRAPHY

Achenbach, T.M. The classification of children's psychiatric symptoms: A factor analytic study. *Psychological Monographs*, 1966, 80, 6, 37 pages.

Achte, K.A. Der Verlauf der Schizophrenien und der Schizophreniformen Psychosen. *Acta Psychiatrica Scandinavica*, Suppl. 155, 1961.

Alanen, Y.O., Rekola, J.K., Stewen, A., Takala, K., & Tuovinen, M. The family in the pathogenesis of schizophrenic and neurotic disorders. *Acta Psychiatrica Scandinavica, Copenhagen*, Suppl. 189, 42, 1966.

Alkire, A.A., Goldstein, M.J., Rodnick, E.H., & Judd, L.L. Social influence and counter-influence within families of four types of disturbed adolescents. *Journal of Abnormal Psychology*, 1971, 77, 32-41.

Allen, G., & Kallmann, F.J. Mongolism in twin sibships. *Acta Genetica et Statistica Medica*, 1957, 7, 385.

Allen, G., & Kallmann, F.J. Frequency and types of mental retardation in twins. *American Journal of Human Genetics*, 1955, 7, 15.

Alvarez, R.R. A comparison of the preference of schizophrenic and normal subjects for rewarded and punished stimuli. Unpublished Ph.D. dissertation, Duke University, 1957.

Angyal, Alice F. Speed and pattern of perception in schizophrenic and normal persons. *Character and Personality*, 1942, 11, 108-127.

Angyal, A., & Blackman, N. Vestibular reactivity in schizophrenia. *Arch. Neurol. Psychiat.*, 1940, 44, 611-620.

Angyal, A., Freeman, H., & Hoskins, R.G. Physiologic aspects of schizophrenic withdrawal. *Arch. Neurol. Psychiat.*, 1940, 44, 621-626.

Angyal, A., & Sherman, M.A. Postural reactions to vestibular stimulation in schizophrenic and normal subjects. *American Journal of Psychiatry*, 1942, 98, 857-862.

Aschner, B.M., Kallmann, F.J., & Roizin, L. Concurrence of Morgagni's syndrome, schizophrenia and adenomatous goiter in monozygotic twins. *Acta genet. med. gemellolog.*, 1953, 2, 431.

Astrup, C., Fossum, A., & Holmboe, R. *Prognosis in junctional psychosis: Clinical, social and genetic aspects.* Springfield, Ill.: Charles C. Thomas, 1962.

Atkinson, R.L., & Robinson, N.M. Paired-associate learning by schizophrenic and normal subjects under conditions of personal and impersonal reward and punishment. *Journal of Abnormal and Social Psychology*, 1961, 62, 322-326.

Ax, A.F., & Banford, J.L. The GSR recovery limb in chronic schizophrenics. *Psychophysiology*, 1970, 7, 145-147.

Babigian, H.M. Schizophrenia in Monroe County. In: *Schizophrenia: Implications of research findings for treatment and teaching.* By M.M. Katz, A. Littlestone, L. Mosher, M.S. Roath, & A.H. Tuma (Eds.). In Press.

Bell, R.Q. Convergence: An accelerated longitudinal approach. *Child Development*, 1953, 24, 142-145.

Bellak, L. *Schizophrenia.* New York: Logos Press, 1958.

Blackwood, W., McMenemy, W.H., Meyer, A., Norman, R.L., & Russel, D.S. *Greenfield's Neuropathology.* Baltimore: Williams and Wilkins, 1967.

Bleuler, M. Vererbungsprobleme bei Schizophrenen. *Z. ges. Neurol. Psychiat.*, 1930, 127, 321-388; Eng. trans. in *Journal of Nervous and Mental Disease*, 1931, 74.

Bleuler, M. Schizophrenia: Review of the work of Prof. Eugen Bleuler. *Arch. Neurol. Psychiat.*, 1931, 26, 610-627.

Bleuler, M. Psychotische Belastung von körperlich Kranken. *Z. ges. Neurol. Psychiat.*, 1932, 146, 780-810.

Bleuler, M. Der Rorschach-Vejrsuch als Unterscheidungsmittel von Konstitution und Prozess. *Z. ges. Neurol. Psychiat.*, 1934, 151, 571-578.

Bleuler, M. Erblichkeit und Erbprognose: Durchschnittsbevölkerung, Schizophrenie, manisch-depressives Irresein, Epilepsie, 1933-1936. *Fortschr. Neurol. Psychiat.*, 1937, 9, 250-664.

Bleuler, M. Erblichkeit und Erbprognose: Schizophrenie, manisch-depressives Irresein, Epilepsie, Durchschnittsbevölkerung. *Fortschr. Neurol. Psychiat.*, 1938, 10, 392-403.

Bleuler, M. Erblichkeit und Erbprognose: Schizophrenie, manisch-depressives Irresein, Epilepsie, Durchschnittsbevölkerung. *Fortschr. Neurol. Psychiat.*, 1939, 11, 287-302.

Bleuler, M. Erblichkeit und Erbprognose: Schizophrenie, manisch-depressives Irresein, Epilepsie, Durchschnittsbevölkerung (1939-1940). *Fortschr. Neurol. Psychiat.*, 1941, 13, 49-63.

Bleuler, M. *Krankheitsverlauf, Persönlichkeit und Verwandtschaft Schizophrener und ihre gegenseitigen Beziehungen.* Leipzig: Thieme, 1941.

Bleuler, M. Das Wesen der Schizophrenieremission nach Schockbehandlung. *Z. ges. Neurol. Psychiat.*, 1941, 173, 553-597.

Bleuler, M. Die spatschizophrenen Krankheitsbilder. *Fortschr. Neurol. Psychiat.*, 1943, 15, 259.

Bleuler, M. Schizophrenes und endokrines Krankheitsgeschehen. *Arch. Klaus-Stift. Vererb.-Forsch.*, 1943, 18, 403.

Bleuler, M. Die Prognose der Psychosen, insbesondere der Schizophrenie. *Periodische Mitteilungen der Schweiz. Lebensversicherungs-Ges.*, 1946, 175-186.

Bleuler, M. Forschungen zur Schizophreniefrage. *Wien. Z. Nervenheilk.*, 1948, 1, 129-148.

Bleuler, M. Bedingt Einheitlichkeit im Erbgang — eine überwundene Schwierigkeit in der Konstitutionsforschung am Menschen. *Arch. Klaus-Stift. Vererb.-Forsch.*, 1949, 24, 355-364.

Bleuler, M. Endokrinologie in Beziehung zur Psychiatrie (Uebersichtsreferat). *Zbt. ges. Neurol. Psychiat.*, 1950, 110, 225.

Bleuler, M. Forschungen und Begriffswandlungen in der Schizophrenielehre, 1941-1950. *Fortschr. Neurol. Psychiat.*, 1951, 19, 385-456.

Bleuler, M. Biologie und Entwicklungslehre der Personlichkeit. *Verh. schweiz. naturforsch. Ges. Bern*, 1956, 66-43.

Bleuler, M. Gedanken zur heutigen Schizophrenielehre — am Beispiel der Konstitutionspathologie erläutert. *Wien. Z. Nervenheilk.*, 1953, 7, 255-270.

Bleuler, M. *Endokrinologische Psychiatrie.* Stuttgart: Thieme, 1954.

Bleuler, M. Zur Psychotherapie der Schizophrenie. *Dtsch. med. Wschr.*, 1954, 79, 841-842.

Bleuler, M. Das Wesen der Serpasil-Behandlung an Schizophrenen. In: Das zweite Serpasil-Symposium in der psychiatrischen Universitätsklinik Burghölzli, Zürich. *Schweiz. med. Wschr.*, 1955, 85, 439-444.

Bleuler, M. Familial and personal background of chronic alcoholics. In: O. Dietheim: *Etiology of chronic alcoholism.* Springfield, Ill.: Charles C. Thomas, 1955, Pp. 110-166.

Bleuler, M. Comparative study of the constitution of Swiss and American alcoholic patients. In: O. Dietheim: *Etiology of chronic alcoholism.* Springfield, Ill.: Charles C. Thomas, 1955, Pp. 167-178.

Bleuler, M.   Research and changes in concepts in the study of schizophrenia, 1941-1950. *Bulletin of the Isaac Ray Medical Library*, 1955, 3, 1-132.

Bleuler, M.   Psychiatrische Irrtümer in der Serotoninforschung. *Dtsch. med. Wschr.*, 1956, 81, 1078-1081.

Bleuler, M.   Comparaison entre les effets de la Chlorpromazine et de la Réserpine en psychiatrie. *Encéphale*, 1956, 45, 334-338.

Bleuler, M.   Eugen Bleuler: Die Begründung der Schizophrenielehre. In: *Gestalter unserer Zeit. Bd. 4: Erforscher des Lebens*. Oldenburg: Gerhard Stalling Verlag, 1956.

Bleuler, M.   Aspects secrets de la psychiatrie. *Evolution Psychiatrique*, 1956, I, 45-50.

Bleuler, M.   Die Problematik der Schizophrenien als Arbeitsprogramm des II. Internationalen Kongresses für Psychiatrie. *Nervenarzt*, 1957, 28, 529-533.

Bleuler, M.   Scopo e tema del nostro congresso. *Pisani*, 1957, 71/3, 481-491.

Bleuler, M.   Aims and topic of our congress. Hamdard, *Medical Digest* (Karachi), May, 1958.

Bleuler, M.   International cooperation in research on schizophrenia. *Bulletin of the Menninger Clinic*, 1958, 22, 43-49.

Bleuler, M.   Endokrinologische Behandlungsverfahren bei psychischen Störungen.   In: *Therapeutische Fortschritte in der Neurologie und Psychiatrie*, hgg. v. H. Hoff; Urban und Schwarzenberg, Wien-Innsbruck, 1960, Pp. 294-305.

Bleuler, M.   Entwicklungslinien psychiatrischer Praxis und Forschung. *Schweiz. med. Wschr.*, 1961, 91, 1549.

Bleuler, M.   Early Swiss sources of Adolf Meyers concepts. *American Journal of Psychiatry*, 1962, 11973, 193-196.

Bleuler, M.   Schizophrenieartige Psychosen und Aetiologie der Schizophrenie. *Schweiz. med. Wschr.*, 1962, 92, 1641-1647.

Bleuler, M.   Conception of schizophrenia within the last fifty years and today. *Proceedings of the Royal Society of Medicine*, 1963, 56, 945-952.

Bleuler, M.   Endokrinologische Psychiatrie. In: *Psychiatrie der Gegenwart – Forschung und Praxis*. Band I/1b; Teil B, S. Springer, Berlin-Gottingen-Heidelberg, 1964, 161-252.

Bleuler, M.   Ursache und Wesen der schizophrenen Geistesstörungen. *Dtsch. med. Wschr.* 89, 40 & 41, 1865-1870 und 1947-1952, 1964.

Bleuler, M.   Neue Therapiemoglichkeiten im Vergleich zu alten in der Psychiatrie. *Dtsch. med. Wschr.*, 1964, 89, 501-505.

Bleuler, M.   Significato della ricerca psicoterapeutica per la teoria sulla schizofrenia e per il paziente schizofrenico.   *Arch. Psicol. Neurol. Psychiat.*, 1966, 27/4-5, 353-368.

Bleuler, M.   Neue Entwicklung des Schizophrenieproblems. *Praxis* (Bern), 1967, 56/10, 326-331.

Bleuler, M.   A 23-year longitudinal study of 108 schizophrenics and impressions in regard to the nature of schizophrenia. In: *The transmission of schizophrenia*, D. Rosenthal, & S.S. Kety (Eds.) Pergamon Press, Oxford, 1968, Pp. 3-12.

Bower, E.M.   *Early identification of emotionally handicapped children in school.* Springfield, Ill.: Charles C. Thomas, 2nd ed., 1969.

Bradford, N.   Comparative perceptions of mothers and maternal roles by schizophrenic patients and their normal siblings. Unpublished Ph.D. dissertation. University of Minnesota, 1965.

Bradley, C.   *Schizophrenia in childhood.*   New York: Macmillan, 1941, Pp. 137-145.

Broadhurst, P.L.   Analysis of maternal effects in the inheritance of behavior. *Animal Behavior*, 1961, 9, 129-141.

Bruner, J.S. Discussion: Infant education as viewed by a psychologist. In: *Education of the infant and young child*. V.H. Denenberg (Ed.). New York: Academic Press, 1970, Pp. 109-116.

Burks, B.S. The relative influence of nature and nurture upon mental developments: A comparative study of foster parent-foster child resemblance and true parent-true child resemblance. *27th Yearbook of the national society for the study of education*, 1928, Pt. 1, 219-316.

Buss, A.H.; & Lang, P.J. Psychological deficit in schizophrenia. I. Affect, reinforcement, and concept attainment. *Journal of Abnormal Psychology*, 1965, 70, 2-24.

Cannon, W.B. *The wisdom of the body* (Rev. ed.). New York: Norton, 1939.

Carrigan, Patricia M. Intraindividual variability in schizophrenia. *Diss. Abstracts*, 1964, 25, 2, 1330. (Order no. 64-8142)

Cavanaugh, D.K. Improvement in the performance of schizophrenics on concept formation tasks as a function of motivational change. *Journal of Abnormal and Social Psychology*, 1958, 57, 8-12.

Chandler, M.J. Egocentricism in normal and pathological child development. Paper presented at the First Symposium of the International Society for the Study of Behavioral Development. Nijmegen, Holland, 1971.

Cicchetti, D.V. Reported family dynamics and psychopathology. *Journal of Abnormal Psychology*, 1967, 72, 282-289.

Clarke, A.R. Conformity behavior of schizophrenic subjects with maternal figures. *Journal of Abnormal and Social Psychology*, 1964, 68, 45-53.

Coghill, G.E. The neuro-embryologic study of behavior: Principles, perspective and aim. *Science*, 1933, 78, 131-138.

Cohen, J. Multiple regression as a general data-analytic system. *Psychological Bulletin*, 1968, 70, 426-433.

Cohen, L.H., & Patterson, M. Effect of pain on the heart rate of normal and schizophrenic individuals. *Journal of General Psychology*, 1937, 17, 273-289.

Coopersmith, S. *The antecedents of self-esteem*. San Francisco: W.H. Freeman Co., 1967.

Cromwell, R.L., Rosenthal, D., Shakow, D., & Zahn, T.P. Reaction time, locus of control, choice behavior, and descriptions of parental behavior in schizophrenic and normal subjects. *Journal of Personality*, 1961, 29, 363-379.

Dean, S.R. Schizophrenia. *American Journal of Psychiatry*, 1957, 114, 557.

Dean, S.R. Schizophrenia research a national necessity. Congressional Record, Proceedings and Debates of the 85th Congress, Second Session, March 20, 1958.

Dean, S.R. Schizophrenia: Mental crippler of youth. *Today's Health*, 1958, 36, 41.

Dean, S.R. Schizophrenia: A major public health problem. *Connecticut Medicine*, 1959, 23, 328-330.

Dempsey, E.W. Homeostasis. In: S.S. Stevens (Ed.) *Handbook of experimental psychology*. New York: Wiley, 1951, Pp. 209-235.

Diderichsen, B. Formelle Karakteristika ved Associationsforløbet hos en gruppe børn med høj risiko for schizophreni, Københavns Universitet, 1967.

Dunn, W.L., Jr. Visual discrimination of schizophrenic subjects as a function of stimulus meaning. *Journal of Personality*, 1954, 23, 48-64.

Engelhardt, R.S. Semantic correlates of interpersonal concepts and parental attributes in schizophrenia. Unpublished Ph.D. dissertation. Duke University, 1959.

Erlenmeyer-Kimling, L., Rainer, J.D., & Kallmann, F.J. Current reproductive trends in schizophrenia: A psychiatric-genetic study. In: P.H. Hoch, & J. Zubin (Eds.) *Psychopathology of Schizophrenia*. New York: Grune & Stratton, 1966.

Falek, A., Kallmann, F.J., Lorge, I., & Jarvik, L.F. Longevity and intellectual variation in a senescent twin population. *Journal of Gerontology*, 1960, 15, 305.

Farina, A. Patterns of role dominance and conflict in parents of schizophrenic subjects. *Journal of Abnormal and Social Psychology*, 1960, 61, 31-38.

Farina, A., & Dunham, R.M. Measurement of family relationships and their effects. *Archives of General Psychiatry*, 1963, 9, 64-73.

Farina, A., & Holzberg, J.D. Interaction patterns of parents and hospitalized sons diagnosed as schizophrenic or non-schizophrenic. *Journal of Abnormal Psychology*, 1968, 73, 114-118.

Fish, B., & Alpert, M. Patterns of neurological development in infants born to schizophrenic mothers. *Recent Advances in Biological Psychiatry*, New York, 1963, Vol. 5.

Fowks, D.C., Watt, N.F., & Maher, B.A. Autonomic arousal in good and poor premorbid schizophrenics. *British Journal of Social and Clinical Psychology*, 1970, 9, 135-147.

Fox, S.S. LSD alteration of optic potentials (cat lateral geniculate); block by schizophrenic serum. *Federation Proceedings*, 1960, 19, 262.

Fraser, F.C., & Fainstat, T.D. Production of congenital defects in the offspring of pregnant mice treated with cortisone. *Pediatrics*, 1951, 8, 527-533.

Fredericson, E. Reciprocal fostering of two inbred mouse strains and its effect on the modification of aggressive behavior. *American Psychologist*, 1952, 7, 241-242 (Abstract).

Freeman, H., & Rodnick, E.H. Effect of rotation on postural steadiness in normal and in schizophrenic subjects. *Arch. Neurol. Psychiat.*, 1942, 48, 47-53.

Fujita, S., & Ging, N.S. Presence of toxic factors in urine from schizophrenic subjects. *Science*, 1961, 134, 1687-1688.

Garmezy, N. Approach and avoidance behavior of schizophrenic and normal subjects under conditions of reward and punishment. *Journal of Personality*, 1952, 20, 253-276.

Garmezy, N. Commentary. *Journal of Nervous and Mental Disease*, 1971, 153, 317-322.

Garmezy, N. Contributions of experimental psychology to understanding the origins of schizophrenia. In: Romano, J. (Ed.) The origins of schizophrenia. *Excerpta Medica International*, 1967.

Garmezy, N. Models of etiology for the study of children who are at risk for schizophrenia. In: *Life history research in psychopathology*, Vol. II. M. Roff, L. Robins, & M.M. Pollack (Eds.) Minneapolis: University of Minnesota Press. In Press.

Garmezy, N. Prediction of performance in schizophrenia. In: *Psychopathology of schizophrenia*. P. Hoch, & J. Zubin (Eds.) New York: Grune & Stratton, 1966, Pp. 129-181.

Garmezy, N. Process and reactive schizophrenia: Some conceptions and issues. In: Katz, M., & Cole, J. (Eds.) *The role and methodology of classification in psychiatry and psychopathology*. U.S. Department of HEW, Government Printing Office. Reprinted (with addendum) in *Schizophrenia Bulletin*, Washington, D.C., NIMH, Vol. 1, A 2, 1970, Pp. 30-74.

Garmezy, N. Research strategies for the study of children who are at risk for schizophrenia. In: *Schizophrenia: Implications of research findings for treatment and teaching.* M.M. Katz, R. Littlestone, L. Mosher, M.S. Roath, & A.H. Tuma (Eds.) In Press.

Garmezy, N. Vulnerability research and the issue of primary prevention. *American Journal of Orthopsychiatry*, 1971, 41 (1), 101-116.

Garmezy, N. Vulnerable children: Implications derived from studies of an internalizing-externalizing symptom dimension. In: *The psychopathology of adolescence*. Zubin, J., & Freedman, A.M. (Eds.) New York: Grune & Stratton, 1970, Pp. 212-239.

Garmezy, N., & Nuechterlein, K.H. Vulnerable and invulnerable children: The fact and fiction of competence and disadvantage. *American Journal of Orthopsychiatry*, (abstract), 1972, 77.

Garmezy, N., & Rodnick, E.H. Premorbid adjustment and performance in schizophrenia: Implications for interpreting heterogeneity in schizophrenia. *Journal of Nervous and Mental Disease*, 1959, 129, 450-466.

Garmezy, N., Weintraub, S.A., Wright, D.M., Tredici, L., & Schiele, B.C. Effects of censure and chlorpromazine on visual discrimination behavior of schizophrenic and alcoholic patients. *Proceedings of the 77th Annual APA Convention*, 1969.

Gerard, R.W., *et al.* The nosology of schizophrenia. *American Journal of Psychiatry,* 1963, 120, 16-29.

Ginsburg, B.E., & Allee, W.C. Some effects of conditioning on social dominance and sub-ordination in inbred strains of mice. *Physiological Zoology,* 1942, 15, 485-506.

Goldfarb, William, & Dorsen, Marilyn M. *Annoted bibliography of childhood schizo-phrenia.* New York: Basic Books, 1956.

Goldstein, M.J. Premorbid adjustment, paranoid status, and patterns of response to pheno-thiazine in acute schizophrenia. *Schizophrenia Bulletin,* 1970, 3, 34-37.

Goldstein, M.J., Gould, E., Alkire, A., Rodnick, E.H., & Judd, L.L. Interpersonal themes in the thematic apperception test stories of families of disturbed adolescents. *Journal of Nervous and Mental Disease,* 1970, 150, 354-365.

Goldstein, M.J., Judd, L.L., Rodnick, E.H., Alkire, A., & Gould, E. A method for studying social influence and coping patterns within families of disturbed adolescents. *Journal of Nervous and Mental Disease,* 1968, 147, 233-251.

Goldstein, M.J., Judd, L.L., Rodnick, E.H., & LaPolla, A. Psychophysiological and be-havioral effects of phenothiazine administration in acute schizophrenics as a function of premorbid status. *Journal of Psychiatric Research,* 1969, 6, 271-287.

Goldstein, M.J., Rodnick, E.H., Judd, L.L., & Gould, E. Galvanic skin reactivity among family groups containing disturbed adolescents. *Journal of Abnormal Psychology,* 1970, 75, 57-67.

Goodman, D. Performance of good and poor premorbid male schizophrenics as a function of paternal vs. maternal censure. *Journal of Abnormal and Social Psychology,* 1964, 69, 550-555.

Grinker, R.R. Psychiatry and our dangerous world. In: *Psychiatric research in our chang-ing world.* Proceedings of an International Symposium. Montreal, 1968, Excerpta Med-ica International Congress Series, No. 187.

Grinker, R.R. (Ed.) *Toward a unified theory of human behavior.* New York: Basic Books, 1960.

Gruzelier, J., & Venables, P. Paper presented at British Psychological Association, London, 1971.

Haggard, E.A., Brekstad, A., & Skard, A. On the reliability of the anamnestic interview. *Journal of Abnormal and Social Psychology,* 1960, 61, 311-318.

Harris, J.E. Size estimation of pictures as a function of thematic content for schizophrenic and normal subjects. *Journal of Personality,* 1957, 25, 651-671.

Hartup, W.W. Peer interaction and social organization. In: *Manual of child psychology,* 3rd Ed. P.H. Mussen (Ed.) New York: John Wiley & Sons, 1970, Pp. 361-456.

Heston, L.L. Psychiatric disorders in foster home reared children of schizophrenic moth-ers. *British Journal of Psychiatry,* 1966, 112, 819-825.

Higgins, J. The concept of process-reactive schizophrenia: Criteria and related research. *Journal of Nervous and Mental Disease,* 1964, 138, 9-25.

Higgins, J. Process reactive schizophrenia: Recent developments. *Journal of Nervous and Mental Disease,* 1969, 149, 450-472.

Higgins, J., & Peterson, J.C. Concept of process-reactive schizophrenia: A critique. *Psy-chological Bulletin,* 1966, 66, 201-206.

Holmberg, G.K., & Gershon, S. Autonomic and psychic effects of yohimbine hydro-chloride. *Psychopharmacologia,* 1961, 2, 93-106.

Honzik, M.P. Developmental studies of parent-child resemblance in intelligence. *Child Development,* 1957, 28, 215-228.

Hoskins, R.G. *The biology of schizophrenia.* New York: Norton, 1946.

Hoskins, R.G., & Jellinek, E.M. The schizophrenic personality with special regard to psychologic and organic concomitants. *Proceedings. Research nerv. ment. Disease*, 1933, 14, 211-233.

Huebner, Dorothy M. Effects of repetition on the association test in schizophrenic and normal subjects. Unpublished master's thesis. Johns Hopkins University, 1938.

Hunting, W.H. Differences in the perceptual recognition responses of good and poor premorbid schizophrenics to anxiety and neutral words. Unpublished doctoral dissertation. University of California (Los Angeles), 1966.

Huston, P.E. The reflex time of the patellar tendon reflex in normal and schizophrenic subjects. *Journal of General Psychology*, 1935, 13, 3-41.

Huston, P.E. Sensory threshold to direct current stimulation in schizophrenic and in normal subjects. *Arch. Neurol. Psychiat.*, 1934, 31, 590-596.

Huston, P.E., & Shakow, D. Learning capacity in schizophrenia; with special reference to the concept of deterioration. *American Journal of Psychiatry*, 1949, 105, 881-888.

Huston, P.E., & Shakow, D. Learning in schizophrenia. I. Pursuit learning. *Journal of Personality*, 1948, 17, 52-74.

Huston, P.E., Shakow, D., & Riggs, L.A. Studies of motor function in schizophrenia. II. Reaction time. *Journal of General Psychology*, 1937, 16, 39-82.

Huston, P.E., & Shakow, D. Studies of motor function in schizophrenia. III. Steadiness. *Journal of General Psychology*, 1946, 34, 119-126.

Huston, P.E., & Singer, Mary M. Effect of sodium amytal and amphetamine sulfate on mental set in schizophrenia. *Arch. Neurol. Psychiat.*, 1945, 53, 365-369.

Ingalls, T.H., Avis, F.R., Curley, F.J., & Temin, H.M. Genetic determinants of hypoxia-induced congenital anomalies. *Journal of Heredity*, 1953, 44, 185-194.

Jarvik, L.F., Kallmann, F.J., Falek, A., & Klaber, M.M. Changing intellectual functions in senescent twins. *Acta Genet. Stat. Med.*, 1957, 7, 421.

Jarvik, L.F., Kallmann, F.J., & Falek, A. Intellectual changes in aged twins. *Journal of Gerontology*, 1962, 17, 289.

Jarvik, L.F., Kallmann, F.J., & Falek, A. Psychiatric genetics and aging. *Gerontologist*, 1962, 2, 164.

Jarvik, L.F., Kallmann, F.J., Lorge, I., & Falek, A. Longitudinal study of intellectual changes in senescent twins. In: C. Tibbits, & W. Donahue (Eds.) *Social and psychological aspects of aging*. New York: Columbia University Press, 1962.

Jarvik, L.F., Falek, A., Kallmann, F.J., & Lorge, I. Survival trends in a senescent twin population. *American Journal of Human Genetics*, 1960, 12, 170.

Joffe, J.M. *Prenatal determinants of behavior*. London: Pergamon Press, 1969.

Johannesen, W.J. Motivation in schizophrenic performance: A review. *Psychological Reports*, 1964, 15, 839-870.

Johanson, Eva. A study of schizophrenia in the male. A psychiatric and social study based on 138 cases with follow-up. *Acta psych. Scand.*, Suppl. 125, 1958.

Jungeblut, C.W., Kallmann, F.J., Roth, B., & Goodman, H.O. Preliminary twin data on the salivary excretion of a receptor-destroying enzyme. *Acta Genet. Stat. Med.*, 1957, 7, 191.

Kallmann, F.J. Accidental stab wounds as cause of death. *Ärztl. Sachverständingen Ztschr.*, 1921, 22, 126. (German)

Kallmann, F.J. On the psychopathology of the superstitious criminal. *Mschr. Psychiat. Neurol.*, 1929, 72, 37. (German)

Kallmann, F.J. On the symptomatology of cerebral cysticercosis. *Mschr. Psychiat. Neurol.*, 1929, 72, 324. (German)

Kallmann, F.J., & Marcuse, H. Sulfosin therapy in general paresis and schizophrenia. *Nervenarzt*, 1929, 2, 149. (German)

Kallmann, F.J., & Salinger, F. Accident-conditioned metastasis in malignant tumors. *Ärztl. Sachverständigen Ztschr.*, 1929, 9, 1. (German)

Kallmann, F.J., & Salinger, F. Diagnostic and forensic aspects of cerebral cysticercosis. *Mschr. Psychiat. Neurol.*, 1930, 76, 38. (German)

Kallmann, F.J. The methods of fever treatment. *Hospitalstitende*, 1932, 75, 1. (German)

Kallmann, F.J. The methods of fever treatment in neurosyphilis. *Mediz. Welt*, 1932, 43, 1. (German)

Kallmann, F.J. The results of fever treatment in the Herzberg Hospital. In: K. Bonhoeffer, & P. Jossmann (Eds.) *Ergebnisse der Reiztherapie bei progressiver Paralyse.* Berlin: S. Karger, 1932. (German)

Kallmann, F.J. The fertility of schizophrenics. In: H. Harmsen, & F. Lohse (Eds.) *Bevölkerungsfragen*, Munich: J.F. Lehmanns, 1936. (German)

Kallmann, F.J. Eugenic birth control in schizophrenic families. *Journal of Contraception*, 1938, 3, 195.

Kallmann, F.J. *The genetics of schizophrenia.* New York: J.J. Augustin, 1938.

Kallmann, F.J. Heredity, reproduction and eugenic procedure in the field of schizophrenia. *Eugenics News*, 1938, 23, 105.

Kallmann, F.J. In memoriam: Dr. Med Wilhelm Weinberg. *Journal of Nervous and Mental Disease*, 1938, Vol. 87.

Kallmann, F.J. Informal discussion of "Sources of mental disease: Their amelioration and prevention." In: F.R. Moulton, & P.O. Komora (Eds.) *Mental health.* Publication No. 9, American Association for the Advancement of Science, 1939.

Kallmann, F.J. Collaborator in *Psychiatric dictionary.* (L.E. Hinsie, & J. Shatzky). New York: Oxford University Press, 1940.

Kallmann, F.J., Barrera, S.E., & Metzger, H. The association of hereditary microphthalmia with mental deficiency. *American Journal of Mental Deficiency*, 1940, 45, 25.

Kallmann, F.J. Editorial. *American Journal of Mental Deficiency*, 1941, 46, 165.

Kallmann, F.J. Knowledge about the significance of psychopathology in family relations. *Marriage and Family Living*, 1941, 3, 81.

Kallmann, F.J. The operation of genetic factors in the pathogenesis of mental disorders. *New York State Journal of Medicine*, 1941, 41, 1352.

Kallmann, F.J., Barrera, S.E., Hoch, P.H., & Kelley, D.M. The role of mental deficiency in the incidence of schizophrenia. *American Journal of Mental Deficiency*, 1941, 45, 514.

Kallmann, F.J., & Barrera, S.E. The heredoconstitutional mechanisms of predisposition and resistance to schizophrenia. *American Journal of Psychiatry*, 1942, 98, 544.

Kallmann, F.J. Genetic mechanisms in resistance to tuberculosis. *Psychiatric Quarterly Supplement*, 1943, 17, 32.

Kallmann, F.J. Twin studies on genetic variations in resistance to tuberculosis. *Journal of Heredity*, 1943, 34, 269.

Kallmann, F.J., & Reisner, D. Twin studies on the significance of genetic factors in tuberculosis. *American Review of Tuberculosis*, 1943, 47, 549.

Kallmann, F.J., & Schonfeld, W.A. Psychiatric problems in the treatment of eunuchoidism. *American Journal of Mental Deficiency*, 1943, 47, 386.

Kallmann, F.J. Review of psychiatric progress, 1943: Heredity and eugenics. *American Journal of Psychiatry*, 1944, 100, 551.

Kallmann, F.J., Schonfeld, W.A., & Barrera, S.E. The genetic aspects of primary eunuchoidism. *American Journal of Mental Deficiency*, 1944, 48, 203.

301

Kallmann, F.J. Review of psychiatric progress, 1944: Heredity and eugenics. *American Journal of Psychiatry*, 1945, 101, 536.

Kallmann, F.J. The genetic theory of schizophrenia. *American Journal of Psychiatry*, 1946, 103, 309.

Kallmann, F.J. Review of psychiatric progress, 1945: Heredity and eugenics. *American Journal of Psychiatry*, 1946, 102, 522.

Kallmann, F.J., & Anastasio, M.M. Twin studies on the psychopathology of suicide. *Journal of Heredity*, 1946, 37, 171.

Kallmann, F.J., & Mickey, J.S. The concept of induced insanity in family units. *Journal of Nervous and Mental Disease*, 1946, 104, 303.

Kallmann, F.J., & Mickey, J.S. Genetic concepts and folie à deux. *Journal of Heredity*, 1946, 37, 298.

Kallmann, F.J. Genetics in relation to mental disorders. *Eugenics News*, 1947, 32, 51.

Kallmann, F.J. Modern concepts of genetics in relation to mental health and abnormal personality development. *Psychiatric Quarterly*, 1947, 21, 1.

Kallmann, F.J. Review of psychiatric progress, 1946: Heredity and eugenics. *American Journal of Psychiatry*, 1947, 103, 513.

Kallmann, F.J., & Anastasio, M.M. Twin studies on the psychopathology of suicide. *Journal of Nervous and Mental Disease*, 1947, 105, 40.

Kallmann, F.J., & Sander, G. The genetics of epilepsy. In: P.H. Hoch, & R.P. Knight (Eds.) *Epilepsy*. New York: Grune & Stratton, 1947.

Kallmann, F.J. Applicability of modern genetic concepts in the management of schizophrenia. *Journal of Heredity*, 1948, 39, 339.

Kallmann, F.J. Current trends in psychiatry and social medicine as observed at the International Conference of Physicians. *Psychiatric Quarterly Supplement*, 1948, 22, 326.

Kallmann, F.J. The genetic aspects of senescence in the light of twin studies. *Mschr. Psychiat. Neurol.*, 1948, 116, 58. (German)

Kallmann, F.J. Genetics in relation to mental disorders. *Journal ment. Sci.*, 1948, 94, 250.

Kallmann, F.J. The genetic theory of schizophrenia. In: C. Kluckhohn, & H.A. Murray (Eds.) *Personality in nature, society, and culture*. New York: Alfred A. Knopf, 1948.

Kallmann, F.J. Heredity and constitution in relation to the treatment of mental disorders. In: P.H. Hoch (Ed.) *Failures in psychiatric treatment*. New York: Grune & Stratton, 1948.

Kallmann, F.J. Review of psychiatric progress, 1947: Heredity and eugenics. *American Journal of Psychiatry*, 1948, 104, 448.

Kallmann, F.J., & Sander, G. Twin studies on aging and longevity. *Journal of Heredity*, 1948, 39, 349.

Kallmann, F.J. Constitutional relationship between schizophrenia and tuberculosis. *De Paul Journal*, 1949, Vol. 3, No. 8.

Kallmann, F.J. Medical genetics and eugenics in relation to mental health problems and senescence. *Eugenics News*, 1949, 33, 15.

Kallmann, F.J. On the frequency of suicide in twins and nontwins. *Mschr. Psychiat. Neurol.*, 1949, 117, 280. (German)

Kallmann, F.J. Review of psychiatric progress, 1948: Heredity and eugenics. *American Journal of Psychiatry*, 1949, 105, 497.

Kallmann, F.J., De Porte, J., De Porte, E., & Feingold, L. Suicide in twins and only children. *American Journal of Human Genetics*, 1949, 1, 113.

Kallmann, F.J., & Feingold, L. Principles of human genetics in relation to insurance medicine and public health. *J. insur. Med.*, 1949, Vol. 4, No. 1.

Kallmann, F.J., & Planansky, K. Utilization of genetic data in insurance medicine. *J. insur. Med.*, 1949, Vol. 4, No. 4.

Kallmann, F.J., & Sander, G. Twin studies on senescence. *American Journal of Psychiatry*, 1949, 106, 29.

Kallmann, F.J. The genetics of psychoses. In: *Proceedings, First International Congress of Psychiatry, Sect. VI.* Paris: Hermann & Cie, 1950.

Kallmann, F.J. The genetics of psychoses. *American Journal of Human Genetics*, 1950, 2, 385.

Kallmann, F.J. Review of psychiatric progress, 1949: Heredity and eugenics. *American Journal of Psychiatry*, 1950, 106, 501.

Kallmann, F.J., & Svendsen, B.B. Progress of genetics in relation to oligophrenia, epilepsy and other neurological disorders, 1939-1946. *Ztschr. ges. Neurol. Psychiat.*, 1950, 110, 1. (German)

Kallmann, F.J. Recent progress in relation to the genetic aspects of mental deficiency. *American Journal of Mental Deficiency*, 1951, 56, 375.

Kallmann, F.J. Relationship between schizophrenia and somatotype. *Modern Medicine*, 1951, 19, 140.

Kallmann, F.J. Review of psychiatric progress, 1950: Heredity and eugenics. *American Journal of Psychiatry*, 1951, 107, 503.

Kallmann, F.J. Twin studies in relation to adjustive problems in man. *Transactions of the New York Academy of Sciences*, 1951, 13, 270.

Kallmann, F.J., Feingold, L., & Bondy, E. Comparative adaptational, social, and psychometric data on the life histories of senescent twin pairs. *American Journal of Human Genetics*, 1951, 3, 65.

Kallmann, F.J. Comparative twin study on the genetic aspects of male homosexuality. *Journal of Nervous and Mental Disease*, 1952, 115, 283.

Kallmann, F.J. The genetic aspects of mental disorders in the aging. *Journal of Heredity*, 1952, 43, 89.

Kallmann, F.J. Genetic aspects of psychoses. In: *The biology of mental health and disease.* New York: Paul B. Hoeber, 1952.

Kallmann, F.J. The genetics of psychoses. In: *Proceedings, First International Congress of Psychiatry, Sect. VI.* Paris: Hermann & Cie, 1952.

Kallmann, F.J. Human genetics as a science, as a profession, and as a social-minded trend of orientation. *American Journal of Human Genetics*, 1952, 4, 237.

Kallmann, F.J. Introductory statement of moderator. Round table discussion on "Psychiatric guidance in problems of marriage and parenthood" (resumé). *Eugenics News*, 1952, 37, 55.

Kallmann, F.J. Review of psychiatric progress, 1951: Heredity and eugenics. *American Journal of Psychiatry*, 1952, 108, 500.

Kallmann, F.J. Twin and sibship study of overt male homosexuality. *American Journal of Human Genetics*, 1952, 4, 136.

Kallmann, F.J., & Bondy, E. Applicability of the twin study method in the analysis of variations in mate selection and marital adjustment. *American Journal of Human Genetics*, 1952, 4, 209.

Kallmann, F.J., & Sander, G. Twin studies of senescence. In: R.G. Kuhlen, & G.G. Thompson (Eds.) *Psychological studies of human development.* New York: Appleton-Century-Crofts, 1952.

Kallmann, F.J. *Heredity in health and mental disorder.* New York: W.W. Norton, 1954.

303

Kallmann, F.J. Review of psychiatric progress, 1952: Heredity and eugenics. *American Journal of Psychiatry*, 1953, 109, 491.

Kallmann, F.J. Genetic principles in manic-depressive psychosis. In: P.H. Hoch, & J. Zubin (Eds.) *Depression*. New York: Grune & Stratton, 1954.

Kallmann, F.J. The genetics of psychotic behavior patterns. In: D. Hooker, & C.C. Hare (Eds.) *Genetics and the inheritance of integrated neurological and psychiatric patterns.* Baltimore: Williams & Wilkins, 1954.

Kallmann, F.J. Heredity and health in mental disorder. In: L. Gedda (Ed.) *Genetica Medica.* Rome: Gregor Mendel Institute, 1954.

Kallmann, F.J. Review of psychiatric progress, 1953: Heredity and eugenics. *American Journal of Psychiatry*, 1954, 110, 489.

Kallmann, F.J. Twin data in the analysis of mechanisms of inheritance. *American Journal of Human Genetics*, 1954, 6, 157.

Kallmann, F.J. Review of psychiatric progress, 1954: Heredity and eugenics. *American Journal of Psychiatry*, 1955, 111, 502.

Kallmann, F.J., & Baroff, G.S. Abnormalities of behavior (in the light of psychogenetic studies). In: C.P. Stone (Ed.) *Annual review of psychology, Vol. VI.* Stanford: Annual Reviews, 1955.

Kallmann, F.J. Genetic aspects of mental disorders in later life. In: O.J. Kaplan (Ed.) *Mental disorders in later life*, (2nd Ed.) Stanford: Stanford University Press, 1956.

Kallmann, F.J. The genetics of aging. *Journal of Chronic Disease*, 1956, 4, 140.

Kallmann, F.J. The genetics of aging. In: J.E. Moore, H.H. Merritt, & R.J. Masselink (Eds.) *The neurologic and psychiatric aspects of the disorders of aging.* Baltimore: Williams & Wilkins, 1956.

Kallmann, F.J. The genetics of human behavior. *American Journal of Psychiatry*, 1956, 113, 496.

Kallmann, F.J. Genetic variations in adjustment to aging. In: J.E. Anderson (Ed.) *Psychological aspects of aging.* Washington, D.C., American Psychological Association, 1956.

Kallmann, F.J. Heredity in disturbed mentality: Eugenic aspects. In: *Enciclopedia Medica Italiana, Vol. VIII.* Florence: Sansoni Edizioni Scientifiche, 1956. (Italian)

Kallmann, F.J. Objectives of the mental health project for the deaf; In: *Proceedings, 37th Convention of American Instructors of the Deaf.* Senate Document No. 99. Washington, D.C.: U.S. Government Printing Office, 1956.

Kallmann, F.J. Psychiatric aspects of genetic counseling. *American Journal of Human Genetics*, 1956, 8, 97.

Kallmann, F.J. Review of psychiatric progress, 1955: Heredity and eugenics. *American Journal of Psychiatry*, 1956, 112, 510.

Kallmann, F.J., Aschner, B.M., & Falek, A. Comparative data on longevity, adjustment to aging and causes of death in a senescent twin population. In: L. Gedda (Ed.) *Novant' anni delle Leggi Mendeliane.* Rome: Gregor Mendel Institute, 1956.

Kallmann, F.J., & Roth, B. Genetic aspects of preadolescent schizophrenia. *American Journal of Psychiatry*, 1956, 112, 599.

Kallmann, F.J. Heredity and aging. *Newsletter of the Gerontological Society*, 1957, 4, 5.

Kallmann, F.J. Medical Arts Congress of Turin: With International Symposium of Medical Genetics. *Eugenics News*, 1957, 4, 162.

Kallmann, F.J. Review of psychiatric progress, 1956: Heredity and eugenics. *American Journal of Psychiatry*, 1957, 113, 595.

Kallmann, F.J. The role of genetics in psychiatry. *American Journal of Psychotherapy*, 1957, 11, 885.

Kallmann, F.J. Twin data on the genetics of aging. In: G.E.W. Wolstenholme, & C.M. O'Connor (Eds.) *Methodology of the study of aging.* Ciba Foundation Colloquia on Ageing, Vol. III. London: J. & A. Churchill, 1957.

Kallmann, F.J., & Baroff, G.S. Heredity and variations in human behavior patterns. *Acta Genet. Stat. Med.,* 1957, 7, 410.

Kallmann, F.J. An appraisal of psychogenetic twin data. *Dis. nerv.* Syst. Suppl., 1958, 19, 9.

Kallmann, F.J. Comments on eugenic abortion from the viewpoint of psychiatric genetics. *Med. Klin.,* 1958, 53, 2064. (German)

Kallmann, F.J. Genetic aspects of schizophrenia. *Med. Hyg.,* 1958, No. 393, 173. (French)

Kallmann, F.J. The genetic viewpoint of the etiology of mental illness. In: *Proceedings, Joint Commission on Mental Health.* Boston, JCMH, 1958.

Kallmann, F.J. In memoriam: Bruno Schulz, 1890-1958. *Arch. Psychiat. Ztschr. ges. Neurol.,* 1958, 197, 121.

Kallmann, F.J. Review of psychiatric progress, 1957: Heredity and eugenics. *American Journal of Psychiatry,* 1958, 114, 586.

Kallmann, F.J. Types of advice given by heredity counselors. *Eugenics Quarterly,* 1958, 5, 48.

Kallmann, F.J. The use of genetics in psychiatry. *Journal ment. Sci.,* 1958, 104, 542.

Kallmann, F.J., & Jarvik, L.F. Twin data on genetic variations in resistance to tuberculosis. In: L. Gedda (Ed.) *Genetica della Tubercolosi e dei Tumori.* Rome: Gregor Mendel Institute, 1958.

Kallmann, F.J., & Sank, D. Genetics, eugenics and psychohygiene. In: H. Meng (Ed.) *Psychohygienische Vorlesungen.* Basel: Benno Schwabe, 1958. (German)

Kallmann, F.J. Genetic aspects of schizophrenia. In: *Proceedings, Second International Congress for Psychiatry,Vol. IV.* Zürich: Orell Füssli Arts Graphiques, 1959.

Kallmann, F.J. The genetics of mental illness. In: S. Arieti (Ed.) *American handbook of psychiatry.* New York: Basic Books, 1959.

Kallmann, F.J. Psychogenetic studies of twins. In: S. Koch (Ed.) *Psychology: A study of a science,Vol. III.* New York: McGraw-Hill, 1959.

Kallmann, F.J. Review of psychiatric progress, 1958: Heredity and eugenics. *American Journal of Psychiatry,* 1959, 115, 586.

Kallmann, F.J. Types of advice given by heredity counselors. In: H.G. Hammons (Ed.) *Heredity counseling.* New York: Paul B. Hoeber, 1959.

Kallmann, F.J., & Jarvik, L.F. Individual differences in constitution and genetic background. In: J.E. Birren (Ed.) *Handbook of aging and the individual: Psychological and biological aspects.* Chicago: University of Chicago Press, 1959.

Kallmann, F.J., & Rainer, J.D. Genetics and demography. In: P.M. Hauser, & O.D. Duncan (Eds.) *The study of population.* Chicago: University of Chicago Press, 1959.

Kallmann, F.J. Important events in genetics. *Archives of Neurology,* 1960, 2, 363.

Kallmann, F.J. Review of psychiatric progress, 1959: Heredity and eugenics. *American Journal of Psychiatry,* 1960, 116, 577.

Kallmann, F.J. Twin studies (human genetics). In: W.H. Crouse (Ed.) *Encyclopedia of science and technology, Vol. VI.* New York: McGraw-Hill, 1960.

Kallmann, F.J. Discussion of "Defining the unit of study in field investigations in the mental disorders." In: J. Zubin (Ed.) *Field studies in the mental disorders.* New York: Grune & Stratton, 1961.

Kallmann, F.J. Discussion of two psychiatric twin studies. *American Journal of Psychiatry,* 1961, 117, 804.

Kallmann, F.J. Genetic factors in aging: Comparative and longitudinal observations on a senescent twin population. In: P.H. Hoch, & J. Zubin (Eds.) *Psychopathology of aging.* New York: Grune & Stratton, 1961.

Kallmann, F.J. Genetic factors in the etiology of mental disorders. *American Journal of Orthopsychiatry*, 1961, 31, 445.

Kallmann, F.J. Heredity in the etiology of disordered behavior. In: P.H. Hoch, & J. Zubin (Eds.) *Comparative epidemiology of the mental disorders.* New York: Grune & Stratton, 1962.

Kallmann, F.J. New goals and perspectives in human genetics. *Acta genet. med. gemellolog.*, 1961, 10, 377.

Kallmann, F.J. Review of psychiatric progress, 1960: Heredity and eugenics. *American Journal of Psychiatry*, 1961, 117, 577.

Kallmann, F.J. Discussion of "Somatic chromosomes in mongolism", In: L.C. Kolb, R. L. Masland, & R.E. Cole (Eds.) *Mental retardation.* Baltimore: Williams & Wilkins, 1962.

Kallmann, F.J. (Ed.) *Expanding goals of genetics in psychiatry.* New York: Grune & Stratton, 1962.

Kallmann, F.J. The future of psychiatry in the perspective of genetics. In: P.H. Hoch, & J. Zubin (Eds.) *The future of psychiatry.* New York: Grune & Stratton, 1962.

Kallmann, F.J. Genetic factors in relation to psychiatric diagnosis. *Dis. nerv. Syst.*, 1962, 23, 594.

Kallmann, F.J. Genetic research and counseling in the mental health field, present and future. In: F.J. Kallmann (Ed.) *Expanding goals of genetics in psychiatry.* New York: Grune & Stratton, 1962.

Kallmann, F.J. The hybrid speciality of psychiatric genetics. *Acta genet. med. gemellolog.*, 1962, 11, 317.

Kallmann, F.J. Introduction, research in genetics. In: R.M. Steinhilber, & G.A. Ulett (Eds.) *Psychiatric research in public service.* Psychiatric Research Report No. 15. Washington, D.C.: American Psychiatric Association, 1962.

Kallmann, F.J. New genetic approaches to psychiatric disorders. In: T.T. Tourlentes, S. L. Pollack, & H.E. Himwich (Eds.) *Research approaches to psychiatric problems.* New York: Grune & Stratton, 1962.

Kallmann, F.J. Recent cytogenetic advances in psychiatry. In: *Proceedings, Third World Congress of Psychiatry, Vol. 1.* Toronto: University of Toronto Press, 1962.

Kallmann, F.J. The William Allan Memorial Award for outstanding work in human genetics. *American Journal of Human Genetics*, 1962, 14, 95.

Kallmann, F.J., Baroff, G.S., & Sank, D. Etiology of mental subnormality in twins. In: F.J. Kallmann (Ed.) *Expanding goals of genetics in psychiatry.* New York: Grune & Stratton, 1962.

Kallmann, F.J., & Glanville, E.V. Review of psychiatric progress, 1961: Heredity and eugenics. *American Journal of Psychiatry*, 1962, 118, 577.

Kallmann, F.J. Genetic aspects of sex determination and sexual maturation potentials in man. In: G. Winokur (Ed.) *Determinants of human sexual behavior.* Springfield, Ill.: Charles C. Thomas, 1963.

Kallmann, F.J. Specialized psychiatric services for the deaf. In: G.M.L. Smith (Ed.) *The psychiatric problems of deaf children and adolescents.* London: The National Deaf Children's Society, 1963.

Kallmann, F.J., & Glanville, E.V. Review of psychiatric progress, 1962: Heredity and eugenics. *American Journal of Psychiatry*, 1963, 119, 601.

Kallmann, F.J., & Rainer, J.D. Psychotherapeutically oriented counseling techniques in the setting of a medical genetics department. In: B. Stokvis (Ed.) *Proceedings, Fifth*

International Congress of Psychotherapy, Vol. IV. Topical problems in psychotherapy. Basel: S, Karger, 1963.

Kallmann, F.J. Main findings and some projections. In: J.D. Rainer, K.Z. Altshuler, & F. J. Kallmann, (Eds.) *Family and mental health problems in a deaf population.* New York State Psychiatric Institute, 1963.

Kallmann, F.J. Some genetic aspects of deafness and their implications for family counseling. In: *Proceedings, International Congress on Education of the Deaf.* Senate Document No. 106. Washington, D.C.: U.S. Government Printing Office, 1964.

Kallmann, F.J., Falek, A., Hurzeler, M., & Erlenmeyer-Kimling, L. The developmental aspects of children with two schizophrenic parents. In: P. Solomon, & B.C. Gluech, Jr. (Eds.) *Recent research on schizophrenia.* Psychiatric Research Report No. 19, Washington, D.C.: American Psychiatric Association, 1964.

Kallmann, F.J., & Goldfarb, C. Review of psychiatric progress, 1963: Heredity and eugenics. *American Journal of Psychiatry,* 1964, 120, 625.

Kallmann, F.J., & Rainer, J.D. The genetic approach to schizophrenia: Clinical, demographic and family guidance problems. In: L.C. Kolb, F.J. Kallmann, & P. Polatin (Eds.) *Schizophrenia.* International Psychiatry Clinics, Vol. I, No. 4. Boston: Little, Brown, 1964.

Kallmann, F.J. Contributor to *Aging and levels of biological organization* (A.M. Brues, & G.A. Sacher, Eds.) Chicago: University of Chicago Press, 1965.

Kallmann, F.J. The genetic theory of schizophrenia. In: R.C. Teevan, & R.C. Birney (Eds.) *Readings for introductory psychology.* New York: Harcourt Brace, & World, 1965.

Kallmann, F.J. Review of psychiatric progress, 1964: Heredity and eugenics. *American Journal of Psychiatry,* 1965, 121, 628.

Kallmann, F.J. Some aspects of genetic counseling. In: J.V. Neel, M.W. Shaw, & W.J. Schull (Eds.) *Genetics and the epidemiology of chronic diseases.* Public Health Service Publication No. 1163. Washington, D.C.: U.S. Government Printing Office, 1965.

Kalter, H. The inheritance of susceptibility to teratogenic action of cortisone in mice. *Genetics,* 1954, 39, 185-196.

Kantor, R.E., & Herron, W.G. *Reactive and process schizophrenia.* Palo Alto, Calif.: Science & Behavior Books, 1966.

Kaswan, J.W., Love, L.R., & Rodnick, E.H. Information feedback as a method of clinical intervention and consultation. In: C. Spielberger (Ed.) *Current topics in clinical and community psychology.* Vol. 3. New York: Academic Press, 1971.

Katz, S.E. Trait attributes assigned to mother, father, and self by schizophrenic and normal subjects. Summa cum laude thesis. University of Minnesota, 1965.

Kety, S.S., Rosenthal, D., Wender, P.H., & Schulsinger, F. The types and prevalence of mental illness in the biological and adoptive families of schizophrenics. *Journal of Psychiatric Research,* 1968, 6 (supplement 1), 345-362.

Klein, E.B., Cicchetti, D.V., & Spohn, H.E. A test of the censure-deficit model and its relation to premorbidity in the performance of schizophrenics. *Journal of Abnormal Psychology,* 1967, 72, 174-181.

Knehr, C.A. Schizophrenic reaction time responses to variable preparatory intervals. *American Journal of Psychiatry,* 1954, 110, 585-588.

Knight, R. Effect of punishment on performance of schizophrenics: A review of the literature. University of Minnesota. Mimeographed, 1968, 116 pages.

Kolb, L.C., Kallmann, F.J., & Polatin, P. (Eds.) *Schizophrenia.* International Psychiatry Clinics, Vol. I, No. 4. Boston: Little, Brown, 1964.

Langfeldt, G. Clinical and experimental investigations on the relation between internal secretions and *dementia praecox. Acta medica Scand. Suppl. XVI,* 1926.

Langfeldt, G. The clinical subdivision of the schizophrenia group. Prémier Congrès mondial de Psychiatrie. Compt. rendues des séances. Paris: Hermann & Cie, 1950.

Langfeldt, G. The diagnosis of schizophrenia. *American Journal of Psychology*, 1951, 108.

Langfeldt, G. *The endocrine glands and the autonomic systems in dementia praecox.* Bergen, Norway: J.W. Eide, 1926.

Langfeldt, G. Die Insulin-Schockbehandlung der Schizophrenie. *Psych.-Neurol. Wochenschrift*, nr. 38, 1936.

Langfeldt, G. Modern viewpoints on the symptomatology and diagnostics of schizophrenia. *Acta Psych. et Neurol. Scand., Suppl. 80*, 1953.

Langfeldt, G. Neue Gesichtspunkte zur Bewertung der Insulinschock Therapie bei Schizophrenie. *Monatschr. für Psych. und Neurol.*, Ed. 98, 1938, p. 352.

Langfeldt, G. La portée d'une dichotomie du groupe des schizophrenies. *L'Evolution Psychiatrique*, 1966, No. 2.

Langfeldt, G. The prognosis of schizophrenia and the factors influencing the course of the disease. Monograph. London: Humphrey Melford, 1937.

Langfeldt, G. The schizophreniform states. Monograph. London: Humphrey Melford, 1939.

Langfeldt, G. Zur Frage der spontanen Remissionen der Schizophreniformen Psychosen mit besonderer Berücksichtigung der Frage nach der Dauer dieser Remissionen. *Ztsch. f. d. g. Neurol. und Psych.*, 1939, 164, Bd., 4 H.

Langfeldt, G., Ford, L., Mazzitelli, Helen, Rohan, Anne Marie. Comparative diagnostic considerations and prognostic evaluations of electro-shock and insulin coma treatments. A Norwegian-American psychiatric-psychological teamwork. *American Journal of Psychology*, 1955.

Lennard, H.K., Beaulieu, M.R., & Embrey, N.G. Interaction in families with a schizophrenic child. *Archives of General Psychiatry*, 1965, 12, 166-183.

Leventhal, A.M. The effects of diagnostic category and reinforcer on learning and awareness. *Journal of Abnormal and Social Psychology*, 1959, 59, 162-166.

Lidsky, A., Hakerem, G., & Sutton, S. Psychopathological patterns of pupillary response to light. Paper presented at Fifth Pupil Colloquium, University of Pennsylvania, May, 1967.

Lidz, T., Fleck, S., & Cornelison, A. *Schizophrenia and the family.* New York: International Universities Press, 1965.

Linder, F.E., & Carmichael, H.T. A biometric study of the relation between oral and rectal temperatures in normal and schizophrenic subjects. *Human Biology*, 1935, 7, 24-46.

Lippitt, R., & Gold, M. Classroom social structure as a mental health problem. *Journal of Social Issues*, 1959, 15, 40-49.

Losen, S.M. The differential effects of censure on the problem solving behavior of schizophrenic and normal subjects. *Journal of Personality*, 1961, 29, 258-272.

MacFarlane, J.W. Perspectives on personal consistency and change: The guidance study. *Vita Humana*, 1964, 115-126.

MacFarlane, J.W., & Clausen, J.A. Childhood influences upon intelligence, personality and mental health. In: *The mental health of the child.* J. Segal (Ed.) Rockville, Maryland, National Institute of Mental Health, 1971, Pp. 131-154.

Malmo, R.B., Shagass, C., & Smith, A.A. Responsiveness in chronic schizophrenia. *Journal of Personality*, 1951, 19, 359-375.

Marcus, L. Attention, set and risk-taking in disturbed, vulnerable and normal children. Ph.D. dissertation proposal. Mimeographed, University of Minnesota Project Competence, 1971.

308

McCarthy, J.F. The differential effects of praise and censure upon the verbal responses of schizophrenics. Unpublished doctoral dissertation, The Catholic University of America, 1963.

McPherson, S. Communication of intents among parents and their disturbed adolescent child. *Journal of Abnormal Psychology*, 1970, 76, 98-105.

Mednick, S.A. Breakdown in children at high risk for schizophrenia: Behavioral and autonomic characteristics and possible role of perinatal complications. *Mental Hygiene*, 1970, 54, 50-63.

Mednick, S. Learning theory approach to research in schizophrenia. *Psychological Bulletin*, 1958, 55, 316-327.

Mednick, S.A. Schizophrenia: A learned thought disorder. In: G. Nielsen (Ed.) *Clinical Psychology*. Proceedings of the XIV International Congress of Applied Psychology, Copenhagen, Munksgaard, 1962.

Mednick, S.A., & McNeil, T.F. Current methodology in research on the etiology of schizophrenia. *Psychological Bulletin*, 1968, 70, 681-693.

Mednick, B., Mednick, S., & Schulsinger, F. Breakdown in high risk subjects: Familial and early environmental factors, 1972, unpublished manuscript.

Mednick, S.A., Mura, E., Schulsinger, F., & Mednick, B. Perinatal conditions and infant development in children with schizophrenic parents. *Social Biology*, 1971, 18, 103-113.

Mednick, S.A., & Schulsinger, F. Some premorbid characteristics related to breakdown in children with schizophrenic mothers. In: *The transmission of schizophrenia*. D. Rosenthal, & S.S. Kety (Eds.) Oxford: Pergamon Press, 1968, Pp. 267-291.

Mednick, S.A., Schulsinger, F., & Lampasso, A. Rate of GSR recovery and avoidant associations. Unpublished manuscript, 1972.

Menninger, K., Mayman, M., & Pruyser, P. *The vital balance: The life process in mental health and illness*. New York: Viking, 1963.

Miles, H.C., & Gardner, E.A. A psychiatric case register. *Archives of General Psychiatry*, 1966, 14, 571-580.

Millard, Mary S., & Shakow, D. A note on color-blindness in some psychotic groups. *Journal of Social Psychology*, 1935, 6, 252-256.

Miller, N.E. Learning of visceral and glandular responses. *Science*, 1969, 163, 434-445.

Milstein, V., Stevens, J., & Sachdev, K. Habituation of the alpha attentuation response in children and adults with psychiatric disorders. *Electroencephalography and Clinical Neurophysiology*, 1969, 26, 12-18.

Mishler, E.G., & Waxler, N. *Family progress and schizophrenia*. New York: Science House, 1968.

Nathanson, I.A. A semantic differential analysis of parent-son relationships in schizophrenia. *Journal of Abnormal Psychology*, 1967, 72, 277-281.

Nuechterlein, K.H. Competent disadvantaged children: A review of research. Summa cum laude thesis. University of Minnesota, 1970.

Phillips, L. Case history data and prognosis in schizophrenia. *Journal of Nervous and Mental Disease*, 1953, 117, 515-525.

Phillips, L. *Human adaptation and its failures*. New York: Academic Press, 1968.

Rainer, J.D., Altshuler, K.Z., & Kallmann, F.J. Psychotherapy for the deaf. In: J.D. Rainer, K.Z. Altshuler, & F.J. Kallmann (Eds.) *Family and mental health problems in a deaf population*. New York: New York State Psychiatric Institute, 1963.

Rainer, J.D., Altshuler, K.Z., & Kallmann, F.J. Psychotherapy for the deaf. In: B. Stokvis (Ed.) *Proceedings, Fifth International Congress of Psychotherapy, Vol. III*. Advances in psychosomatic medicine. Basel: S. Karger, 1963.

309

Rainer, J.D., Altshuler, K.Z., & Kallmann, F.J. (Eds.) *Family and mental health problems in a deaf population.* New York: New York State Psychiatric Institute, 1963.

Rainer, J.D., & Kallmann, F.J. Behavior disorder patterns in a deaf population. *U.S.P.H.S. Rep.*, 1957, 72, 585.

Rainer, J.D., & Kallmann, F.J. Constructive psychiatric program for a deaf population. In: *Proceedings, 38th Convention of American Instructors of the Deaf.* Senate Document No. 66. Washington, D.C.: U.S. Government Printing Office, 1958.

Rainer, J.D., & Kallmann, F.J. The role of genetics in psychiatry. *Journal of Nervous and Mental Disease*, 1958, 126, 403.

Rainer, J.D., & Kallmann, F.J. Genetic and demographic aspects of disordered behavior patterns in a deaf population. In: B. Pasamanich (Ed.) *Epidemiology of mental disorder.* Publication No. 60. Washington, D.C.: American Association for the Advancement of Science, 1959.

Rainer, J.D., & Kallmann, F.J. Observations, facts and recommendations derived from a mental health project for the deaf. *Trans. Amer. Acad. Ophth. Otolar.*, 1959, 63, 179.

Rainer, J.D., & Kallmann, F.J. Preventive mental health planning. In: J.D. Rainer, K.Z. Altshuler, & F.J. Kallmann (Eds.) *Family and mental health problems in a deaf population.* New York: New York State Psychiatric Institute, 1963.

Rainer, J.D., & Kallmann, F.J. The role of genetics in thyroid disease. In: S.C. Werner (Ed.) *The thyroid*, (2nd Ed.) New York: Hoeber, Harper & Row, 1962.

Ressler, R.H. Genotype-correlated parental influences in two strains of mice. *Journal of Comparative and Physiological Psychology*, 1963, 56, 882-886.

Retterstol, N. *Paranoid and paranoiac psychoses.* Springfield, Ill.: Charles C. Thomas, 1966.

Rickers-Ovsiankina, Maria. Studies on the personality structure of schizophrenic individuals. II. Reaction to interrupted tasks. *Journal of General Psychology*, 1937, 16, 179-196.

Rimland, Bernard. *Infantile autism.* New York: Appleton-Century-Crofts, 1964, Pp. 237-265.

Rodnick, E.H. Cognitive and perceptual response set in schizophrenics. In: *Cognition, personality & clinical psychology.* R. Jessor & S. Feshbach (Eds.) San Francisco: Jossey-Bass, 1967, Pp. 173-209.

Rodnick, E.H. The effect of metrazol shock upon habit systems. *Journal of Abnormal and Social Psychology*, 1942, 37, 560-565.

Rodnick, E.H. The psychopathology of development: Investigating the etiology of schizophrenia. *American Journal of Orthopsychiatry*, 1968, 38, 784-798.

Rodnick, E.H., & Garmezy, N. An experimental approach to the study of motivation in schizophrenia. *Nebraska Symposium on Motivation.* M.R. Jones (Ed.) Lincoln, Neb.: University of Nebraska Press, 1957, Pp. 109-184.

Rodnick, E.H., & Shakow, D. Set in the schizophrenic as measured by a composite reaction time index. *American Journal of Psychiatry*, 1940, 97, 214-225.

Roe, A. Children of alcoholic parentage raised in foster homes. In: *Alcoholism, science, and society*, published by Quarterly Journal of Studies on Alcohol, 1945, Pp. 115-127.

Rolf, J.E. The academic and social competence of children vulnerable to schizophrenia and other behavior pathologies. *Journal of Abnormal Psychology.* In Press.

Rolf, J.E. The academic and social competence of school children vulnerable to behavior pathology. Unpublished Ph.D. dissertation. University of Minnesota, 1969.

Rosenthal, D. *Genetic theory and abnormal behavior.* New York: McGraw-Hill, 1970.

Rosenthal, D., Lawlor, W.G., Zahn, T.P., & Shakow, D. The relationship of some aspects of mental set to degree of schizophrenic disorganization. *Journal of Personality*, 1960, 28, 26-38.

Rosenthal, D., Wender, P.H., Kety, S.S., Schulsinger, F., Welner, J., & Östergaard, L. Schizophrenics' offspring reared in adoptive homes. In: D. Rosenthal, & S.S. Kety (Eds.) *The transmission of schizophrenia.* London: Pergamon Press, 1968, Pp. 377-391.

Royce, J.R., & Covington, Genetic differences in the avoidance conditioning of mice. *Journal of Comparative and Physiological Psychology*, 1960, 53, 197-200.

Sands, S.L., & Rodnick, E.H. Concept and experimental design in the study of stress and personality. *American Journal of Psychiatry*, 1950, 106, 673-679.

Sank, D., & Kallmann, F.J. Genetic and eugenic aspects of early total deafness. *Eugenics Quarterly*, 1956, 3, 69.

Sank, D., & Kallmann, F.J. The role of heredity in early total deafness. *Volta Review*, 1963, 65, 461.

Schaefer, S.M.J. MMPI profiles of good and poor premorbid schizophrenic patients. Summa cum laude thesis. University of Minnesota, 1965.

Schaie, K.W., & Strother, C.R. A cross-sequential study of age changes in cognitive behavior. *Psychol. Bull.*, 1968, 70, 671-680.

Schnack, G.F., Shakow, D., & Lively, Mary L. Studies in insulin and metrazol therapy. II. Differential effects on some psychological functions. *Journal of Personality*, 1945, 14, 125-149.

Shakow, D. Psychological deficit in schizophrenia. *Behavioral Science*, 1963, 8, 275-305.

Shakow, D. The nature of deterioration in schizophrenic conditions. *Nerv. Ment. Dis. Monogr.*, 1946, No. 70.

Shakow, D. Segmental set: A theory of psychological deficit in schizophrenia. *Archives of General Psychiatry*, 1962, 6, 1-17.

Shakow, D. How phylogenetically older parts of the brain relate to behavior. Paper read at American Association for the Advancement of Science, Washington, D.C., December, 1958.

Shakow, D. Normalisierungstendenzen bei chronisch Schizophrenen: Konsequenzen für die Theorie der Schizophrenie. *Schweiz. Z. Psychol. Anwend.*, 1958, 17, 285-299.

Shakow, D., & Huston, P.E. Studies of motor function in schizophrenia. I. Speed of tapping. *J. gen. Psychol.*, 1936, 15, 63-106.

Shakow, D., & Rosenzweig, S. Play technique in schizophrenia and other psychoses. II. An experimental study of schizophrenic constructions with play materials. *American Journal of Orthopsychiatry*, 1937, 7, 36-47.

Skeels, H.M. Mental development of children in foster homes. *Journal genet. Psychol.*, 1936, 49, 91-106.

Skodak, M. Children in foster homes: A study of mental development. *University of Iowa Studies of Child Welfare*, 1939, 16, No. 1.

Skodak, M., & Skeels, H.M. A final follow-up study of one hundred adopted children. *Journal gent. Psychol.*, 1949, 75, 85-125.

Sontag, L.W. Differences in modifiabllity of fetal behavior and physiology. *Psychosomatic Medicine*, 1944, 6, 151-154.

Spain, B. Eyelid conditioning and arousal in schizophrenic and normal subjects. *Journal of Abnormal Psychology*, 1966, 71, 260-266.

Spector, R.G. Enzyme chemistry of anoxic brain injury. In: C.W.M. Adams (Ed.) *Neurohistochemistry.* New York: Elsevier, 1965.

Stoller, F.H. The effect of maternal evaluation on schizophrenics and their siblings. Unpublished doctoral dissertation. University of California (Los Angeles), 1964.

Strömgren, E. Schizophreniform psychoses. Celebration volume for Gabriel Langfeldt. *Acta Psych. Scand.*, Vol. 41, fasc. 3, 1965.

Teele, J.E., Schleifer, M.J., Corman, L., & Larson, K. Teacher ratings, sociometric status, and choice-reciprocity of anti-social and normal boys. *Group Psychotherapy*, 1966, 19 (3-4), 183-197.

Tizard, J., & Venables, P.H. Reaction time responses by schizophrenics, mental defectives, and normal adults. *American Journal of Psychiatry*, 1956, 112, 803-807.

Venables, P.H. Psychophysiological aspects of schizophrenia. *British Journal of Medical Psychology*, 1966, 39, 289-297.

Venables, P.H., & Wing, J.K. Level of arousal and the sub-classification of schizophrenia. *Archives of General Psychiatry*, 1962, 7, 114-121.

Watt, N.F., Stolorow, R.D., Lubensky, Amy W., & McClelland, D.C. School adjustment and behavior of children hospitalized for schizophrenia as adults. *American Journal of Orthopsychiatry*, 1970, 40, 637-657.

Wegrocki, H.J. Generalizing ability in schizophrenia: An inquiry into the disorders of problem thinking in schizophrenia. *Arch. Psychol.*, 1940, No. 254.

Weintraub, S.A. Cognitive and behavioral impulsivity in internalizing-externalizing and normal children. Unpublished Ph.D. dissertation. University of Minnesota, 1968.

Welner, J., & Stromgren, E. Clinical and genetic studies on benign schizophreniform psychoses based on a follow-up. *Acta Psych. Scand.*, 1958, 33, 377-399.

Wenar, C. *Competence at one.* Merrill Palmer Quarterly, 1964, 10, 329-342.

Wenar, C. *Personality development.* Boston: Houghton Mifflin Co., 1971.

Wender, P.H., Rosenthal, D., & Kety, S.S. A psychiatric assessment of the adoptive parents of schizophrenics. In: D. Rosenthal, & S.S. Kety (Eds.) *The transmission of schizophrenia.* London: Pergamon Press, 1968, Pp. 235-250.

White, B.L. An analysis of excellent early educational practices: Preliminary report. *Interchange*, 1971, 2, 71-88.

White, R.W. The experience of efficacy in schizophrenia. *Psychiatry*, 1965, 28, 199-211.

Willey, R.R. An experimental investigation of the attributes of hypnotizability. Unpublished doctoral dissertation. University of Chicago, 1951.

Woodrow, H. The measurement of attention. *Psychol. Monogr.*, 1914, 17, No, 5 (Whole No. 76).

Wright, D.M. Impairment in abstract conceptualization in the parents of poor-premorbid male schizophrenics. Unpublished Ph.D. dissertation. University of Minnesota, 1970.

Yarrow, Marian R., Campbell, J.D., & Burton, R.W. Recollections of childhood: A study of the retrospective method. *Monographs of the Society for Research in Child Development*, 1970, 35, No. 5, 83 pp.

Zahn, T.P., Rosenthal, D., & Lawlor, W.G. Electrodermal and heart-rate orienting reactions in chronic schizophrenia. *Journal of Psychiatric Research*, 1968, 6, 117-134.

Zahn, T.P., Rosenthal, D., & Lawlor, W.G. GSR orienting reactions to visual and auditory stimuli in chronic schizophrenic and normal subjects. Paper read at Society for Psychophysiological Research, Denver, Colorado, October, 1962.

Zahn, T.P., Rosenthal, D., & Shakow, D. Effects of irregular preparatory intervals on reaction time in schizophrenics. *Journal of Abnormal and Social Psychology*, 1963, 67, 44-52.

Zahn, T.P., Rosenthal, D., & Shakow, D. Reaction time in schizophrenic and normal subjects in relation to the sequence of series of regular preparatory intervals. *Journal of Abnormal and Social Psychology*, 1961, 63, 161-168.

Zahn, T.P., Rosenthal, D., & Shakow, D. Reaction time in schizophrenic and normal subjects in relation to the sequence of series of regular preparatory intervals. *Journal of Abnormal and Social Psychology*, 1961, 63, 161-168.

Zahn, T.P., Shakow, D., & Rosenthal, D. Reaction time in schizophrenic and normal subjects as a function of preparatory and intertrial intervals. *Journal of Nervous and Mental Disease*, 1961, 133, 283-287.

zur Nieden, M. The influence of constitution and environment upon the development of adopted children. *Journal of Psychology*, 1951, 31, 91-95.

AFTERWORD

Schizophrenia is more than a mental health problem. It is a major public health problem ranking in importance, prevalence and economic loss with cancer and heart disease.

The special tragedy of schizophrenia is its predilection for youth. It is the greatest single threat in the entire field of medicine to potentially productive young people. It may well be called the mental crippler of youth. It stands supreme in its toll of human misery. There is hardly a family that has not been directly or indirectly touched by it.

The purpose of our Award is to stimulate and reward multi-disciplinary research concerned with studies, investigations and experiments relating to the cause, diagnosis, treatment, control, prevention, cure and other many-faceted problems of schizophrenia.

Until recently schizophrenia was the most neglected of all major afflictions. It was not until 1958 that Congress allocated funds specifically for schizophrenia. In responding to my testimony on the subject, Congressman John E. Fogarty, the Chairman of the Subcommittee on Appropriations for Labor, Health, Education and Welfare, said, "This is the first time to my knowledge that anyone has appeared before us to talk on just the specific problem of schizophrenia." In his report to the 85th Congress, March 25, 1958, Chairman Fogarty stated:

> The Committee will expect that approximately $1,300,000 of the increase provided will be spent in increasing research on schizophrenia above the level contemplated in the budget. The Committee lends full support to all approaches to this problem that are sanctioned by competent scientific advice, for this disease is one of the most terrible afflictions of man and one of the most costly to society.

It was the first time in world history that any national government had earmarked funds specifically for schizophrenia (Dean, 1957; 1958; 1959).

We have come a long way since then, as the prize lectures in this volume indicate. We still have a long way to go. Schizophrenia remains a vast frontier harboring a mystery that may be the key to all afflictions of the mind. Our Award is dedicated to the hope that men of vision will eventually solve that mystery.

Acknowledgements: The preparation of this volume depended on the cooperation of several individuals, especially the recipients of the Award whose papers are recorded herein. Special thanks are also due to the following for their advice regarding editing and publication: Dr. James G. Miller, Dr. Raymond W. Waggoner, Dr. Gene L. Usdin and Dr. Jules H. Masserman. Last but far from least, I must express my grateful appreciation to my secretary, Valerie J. Anders, for her ability to steer a clear course through the maze of details encountered in such a project.

Stanley R. Dean, M.D.
Miami, Florida
March, 1973

INDEX

316

317

320

321